Instructor's Resource Guide

Sandy Boyd, Ed.D.

Criminal Justice Today

An Introductory Text for the Twenty-First Century

Ninth Edition

Frank Schmalleger, Ph.D.

Professor Emeritus,
The University of North Carolina at Pembroke

PEARSON
Prentice
Hall

Upper Saddle River, New Jersey 07458

10 9 8 7 6 5 4 3 2
ISBN 0-13-171966-1

Contents

Introduction

This *Instructor's Resource Guide* (IRG) to accompany the ninth edition of *Criminal Justice Today* by Frank Schmalleger is designed to make your job more manageable. It provides a comprehensive summary of the information in the textbook and is organized so that you can use the IRG as an easy-access reference to the issues presented in the textbook and to complementary materials. This will help to make your teaching more effective. Here we provide the links from the textbook to the various supplements included in the Schmalleger package. It would be difficult for you to take advantage of the large number of learning supplements if we did not provide you with an effective road map. This resource guide is that road map.

The chapters of the resource guide correspond directly to the textbook chapters. Each chapter of the IRG has the following sections:

Outline   This is the same general outline as found at the beginning of each chapter in the text.

Learning Objectives   This section provides a list of overall learning objectives for each chapter. The objectives listed here also appear in the *Student Study Guide* (SSG).

Chapter Summary   Each chapter summary, also provided in the *Student Study Guide*, highlights the main points of the chapter. It includes definitions, significant cases, and important research findings. Encourage students to read the summary in the SSG before they read the chapter in the textbook, and then have them read the summary again immediately after they have read the chapter in the textbook. Doing so will reinforce their understanding and comprehension of the material.

Teaching Outline   The teaching outline is a detailed description of the information in each chapter of the textbook. We highlight the main topics, describe the information briefly, and provide reminders of the examples used in the textbook. In addition, all of the key terms and key cases discussed in the textbook are provided in the appropriate places in the lecture outline; they are also in the *Student Study Guide*. Instructional Cues are woven into each chapter's teaching outline. They suggest points to emphasize, extra materials to include, or strategies to further discuss an issue. Also included are Instructional Cues Linked to the SSG, which use the activities of the *Student Study Guide*.

Learner Activities   The IRG contains the learner activities that appear in the *Student Study Guide* for each textbook chapter. You can assign these activities as homework, extra-credit activities, or research projects. Some of the activities are essay questions that require students to think more deeply about the issues.

Learning Activities Utilizing the World Wide Web   There are additonal activities for teaching that are similar to those in the *Student Study Guide*, which can be used in the classroom or as out-of-class assignments. These activities (1) help students appreciate the depth of justice-related information available at their fingertips, (2) provide virtual tours of noted criminal justice agencies, (3) facilitate exploration of the wide diversity of opinion surrounding justice issues in today's world, and (4) expand on the material covered in the textbook. Finally, there is an additional list of websites that are related to the chapter topic.

Suggested Answers to Chapter Discussion Questions   *Criminal Justice Today* contains a number of end-of-chapter discussion questions. Although students' personal opinions may play a role in their answers to these questions, most responses can be assessed in terms of basic information and common themes found throughout the textbook. Here we suggest some answers to each of the discussion questions, keeping in mind the main points of the chapter.

Key—Student Study Guide Questions   The *Student Study Guide* contains 30 multiple-choice, true-or-false, and short-answer questions for each chapter. This section in the IRG includes those questions and the answers.

Key—Crossword Puzzle and Word Search   At the end of each chapter of the *Student Study Guide*, there is a crossword puzzle and a word search puzzle. We provide these puzzles as a fun way to test students' comprehension; the wording of the clues doesn't always echo the language of the textbook but expresses the concepts students must identify. The puzzles with their answers are in the last section of each chapter of the IRG.

In Appendix A, you will find Popular Media in the Classroom. There are so many resources to choose from in current popular media. In this section of the IRG are suggestions, grouped by chapter, for you to choose from as you prepare for your classroom teaching. The list of media can be endless! The challenge remains only in choosing the best media, from those that are relevant to the topic, to support your teaching.

Finally, to accompany the the ABC Video Library that accompanies the textbook, you will find *Video Library Instructor's Guide*. Each of the five video guides includes suggestions for use by chapter, a summary, and discussion prompts. There are also websites that can be accessed for further information on the topic.

We hope that the materials in this resource guide are useful and contribute to your enjoyment of teaching about criminal justice today.

If you have any suggestions on how this *Instructor's Resource Guide* can be more helpful to you, please send your comments to:

Justice Research Association
Suite 104/Box 125
6231 PGA Blvd.
Palm Beach Gardens, FL 33418

schmalleger@cjtoday.com

Sandy Boyd, Ed.D.   Frank Schmalleger, Ph.D
College of Marin   Justice Research Association

Sample Syllabus

The following is a sample syllabus that can be used with *Criminal Justice Today*, 9/e. In general, a syllabus should contain information about the course (name, number, section, location, and meeting times), the instructor (name, contact information, office hours, and office location), and course materials (required readings, course description, assignments, grading, other class policies, and a reading schedule).

Syllabus: Fall 2007

Course Information

Course Name: Introduction to Criminal Justice
Course Number: CJ101
Section Number: 0003
Meeting Times: Monday, Wednesday, Friday 12:00–1:00
Meeting Location: University Hall 242

Instructor Information

Instructor Name: Dr. Mary Welsh
Office Location: Memorial Hall 018
Office Hours: Monday and Wednesday, 2–5
Telephone Number: 222-3333
E-mail Address: mwelsh@university.com

Course Materials

Required Readings

1. Schmalleger, Frank. 2007. *Criminal Justice Today* (9th ed.). Upper Saddle River, NJ: Prentice Hall.
2. Schmalleger, Frank, and Steve Chermak. 2007. *Student Study Guide for Criminal Justice Today* (9th ed.). Upper Saddle River, NJ: Prentice Hall.

Course Description

This course provides an introduction to the criminal justice system. The primary goal of this course is to develop a general understanding of the criminal justice system's response to crime in society. It is important to note that the general theme of this course involves the delicate balance between community interests and individual rights that criminal justice decision making requires. We will explore this theme by examining the criminal justice process in some detail, focusing on how the system is structured to respond to crime. This requires an understanding of the core elements of the criminal justice system: police, courts, and corrections.

We will explore the criminal justice system in five parts.

Part 1   In Part 1 we will examine crime in America. We will briefly touch on the basic functions of each component of the criminal justice system, discuss the definition of crime and different kinds of crime, and then explore the causes of crime.

Part 2   This part of the course will focus on the beginning stages of the criminal justice process, exploring policing and police decision making. We will explore the history and structure of policing, police management, and legal aspects of policing.

Part 3   This section of the course will address adjudication. Here we will explore the operation of the court system by examining the courtroom work group, all stages of the court process, and progression of cases through the system.

Part 4   This section of the course will explore corrections. We will discuss probation, parole, community corrections, prisons, and jails. We will also give considerable attention to life in male and female institutions.

Part 5   In the final section of the course, we will examine special criminal justice issues. These issues include juvenile justice, drugs and crime, multinational criminal justice, and the future of criminal justice.

Course Requirements

- Five Examinations (100 points each)
- Ten Homework Assignments (20 points each)
- Attendance and Participation (50 points)

Grading Scale

It is very important that you describe clearly the method you will use to assign grades. If you prefer using a straight percentage scale (e.g., 90%, 80%, etc.), be sure to highlight the point totals that fall above and below each cutoff. Similarly, if you assign plus and minus grades, it is best to state the distribution completely. Finally, you should include information on whether you use a curve to assign examination or final grades.

Description of Course Requirements

Examinations   There will be five multiple-choice and true-or-false examinations. We will have an examination after we complete each part of the course. There will be 50 questions on an examination (each question will be worth two points), and the examination will cover materials presented in lecture and the textbook.

Homework Assignments   Each chapter of the *Student Study Guide* has four student activities and an Internet activity, which involve analyzing the information provided in the textbook. You should have at least two of these activities completed before we finish that chapter. I will randomly collect ten of these activities during the course of the semester. Each assignment will be worth up to 20 points. (*Note*: If you prefer not to use this "pop quiz" method, you can assign the activities that suit your teaching style and your class.)

Attendance and Participation   A portion of your final grade will be based on your attendance and participation in the class. Read the textbook before class, and be prepared to ask and answer questions.

Policies and Procedures

Policies are discretionary items, but often a written statement is an effective way to avoid ambiguity and problems. Policies and procedures you might address in this section include attendance, make-up examinations or missed assignments, participation, academic integrity, and classroom civility.

Course Reading Schedule

Week	Topic(s)	Readings
1	What Is Criminal Justice?	Chapter 1
2	The Crime Picture	Chapter 2
3	The Search for Causes	Chapter 3
4	Criminal Law	Chapter 4
5	Policing: History and Structure	Chapter 5
6	Policing: Purpose and Organization	Chapter 6
7	Policing: Legal Aspects	Chapter 7
	Policing: Issues and Challenges	Chapter 8
8	The Courts: Structure and Participants	Chapter 9
9	Pretrial Activities and the Criminal Trial	Chapter 10
10	Sentencing	Chapter 11
11	Probation, Parole, and Community Corrections	Chapter 12
12	Prisons and Jails	Chapter 13
13	Prison Life	Chapter 14
14	Juvenile Justice	Chapter 15
	Drugs and Crime	Chapter 16
15	Terrorism and Multinational Criminal Justice	Chapter 17
	The Future of Criminal Justice	Chapter 18

Supplements

Instructor Supplements

Instructor's Manual	0-13-171966-1
ABC Video	0-13-171960-2
PH TestGen	0-13-171963-7
Electronic IM with PPS	0-13-171953-X
Test Item File	0-13-171952-1
Blackboard	
Course Compass	
Web CT	

Student Supplements

Student Study Guide	0-13-171961-0
Time of Criminal Justice	0-13-117457-6
What Every Law Enforcement Officer Should Know about DNA Evidence (CD-ROM)	0-13-114469-3
Careers in Criminal Justice CD-ROM	0-13-119513-1
Evaluating Online Resources	0-13-184460-1
CJ Student Writer's Manual	0-13-124506-6
CJ Dictionary	0-13-192132-0
CJ System Wall Chart	0-13-170161-4

State Specific Supplements

California	0-13-171954-8
Florida	0-13-171956-4
Illinois	0-13-171955-6
Indiana	0-13-170168-1
Maryland	0-13-170169-X
Massachusetts	0-13-170170-3
Michigan	0-13-114031-0
New York	0-13-171958-0
North Carolina	0-13-114030-2
Ohio	0-13-048312-5
Pennsylvania	0-13-170166-5
Texas	0-13-171957-2

CHAPTER 1

What Is Criminal Justice?

LEARNING OBJECTIVES

After reading this chapter, you should be able to:

- Identify the theme on which this textbook builds
- Highlight the differences between the individual-rights and public-order perspectives
- Explain society's need for a system of order maintenance, and detail the role of law within that system
- Describe the personal sacrifices necessitated by public order
- Expound upon the relationship of criminal justice to social justice and other wider notions of equity and fairness
- Explain the structure of the criminal justice system in terms of its major components
- Describe the differences between the consensus and conflict models of the criminal justice system
- Describe the process of American criminal justice, including the stages of criminal case processing
- Explain the meaning of due process of law, and identify where due process guarantees can be found in the American legal system
- Explain how multiculturalism and diversity present special challenges to, and opportunities for, the American system of criminal justice

Chapter Summary

Chapter 1 accomplishes five objectives. First, it describes the major theme of the book. Second, it discusses whether the criminal justice process functions as a system. Third, it provides an overview of the textbook and the criminal justice process. Fourth, it explains the differences between criminology and criminal justice. Finally, it explains how multiculturalism presents unique challenges and opportunities for the criminal justice system.

The author describes the major theme that will be revisited throughout the textbook. This theme, individual rights versus public order, provides a framework for thinking about difficult criminal justice issues. This framework involves balancing individual rights (i.e., the right of individuals to be protected from overzealous and intrusive government agents) against community interests (i.e., the right of society to feel secure from crime). Individual rights and community interests are delicately balanced in our **criminal justice system**. When a movement is made to expand individual rights, such as in the 1960s, community interests are affected. Conversely, and more recently, as community interests have expanded, individual rights have been limited. To help put these "shifts of the pendulum" in perspective, this chapter discusses a series of celebrated cases such as the Oklahoma City bombing and the September 11 attacks. The way one balances these two competing interests revolves around each person's conception of justice. What is fair? Can the system be fairer? Everyone—including politicians, victims, defendants, police officers, prosecutors, and judges—attempts to balance individual and community interests, which affects how justice is applied. Individuals who prefer to protect freedoms and liberties are called **individual-rights advocates**. Individuals who believe that the interests of society should take precedence over liberties are called **public-order advocates**. It is important to realize that (1) understandings of justice are different for everyone and (2) our definitions are molded by our life experiences.

The criminal justice system is the mechanism in place for meting out justice when violations of criminal law occur. Yet does the criminal justice system function as a system? Supporters of a **consensus model** of justice say yes. This model argues that the system is predictable, that there is a high level of cooperation among agencies and individuals in the system, and that the components of the system—police, courts, and corrections—operate without conflict. Conversely, the **conflict model** of criminal justice views the operation of these components from a different perspective. Supporters of this model argue that the goals of criminal justice agencies and the individuals working within them differ and that the system's processes are affected by outside influences such as political pressure, informal arrangements, media coverage of high-profile cases, and discretion.

Both models have some value in helping us understand the operation of the criminal justice system. There are times when the agencies of criminal justice work closely together, representing a consensus model. For example, when criminal justice crises arise, such as when the federal building in Oklahoma City was bombed or the World Trade Center and the Pentagon were attacked, all components were focused on similar goals. However, at other times the goals of each agency conflict. For example, a prosecutor may want police officers to crack down on juvenile crime. Police officers, however, may feel that other crimes, perhaps drunk driving, should take priority.

The author provides an overview of the book and introduces you to the stages in the justice process. It is important that you familiarize yourself with these stages. In general, the criminal justice process starts when a citizen (victim or witness) calls the police to report a crime. The police are responsible for conducting the investigation, making an arrest (if they can establish probable cause), and **booking** the suspect. The court process begins when this suspect appears before a judge at the first appearance. Here, the judge decides what should be done with the suspect pending the outcome of the case. A **grand jury** or **preliminary hearing** will then be conducted to determine whether the criminal justice process should continue. An **information** can result from a preliminary hearing, and an **indictment** can result from a grand jury hearing. The suspect then will be arraigned on the charges. A trial will be held, and if the person is found (or pleads) guilty, then sentencing occurs. It is then the responsibility of the corrections component of the criminal justice system to carry out the sentence.

This chapter also discusses Herbert Packer's two models of the criminal justice system. The first model is the **crime-control model**, which prioritizes efficiency in order to maintain social order. In contrast, Packer's **due process model** prioritizes individual rights and protecting innocent citizens.

Teaching Outline

    I. Introduction (p. 6)
- Discuss the meaning of crime, and highlight the role that the criminal justice system has in responding to crime.

Crime   Conduct in violation of the criminal laws of a state, the federal government, or a local jurisdiction, for which there is no legally acceptable justification or excuse. (p. 7)

    II. A Brief History of Crime in America (p. 7)
- Define individual rights.

Individual Rights   The rights guaranteed to all members of American society by the U.S. Constitution (especially those found in the first ten amendments to the Constitution, known as the *Bill of Rights*). These rights are particularly important to criminal defendants facing formal processing by the criminal justice system. (p. 8)

INSTRUCTIONAL CUE

A good strategy to help students understand the dichotomy of individual-rights advocates and public-order advocates is to hold a debate in class. Divide the class in half and assign one half to be individual-rights advocates and the other to be public-order advocates. A good issue for them to take a position on is drunk driving. Explain to students how the criminal justice system's response to drunk driving has evolved significantly during the last 30 years. Emphasize that drunk driving was virtually ignored in the 1970s; when an incident came to the attention of the criminal justice system, either it would be ignored or the drunk driver would receive a short sentence. Today drunk driving is considered a serious crime and is given high priority in many cities. Ask the half of the class that represents the individual-rights advocates to argue that the new emphasis on drunk driving is excessive. Ask the half of the class viewing the issue as public-order advocates to provide reasons that strict enforcement of drunk-driving laws is a reasonable criminal justice response.

INSTRUCTIONAL CUE LINKED TO THE STUDENT STUDY GUIDE

Use Student Activity 1 in the Student Study Guide to highlight the differences between individual-rights advocates and public-order advocates. This is a good activity to generate class discussion. After students have completed this assignment, ask the group to identify the strategies they would use to respond to terrorism. After you have a good list of various strategies, ask the students which ones are consistent with public-order advocates and which are consistent with individual-rights advocates. For example, a public-order advocate might recommend increasing the length of sentences for terrorists. On the other hand, an individual-rights advocate might be concerned about the impact that the USA PATRIOT Act will have on civil liberties.

INSTRUCTIONAL CUE LINKED TO THE STUDENT STUDY GUIDE

Use the second student activity in the Student Study Guide to illustrate the difficulties of balancing individual and community rights. This could be either an in-class writing assignment or a homework assignment. After students complete this assignment, use the exercise to generate discussion. First, brainstorm with the students to generate various definitions of justice. For example, you might have several students write their definitions of justice on a board or transparency. Second, generate discussion about the case provided in the Student Study Guide. You might want to refresh their memories on the facts of the case. Ask students whether the sentence was just. Then change the situation. For example, explain how Dale Parak had an extensive criminal record, including a prior murder conviction (he served 14 years for this conviction). Was the sentence just? Or tell them that Dale Parak also had cancer and had about two years to live. Was the sentence just?

- Provide students with a historical perspective of crime in the last half century. An effective way to highlight the changes is to simply provide a timeline of critical events—those discussed in this section. Discuss the importance of these high-profile cases and how they influence public understanding of criminal justice. Ask students what other high-profile crime events they remember.
- Engage students in a discussion of why crime and criminal justice are such important political issues. Ask them how the political process can be influenced by high-profile media events, such as any of the incidents discussed at the beginning of the chapter. Discuss the September 11 attacks with students, and then describe how politicians responded by enacting the **USA PATRIOT Act of 2001**.

USA PATRIOT Act of 2001   A federal law (Public Law 107-56), enacted in response to terrorist attacks on the World Trade Center and the Pentagon on September 11, 2001. The law, officially titled The Uniting and Strengthening America by Providing Appropriate Tools Required to Intercept and Obstruct Terrorism Acts, substantially broadens the investigative authority of law enforcement agencies throughout America and is applicable to many crimes other than terrorism. (p. 9)

III. The Theme of This Book (p. 10)

- Discuss the major focus of the book, which is the recognition by society of the need to balance (1) the rights of individuals faced with criminal prosecution against (2) the valid interests of society in preventing crimes and in reducing the harm caused by criminal activity (individual rights versus public order).
- Highlight the key differences between individual-rights advocates and public-order advocates.

Individual-Rights Advocate   One who seeks to protect personal freedoms within the process of criminal justice. (p. 11)

Public-Order Advocate   One who believes that under certain circumstances involving a criminal threat to public safety, the interests of society should take precedence over individual rights. (p. 11)

IV. Social Justice (p. 12)

- Discuss justice, and ask students what justice means to them.

Justice   The principle of fairness; the ideal of moral equity. (p. 14)

- Explain the differences between criminal justice and social justice. Contrast the focus of criminal justice (violations of the criminal law) and civil justice (fairness in relationships among citizens, government agencies, and businesses in private matters).

Social Justice   An ideal that embraces all aspects of civilized life and that is linked to fundamental notions of fairness and to cultural beliefs about right and wrong. (p. 14)

Criminal Justice   In the strictest sense, the criminal (penal) law, the law of criminal procedure, and the array of procedures and activities having to do with the enforcement of this body of law. Criminal justice cannot be separated from social justice because the kind of justice enacted in our nation's criminal courts is a reflection of basic American understandings of right and wrong. (p. 14)

Civil Justice   The civil law, the law of civil procedure, and the array of procedures and activities having to do with private rights and remedies sought by civil action. Civil justice cannot be separated from social justice because the kind of justice enacted in our nation's civil courts is a reflection of basic American understandings of right and wrong. (p. 14)

- Discuss the concept of the administration of justice and stress justice as the ultimate goal of criminal justice.

Administration of Justice   The performance of any of the following activities: detection, apprehension, detention, pretrial release, post-trial release, prosecution, adjudication, correctional supervision, or rehabilitation of accused persons or other criminal offenders. (p. 14)

    V. American Criminal Justice: System and Functions (p. 15)

        A. The Consensus Model (p. 15)

- Explain the criminal justice system in terms of its component subsystems: law enforcement, courts, and corrections.

Criminal Justice System   The aggregate of all operating and administrative or technical support agencies that perform criminal justice functions. The basic divisions of the operational aspects of criminal justice are law enforcement, courts, and corrections. (p. 15)

Consensus Model   A criminal justice perspective that assumes that the system's subcomponents work together harmoniously to achieve the social product we call *justice*. (p. 16)

        B. The Conflict Model

- Stress that the consensus model envisions the subcomponent agencies as all functioning in order to achieve the goal of justice and the conflict model envisions the components as serving their own interests.

Conflict Model   A criminal justice perspective that assumes that the system's components function primarily to serve their own interests. According to this theoretical framework, justice is more a product of conflicts among agencies within the system than it is the result of cooperation among component agencies. (p. 16)

INSTRUCTIONAL CUE

An effective way to illustrate differences between the consensus and conflict models is to discuss the criminal justice system in general and in specific terms. In general, the goals of the system include responding to crime in society, fairness, and justice. One could argue that the subcomponents are in consensus by including these general goals as part of their mandate. However, the subcomponents also approach these goals in very different ways; thus, there is conflict. Police focus on putting people behind bars; a prosecutor is willing to plea-bargain to increase the efficiency of the system, frequently resulting in the release of convicted offenders to the community; and correctional institutions are concerned with overcrowded facilities.

INSTRUCTIONAL CUE LINKED TO THE STUDENT STUDY GUIDE

Use Student Activity 3 in the Student Study Guide to help illustrate the disagreement in goals that is characteristic of the conflict model. This activity can be a class project or a group assignment. It is a good assignment to help students understand the conflict and consensus models better, and they will also gain a broader appreciation for the various activities of the system.

    VI. American Criminal Justice: The Process (p. 16)

        A. Investigation and Arrest (p. 16)

INSTRUCTIONAL CUE

Use a hypothetical couple and criminal activity to walk through the Criminal Justice process. For example, John (20 years old) and Jane (14 years old) rob a liquor store. Discuss the likelihood that because Jane is a juvenile she will be processed through the juvenile justice system (discussed at length in Chapter 15). John Doe, however, will be processed in the adult system.

- Describe arrest warrants.

Warrant   In criminal proceedings, a writ issued by a judicial officer directing a law enforcement officer to perform a specified act and affording protection from damages if he or she performs it. (p. 17)

- Present a short history of limits to freedom when arrested and the resultant U.S. Supreme Court decision, *Miranda* v. *Arizona.*
    1. Booking

Booking   A law enforcement or correctional administrative process officially recording an entry into detention after arrest and identifying the person, the place, the time, the reason for the arrest, and the arresting authority. (p. 17)

   B. Pretrial Activities (p. 17)
     1. First Appearance
- Explain how the court process begins, and discuss what occurs at the first appearance. Discuss the bail process.

Bail   The money or property pledged to the court or actually deposited with the court to effect the release of a person from legal custody. (p. 17)

     2. Preliminary Hearing

Preliminary Hearing   A proceeding before a judicial officer in which three matters must be decided: (1) whether a crime was committed, (2) whether the crime occurred within the territorial jurisdiction of the court, and (3) whether there are reasonable grounds to believe that the defendant committed the crime. (p. 18)

Probable Cause   A set of facts and circumstances that would induce a reasonably intelligent and prudent person to believe that a particular other person has committed a specific crime. Also, reasonable grounds to make or believe an accusation. Probable cause refers to the necessary level of belief that would allow for police seizures (arrests) of individuals and full searches of dwellings, vehicles, and possessions. (p. 18)

     3. Information or Indictment
- Explain the difference between an indictment and an information.

Indictment   A formal, written accusation submitted to the court by a grand jury, alleging that a specified person has committed a specified offense, usually a felony. (p. 18)

Information   A formal, written accusation submitted to a court by a prosecutor, alleging that a specified person has committed a specified offense. (p. 18)

Grand Jury   A group of jurors who have been selected according to law and have been sworn to hear the evidence and to determine whether there is sufficient evidence to bring the accused person to trial, to investigate criminal activity generally, or to investigate the conduct of a public agency or official. (p. 18)

     4. Arraignment

Arraignment   Strictly, the hearing before a court having jurisdiction in a criminal case, in which the identity of the defendant is established, the defendant is informed of the charge and of his or her rights, and the defendant is required to enter a plea. Also, in some usages, any appearance in criminal court prior to trial. (p. 18)

   C. Adjudication (p. 19)
- Introduce the concept of precedent as understandings built up through common usage and also as decisions rendered by courts in previous cases.

Trial   In criminal proceedings, the examination in court of the issues of fact and relevant law in a case for the purpose of convicting or acquitting the defendant. (p. 19)

    D. Sentencing (p. 19)
- Discuss the difference between consecutive and concurrent sentences.

Consecutive Sentence   One of two or more sentences imposed at the same time, after conviction for more than one offense, and served in sequence with the other sentence. Also, a new sentence for a new conviction, imposed upon a person already under sentence for a previous offense, which is added to the previous sentence, thus increasing the maximum time the offender may be confined or under supervision. (p. 20)

Concurrent Sentence   One of two or more sentences imposed at the same time, after conviction for more than one offense, and served at the same time. Also, a new sentence for a new conviction, imposed upon a person already under sentence for a previous offense, served at the same time as the previous sentence. (p. 20)

    E. Corrections (p. 20)
- Discuss sentencing options.
1. Probation and Parole

INSTRUCTIONAL CUE LINKED TO THE STUDENT STUDY GUIDE

Use Student Activity 4 in the Student Study Guide to help illustrate the stages of the criminal justice process.

  VII. Due Process and Individual Rights (p. 21)

Due Process   A right guaranteed by the Fifth, Sixth, and Fourteenth Amendments of the U.S. Constitution and generally understood, in legal contexts, to mean the due course of legal proceedings according to the rules and forms established for the protection of individual rights. In criminal proceedings, due process of law is generally understood to include the following basic elements: a law creating and defining the offense, an impartial tribunal having jurisdictional authority over the case, accusation in proper form, notice and opportunity to defend, trial according to established procedure, and discharge from all restraints or obligations unless convicted. (p. 21)

    A. The Role of the Courts in Defining Rights (p. 22)
    B. The Ultimate Goal: Crime Control through Due Process (p. 22)

Crime-Control Model   A criminal justice perspective that emphasizes the efficient arrest and conviction of criminal offenders. (p. 22)

Due Process Model   A criminal justice perspective that emphasizes individual rights at all stages of the justice system processing. (p. 22)

INSTRUCTIONAL CUE

A good way to illustrate the due process model is by discussing a case of a defendant who was wrongfully convicted. Highlight how DNA technology has assisted law enforcement on the one hand but also helped innocent people who were convicted. You could also discuss the case of Rubin "Hurricane" Carter, who is the subject of the movie *The Hurricane.*

Social Control   The use of sanctions and rewards within a group to influence and shape the behavior of individual members of that group. Social control is a primary concern of social groups and communities, and it is their interest in the exercise of social control that leads to the creation of both criminal and civil statutes. (p. 22)

INSTRUCTIONAL CUE

Provide a list of criminal justice issues, for example, habitual offender statutes such as three-strikes laws, the *Miranda* warnings, the exclusionary rule, mandatory domestic violence arrests, speedy trials, police crackdowns, drunk-driving roadblocks, and providing of attorneys to indigents. Discuss whether each issue is more consistent with the due process model or the crime-control model.

VIII. The Role of Research in Criminal Justice (p. 22)
- Explain the differences between criminal justice (p. 14) and criminology.

Criminology   The scientific study of the causes and prevention of crime and the rehabilitation and punishment of offenders. (p. 24)

A. Research and Professionalism
- Discuss the study *Preventing Crime: What Works, What Doesn't, What's Promising* by Larry Sherman.

IX. Multiculturalism and Diversity in Criminal Justice (p. 24)
- Define multiculturalism, and highlight the importance of multiculturalism to criminal justice processes.

Multiculturalism   The existence within one society of diverse groups that maintain unique cultural identities while frequently accepting and participating in the larger society's legal and political system. Multiculturalism is usually used in conjunction with the term *diversity* to identify many distinctions of social significance. Adapted from Robert M. Shusta et al., Multicultrual Law Enforcement, 2nd ed. (Upper Saddle River, NJ: Prentice Hall, 2002), p. 443. (p. 25)

Learner Activities

Activity 1

One of the most important issues faced by the criminal justice system is how best to respond to terrorism. Since the attacks of September 11, the public believes that terrorism is a significant threat in the United States. What do you think? Answer questions in the space provided below. You may want to look at the following websites for background information: The Prentice Hall Cybrary, at http://www.cybrary.info, has an extensive collection of articles on terrorism posted; also the National Criminal Justice Reference Service, at http://www.ncjrs.org, has information on terrorism.

1. Is terrorism a serious problem in this country? Why or why not?
2. What ten things can the criminal justice system do to respond to terrorism?
3. Of the ten items you cited, which one do you think might be most effective? Why?
4. Why is it so difficult to respond to terrorism?

_____

_____

_____

_____

_____

_____

Activity 2

What is your definition of justice? Consider the facts of the following case:

Dale and Mike Parak were twin brothers and best friends. They spent their entire lives looking out for each other's interests. When growing up, the two were inseparable. They played sports together, double-dated frequently, and attended the same university. They grew closer as they aged, they got married at about the same time, and eventually both were divorced. After they retired from their jobs, they decided to live together to save money and because they still enjoyed each other's company.

When he was 70 years old, Mike was diagnosed with cancer. Doctors predicted that he had about six months to live. The brothers, however, agreed that Mike should not suffer. Mike and Dale wrote and signed a note stating that they decided to commit suicide. Dale broke 20 tranquilizers into Mike's evening meal and watched as he ate it. Yet when Dale checked on Mike one hour later, Mike was still alive. Dale panicked. He took a .38-caliber revolver from his desk and shot Mike, killing him instantly. Dale then went into the kitchen and took a handful of tranquilizers. He did not die. He awoke the next morning as somebody pounded on the front door. It was a neighbor who, seeing that Dale was dazed and confused, decided to call an ambulance and the police.

The responding police officer conducted an investigation, and Dale was arrested and charged with the murder of his brother, Mike. The prosecutor, although noting it to be a difficult case, pursued the case because she thought no citizen had the right to decide when someone should die. Dale Parak pleaded guilty to first-degree manslaughter and was sentenced to five years in a maximum-security prison. (Note that this was the lowest sentence that could be given to a defendant convicted of his crime.)

1. According to the definition of justice you provided, was this sentence just? Why or why not?
2. If you were the prosecutor in this case, would you have charged Dale Parak? Why or why not?
3. If you were the judge in this case, how would you have sentenced Dale Parak? Why?

_____

_____

_____

_____

_____

_____

Activity 3

An effective way for you to understand the conflict of goals that is characteristic of the different criminal justice components is to talk to criminal justice professionals about their priorities and expectations. This assignment requires you to interview at least one representative of law enforcement, one of the court, and one of a corrections agency. For example, you could interview a police officer, a prosecuting attorney, and a correctional officer. Or you could interview a sheriff's deputy, a judge, and a probation officer. Any combination of representatives would be fine. Prepare questions in advance to find out about the background characteristics of these individuals, why they chose their careers, and the types of activities they do in a typical day. Finally, ask them about the organization's goals. For example, you could ask, What would you say are the five most important goals of this organization?

When you complete your interviews, discuss what you discovered in the space below. Did the three people you interviewed have the same goals? If so, were these goals prioritized in the same manner?

_____
_____
_____
_____
_____
_____

Activity 4

Crime and justice are subjects that are frequently presented on television. Prime-time television shows, soap operas, music videos, and cartoons often portray images of crime and criminal justice.

In the space below, list at least three television shows that you have seen that depict the police, courts, and correctional components of the criminal justice system (three television shows for each component). How do these shows present each component? Are the images positive or negative? What stages of the process are depicted? Do you think these images are fair representations of criminal justice? Why or why not?

_____
_____
_____
_____
_____
_____

Internet Activity

Visit the Prentice Hall Cybrary at http://www.cybrary.info. Choose a topic that is relevant to the material provided in Chapter 1. Describe the types of resources available on that topic.

_____
_____
_____
_____
_____

Distance Learning Activity

Visit the World Wide Web or the Prentice Hall Cybrary at http://www.cybrary.info to collect information on the criminal justice system's response to terrorism after the attacks at the World Trade Center and the Pentagon. Find at least one article that highlights individual-order concerns and one that highlights public-order concerns. After you have completed the assignment, participate in a class discussion to compare and contrast the findings from the different essays if your instructor asks you to do so.

_____

_____

_____

_____

_____

_____

Learning Activities Utilizing the World Wide Web

There are student-based activities in the Student Study Guide (Internet Activity, Distance Learning Activity, CJ Today on the World Wide Web) that are similar in focus to those that follow. However, the following are presented as instructor-led activities, to be used in a classroom with online access.

Visit the Prentice Hall Cybrary at http://www.cybrary.info. Choose a topic that is relevant to the material provided in Chapter 1. In class, display the types of resources available on that topic.

Visit the Prentice Hall Cybrary at http://www.cybrary.info. Collect information on the criminal justice system's response to terrorism after the attacks at the World Trade Center and the Pentagon. Find at least one article that highlights individual-order concerns and one that highlights public-order concerns. In class, display (or duplicate) the articles, and have students compare and contrast the findings from the different articles.

Visit the *Criminal Justice Today* website at http://cjtoday.com. You'll find links to study aids tailored to each chapter in the text, Web Extras and Library Extras, crime and justice news, and the Prentice Hall Cybrary.

Other websites for organizations and agencies related to the material in Chapter 1 include:

American Civil Liberties Union (ACLU)	http://www.aclu.org
Justice for All	http://www.jfa.net.
Preventing Crime: "What Works, What Doesn't"	http://cjcentral.com/sherman/ sherman.htm
U.S. Department of Justice	http://www.usdoj.gov
Bureau of Justice Statistics	http://www.ojp.usdoj.gov/bjs
National Criminal Justice Reference Service	http://www.ncjrs.org
Terrorism Files	http://www.terrorismfiles.org
National Center for Victims of Crime	http://www.ncvc.org
Office for Victims of Crime (OVC)	http://www.ojp.usdoj.gov/ovc
Violence, Public Health, and the Media	http://www.annenberg.nwu. edu/pubs

Suggested Answers to Chapter Discussion Questions

1. **What is the theme on which this textbook builds?**

   The main theme of *Criminal Justice Today* is individual rights versus public order. The theme stresses the need to balance the protection of each individual's constitutional rights with the protection of society as a whole. Ensuring that the basic rights of individuals are not infringed upon while society is protected through the maintenance of public order requires a delicate balancing act.

How does the theme facilitate the study of criminal justice?

The study of criminal justice involves examination of the processes by which the various components of the system interact to maintain the balance between individual rights and public order. In considering the potential impact of social issues and technological changes on future crime, administrators must also address systemic changes mandated by increased social awareness of and sensitivity to the multicultural makeup of American society.

2. **Describe the individual-rights and public-order perspectives. What are the central features of each?**

The central feature of the individual-rights perspective is the focus on its protection of personal freedoms. This perspective is concerned about unnecessarily restrictive government actions that limit or eliminate these freedoms. The central feature of the public-order perspective is in the acknowledgment that the interests of society should take precedence over individual rights.

How do they differ?

These perspectives are in conflict. The individual-rights perspective is willing to sacrifice public safety in order to protect important personal freedoms. The public-order perspective is willing to eliminate or limit rights to increase public safety.

3. **Why is public order necessary? Do we have enough public order or too little? How can we tell?**

Public order provides a firm footing for interpersonal and interinstitutional relationships, hence contributing to social and economic growth and stability. Laws lend predictability to society and allow for effective planning within society's legal framework.

Without order, predictability evaporates—and along with it go safety and security. Individuals and organizations would find themselves unable to plan or to function in consort with one another. The strongest would rule, and the weak would be subject to their whims. Threats and the fear engendered by potential threats would take the place of law. Similarly, in a disordered society, America's declared belief that "all men are created equal" would be a hollow notion, as the lack of order would negate society's ability to ensure equality in the treatment of its members. Unequal treatment of any social group is oppressive, and history has shown that such oppression, over time, sparks rebellion and may even lead to anarchy or a new social order.

As with some of the preceding discussion questions, this question is a matter of perspective. Residents of high-crime, gang-ruled urban areas in south-central Los Angeles, Detroit, and elsewhere might well argue that public order is virtually nonexistent in their experience. Interestingly, those same residents might also complain that too much public order invades their lives—in the unwanted form of order imposed by gangs.

Likewise, deadbeat dads arrested for failing to pay court-ordered child support might believe that public order is out of control and invasive. Meanwhile, fugitive felons brazenly walking the streets knowing that the overloaded system helps them remain free are certain that there is just enough public order to suit them.

Our sense of whether there is too much or too little public order, then, is driven by our personal experiences with the systems and agencies that impose public order on each of us.

What might a large, complex society such as ours be like without laws and without a system of criminal justice? Would you want to live in such a society? Why or why not?

Most people would view the abolition of law and the dismantling of government as regression to a less civilized state. The term *lawlessness*, commonly used to describe riots and other forms of social disorder, generally evokes an image of an undesirable social state.

Popular fiction writers often employ the theme of a lawless society without governmental agencies to maintain order as the premise of their books and movies. Usually, the social state is depicted as having deteriorated to near-anarchy, with the predatory strong ruling the powerless weak. In such scenarios, a crude criminal justice system is typically depicted as a vigilante system used arbitrarily by the strong with little regard for justice.

There are those, however, who yearn for release from governmental controls. Real-life antigovernment militia members and radical antitax advocates, such as the Montana Freemen political group, seem to view a lawless society as a virtual utopia. They oppose intrusion by the various levels of government and the laws each level imposes. Such intrusion, they believe, inherently denies them the right to live as free men and women unencumbered by externally mandated social obligations that they are forced to honor. The theme of the strong ruling the weak is accepted in these circles as the natural order, that is, the "survival of the fittest."

4. **What must we, as individuals, sacrifice to facilitate public order?**

True and complete freedom means living without constraints of any kind. Public order, however, relies on a social bond between society and the individual. That bond involves the submission of society's members to controls imposed by laws, governmental regulations, and social customs. Although society protects us through its laws and through the mechanisms it establishes to enhance security (such as the justice system), it is our duty to responsibly follow the law and to contribute to public safety.

Do we ever give up too much in the interest of public order? If so, when?

History is replete with examples of citizens giving up too much to achieve order. Within the context of their limited society, the citizens of Nazi Germany may have considered the stringent controls imposed by the Nazi state—including the extermination of German Jews—to be essential to their way of life. In the greater context of the world community, however, those controls were seen as excessive, even horrific.

Ethnic cleansing programs in various countries during the second half of the twentieth century, as well as the infamous apartheid laws formerly practiced in South Africa, exemplify the efforts of oppressive regimes to achieve their own forms of public order. Such activities typically evoke condemnation as a world response, on grounds that they violate elemental human rights. The practitioners of such activities, however, argue that the pursuit of their narrowly defined state of public order justifies their abhorrent practices.

5. **What is justice? What aspects of justice does this chapter discuss?**

Justice focuses on the principle of fairness and the ideal of moral equity. The chapter focuses on social justice, criminal justice, and civil justice.

How does criminal justice relate to social justice and other wider notions of equity and fairness?

Social justice embraces all aspects of civilized life and is linked to broader notions of fairness and right and wrong. Criminal justice is one aspect of this wider form of justice. Criminal justice is an important mechanism by which justice can be achieved. Not only do victims, defendants and others seek and expect fairness from the criminal justice system, but the activities and actions of the criminal justice system often spark society to consider what is considered equal justice.

6. **What are the main components of the criminal justice system? How do they interrelate?**

The criminal justice system encompasses three main components: police, courts, and corrections. These three components interrelate in several ways. First, they interact in the processing of specific cases. For example, police officers conduct investigations and make arrests. Offenders then must be processed by the court system, but police officers play a critical role in this process, as they might confer with prosecutors or testify at motion hearings or trials. If an offender is convicted, prosecutors might recommend the sentence and judges may consider prison overcrowding issues when deciding the final sentence. Second, these components interact at a policy level. The formal and informal decision-making processes of each component can impact the strategies and priorities of the other components. Third, the components are increasingly working together in various ways to respond to specific types of crimes. For example, drug, gun, and violent crime task forces often include line-level and command staff from the different components.

How might they conflict?

The interactions between components often result in conflict. Each component focuses on achieving different goals, and the priorities of the different components may not be consistent. A new criminal justice strategy might be implemented by one component, but the goals of that program may not be consistent with the other components.

7. **This chapter describes two models of the criminal justice system. What are they, and how do they differ?**

This chapter describes the *consensus model*, which assumes that the component parts of the criminal justice system strive toward a common goal and that the movement of cases and people through the system is smooth due to cooperation between the various components of the system, and the *conflict model*, which says that criminal justice agency interests tend to make actors within the system self-serving and that pressures for success, promotion, pay increases, and general accountability fragment the efforts of the system as a whole, leading to a criminal justice nonsystem.

Which model do you think is more useful? Which is more accurate? Why?

Given the great variation in attitudes about crime and punishment, varying propensities toward liberalism or conservatism, the strength of local government leadership, the degree of citizen activism or ambivalence, and so on, it would be difficult to label either model as "more realistic" than the other. To a large extent, it's a matter of perspective.

For example, many view the consensus model as the ideal of the criminal justice system and the conflict model as the reality. An incumbent state attorney general running for reelection, therefore, might well depict the criminal justice system within his or her state as a shining example of the consensus model at its best—while his or her opponent depicts it as a chaotic example of the conflict model at its worst.

Many academicians, in contrast, will say that the conflict model is more realistic—that is, it depicts the criminal justice system in terms of its everyday realities. In fact, the various agencies that make up the justice system are often at odds and are concerned only with their own interests rather than with system-wide goals. Similarly, individual agencies rarely focus on society-wide values such as social justice and procedural fairness; instead they are primarily concerned with meeting legislative, budgetary, and administrative requirements.

8. **List the stages of case processing that characterize the American system of criminal justice, and describe each stage.**

   a. Investigation, arrest, and booking. The process generally begins with the investigation of a crime. A witness or victim might report a crime, a patrol officer may discover a crime, or police officers might use undercover operations to discover crime. An arrest involves taking a person into custody. Booking involves taking pictures and fingerprints and recording personal information.

   b. First appearance, preliminary hearing, and arraignment. At the first appearance, the judge tells suspects of the charges, will advise them of their rights, and will decide bail. The purpose of the preliminary hearing is to determine whether there is sufficient evidence to continue the criminal justice process. At the arraignment, the suspect hears the charges and is asked to enter a plea.

   c. Adjudication. Cases are resolved by either plea bargaining or trial. Cases that go to trial are governed by the rules of evidence, procedural law, and precedent. Trials are best thought of as a contest between prosecuting and defense attorneys.

d. Sentencing. Once a person pleads guilty or is convicted at trial, the judge must impose a sentence. Judges have a wide range of sentences available to them, but their discretion is limited by statute and guidelines. Defendants do have the right to appeal.

e. Corrections. Corrections begin after a sentence is imposed. Among the options available to judges are prison and probation.

9. What is meant by "due process of law"? Where in the American legal system are guarantees of due process found?

Due process means procedural fairness. Due process of law includes a law creating and defining an offense, an impartial tribunal, accusation in proper form, notice and opportunity to defend, trial according to established procedures, and discharge or conviction. These rights are guaranteed by the Fifth, Sixth, and Fourteenth Amendments.

10. What is multiculturalism? What is social diversity?

E pluribus unum—out of many, one. The familiar American motto suggests a homogenized society bonded together as a unified national community. That ideal is most often visible in times of crisis, such as during America's involvement in the Second World War or following the 1995 bombing of Oklahoma City's Murrah Federal Building.

On a daily basis, however, the reality is that American society is an amalgam of ethnic, racial, religious, and cultural influences. What else could be expected in a nation of immigrants? Now, in these early days of the twenty-first century, we are seeing these influences gain strength because of the dramatic social changes wrought by the civil rights movement of the mid-twentieth century and the emergence of the Information Age in the late twentieth century. As a result, American society now has a much greater awareness of both the realized and potential contributions of the diverse elements from which it grew, as well as increasing respect for, and sensitivity to, these differences.

The text defines multiculturalism as the existence within one society of diverse groups that maintain unique cultural identities while frequently accepting and participating in the larger society's legal and political system. Diversity is simply the condition of being different. The diversity within American society, then, makes the United States a textbook example of multiculturalism.

What impact do multiculturalism and diversity have on the practice of criminal justice in contemporary American society?

Few governmental systems are as impacted by multiculturalism and diversity as is the criminal justice system. Perhaps the most dramatic effects are noted in the field of law enforcement. Continuing revelations of past or current wrongs committed by police against individual members of the public—wrongs unarguably shown to have been motivated by racial or ethnic bias—have significantly eroded public trust in policing agencies. Some current policing methods, particularly racial profiling, are thought by many to reflect ongoing institutional bias and are increasingly being successfully challenged in court.

That is not to suggest that law enforcement administrators are negligent or insensitive to issues arising from our diversity. To the contrary, significant strides have already been made in many agencies and continue at all jurisdictional levels. New York City police responses in the wake of the World Trade Center attacks in 2001, for example, were notably restrained when compared to law enforcement responses following the bombing of the Murrah Federal Building. In the latter case, an almost universal presumption that Arab terrorists were the likely perpetrators led to equally universal embarrassment when the actual bomber turned out to be a non-Muslim homegrown military veteran. In the New York instance, however, civic leaders and police administrators moved quickly to quash reprisals against Arab-Americans and to foster impartiality among investigators pursuing leads in the case.

The courts, too, particularly at the appellate level, are confronted with multicultural factors that demand consideration as rulings are made. A ruling against an offender charged with violating American law by practicing an ethnic or religious tradition can create backlash within the affected ethnic community. The centuries-old practice of female circumcision, for example, typifies the kind of issue that presents a clear conflict between American law and cultural tradition.

Correctional leaders must also address multiculturalism on a daily basis. Even such a seemingly benign activity as developing the daily menu for feeding the inmate population, for example, can present serious problems. In the face of endless lawsuits and court rulings, leaders must sometimes scramble to meet inmates' religious or ethnic needs while trying to operate within the constraints of limited budgets.

Challenges facing justice professionals include such complex issues as how to police communities or neighborhoods with values different from those of mainstream society; whether immigrants and foreign national visitors can be justly judged in court proceedings that apply standards and laws that may be completely foreign to them; the widespread—and growing—need for language translation (certainly a ripe opportunity for the adaptation of technological innovations); the problem of gang influences in prison populations comprised of vastly different cultural groupings; and the need for cultural sensitivity among criminal justice practitioners. Justice professionals will face these and innumerable additional challenges in the pursuit of equity for all members of our complex society.

Multiculturalism presents both profound problems and significant opportunities for American justice administrators. While some argue that oversensitivity to multiculturalism and diversity has a corrosive effect that weakens the justice system, others see our growing social awareness as a catalyst for change that will yield greater justice for all.

Like all segments of society—business and industry, education, the military, and so on—the criminal justice system's adoption of functional changes to accommodate evolving social concerns is a complex process that inevitably moves far too slowly for some and way too fast for others. It is critical to note, though, that the process has begun and is continuing.

Key—Student Study Guide Questions

True or False

_____ 1-1. A preliminary hearing involves a group of jurors selected from the community. **(False, p. 18)**

_____ 1-2. Expanding the rights of defendants to protect them from injustice would be most closely associated with a crime-control model of criminal justice. **(False, p. 22)**

_____ 1-3. The *Miranda* decision only requires that police personnel advise a person of his or her rights at the time of the arrest. **(False, p. 17)**

_____ 1-4. Parole differs from probation in that paroled offenders serve a portion of their prison sentences before being released. **(True, p. 20)**

_____ 1-5. Criminal justice is narrower than social justice because it is concerned only with violations of criminal law. **(True, p. 14)**

_____ 1-6. The consensus model of the study of criminal justice assumes that the system's subcomponents function primarily to serve their own interests. **(False, p. 16)**

_____ 1-7. Bail is a mechanism that defendants use to avoid advancing into the later stages of the criminal justice process. **(False, p. 17)**

_____ 1-8. Indictments are filed based on the outcome of a preliminary hearing. **(False, p. 18)**

____ 1-9. A concurrent sentence is a sentence that requires an offender who has been found guilty of more than one charge to serve one sentence after another is completed. **(False, p. 20)**

____ 1-10. Criminology is the application of scientific techniques to the investigation of a crime. **(False, p. 24)**

Multiple Choice

1-11. What decision is made at a suspect's arraignment?
 a. The suspect is required to enter a plea.
 b. The suspect is informed of the charges against him or her.
 c. The suspect is informed of his or her rights.
 d. All of the above are decisions made at arraignment. (p. 18)

1-12. Which of the following models assumes a systems model of criminal justice?
 a. due process model
 b. individual-rights model
 c. conflict model
 d. consensus model (p. 16)

1-13. Who would suggest that under certain circumstances involving criminal threats to public safety, the interests of society should take precedence over individual rights?
 a. a crime-control advocate
 b. a justice-ideal advocate
 c. an individual-rights advocate
 d. a public-order advocate (p. 11)

1-14. Who would support the full protection of personal freedoms and civil rights within the criminal justice process?
 a. a crime-control advocate
 b. a justice-ideal advocate
 c. an individual-rights advocate (p. 11)
 d. a public-order advocate

1-15. In the criminal justice process, a(n) _____ has to occur before a(n) _____.
 a. arraignment; preliminary hearing
 b. sentencing; trial
 c. arrest; first appearance (p. 17)
 d. booking; arrest

1-16. Upon being convicted of robbery and burglary, Jalen Arow is sentenced to seven years for the robbery and five years for the burglary. The sentence for burglary will be served right after the robbery sentence. This is an example of
 a. an unfair sentence.
 b. a discriminatory sentence.
 c. a consecutive sentence. (p. 20)
 d. a concurrent sentence.

1-17. Who is credited with creating the crime-control model of criminal justice?
 a. Earl Warren
 b. Jerome Skolnick
 c. Colin Ferguson
 d. Herbert Packer (p. 23)

1-18. A _____ is a group of jurors selected to hear the evidence and to determine whether there is sufficient evidence to bring the accused person to trial.
 a. jury
 b. public forum
 c. grand jury (p. 18)
 d. preliminary hearing

1-19. The conflict model of criminal justice
   a. assumes that the efforts of the component parts of the system are fragmented, leading to a criminal justice nonsystem. (p. 16)
   b. assumes that the movement of cases and people through the system is smooth due to cooperation among components of the system.
   c. assumes that all parts of the system work together toward a common goal.
   d. assumes police officers are the dominant actors in the criminal justice system.

1-20. A(n) _____ is a writ issued by a judicial officer directing a law enforcement officer to perform a specified act and affording the officer protection from damages if he or she performs it.
   a. indictment
   b. warrant (p. 17)
   c. pretrial release order
   d. information

Fill-In

1-21. Under certain circumstances involving criminal threats to public safety, _____ suggest that the interests of society should take precedence over individual rights. **(public-order advocates, p. 11)**

1-22. The _____ is a perspective on the study of criminal justice that assumes that the system's subcomponents work together harmoniously to achieve that social product we call *justice*. **(consensus model, p. 16)**

1-23. The crime-control model was first brought to the attention of the academic community by _____. **(Herbert Packer, p. 23)**

1-24. _____ are those who seek to protect personal freedoms within the process of criminal justice. **(Individual-rights advocates, p. 11)**

1-25. Jerome Skolnick's classic study of clearance rates provides support for the idea of a(n) _____. **(criminal justice nonsystem, p. 16)**

1-26. _____ is the step of the criminal justice process that occurs immediately after arrest. **(Booking, p. 17)**

1-27. _____ is an ideal that embraces all aspects of civilized life and that is linked to fundamental notions of fairness and to cultural beliefs about right and wrong. **(Social justice, p. 14)**

1-28. _____ is a legal criterion residing in a set of facts and circumstances that would cause a reasonable person to believe that another person has committed a specific crime. **(Probable cause, p. 18)**

1-29. The money or property pledged to the court to effect the release of person from legal custody is called _____. **(bail, p. 17)**

1-30. The _____ assumes that the criminal justice system's subcomponents function primarily to serve their own interests. **(conflict model, p. 16)**

Key—Crossword Puzzle

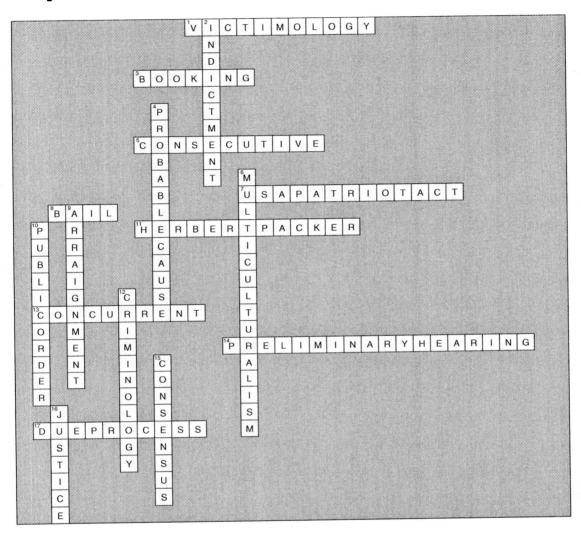

Across

1. Scientific study of crime victims and the victimization process.
3. When a law enforcement official records an entry into detention after arrest.
5. Type of sentence whereby offenders are ordered to serve one sentence after another.
7. Federal law enacted in response to the terrorist attacks on the World Trade Center and the Pentagon on September 11, 2001.
8. Money or property pledged to the court to effect the release of a person from legal custody.
11. Scholar responsible for creating the crime-control and due process models.
13. Type of sentence that runs at the same time.
14. Also called the preliminary examination.
17. Constitutional requirement of fairness and equity.

Down

2. Grand jury returns a(n) _____.
4. Legal basis for an apprehension by the police.
6. Word usually used in conjunction with diversity.
9. First appearance of the defendant before the court that has the authority to conduct a trial.
10. Type of advocate that stresses the interests of society.
12. Scientific study of the causes and prevention of crime and the rehabilitation and punishment of offenders.
15. Model emphasizing a systems perspective.
16. Principle of fairness.

Key—Word Search Puzzle

```
I N D I V I D U A L R I G H T S A D V O C A T E L W D R L X
C R I M E C O N T R O L M O D E L Y L X U V B U Z T A L J G
W P Z M Q U K Q M E C A X L O H E U W X C A O O A X H D C E
Z B Q N B G A E Z I H I A D C V H L A Q J Y O N M H Z V U E
C P F G M G Z B A M A I U E X F X T Y V F N K J J D O G C C
O N R K W M L L A E R O Z V F Z T U D Y S B I Z E L O L B V
N E E Q I F S F T P N Z T O K K N A S D D N Z B K O T P L
S P F P B F V V P S B Y G P M T I N H D B L G R K L J R H M
E Y B K P A R B T Q A F C R I M I N O L O G Y Y G H Z T G H
C U U V X J B B R D W C O N C U R R E N T S E N T E N C E G
U O B I E Y C L H D L K U G V E X U Q I N D I C T M E N T U
T S N S P J I O E I I Z L X M C V G R Q N A R U N I D H S A
I H M S T U S F A C O S M L P G N R H A I E I N O X O H W X
V M U D E B B N T A E J T R M V A P Z R W L J X X R C V O
E O L V Y N P L Y J X U T B E K O N O R C R C C K W L M T W
S C T O T C S G I J P Q S I L L Y D N I N T A G X N F U Z E
E O I P J R D U B C G P Y E I G H J O M F C O I Q O T T C D
N N C F L I K L S O O G Q W M O A U O X A R E N G G J I V Y
T F U R J M O W U M E R G K I B T R S A M I G L H N T N A G
E L L M I E F E P O P D U N X M Y A P E M F B I S M O C I
N I T R T N O G I O F D S E A U Z D K P H E D T U W U E F E
C C U B O A P W Z T H Y E F R C Z B N J O E J N R R F N C
E C T R O V L F G B V C U D L Y A U L L H S F V K I B I O L T
Y M A T P J F P E Z U W C W H T D U S A P A T R I O T A C T
I O L Q C U E L K E K S S X E N M V V L E Y K I Y X B T F B
H D I B C S Y Z A F D M O U A D K E O C N C V Z K X P N E J
S E S G P T Y W S L Y I A P R I K W Z C D Y G V D U X R N L
M L M N T I K T S J W F S J I P F G P F A P A M X Q H J S A
B E J D T C C K Z K L I N I N K N C L V I T R H F H Z T H O
T H Y F F E A Q G M X T E X G X M X S J C S E I G B G Q X O
```

Arraignment

Bail

Booking

Concurrent Sentence

Conflict Model

Consecutive Sentence

Consensus Model

Crime

Crime-Control Model

Criminal Justice

Criminology

Grand Jury

Indictment

Individual-Rights Advocate

Justice

Multiculturalism

Preliminary Hearing

Probable Cause

Public-Order Advocate

Trial

USA PATRIOT Act

CHAPTER 2

The Crime Picture

LEARNING OBJECTIVES

After reading this chapter, you should be able to:

- Name and compare the two major national crime data-gathering programs in the United States today
- Explain what crime statistics can tell us about crime in America
- Discuss some of the limitations inherent in statistical reports of crime
- Describe the FBI's Crime Index, and list the eight major crimes that make up the index
- Explain why crime statistics are generally expressed as rates instead of simple numerical tabulations
- Describe the two major categories of Part I offenses in the Uniform Crime Reports
- Explain the hierarchy rule, and discuss how it affects crime reporting
- Discuss the meaning of the term *clearance rate*
- Explain how the National Incident-Based Reporting System operates, and describe how it differs from the traditional Uniform Crime Reporting Program
- Identify the special categories of crime discussed in this chapter

Chapter Summary

Justin Stacato was standing at a bus stop when four teenagers approached him and asked for his wallet. Although he said he didn't want any trouble and gave them his wallet without resistance, one of the teenagers hit Justin in the head with a baseball bat. He was knocked unconscious and was rushed to the hospital for his injuries.

How would these crimes be classified by the criminal justice system? Chapter 2 in the text describes various crime-classification instruments. For example, if Justin or the hospital reported this incident to the police, it could eventually be part of that department's annual uniform crime statistics submitted to the FBI. Or if Justin's household was one of the households selected for the **National Crime Victimization Survey (NCVS)**, then his victimization could be included as part of these victimization statistics (if he reported it to interviewers). If the teenagers were arrested, a prosecutor might charge the youths with **aggravated assault** and **robbery**. If the reported facts were more detailed and included the information that Justin was an African-American male and the teenagers spray painted a racial epithet on his back while he was unconscious, this crime might be classified as a **hate crime**.

The two primary sources of data used to understand the crime picture in America are official statistics and victimization statistics. The most cited and well-known official source of data is the **Uniform Crime Reports (UCR)**, compiled annually by the FBI. There are approximately 16,000 police departments throughout the United States that voluntarily submit statistics on crimes reported to them. The FBI compiles these statistics and then reports the figures as either **Part I offenses** or **Part II offenses**.

The best-known source of victimization statistics is the National Crime Victimization Survey (NCVS). This survey asks citizens directly about their victimization experiences, including characteristics of the perpetrator, the crime, and the incident. This survey includes information on six crimes: rape, robbery, assault, burglary, larceny, and motor vehicle theft.

Although both of these sources provide some general understanding of the crime problem, they have limitations. In developing the UCR, the FBI relies on the willingness of police departments to report and assumes that the information is accurately represented. But citizens do not report all crimes because, for a variety of reasons, they do not want to involve the police. Fear of retaliation, embarrassment, and belief that the police cannot do anything about it anyway are cited as reasons for not reporting crimes. These factors reduce the accuracy of UCR data. Victimization statistics might present a more accurate portrait of crimes not reported to the police, but this source of data has other limitations. Respondents, for example, might lie or exaggerate the circumstances of their victimization.

The text also provides general descriptions of the eight index offenses and interesting descriptive information about each offense category. **Murder, forcible rape, aggravated assault, robbery, larceny, burglary, motor vehicle theft**, and **arson** are discussed in detail. Murders, for example, do not occur frequently (compared to the other index offenses), but when they do, the police are able to clear a large percentage of them. When a murder does occur, young males (18 to 24 years old) are most likely to have committed this type of crime.

This chapter also has a section on women and crime, discussing women as victims and offenders. Although women are not as likely as men to be victimized, they are more likely to be injured by crime and to be in fear of crime. Women are much less likely than males to commit one of the eight index offenses, although the rate at which women commit these types of crime is increasing rapidly.

The text also introduces other ways of understanding the crime picture. It examines the criminal justice system's interest in hate crimes, elderly crimes, terrorism, and cybercrime.

Although statistics are important to a general understanding of crime, their value is tempered by their inability to indicate clearly how crime affects individuals. Was Justin able to recover from his crimes physically? Psychologically? Emotionally? Was the criminal justice system responsive to his personal needs?

Teaching Outline

I. Introduction (p. 34)

    A. Crime Data and Social Policy (p. 34)

- Data provide a picture of crime in society.
- They are used as a tool to make social policy decisions.

INSTRUCTIONAL CUE

Discuss common misconceptions about crime caused by our heavy reliance on the news media for information about crime. Research on the types of crime presented in the news consistently indicates an inverse relationship between the amount of crime that occurs and what the media present. For example, murder is the index offense least likely to occur, but it is the crime most likely to be presented in the news. What implications does this have for public opinion on crime? On criminal justice policy making? You can also explore the differences between statistics on crime and the media's coverage of crime by having students complete Student Activity 1.

INSTRUCTIONAL CUE LINKED TO THE STUDENT STUDY GUIDE

Use Student Activity 1 to illustrate that the news media are important sources of information that the public uses to form opinions about crime but that they also provide a distorted view of crime.

- Provide an overview of data sources. Briefly discuss the Uniform Crime Reports, the National Crime Victimization Survey, and the Sourcebook of Criminal Justice Statistics.

Uniform Crime Reports (UCR) An annual FBI publication that summarizes the incidence and rate of reported crimes throughout the United States. (p. 35)

National Crime Victimization Survey (NCVS) An annual survey of selected American households conducted by the Bureau of Justice Statistics to determine the extent of criminal victimization—especially unreported victimization—in the United States. (p. 35)

Bureau of Justice Statistics (BJS) A U.S. Department of Justice agency responsible for the collection of criminal justice data, including the annual National Crime Victimization Survey. (p. 35)

II. The Uniform Crime Reports (p. 36)

    A.. Development of the UCR Program (p. 36)

- Since 1930 the FBI has been compiling statistics on crimes known to the police.
- Police departments (about 16,000) voluntarily submit to the FBI information on the crimes that have been reported to them.
- The FBI develops the Crime Index, which represents the total number of Part I offenses that have been reported to the police.

Crime Index (UCR) An inclusive measure of the violent and property crime categories, or Part I offenses, of the Uniform Crime Reports. The Crime Index has been a useful tool for geographic (state-to-state) and historical (year-to-year) comparisons because it employs the concept of a crime rate (the number of crimes per unit of population). However, the addition of arson as an eighth index offense and the new requirements with regard to the gathering of hate-crime statistics could result in new Crime Index measurements that provide less-than-ideal comparisons. (p. 38)

    B. Historical Trends (p. 38)

- The FBI compiles these data and makes data available in a variety of forms.

- Most UCR information is reported as a rate of crime.
- Discuss the three major shifts in crime rates that have occurred since the UCR began.
- Mention that a fourth shift may be starting now.

C. UCR Terminology (p.40)

- Mention the FBI Crime Clock as a shorthand way of diagramming crime frequency in the United States.
- Discuss the rate of occurrence of typical violent crimes, such as murder, forcible rape, robbery, and aggravated assault.

Violent Crime   A UCR offense category that includes murder, rape, robbery, and aggravated assault. (p. 41)

- List typical property crimes, such as burglary, larceny, shoplifting, motor vehicle theft, and arson.

Property Crime   UCR offense category that includes burglary, larceny, auto theft, and arson. (p. 41)

- Explain the hierarchy rule.
- Explain the term *clearance rate*.

Clearance Rate   A traditional measure of investigative effectiveness that compares the number of crimes reported or discovered to the number of crimes solved through arrest or other means (such as the death of the suspect). (p. 41)

INSTRUCTIONAL CUE

Gather state statistics on the eight index crimes and include trend data. Compare and contrast the state figures and the national figures. Does crime in your state have patterns similar to those of national crime? Highlight the declining crime rates.

D. Part I Offenses (p.43)

Part I Offenses   A set of UCR categories used to report murder, rape, robbery, aggravated assault, burglary, larceny-theft, motor vehicle theft, and arson, as defined under the FBI's Uniform Crime Reporting Program. (p. 43)

1. Murder (p. 43)

Murder   The unlawful killing of a human being. Murder is a generic term that in common usage may include first- and second-degree murder, manslaughter, involuntary manslaughter, and other similar offenses.

- Approximately 16,000 murders occur per year, and it is the smallest numerical category of Part 1 offenses.
- Murders are more likely to occur in the warmer months than in the colder months.
- The weapon used to commit a large percentage of murders is a gun.
- Few murders are committed by strangers.
- It is the index crime least likely to occur but most likely to be cleared.
- Mention the 2004 change in federal homicide law, which added the fetal homicide statute.

2. Forcible Rape (p. 44)

Rape   Unlawful sexual intercourse, achieved through force and without consent. Broadly speaking, the term *rape* has been applied to a wide variety of sexual attacks and may include same-sex rape and the rape of a male by a female. Some jurisdictions refer to same-sex rape as *sexual battery*. (p. 44)

Forcible Rape (UCR)   The carnal knowledge of a female forcibly and against her will. For statistical reporting purposes, the FBI defines *forcible rape* as "unlawful sexual intercourse with a female, by force and against her will, or without legal or factual consent." Statutory rape differs from forcible rape in that it generally involves nonforcible sexual intercourse with a minor. (p. 44)

Sexual Battery   Intentional and wrongful physical contact with a person, without his or her consent, that entails a sexual component or purpose. (p. 44)

- Explain that rape is the least reported of all offenses, due primarily to fear or embarrassment but also to poor handling by the justice system.
- Explain that rape report rates are increasing somewhat, due in part to changes in the way the system responds to rape.
- Explain that rape is a planned violent crime that serves the offender's need for power rather than sexual gratification.
- Discuss date rape.

Date Rape   Unlawful forced sexual intercourse with a female against her will that occurs within the context of a dating relationship. Date rape, or acquaintance rape, is a subcategory of rape that is of special concern today. (p. 45)

   3. Robbery (p. 46)

Robbery (UCR)   The unlawful taking or attempted taking of property that is in the immediate possession of another by force or violence and/or by putting the victim in fear. Armed robbery differs from unarmed, or strong-arm, robbery with regard to the presence of a weapon. Contrary to popular conceptions, highway robbery does not necessarily occur on a street—and rarely in a vehicle. The term *highway robbery* applies to any form of robbery that occurs outdoors in a public place. (p. 46)

- Explain that robbery is a personal crime, that individual citizens are typical targets of robbers, and that guns are discharged in 20% of robberies.
- Robbery is primarily an urban offense, and arrestees are primarily male and members of minority groups.

   4. Aggravated Assault (p. 48)

Aggravated Assault (UCR)   The unlawful, intentional inflicting, or attempted or threatened inflicting, of serious injury upon the person of another. While *aggravated assault* and *simple assault* are standard terms for reporting purposes, most state penal codes use labels like *first-degree* and *second-degree* to make such distinctions. (p. 49)

Assault (UCR)   An unlawful attack by one person upon another. Historically, *assault* meant only the attempt to inflict injury on another person; a completed act constituted the separate offense of battery. Under modern statistical usage, however, attempted and completed acts are grouped together under the generic term *assault*. (p. 49)

- Explain the differences between simple and aggravated assault.
- Cite the relatively high clearance rates for assaults.

   5. Burglary (p. 49)

Burglary (UCR)   The unlawful entry of a structure to commit a felony or a theft (excludes tents, trailers, and other mobile units used for recreational purposes). For the UCR, the crime of burglary can be reported if (1) an unlawful entry of an unlocked structure has occurred, (2) a breaking and entering (of a secured structure) has taken place, or (3) a burglary has been attempted. (p. 49)

- Explain that burglary is a property crime and that the burglar usually "fences" stolen materials.
- Cite annual losses totaling over $3 billion.
- Cite the typically low clearance rates of burglary.

- Explain the differences among forcible entry, unlawful entry where no force is used, and attempted forcible entry.

6. Larceny-Theft (p. 50)

Larceny-Theft (UCR)   The unlawful taking or attempted taking, carrying, leading, or riding away of property, from the possession or constructive possession of another. Motor vehicles are excluded. Larceny is the most common of the eight major offenses, although probably only a small percentage of all larcenies are actually reported to the police because of the small dollar amounts involved. (p. 50)

- Explain that larceny, also called theft, is the most common of all offenses and is often not reported because losses are small.
- Explain the difference between simple and grand larceny.
- Discuss why larceny is a catch-all category of the UCR.
- Explain that the most common larceny is theft of motor vehicle parts.

Identity Theft   A crime in which an imposter obtains key pieces of information, such as Social Security and driver's license numbers, to obtain credit, merchandise, and services in the name of the victim. The victim is often left with a ruined credit history and the time-consuming and complicated task of repairing the financial damages. (p. 51)

- Discuss the 2005 penalty enhancement for identity theft

7. Motor Vehicle Theft (p. 52)

Motor Vehicle Theft (UCR)   The theft or attempted theft of a motor vehicle. *Motor vehicle* is defined as a self-propelled road vehicle that runs on land surface and not on rails. The stealing of trains, planes, boats, construction equipment, and most farm machinery is classified as larceny under the UCR Program, not as motor vehicle theft. (p. 53)

- Explain why motor vehicle thefts have such high reporting rates.
- Discuss the reasons why motor vehicle thefts have such low clearance rates.
- Discuss carjacking.
- Explain that under the UCR Program the stealing of trains, planes, boats, construction equipment, and most farm machinery is classified as larceny, not as motor vehicle theft.

8. Arson (p. 53)

Arson (UCR)   The burning or attempted burning of property, with or without the intent to defraud. (p. 53)

- The most common category of arson is the intentional and unlawful burning of structures; the second most common category is the arson of vehicles.

INSTRUCTIONAL CUE

Have students decide which Part I offense crime is occurring in the following situations:

A college freshman visits a friend's residence hall and forces her to have sexual intercourse. **(forcible rape)**

A woman is caught after she puts a gun to an elderly man's head and takes his wallet and watch. **(robbery)**

A man drives his car into a group of teenagers. Six teenagers have to be taken to the hospital for treatment of their injuries. **(aggravated assault)**

A 14-year-old girl steals a Porsche 944 from a car dealership. **(motor vehicle theft)**

A 14-year-old boy steals a bulldozer. **(larceny)**

A man walks through an open door of a home and steals cash and other valuables and raids the refrigerator. **(burglary)**

An 18-year-old girl gave birth to a baby boy in her mother's fourth-floor apartment and tossed the child out the window, and the baby died. **(murder)**

A woman walks out of a coatroom with a leather jacket that does not belong to her. **(larceny)**

A man sets his neighbor's Christmas tree on fire. **(arson)**

A woman borrows a neighbor's boat to go fishing, and the neighbor did not give her permission to use it. **(larceny)**

     E. Part II Offenses (p. 53)
- Describe the FBI's Part II offenses.

Part II Offenses   A set of UCR categories used to report data concerning arrests for less serious offenses. (p. 53)

     F. NIBRS: The New UCR (p. 54)

National Incident-Based Reporting System (NIBRS)   An incident-based reporting system that collects data on every single crime occurrence. NIBRS data will soon supersede the kind of traditional data provided by the FBI's Uniform Crime Reports. (p. 54)

- NIBRS will provide significantly more data than the UCR on each incident.
- NIBRS eliminates the need for a "hierarchy rule."
- Discuss how the new reporting system replaces Part I and Part II offenses with 22 general offenses.

  III. The National Crime Victimization Survey (p. 56)
- Explain that it is based on victim self-reports rather than police reports and that it was started in 1972 to uncover the dark figure of crime.

Dark Figure of Crime   Crime that is not reported to the police and that remains unknown to officials. (p. 56)

- Cite its ability to show that many more crimes occur than are reported.
- Explain that the Bureau of Justice Statistics gathers these data from a semiannual national sample of more than 50,000 households.
- Explain that it includes data on six crimes: rape, robbery, assault, burglary, personal and household larceny, and motor vehicle theft.
- Discuss how NCVS crime rates indicate that they have reached their lowest level since the survey began.

INSTRUCTIONAL CUE LINKED TO THE STUDENT STUDY GUIDE

Use Student Activity 3 to illustrate the types of data that can be collected in victimization surveys. This activity would probably be more successful as a class or group project than as an individual assignment. Students can design the questionnaire during one class meeting and then collect the data between class sessions. You can ask questions about the results at the next class session.

  IV. Comparisons of the UCR and NCVS (p. 57)
- Both provide crime estimates.
- Both are limited by the types of crimes they measure.
- Both are limited by those they exclude from measurement.
- Both are limited by the methods they use to gather crime data.
- Since UCR data are based primarily on citizens' crime reports, often people do not report the crime to the police. Even if they report, they may not be accurate.

- UCR reports are filtered through a number of bureaucratic levels.
- Certain types of crime are reported rarely, if at all.
- Problems with the NCVS include the following: The survey selectively includes data from people willing to answer the questions, some victims are afraid to report, and the survey tends to include information from more reclusive respondents.

INSTRUCTIONAL CUE

Ask students whether the following statistics would be found in the UCR or the NCVS.

In 2005, 254 infants were murdered. **(UCR)**

Approximately 40% of crimes are reported to the police. **(NCVS)**

Fifty-six percent of aggravated assaults are cleared by arrest. **(UCR)**

The arson rate in 2005 was 5,660. **(UCR)**

V. Special Categories of Crime (p. 59)

Crime Typology   A classification of crimes along a particular dimension, such as legal categories, offender motivation, victim behavior, or the characteristics of individual offenders. (p. 59)

- Women are victimized far less frequently than men but are more likely to be injured during victimization.
- They are more likely than men to make modifications in their lifestyles because of fear of crime.

Stalking   Repeated harassing and threatening behavior by one individual against another, aspects of which may be planned or carried out in secret. Stalking might involve following a person, appearing at a person's home or place of business, making harassing phone calls, leaving written messages or objects, or vandalizing a person's property. Most stalking laws require that the perpetrator make a credible threat of violence against the victim or members of the victim's immediate family. (p. 59)

- Discuss findings from the National Violence Against Women Survey and the Violence Against Women Act.

Cyberstalking   The use of the Internet, e-mail, and other electronic communication technologies to stalk another person. (p. 62)

- Criminal victimization declines with age.
- Elderly people are less likely to protect themselves when they are victims of violent crime.
- The elderly face special kinds of victimization that only rarely affect younger adults.

Hate Crime   A criminal offense in which the motive is hatred, bias, or prejudice based on the actual or perceived race, color, religion, national origin, ethnicity, gender, or sexual orientation of another individual or group of individuals. Also called bias crime. (p. 63)

- Discuss the increase of violence against Arab-Americans following the September 11 attacks.
- Discuss law enforcement's growing concern about white separatist groups.
- Explain the Supreme Court decisions discussed in this section: In *R.A.V.* v. *City of St. Paul*, the Court struck down a city ordinance that prevented the bias-motivated display of symbols or objects. In contrast, however, the Court in *Wisconsin* v. *Mitchell* held that a man charged with a racially motivated beating of a white man could be punished with additional severity.

In *Forsyth County, Georgia* v. *Nationalist Movement*, the Court held that a county requirement regulating parades was unconstitutional because it regulated freedom of speech, and in *Capitol Square Review and Advisory Board* v. *Pinette*, the Court reiterated its position stated in the case of *Forsyth County, Georgia* v. *Nationalist Movement*. In this case, the Court stated that Ku Klux Klan organizers could legitimately erect an unattended cross.

Corporate Crime   A violation of a criminal statute by a corporate entity or by its executives, employees, or agents acting on behalf of and for the benefit of the corporation, partnership, or other form of business entity. (p. 64)

White-Collar Crime   Violations of the criminal law committed by a person of respectability and high social status in the course of his or her occupation. Also, nonviolent crime for financial gain utilizing deception and committed by anyone who has special technical and professional knowledge of business and government, irrespective of the person's occupation. (p. 64)

Organized Crime   The unlawful activities of the members of a highly organized, disciplined association engaged in supplying illegal goods and services, including gambling, prostitution, loan-sharking, narcotics, and labor racketeering, and in other unlawful activities. (p. 65)

Transnational Organized Crime   Unlawful activity undertaken and supported by organized criminal groups operating across national boundaries. (p. 65)

- The Brady Handgun Violence Prevention Act was passed in 1994. It provided a five-day waiting period and a national incident criminal background check system.
- Discuss the research that indicates that most offenders obtained weapons from friends or family members and that a growing number of violent criminals are carrying handguns.
- Discuss the links between drugs and crime.
- Explain that a large percentage of homicides are drug related.

Computer Crime   Any crime perpetrated through the use of computer technology. Also, any violation of a federal or state computer-crime statute. Also called cybercrime. (P.67))

INSTRUCTIONAL CUE LINKED TO THE STUDENT STUDY GUIDE

Have students complete Student Activity 5. This would be an excellent assignment to review the material from Chapter 2.

Learner Activities

Activity 1

Pick a newspaper that interests you. You could use your campus newspaper, a local city newspaper, or a national newspaper such as *USA Today*. In addition, most newspapers post articles on the Web.

Collect 30 crime articles from your newspaper. Read the articles you have collected, and then answer the following questions.

1. What types of crime are presented in the news?
2. What characteristics of crime victims are presented in the news? What characteristics of defendants are presented in the news?
3. Compare what you have discovered with the statistical information discussed in Chapter 2. Do the news media provide an accurate picture of crime in society?

_____

_____

_____

_____

_____

_____

Activity 2

Determine the number of index crimes reported to your university police department for each of the last five years. This information should be readily available to you from the police department, and it probably is posted on its website. Universities have been required to publish annual security reports since 1992. If you are having difficulties finding this information, check the Security on Campus website at http://www. campussafety.org. Click on the College and University Campus Crime Statistics link. Include in your statistics the number of murders, forcible rapes, aggravated assaults, robberies, burglaries, motor vehicle thefts, larcenies, and arson cases that have been reported each of the last five years. Answer the following questions, using these data, in the space provided below. Is your campus safe? Do the data show increases, decreases, or no change in the number of crimes committed on your campus? What types of things does your university do to make the campus safe for students?

_____

_____

_____

_____

_____

_____

Activity 3

Create a victimization questionnaire that you can use to determine the amount and types of victimization that occur on campus. Be sure to ask about the types of victimization experienced, the circumstances of each incident (where did the incident occur? what time?), and whether the student reported the incident to the police. In addition, collect demographic data so that you will be able to classify the responses by sex, age, and race. After you have completed the questionnaire, administer it to at least 50 students and then tabulate the results. What did you learn about victimization from the surveys? What types of victimization were reported? Were there differences by sex? Race? Age?

_____

_____

_____

_____

_____

_____

Activity 4

Read the articles posted at **Library Extras 2–6** and **2–9** at cjtoday.com, and then answer the following questions. What did you learn about violence against women in the United States? What are the major consequences of violence against women? How has the gender gap in crime changed over time?

_____

_____

_____

_____

_____

_____

Activity 5

Visit the Prentice Hall Cybrary at http://www.cybrary.info. Click on Statistics. This section provides helpful information and interesting links to a variety of statistical data sources. Included here is a variety of crime statistics from throughout the world. For example, there are data from the British Crime Survey and the World Crime Survey. For this assignment, you are to collect crime data for any country of your choice other than the United States. In the space below, first discuss the amount and types of crimes in that country. Second, compare the crime picture of that country to what we have learned in this chapter about the United States according to the Uniform Crime Report statistics and National Crime Victimization Survey's data.

_____

_____

_____

_____

_____

_____

Internet Activity

Visit the Prentice Hall Cybrary (http://www.cybrary.info) and use its search feature to find links to both the Uniform Crime Reports and the Sourcebook of Criminal Justice Statistics. Visit both sites in order to gather information about murder. How much information is available at these sites? What does it consist of? What are the similarities and the differences in the availability of information on the crime of murder between these two sites? Generally speaking, how do the two sites compare? Which one did you find more useful? Why?

_____

_____

_____

_____

_____

Distance Learning Activity

Read some of the following materials about new and promising strategies implemented to respond to juvenile homicide: (1) Blueprints for Violence Prevention (see section on model program descriptions) at http://www.ncjrs.org/html/ojjdp/jjbul2001_7_3/contents.html; (2) Gun Use by Male Juveniles (see section on promising gun strategies) at http://www.ncjrs.org/html/ojjdp/jjbul2001_7_2/contents.html; (3) Homicides of Children and Youth at http://www.ncjrs.org/pdffiles1/ojjdp/187239.pdf; (4) Youth Gang Homicides in the 1990s at http://www.ncjrs.org/txtfiles1/ojjdp/fs200103.txt; and (5) Office of Juvenile Justice and Delinquency Prevention page at http://ojjdp.ncjrs.org/ojstatbb/index.html. After reading these materials, answer the following questions: What data about the juvenile homicide problem exist? Describe the major trends in the incidence of juvenile violence over the last ten years. What innovative strategies have been used to respond more effectively to the juvenile homicide problem?

_____

_____

_____

_____

_____

_____

Learning Activities Utilizing the World Wide web

There are student-based activities in the Student Study Guide (Internet Activity, Distance Learning Activity, CJ Today on the World Wide Web) that are similar in focus to those that follow. However, the following are presented as instructor-led activities, to be used in a classroom with online access.

Visit the Prentice Hall Cybrary at http://www.cybrary.info and use its search feature to find links to both the Uniform Crime Reports and the Sourcebook of Criminal Justice Statistics. Collect information on murder from both sites. Display this information in class and discuss the following:

How much information is available at these sites?

What does it consist of?

What are the similarities and the differences in the availability of information on the crime of murder between these two sites?

Generally speaking, how do the two sites compare?

Which one do you find more useful? Why?

Read some of the following materials about new and promising strategies implemented to respond to juvenile homicide:

1. Blueprints for Violence Prevention (see section on model program descriptions) at http://www.ncjrs.org/html/ojjdp/jjbul2001_7_3/contents.html

2. Gun Use by Male Juveniles (see section on promising gun strategies) at http://www.ncjrs.org/html/ojjdp/jjbul2001_7_2/contents.html

3. Homicides of Children and Youth at http://www.ncjrs.org/pdffiles1/ojjdp/187239.pdf

4. Youth Gang Homicides in the 1990s at http://www.ncjrs.org/txtfiles1/ojjdp/fs200103.txt

5. The Office of Juvenile Justice and Delinquency Prevention page at http://ojjdp.ncjrs.org/ojstatbb/index.html

Display parts of each site in class and discuss the following:

What data about the juvenile homicide problem exist?

Describe the major trends in the incidence of juvenile violence over the last ten years.

What innovative strategies have been used to respond more effectively to the juvenile homicide problem?

Visit the Criminal Justice Today website at http://cjtoday.com. You'll find links to study aids tailored to each chapter in the text, Web Extras and Library Extras, crime and justice news, and the Prentice Hall Cybrary.

Other websites for organizations and agencies related to the material in Chapter 2 include:

Sourcebook of Criminal Justice Statistics	http://www.albany.edu/sourcebook
Uniform Crime Reports	http://www.fbi.gov
NIBRS (coming UCR changes)	http://www.nibrs.search.org
Bureau of Justice Statistics	http://www.ojp.usdoj.gov/bjs
Bureau of Justice Assistance	http://www.ojp.usdoj.gov/BJA
FBI Hate Crime Statistics	http://www.fbi.gov/ucr/hatecm.htm
Fedstats	http://www.fedstats.gov
Violence Policy Center	http://www.vpc.org

Suggested Answers to Chapter Discussion Questions

1. **What are the two major crime data-gathering programs in the United States? How do they differ? How are they alike?**

   The two major sources of crime statistics are the Federal Bureau of Investigation's Uniform Crime Reporting Program (UCR) and the Bureau of Justice Statistics' National Crime Victimization Survey (NCVS).

   Differences between the two sources include:

   - Differences in crimes reported: The UCR data include statistics on homicides and incomplete data on arsons; the NCVS does not report homicide or arson data.

   - Differences in data-gathering methodology: The UCR reflects specific crimes reported to law enforcement agencies throughout the country; the NCVS reflects the results of interviewer surveys from "households touched by crime."

   - Differences in scope: The UCR includes only crimes reported; the NCVS includes crimes that were not necessarily reported to the police but that have been uncovered using door-to-door surveys.

   - Differences in information: The UCR reports data on crimes cleared and persons arrested; the NCVS does not. However, the NCVS provides greater detail about victims and their characteristics.

   Similarities between the two sources include the fact that they report data on many of the same types of crime.

2. **What can crime statistics tell us about the crime picture in America?**

   Analysis of crime data yields discernible patterns of crime and victimization rates and the demography of both crime victims and criminals. Changes in the frequency or types of crime in specific geographic regions are easily detectable, as are changes in the participation of specific demographic groupings in criminality. Statistics are also able to show how public perceptions of crime are not always realistic and the influence of the media in creating those perceptions.

How has that picture changed over time?

Since its inception in 1930, the UCR Program has enabled researchers to identify major shifts in crime rates. The first was a pronounced reduction in crime rates after the crime-prone young male segment of the population entered military service in large numbers during World War II. The second shift was a dramatic increase as the postwar baby-boom generation entered its teen years—the crime-prone age range—in the 1960s. Another escalation was detected in the 1980s, when drug-related violent crimes increased significantly, peaking about 1991. Through the remainder of the 1990s, major crime rates initially stabilized and then began showing declines in almost all categories.

3. **What are the potential sources of error in the major reports on crime?**

UCR data are flawed for a number of reasons. Because they reflect only crimes reported to law enforcement agencies, they omit crimes that are not reported. For example, a drug dealer is unlikely to file a report if someone steals his or her drug supply. Likewise, the victim of the theft of a $20 item will probably not file a report because the amount of the deductible on his or her insurance (if he or she has it) likely exceeds the amount of the loss. So-called victimless crimes such as prostitution and gambling are also rarely reported.

Further, the hierarchy rule, which mandates that only the most serious crime be reported in cases where multiple crimes are committed, prevents the counting of criminal events known to have occurred. And the rates of sexual assault offenses other than rape are obscured because they are lumped into the assault category rather than being clearly defined as sexually motivated attacks. Some of these problems are being addressed by adoption of the National Incident-Based Reporting System (NIBRS), an update of the UCR Program that is being implemented even as this text goes to press.

NCVS data suffer from the potential for receiving false or exaggerated reports, from unintentional inaccuracies resulting from the faulty memories of people who submit reports, from misinterpretation of events by people who make the reports, and by the erroneous assessment of criminality to an event that was genuinely accidental.

Can you think of some popular usage of those statistics that might be especially misleading?

It has become commonplace for the news media to report declines in the overall rate of crime in the United States. Such reports, of course, are based on "official" crime statistics—especially those made available through the UCR. Because data on crime rates, however, are based primarily on the reported rates of specific crimes (such as murder, rape, and robbery), any increase or change in the rates of novel forms of crimes not covered by the program will not be visible. Hence, the recent rise in high-technology crimes is not obvious because it does not fall into one of the categories of crime reported under the UCR Program.

Individual reporting categories lend themselves to similar difficulties. An example might be the use of UCR rape data in the media's reporting of sexual criminal activity. Because crimes such as sexual battery, sodomy, oral copulation, and same-sex rape are not included in rape data, a news report based solely on the numbers reflected in the rape category would clearly be misleading.

4. **What is the Crime Index, and how is it computed? What crimes make up the Crime Index?**

The Crime Index is an inclusive measure of the violent and property crime categories of the UCR, also known as Part I offenses. Originally, seven major offenses—murder, forcible rape, robbery, aggravated assault, burglary, larceny-theft, and motor vehicle theft—were listed. In 1979 Congress mandated the addition of arson as the eighth reported offense. The index employs the concept of a crime rate (the number of crimes per unit of population) in the computation of its data.

Why is it difficult to add offenses to (or remove them from) the index without lessening its value as a comparative tool?

Less-than-ideal comparisons may result from the inclusion of new offenses or removal of previously reported offenses. In the case of additions, this would cause uncertainty regarding whether occurrences of the newly categorized offense were previously reported in another crime category, thereby skewing comparisons of data in the former reporting category before and after the realignment. For obvious reasons, the removal of a crime category would negate postremoval comparisons.

5. **Why are many crime statistics expressed as rates? How does the use of crime rates instead of simple numerical tabulation improve the reporting of crime data?**

Expressing crime statistics as rates permits comparisons among areas, across time, and among populations of widely varied sizes. Pure numbers can be grossly misleading. In a city with a population of 7 million, 600 murders would equate to a murder rate of 8.57 per 100,000. If 30 murders occur in a city with a population of 300,000, the rate would be 10 per 100,000. Observers might fixate on the huge number of murders in the larger city—600—and inaccurately believe the city to be more dangerous than the smaller city. In fact, the smaller city, with its higher rate per 100,000, presents a greater risk of being murdered.

This ability to evaluate crime data on a universal scale clarifies the true meaning of the hard numbers, defuses emotional responses to large numbers, and enables the researcher to interpret more accurately what those numbers really mean.

6. **What are the two major crime categories in Part I offenses in the Uniform Crime Reports?**

Part I offenses are categorized as violent (or personal) crimes and property crimes.

Do some property crimes have a violent aspect?

Certain property crimes often include a violent aspect. Examples include:

- A motor vehicle theft by carjacking that results in the injury or death of the vehicle's owner.
- A burglary that involves a violent confrontation between the property owner and the burglar.
- An arson that results in the injury or death of a person.
- A larceny by purse snatching that results in injury to the purse's owner.

Are there any personal crimes that could be nonviolent? If so, what might they be?

For a crime to be categorized as a violent crime, it is not necessary for actual injury or death to occur. Violence can extend from the mere threat of physical harm or from intimidation that leads the victim to believe he or she will suffer physical harm if he or she resists. Consequently, personal crimes are inherently violent.

7. **What is the hierarchy rule in crime-reporting programs? What purpose does it serve?**

The hierarchy rule mandates reporting only the most serious crime in cases where multiple crimes are committed. For example, if the criminal event included kidnapping, rape, and murder, only the murder would be recorded. Although the original intent of the hierarchy rule has been obscured, it was likely created as an accommodation to the manual crime-reporting processes that existed in the 1930s, when the UCR was created.

What do you think of the modifications in the hierarchy rule that are occurring today under the National Incident-Based Reporting System?

The NIBRS mandate to report all crimes committed during a criminal event will improve the accuracy of the crime "count," but at the cost of reducing the comparability of pre- and post-NIBRS data.

8. **What is a clearance rate? What does it mean to say that a crime has been cleared? In what ways can a crime be cleared?**

   When a crime has been cleared, it has been solved. A crime can be cleared by arrest or by exceptional circumstances (as when the suspect has been killed during the commission of the crime, when the suspect was not arrested but later died, or when the suspect is known but has fled U.S. jurisdiction and is likely to be unarrestable as a result).

9. **What is the National Incident-Based Reporting System? How does it differ from the traditional Uniform Crime Reporting System?**

   The National Incident-Based Reporting System is an incident-based reporting system that will supersede the traditional data provided by the FBI's Uniform Crime Reports. Under the new enhanced system, law enforcement agencies will provide detailed information about the crime and arrest activities at the incident level. The traditional UCR Program was summary based, and NIBRS is incident driven. The NIBRS also replaces the old Part I and Part II offenses with 22 general offenses. NIBRS also eliminates the need for the hierarchy rule.

10. **What are the special categories of crime that this chapter discusses? Why are they important?**

    The chapter discusses several special categories of crime, including crime against women, crime against the elderly, hate crime, corporate and white-collar crime, organized crime, gun crime, drug crime, high-technology and computer crime, and terrorism. These categories are important because they provide us with additional ways to think about crime and how the criminal justice system responds to crime. The importance of these special categories is also illustrated by thinking of them as crime typologies. Various typologies are used to describe the characteristics of criminal offending. Creating such special categories increases the importance of these types of crime and provides a common ground for scholars and policymakers to discuss them.

Key—Student Study Guide Questions

True or False

____ 2-1. Rapes are significantly more likely than motor vehicle thefts to be reported to the police. **(False, p. 44)**

____ 2-2. Robbery is a crime against property; burglary is a personal crime. **(False, p. 46)**

____ 2-3. Violent crimes are generally more serious than property offenses. **(True, p. 41)**

____ 2-4. The NIBRS eliminates the need for the UCR hierarchy rule. **(True, p. 54)**

____ 2-5. The elderly are generally less likely to be victimized by violent and property crime. **(False, p. 62)**

____ 2-6. Although women are far less frequently victimized by crime than men, they are more likely to be injured by crime. **(True, p. 59)**

____ 2-7. Drug-related and other victimless crimes are all considered Part I offenses by the Federal Bureau of Investigation. **(False, pp. 40–41)**

____ 2-8. Clearance rates refer to the proportion of crimes reported to the police. **(False, p. 41)**

____ 2-9. The National Crime Victimization Survey is compiled annually by the Bureau of Justice Statistics. **(True, p. 56)**

____ 2-10. Murder and aggravated assault are both considered Part I violent crime offenses. **(True, p. 40)**

Multiple Choice

2-11. Which of the following offense categories includes crimes such as larceny and arson?
a. hate crime
b. organized crime
c. violent crime
d. property crime (p. 41)

2-12. Which of the following agencies is responsible for compiling the Uniform Crime Reports?
a. U.S. Marshals Service
b. Office of Juvenile Justice and Delinquency
c. Bureau of Justice Statistics
d. Federal Bureau of Investigation (p. 36)

2-13. Which of the following is not one of the Uniform Crime Reports Part I offenses?
a. drug possession (pp. 40–41)
b. motor vehicle theft
c. murder
d. rape

2-14. What is the reason rape victims give most often for not reporting the crime to the police?
a. not worth the victim's time
b. fear of reprisal
c. fear of embarrassment (p. 44)
d. police cannot do anything about it

2-15. Which of the following is not a problem with traditional Uniform Crime Reports statistics?
a. Certain crimes are rarely reported to the police.
b. When a number of crimes are committed in the same incident, only the most serious crime will be included in UCR data.
c. Victims may believe that the police cannot do anything about a crime, so they do not report it to them.
d. Certain types of crimes, such as victimless crimes, are not included in the UCR.
e. All of the above are problems. (pp. 57–59)

2-16. Which Part I offense is most likely to be reported by a victim to the police?
a. robbery
b. motor vehicle theft (p. 53)
c. larceny
d. rape

2-17. The National Crime Victimization Survey does not include information about which crime?
a. robbery
b. murder (p. 56)
c. household larceny
d. motor vehicle theft

2-18. The stealing of farm machinery would be classified under what category of the UCR?
a. burglary
b. robbery
c. larceny (p. 53)
d. motor vehicle theft

2-19. Megan Anderson unlawfully entered a computer services building and stole a laser printer. What crime did she commit?
   a. aggravated assault
   b. forcible rape
   c. robbery
   d. burglary (p. 49)

2-20. Which of the following is not a victimless crime?
   a. gambling
   b. motor vehicle theft (p. 53)
   c. drug use
   d. prostitution

Fill-In

2-21. _____ is the least reported of all violent index crimes. **(Forcible rape, p. 44)**

2-22. _____ is intentional and wrongful physical contact with a person, without his or her consent, that entails a sexual component or purpose. **(Sexual battery, p. 45)**

2-23. _____ is unlawful forced sexual intercourse with a female against her will that occurs in the context of a dating relationship. **(Date rape, p. 45)**

2-24. The type of assault that includes the use of a weapon or the need for medical assistance for the victim is called _____. **(aggravated assault, p. 49)**

2-25. _____ are criminal offenses in which there is evidence of the perpetrator's prejudice based on the race, religion, sexual orientation, or ethnicity of the victim(s). **(Hate crimes, p. 63)**

2-26. The most common of the eight major index offenses is _____. **(larceny, p. 50)**

2-27. _____ is the use of the Internet, e-mail, and other electronic communication technologies to stalk another person. **(Cyberstalking, p. 62)**

2-28. Sexual intercourse with a female who is under the age of consent—regardless of whether she is a willing partner—is called _____. **(statutory rape, p. 46)**

2-29. The index offense that is most likely to be reported by a victim to the police is _____. **(motor vehicle theft, p. 53)**

2-30. The type of assault that is usually limited to pushing or shoving is _____. **(simple assault, p. 49)**

Key—Crossword Puzzle

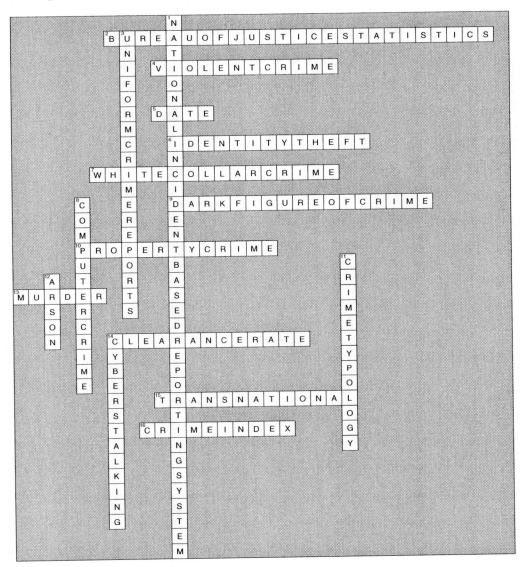

Across

2. Agency responsible for collecting the National Crime Victimization Survey.

4. Murder, rape, robbery, or aggravated assault.

5. Type of rape within the context of a relationship.

6. Crime most likely to ruin a victim's credit history.

7. Type of crime first defined by Edwin Sutherland in 1939.

9. Crimes not reported to police that remain unknown to officials are part of the _____.

10. Burglary, larceny, auto theft, or arson.

13. Unlawful killing of a human being.

14. Number of crimes reported divided by the number of crimes solved.

15. Type of organized crime.

16. Another name for the Part 1 offenses of the UCR.

Down

1. New Uniform Crime Reports.

3. FBI's national source of crime data.

8. Also called cybercrime.

11. Classification scheme used in the study and description of criminal behavior.

12. Burning or attempted burning of property, with or without the intent to defraud.

14. Use of the Internet to stalk a person.

Key—Word Search Puzzle

```
Z H O C J E Y V A T D A U S A S Y V B Z U V G X X R K B Q X
T D L L G K P W A T G O Q E P Y E S F V Q N Y G P G O F J S
P G A T Y O Y D U S C W A M V C O O Z L I A U I F H E N K I
M Y A W C K C J A K L D J Z N Y D A W K R W T F X O N M F Z
T W E N I O W L N R U Z N L F E Z G L X U N S V F A W C Q B
N O I G E V M N X Y K D X G L V Z A K K Q F S V H I R A P S
C A X Z Z U R P Q Q Y F P S L Q T N T O X G M V O Q V S V H
C S K S P B J U U R P F I Y Y S H F W S T A U Z S Y P C O C
S C O C A N B R A T R Y R G R H E V Y U T M S B Q D N M C N
I L O U V H T L T Y E J M E U H W S E B A U Y S N H H S X I
Z E K Q S T G F Q I B R B O T R Q W N E Y R B I A X E L U L
Y A N I A R W G W O I Y C Y T I E D Y T N D T Y E U K I A O
F R K L U Y I I N L C V N R R O S O G N P E P M A M L N V N
O A H B U X A M D N C E S P I P R W F G K R L S X R J T I K
Q N D A K U X F I N C U T A S M H V H C F U T K F K R W O F
F C I U R G E N R R E F U F M I E T E Q R O J Y E C E Y G V
A E V L T O N O A A E W D C A M L Y S H C I T A A B C M J X
F R L T B L B L J H I G Y X F Z C P X V I R M F O R I U S H
E A G A J C A B T O V B O Z I J D O P K D C I E C K N H Q K
N T F H T F N Y E U T H U P U V V L T P L P L M R L U E S I
J E Q H K M T P D R B X B A C P H O V I S U L E B U J L D
C N N Q Z I I P I A Y T A J R M H G K I S T C Y T I A J W A
X B Y H T E F R X H R E O S A R Z Y H G S B A Y E H N U U Q
J B Y N I X L D M T X C D R P U B G E A V O E L J N E D Y T
J M E O Y O W Z B L V R T F E O W W T A W P V R K Y Y F E Z
T D S A S E X U A L B A T T E R Y J N I B R S O G I N Z T X
I J M G J U X N F E G T T X Q I M O C U M H K J X H N J N Q
F M U B Q C A A G G R A V A T E D A S S A U L T P H B G Q F
C K F Y T B U R E A U O F J U S T I C E S T A T I S T I C S
N Q V P D T K T T V N B O P W N N O F T L P J Y I K J G Y Q
```

Aggravated Assault

Arson

Bureau of Justice Statistics

Burglary

Clearance Rate

Computer Crime

Crime Index

Cyberstalking

Dark Figure of Crime

Identity Theft

Larceny-Theft

Motor Vehicle Theft

Murder

NCVS

NIBRS

Rape

Robbery

Sexual Battery

Stalking

CHAPTER 3

The Search for Causes

LEARNING OBJECTIVES

After reading this chapter, you should be able to:

- List the various categories of theoretical approaches used to explain crime
- Describe the basic features of biological theories of crime causation
- Describe the basic features of psychological explanations for crime
- Describe the basic features of sociological theories of crime causation
- Identify two emergent theories of crime causation

Chapter Summary

Chapter 3 provides an overview of theories used to explain the causes of crime. Chapter 3 first discusses the criminological theories of the **Classical School**, including the works of **Cesare Beccaria** and **Jeremy Bentham**. The text discusses the five basic assumptions of classical theory:

1. Crime is caused by the individual exercise of free will.
2. Pain and pleasure are the two central determinants of human behavior.
3. Crime disparages the quality of the bond that exists between individuals and society.
4. Punishment is necessary to deter violators of the law and to serve as an example to others.
5. Crime prevention is possible through swift and certain punishment.

Theories in the **Biological School** search for physical or biological explanations of crime. Influenced by medical and technological advances, these theories have evolved over time. Compare the early biological theories of **Gall, Lombroso**, and **Sheldon** to contemporary biochemical theories. Gall argued that skull shape determined personality and behavior. Lombroso considered various parts of the body in his **atavistic** explanation for crime. Criminals, he argued, were throwbacks to earlier stages of evolution. William Sheldon used **somatotyping** (or body typing) to categorize each individual's physique by its mesomorphic, endomorphic, and ectomorphic characteristics. Sheldon found that juveniles with dominant mesomorphic physiques were most likely to commit crime. Richard Dugdale has considered biological inheritance as applied to criminal families in his examination of the Jukes family tree and Henry Goddard's study of the Kallikaks.

Biological theories have advanced with medical technology. For example, chromosome theories look to internal gene structure to understand the causes of crime. The XYY chromosome theory was popular in the 1960s and early 1970s, but later studies question the ability of the XYY theory to predict criminal behavior. Other biological theories have examined the effects of chemical imbalances, hormones, and allergic reactions to food on criminal behavior.

Psychological explanations argue that criminal behavior results from inappropriately conditioned behavior or from abnormal, dysfunctional, and inappropriate mental processes. One thread of psychological theories presented in the text is **behavioral conditioning**. Another thread focuses on personality disturbances and diseases of the mind. People who believe in conditioning hold that the frequency of any behavior can be increased through rewards, punishments, and/or association with other stimuli. **Sigmund Freud** argued that personality was developed from the interaction of the id, the ego, and the superego. One source of criminal behavior is the ability of a person's superego to control his or her id.

Sociological explanations of crime examine the effects on behavior of environmental forces such as poverty, urban decay, and unemployment. For example, **Shaw** and **McKay's** social ecology theory argues that certain areas of a city—those with high rates of poverty, unemployment, and lack of schooling—are socially disorganized and likely to produce crime. **Merton**, borrowing the concept of **anomie** from Emile Durkheim, argued that since the means to achieve goals are not equally available to all groups, individuals are forced to use illegitimate means, such as crime, to accomplish goals. On the other hand, **subcultural theories** argue that the goals of various groups are different and some groups view committing crime as a legitimate goal. For example, **Marvin Wolfgang** and Franco Ferracuti found that murder was an acceptable goal for certain groups.

Chapter 3 also discusses **social process theories, conflict theories**, and some emerging theories such as **feminist criminology. Social process theories** explain deviant behavior by highlighting the process of interaction between individuals and society. **Conflict theories** consider law a tool of the powerful, which is used by the powerful to further their own interests. **Feminist criminology** emphasizes gender issues in criminology. None of these theories provides a definitive explanation of why people commit crimes. However, understanding how these theories explain the causes of crime is important because they have an impact on the development of criminal justice policy and the criminal justice system's response to crime.

Teaching Outline

I. Introduction (p. 80)

- Define deviance, and explain the difference between criminal and deviant behavior.

Deviance   A violation of social norms defining appropriate or proper behavior under a particular set of circumstances. Deviance often includes criminal acts. Also called *deviant behavior.* (p. 80)

- Explain the range of theories available to explain criminal behavior.

INSTRUCTIONAL CUE

Show the class a picture of a well-known criminal (for example, Al Capone, Jeffrey Dahmer, Charles Manson). Describe his or her criminal activities and any background information you can find about him or her. In general terms, discuss how the various theoretical schools would attempt to explain that person's behavior. For example, the biological theorists might argue that Jeffrey Dahmer was born to be a serial murderer. However, sociological theorists would argue that Dahmer was shaped by his environment.

INSTRUCTIONAL CUE LINKED TO THE STUDENT STUDY GUIDE

Use the first student activity in the Student Study Guide to help illustrate the process of theory building. This assignment should generate considerable discussion. You could even ask students to submit the lyrics of their favorite songs and have them underline words and phrases relevant to the materials covered in class.

II. Criminological Theory (p. 82)

Theory   A set of interrelated propositions that attempt to describe, explain, predict, and ultimately control some class of events. A theory gains explanatory power from inherent logical consistency and is "tested" by how well it describes and predicts reality. (p. 82)

INSTRUCTIONAL CUE

Establish criteria for a "good" theory. Ask students to suggest what makes one theory better than another.

Hypothesis   An explanation that accounts for a set of facts and that can be tested by further investigation; also, something that is taken to be true for the purpose of argument or investigation. *Source: The American Heritage Dictionary and Electronic Thesaurus on CD-ROM* (Boston: Houghton Mifflin, 1987).(p. 82)

- Explain the use of research to test hypotheses.

Research   The use of standardized, systematic procedures in the search for knowledge. (p. 82)

Interdisciplinary Theory   An approach that integrates a variety of theoretical viewpoints in an attempt to explain crime and violence. (p. 83)

III. The Classical School (p. 86)

Classical School   An eighteenth-century approach to crime causation and criminal responsibility that grew out of the Enlightenment and that emphasized the role of free will and reasonable punishments. Classical thinkers believed that punishment, if it is to be an effective deterrent, has to outweigh the potential pleasure derived from criminal behavior. (p. 86)

- Basic assumptions:
  - Crime is caused by an inappropriate exercise of free will.
  - Pain and pleasure are two central determinants of human behavior.
  - Crime is an immoral form of behavior.
  - Punishment is required to deter violators of law from future crimes and to serve as an example to potential violators.
  - Crime prevention is possible through swift and certain punishment.
  A. Cesare Beccaria: Crime and Punishment (p. 86)
     - Wrote *Essays on Crimes and Punishment*
     - Stated that punishment should deter but not be excessive
     - Is considered the founder of the Classical School
  B. Jeremy Bentham: Hedonistic Calculus (p. 86)
     - Devised the hedonistic calculus
     - Believed the philosophy of social control is utilitarianism
     - Like Beccaria, believed that punishment should be swift and certain
  C. The Neoclassical Perspective (p. 86)
     - Explain this perspective, and discuss rational choice and routine activities theory.

Neoclassical Criminology   A contemporary version of classical criminology that emphasizes deterrence and retribution and that holds that human beings are essentially free to make choices in favor of crime and deviance or conformity. (p. 86)

Rational Choice Theory   A perspective on crime causation that holds that criminality is the result of conscious choice. Rational choice theory predicts that individuals will choose to commit crime when the benefits of doing so outweigh the costs of disobeying the law. (p. 86)

Routine Activities Theory   A neoclassical perspective that suggests that lifestyles contribute significantly to both the volume and the type of crime found in any society. (p. 87)

  D. Social Policy and Classical Theories (p. 87)
     - Most criminal justice policy is built around the conceptual basis provided by the Classical School.

INSTRUCTIONAL CUE LINKED TO THE STUDENT STUDY GUIDE

The section on each theory ends with a discussion of the implications of that theory for social policy. For example, the section about psychological theory ends with the discussion of social policy and psychological theory. After you complete the discussion of a type of theory, or when you have completed this chapter, assign Student Activity 2. This is also a good exercise to illustrate the links between criminal justice and criminology (discussed in Chapter 1).

  IV. Biological Theories (p. 87)

Biological School   A perspective on criminological thought that holds that criminal behavior has a physiological basis. (p. 87)

- Assumptions:
  - Human behavior is genetically based.
  - A penchant for crime may be inherited.
  - Criminals and deviants are in more primitive developmental stages in the evolutionary process than most people.
  A. Franz Joseph Gall: Phrenology (p. 87)

- Argued bodily constitution might reflect personality
- Developed cranioscopy

Phrenology   The study of the shape of the head to determine anatomical correlates of human behavior. (p. 88)

      B. Cesare Lombroso: Atavism (p. 88)
- Founder of the Positivist School of criminology

Atavism   A condition characterized by the existence of features thought to be common in earlier stages of human evolution. (p. 89)

Positivist School   An approach to criminal justice theory that stresses the application of scientific techniques to the study of crime and criminals. (p. 89)

- Is considered the "father of modern criminology"
- Identified a large number of atavistic traits that can lead to crime
  1. The Evidence for and against Atavism
      C. Criminal Families (p. 90)
- Highlight Richard Dugdale's examination of the Jukes family and Henry Goddard's examination of the Kallikaks family.
      D. William Sheldon: Somatotypes (p. 90)

Somatotyping   The classification of human beings into types according to body build and other physical characteristics. (p. 90)

- Describe mesomorphs.
- Describe endomorphs.
- Describe ectomorphs.

INSTRUCTIONAL CUE

To illustrate each type of body in Sheldon's theory, use celebrity figures. You could also assign students to cut out magazine pictures that depict each body type.

      E. Social Policy and Biological Theories (p. 90)
- Tied to the eugenics movement

INSTRUCTIONAL CUE

As a discussion starter, use the example of the death penalty or of life in prison without the possibility of parole for offenders who are thought to be criminal by virtue of some biological defect.

   V. Psychobiological Theories (p. 91)
      A. Chromosome Theory (p. 91)
- Explain why men with the XYY chromosomal makeup are identified as "supermales."

Supermale   A human male displaying the XYY chromosome structure. (p. 91)

- Explain the limited value of this theory.
      B. Biochemical Factors and Imbalances (p. 91)

INSTRUCTIONAL CUE

Discuss various biochemical factors thought to be linked with behavior (for example, allergic reactions, effects of vitamins).

C. Heredity and Other Physical Factors (p. 92)
- Describe this as an effort to combine biology and environment.
- Explain the research of both James Q. Wilson and Richard Herrnstein.

D. Social Policy and Psychobiological Theories (p. 93)
VI. Psychological Theories (p. 93)

Psychological School   A perspective on criminological thought that views offensive and deviant behavior as the product of dysfunctional personalities. Psychological thinkers identify the conscious, and especially the subconscious, contents of the human psyche as major determinants of behavior. (p. 93)

- Assumptions:
  - The individual is the primary unit of analysis.
  - Personality is the major motivational element in individuals.
  - Crimes result from inappropriately conditioned behavior.
  - Defective or abnormal mental processes may have a variety of causes.

A. Behavioral Conditioning (p. 93)

Behavioral Conditioning   A psychological principle that holds that the frequency of any behavior can be increased or decreased through reward, punishment, and/or association with other stimuli. (p. 93)

- Discuss Pavlov's work with dogs.

B. Freudian Psychoanalysis (p. 93)
- Suggests that crime could result from three conditions:
  - A weak superego that cannot control the id
  - Sublimation
  - The death wish

Psychoanalysis   A theory of human behavior, based upon the writings of Sigmund Freud, which sees personality as a complex composite of interacting mental entities. (p. 93)

C. Psychopathology and Crime (p. 94)
- Describe development of the concept of psychopathic personality.

Psychopathology   The study of pathological mental conditions—that is, mental illness. (p. 94)

Psychopath   A person with a personality disorder, especially one manifested in aggressively antisocial behavior, which is often said to be the result of a poorly developed superego. (p. 95)

INSTRUCTIONAL CUE

Discuss the Psychological School's claim that crime occurs because of a diseased mind or disordered personality.

D. The Psychotic Offender (p. 95)

Psychosis   A form of mental illness in which sufferers are said to be out of touch with reality. (p. 95)

Schizophrenic   A mentally ill individual who suffers from disjointed thinking and possibly from delusions and hallucinations. (p. 96)

E. Psychological Profiling (p. 96)

Psychological Profiling The attempt to categorize, understand, and predict the behavior of certain types of offenders based upon behavioral clues they provide. (p. 96)

- Explain how Adolf Hitler became the first subject for psychological profiling when Allied leaders employed it in an effort to find possible weaknesses in his psyche.
  F. Social Policy and Psychological Theories (p. 96)
  - Describe the Psychological School's orientation toward individual treatment, which is to expose the individual offender to various forms of therapy.

Dangerousness The likelihood that a given individual will later harm society or others. Dangerousness is often measured in terms of recidivism, the likelihood of additional crime commission within five years following arrest or release from confinement. (p. 96)

VII. Sociological Theories (p. 96)

Chicago School A sociological approach that emphasizes demographics (the characteristics of population groups) and geographics (the mapped locations of such groups relative to one another) and that sees the social disorganization that characterizes delinquency areas as a major cause of criminality and victimization. (p. 96)

Social Disorganization A condition said to exist when a group is faced with social change, uneven development of culture, maladaptiveness, disharmony, conflict, and lack of consensus. (p. 97)

- Assumptions:
  - Social groups, social institutions, the arrangements of society, and social roles all provide the proper focus for criminological study.
  - Group dynamics, group organization, and subgroup relationships form the causal nexus out of which crime develops.
  - The structure of society and its relative degree of organization or disorganization are important factors that contribute to the prevalence of criminal behavior.
  A. Social Ecology Theory (p. 97)
  - Mapping occurs according to social characteristics.
  - Explain "zone two" crime rate.
  - Crime depends on aspects of social structure.
  - Elements include poverty, illiteracy, lack of schooling, unemployment, and illegitimacy.
  B. Anomie Theory (p. 97)

Anomie A socially pervasive condition of normlessness. A disjuncture between approved goals and means. (p. 97)

- Merton applied anomie to criminology.
- Anomie is a disjuncture between approved goals and means.
- Discuss the characteristics of innovators—retreatist, ritualist, and rebel.
  C. Subcultural Theory (p. 98)

Defensible Space Theory The belief that an area's physical features may be modified and structured so as to reduce crime rates in that area and to lower the fear of victimization that residents experience. (p. 99)

Broken Windows Thesis A perspective on crime causation that holds that physical deterioration in an area leads to higher crime rates and an increased concern for personal safety among residents. (p. 99)

• Discuss Cohen's term *reaction formation*.

Reaction Formation The process whereby a person openly rejects that which he or she wants or aspires to but cannot obtain or achieve. (p. 100)

- A subculture consists of a group of people who share a system of values and norms that are at variance with the larger culture.
- Subcultural explanations of crime posit the existence of group values supportive of criminal behavior.

Subculture of Violence A cultural setting in which violence is a traditional and often accepted method of dispute resolution. (p. 100)

- Discuss gangs and the gang lifestyle to illustrate subcultural theory.

D. Social Policy and Sociological Theory (p. 100)
- Asserts that social action is a panacea

VIII. Social Process Theories (p. 101)

Social Process Theory A perspective on criminological thought that highlights the process of interaction between individuals and society. Most social process theories highlight the role of social learning. (p. 101)

A. Differential Association Theory (p. 101)
- Crime is a product of socialization.
- Crime is the natural consequence of an individual's interaction with criminal lifestyles.

Social Learning Theory A psychological perspective that says that people learn how to behave by modeling themselves after others whom they have the opportunity to observe. (p. 101)

B. Restraint Theories (p. 102)
1. Containment Theory
- Focuses on constraints rather than causes
- Inner and outer containment

Containment The aspects of the social bond and of the personality that act to prevent individuals from committing crimes and that keep them from engaging in deviance. (p. 102)

2. Social Control Theory
- Focuses on bonds between individuals and society
- Types of bonds
- Emotional attachments
- A commitment to appropriate lifestyles
- Involvement or immersion in conventional values
- A belief in the correctness of social obligations
3. Neutralization Techniques
- Explain these techniques as rationalizations that allow offenders to shed feelings of guilt and any sense of responsibility.

C. Labeling Theory (p. 103)

Labeling Theory A social process perspective that sees continued crime as a consequence of the limited opportunities for acceptable behavior that follow from the negative responses of society to those defined as offenders. (p. 103)

- It focuses on constraints rather than causes.
- Describe how the criminal label produces consequences for labeled individuals that may necessitate their continued criminality.

Moral Enterprise   The process undertaken by an advocacy group to have its values legitimated and embodied in law. (p. 103)

      D. The Life Course Perspective (p. 104)

Social Development Theory   An integrated view of human development that points to the process of interaction among and between individuals and society as the root cause of criminal behavior. (p. 104)

Life Course Perspective   An approach to explaining crime and deviance that investigates developments and turning points in a person's life. (p. 104)

- Stress how criminal behavior follows an identifiable pattern throughout a person's life cycle.
- Explain the three distinct pathways to delinquency
  The authority conflict pathway
  The covert pathway
  The overt pathway

  IX. Conflict Theories (p. 106)

Conflict Perspective   A theoretical approach that holds that crime is the natural consequence of economic and other social inequities. Conflict theorists highlight the stresses that arise among and within social groups as they compete with one another for resources and survival. The social forces that result are viewed as major determinants of group and individual behavior, including crime. (p. 106)

- Key elements:
  - Society is composed of diverse social groups, and diversity is based on distinctions that people hold to be significant.
  - Conflict between and among groups is unavoidable because of their different interests and values.
  - The fundamental nature of group conflict centers on the exercise of political power.
  - Law is a tool of power that furthers the interests of those powerful enough to make it.

      A. Radical Criminology (p. 107)

Radical Criminology   A conflict perspective that sees crime as engendered by the unequal distribution of wealth, power, and other resources, which adherents believe is especially characteristic of capitalist societies. (p. 107)

- Radical criminology blames criminality and deviant behavior on officially sanctioned cultural and economic arrangements.
- Distribution of wealth and power in society is held to be the primary cause of criminal behavior.

INSTRUCTIONAL CUE

Explain that radical criminologists see the causes of crime as rooted in social inequities. Ask students what form of "treatment" radical criminologists might suggest for convicted offenders.

      B. Peacemaking Criminology (p. 107)

Peacemaking Criminology   A perspective that holds that crime-control agencies and the citizens they serve should work together to alleviate social problems and human suffering and thus reduce crime. (p. 107)

- Official agents of social control need to work with both victims and victimizers to achieve a new world order that is just for all.

    C. Social Policy and Conflict Theories (p. 108)
- Assumes inequalities in society cause crime
- Sees revolution as a potential solution to social inequality

  X. Emergent Perspectives (p. 109)
    A. Feminist Criminology (p. 109)

Feminist Criminology   A developing intellectual approach that emphasizes gender issues in criminology. (p. 109)

    B. Constitutive Criminology (p. 111)

Constitutive Criminology   The study of the process by which human beings create an ideology of crime that sustains the notion of crime as a concrete reality. (p. 111)

    C. Postmodern Criminology (p. 111)

Postmodern Criminology   A brand of criminology that developed following World War II and that builds upon the tenets inherent in postmodern social thought. (p. 111)

Deconstructionist Theories   Emerging approaches that challenge existing criminological perspectives to debunk them and that work toward replacing them with concepts more applicable to the postmodern era. (p. 111)

Learner Activities

Activity 1

Chapter 3 begins by linking media images and criminal behavior. For example, it discusses the criticism that rap music and heavy-metal music poison the minds of our youth. Historically, rock and roll and other types of music have been criticized in a similar manner. Are crime, sex, and violence dominant themes in music? Be sure to provide examples. Do you believe that heavy-metal and rap music can cause juveniles to commit crimes? Why or why not?

_____

_____

_____

_____

_____

Activity 2

Choose one of the theories discussed in Chapter 3. Assume that research has established that this theory has unequivocally identified the cause of crime. Now that you are certain about the cause of crime, what changes would you recommend in the criminal justice system and society to reduce the crime problem in the United States? Be sure to fully explain your theory, and then discuss what changes should be made in the criminal justice system. (*Hint:* The discussion in the text of each general type of theory and social policy would be helpful here. For example, if you were to argue that biological theories are definitive, the section on social policy and biological theories would be a helpful starting point for completing this assignment.)

_____

_____

_____

_____

_____

Activity 3

Visit the website http://www.crimetheory.com and click on the Learning Section, and then Explorations in Criminal Theory. Choose one of the sections that explores a theory or theorist presented in Chapter 3. Which theory or theorist did you examine? Why did you make that choice? What new information did you learn about that theory or theorist? Does this new information change your opinions of this theory or theorist? Are you more, or less, convinced of the validity of the theory or theorist?

_____

_____

_____

_____

_____

_____

Activity 4

When they occur, serial murders get more media attention than any other type of crime. Indeed, not only is serial murder a high-priority news topic, it is often the subject of movies and novels. Your assignment is to first locate at least ten newspaper articles about serial murder. You could use any newspaper database, such as Lexus-Nexus, to do this search. However, if you don't have direct access to a specific newspaper database, then search the Web. After you have collected these articles, answer the following questions. Why is serial murder so intriguing to news and popular media organizations? How do your articles present serial murder? What theories of serial murder are discussed in these articles?

_____

_____

_____

_____

_____

Internet Activity

Research serial killers on the Web. What kind of information is available? What are the best sites for such information?

Print out (or save to disk) the information on serial killers that you find on the Web. Prepare a notebook (or disk file) of this information, and include a section on individual serial killers throughout history. Your instructor may ask you to submit your notebook.

_____

_____

_____

_____

_____

_____

Distance Learning Activity

Visit the Crime Theory page. This web page is located at http://www.crimetheory.com. Visit the Explorations link and complete one of the posted exercises. Submit a summary of what you learned about criminological theory by completing the exercise.

_____

_____

_____

_____

_____

_____

Learning Activities Utilizing the World Wide Web

There are student-based activities in the Student Study Guide (Internet Activity, Distance Learning Activity, CJ Today on the World Wide Web) that are similar in focus to those that follow. However, the following are presented as instructor-led activities, to be used in a classroom with online access.

Prior to class, research serial killers on the Web. Display in class the kinds of information available. Poll the class; then discuss what they consider the best sites for such information.

Visit the Crime Theory page. This web page is located at http://www.crimetheory. com. Visit the Explorations link and complete one of the posted exercises. Submit a summary of what you learned about criminological theory by completing the exercise.

Other websites for organizations and agencies related to the material in Chapter 3 include:

Rand Corporation	http://www.rand.org
Human Genome Project	http://www.ornl.gov/TechResources /Human_Genome
Crime Theory	http://www.crimetheory.com
Crime Times	http://www.crime-times.org
Biology, Behavior, and the Criminal Law	http://www.gruterinstitute.org/ news/vls.html
Genocide Research Project	http://www.people.memphis.edu/ ~genocide
Western Criminology Review	http://wcr.sonoma.edu
American Society of Criminology	http://asc41.com

Suggested Answers to Chapter Discussion Questions

1. **This chapter describes various categories of theoretical approaches used to explain crime. What are they?**

   The eight general categories of criminological theories presented in this chapter include Classical, Biological, Psychobiological, Psychological, Sociological, Social Process, Conflict, and Emergent.

2. **Describe the basic features of biological theories of crime causation. What are the shortcomings of this perspective? Do you think that biological theories have much explanatory power? Why or why not?**

   Basic Features:
   - Human behavior, including criminal tendencies, is genetically based.
   - A penchant for crime may be inherited.
   - Criminals and deviants are in more primitive developmental stages in the evolutionary process than most people.

   Shortcomings:
   - It suggests the need for extreme social policies, such as the eugenics movement.

   Explanatory Power:
   - There is little empirical support for biological theories of crime causation, and much of the early research on these theories was poorly designed.

3. **Describe the basic features of psychological explanations for crime. What are the shortcomings of this perspective? Do you think that psychological theories have much explanatory power? Why or why not?**

   Basic Features:
   - The individual is the primary unit of analysis.
   - Personality is the major motivational element in individuals.
   - Crimes result from inappropriately conditioned behavior.
   - Defective or abnormal mental processes may have a variety of causes.

   Shortcomings:
   - It is dependent on the ability to predict future behavior based on past behavior, with allowance for the effects of therapeutic intervention—an inexact science, at best.

   Explanatory Power:
   - These theories tend to be individualistic. Profiling is incredibly challenging, but the very best profilers can reliably describe an offender's social and psychological characteristics. It is, however, very difficult to predict the future dangerousness of an individual.

4. **Describe the basic features of sociological theories of crime causation. What are the shortcomings of this perspective? Do you think that sociological theories have much explanatory power? Why or why not?**

   Basic Features:
   - Social groups, social institutions, the arrangements of society, and social roles all provide the proper focus for criminological study.
   - Group dynamics, group organization, and subgroup relationships form the causal nexus out of which crime develops.
   - The structure of society and its relative degree of organization or disorganization are important factors that contribute to the prevalence of criminal behavior.

   Shortcomings:
   - It may lead to expensive but sometimes ineffective social programs intended to eliminate crime.

Explanatory Power:
- Most contemporary analysts, however, would probably select sociological explanations of crime as having the most explanatory power because the sociological perspective recognizes the influence of culture and environment on both personality and individual choices.

5. What is meant by "emergent theories"? Identify two emergent theories of crime causation.

Emergent theories are new, developing criminological theories that challenge and/or expand extant theories that have dominated explanations of criminal behavior. Feminist criminology and constitutive criminology are two examples of emergent theories.

Key—Student Study Guide Questions

True or False

____ 3-1. Anomie exists when there is a disjuncture between the goals of society and the means to achieve those goals. **(True, p. 97)**

____ 3-2. Differential association theory was developed by Edwin Sutherland. **(True, p. 101)**

____ 3-3. Techniques of neutralization are rationalizations that allow offenders to shed feelings of guilt for their behavior. **(True, p. 103)**

____ 3-4. Cesare Lombroso is considered the founder of the Classical School of criminology. **(False, p. 86)**

____ 3-5. Phrenologists study the shape of the skull to predict criminal behavior. **(True, p. 87)**

____ 3-6. A basic assumption of the Biological School is that offensive and deviant behavior is the product of environmental forces. **(False, p. 88)**

____ 3-7. Cesare Beccaria is considered the father of criminology. **(False, p. 88)**

____ 3-8. Peacemaking criminology is one of the biological theories of crime. **(False, p. 107)**

____ 3-9. Robert Merton's ritualist accepts both the goals and the means that society considers legitimate. **(False, p. 98)**

____ 3-10. Ectomorphs have bodies that are characterized by thinness, fragility, and delicacy. **(True, p. 90)**

Multiple Choice

3-11. All of the following theorists are biological criminologists except
a. Cesare Lombroso.
b. William Sheldon.
c. Franz Gall.
d. Jeremy Bentham. (p. 86)

3-12. Atavism is
a. a condition characterized by an individual with a dysfunctional superego.
b. a condition characterized by features thought to be common in earlier stages of human evolution. (p. 88)
c. a term used to describe males with an extra Y chromosome.
d. a term used to describe ectomorphic body types.

3-13. Which school explains criminal behavior by looking at gene structure, hormones, and inheritance?
a. Social-Psychological School
b. Classical School
c. Biological School (p. 87)
d. Psychological School

3-14. Which school emphasizes the roles of free will and reasonable punishments?
a. Sociological School
b. Classical School (p. 86)
c. Biological School
d. Psychological School

3-15. Which of the following sociological theories argues that crime is most likely to occur in "zones of transition"?
a. subcultural
b. profiling
c. anomie
d. social ecology (p. 97)

3-16. _____ theory proposes that when an individual's bond to society weakens, the likelihood of crime increases.
a. Labeling
b. Differential association
c. Containment
d. Social control (p. 102)

3-17. Which of Sheldon's body types has a relative predominance of muscle, bone, and connective tissue?
a. mesomorphs (p. 90)
b. risomorphs
c. endomorphs
d. ectomorphs

3-18. According to Robert Merton, a(n) _____ accepts both the goals of society and society's acceptable means to achieve them.
a. retreatist
b. ritualist
c. conformist (p. 98)
d. innovator

3-19. Who would be considered a contemporary, or modern-day, biological theorist?
a. Richard Herrnstein
b. Sarnoff Mednick
c. James Q. Wilson
d. all of the above (p. 92)

3-20. All of the following theories can be considered social process theories except
a. differential association.
b. containment.
c. social ecology. (p. 97)
d. social control.

Fill-In

3-21. Who worked with Clifford Shaw to develop social ecology theory?
_____ **(Henry McKay, p. 97)**

3-22. Who developed differential association theory? _____ **(Edwin Sutherland, p. 101)**

3-23. Whose name is most widely associated with the field of psychology?
_____ **(Sigmund Freud, p. 93)**

3-24. Who argued that crime results from social definition, through law, of unacceptable behavior? _____ **(Howard Becker, p. 103)**

3-25. Who applied anomie to criminology? _____ **(Robert Merton, p. 97)**

3-26. The author of *Sisters in Crime* is _____. **(Freda Adler, p. 109)**

3-27. Who is the father of modern criminology? _____ **(Cesare Lombroso, p. 88)**

3-28. _____ founded the Classical School of criminology. **(Cesare Beccaria, p. 86)**

3-29. _____ is the violation of social norms that define appropriate or proper behavior under a particular set of circumstances. **(Deviance, p. 80)**

3-30. _____ is one theorist who has popularized peacemaking criminology. **(Hal Pepinsky, p. 107)**

Key—Crossword Puzzle

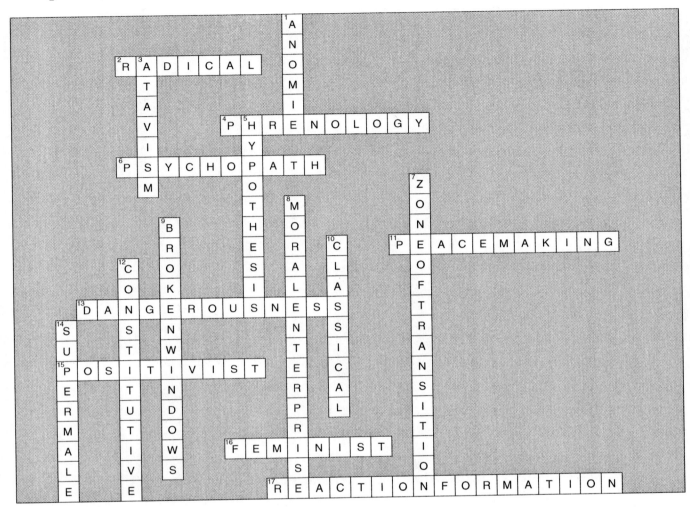

Across

2. Also called Marxist criminology.
4. Study of the shape of the head to determine anatomical correlates of human behavior.
6. Also called sociopath.
11. Perspective that holds that crime-control agencies and the citizens they serve should work together to alleviate social problems and human suffering and thus reduce crime.
13. Usually measured in terms of recidivism.
15. Approach to criminal justice theory that stresses the application of scientific techniques to the study of crime and criminals.
16. Theory that emphasizes gender issues in criminology.
17. Term coined by Albert Cohen.

Down

1. Normlessness.
3. Existence of features thought to be common in earlier stages of human evolution.
5. Something that is taken to be true for the purpose of argument or investigation.
7. "Zone 2" in Shaw and McKay's theory.
8. Process undertaken by an advocacy group to have its values legitimated and embodied in law.
9. J. Q. Wilson's thesis.
10. Crime-causation theory linked to the Enlightenment.
12. Type of criminology that studies the process by which human beings create an ideology of crime that sustains the notion of crime as a concrete reality.
14. Male believed to have an extra Y chromosome.

KEY—Word Search Puzzle

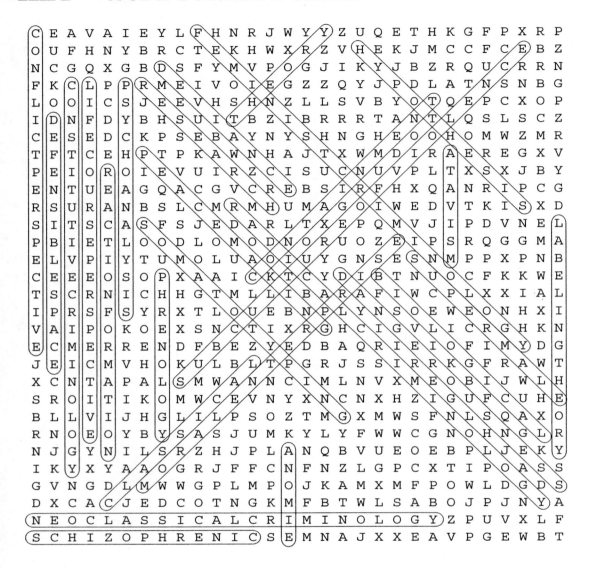

Anomie

Atavism

Biological

Classical

Conflict Perspective

Constitutive Criminology

Containment

Dangerousness

Defensible Space

Deviance

Feminist Criminology

Hypothesis

Labeling Theory

Life Course Perspective

Moral Enterprise

Neoclassical Criminology

Peacemaking

Phrenology

Psychoanalysis

Radical Criminology

Reaction Formation

Research

Schizophrenic

Somatotyping

Subculture of Violence

Supermale

Theory

CHAPTER 4

Criminal Law

OUTLINE

- Introduction
- The Nature and Purpose of Law
- The Rule of Law
- Types of Law
- General Categories of Crime
- General Features of Crime
- Elements of a Specific Criminal Offense
- Types of Defenses to a Criminal Charge

LEARNING OBJECTIVES

After reading this chapter, you should be able to:

- Explain the impact of common law on contemporary American criminal justice
- Discuss the nature of the rule of law, and describe its purpose in Western democracies
- Identify the various types of law, and explain the purpose of each
- List the five categories of criminal law violations
- List the eight general features of crime
- Explain the concept of *corpus delicti*
- Discuss the four broad categories of criminal defenses that our legal system recognizes
- Explain the legal concept of insanity, and distinguish it from psychiatric explanations of mental illness

Chapter Summary

Imagine our society without laws. How would order be maintained? How would individuals be protected from harm? How would society be protected? Law provides these protections, insulating society from mass chaos. Chapter 4 discusses many areas of law including the nature and purpose of law, the rule of law, types of law, and general categories of crime.

Chapter 4 explains why we have laws. Laws are needed to prevent the victimization of innocent people. Laws also ensure that the philosophical, moral, and economic perspectives of those who created the laws are protected. They also uphold established patterns of social privilege and sustain existing power relationships. Laws can also promote change in society or help society adapt to change. For example, new laws have been created in response to the computer revolution. Many criminal laws were created to adapt to rapid social and technological changes.

The text also discusses different types of law. **Common law** is the traditional body of unwritten historical precedents created from everyday social customs, rules, and practice. **Criminal law**, which is the focus of this chapter, is concerned with offenses against society. The criminal justice processing machinery operates according to criminal law. Chapter 4 also distinguishes criminal law from civil law. **Civil law** provides legal guidance regulating the relationships between individuals. Sometimes criminal and civil cases overlap. An individual could be charged under criminal law but also sued in civil court by the victim. **Case law** involves the decisions of courts that provide guiding principles to future decisions, and administrative law is the body of law that regulates industry, business, and individuals.

Chapter 4 also provides a discussion of general categories of crime. Specifically, the text discusses five categories of violation: **misdemeanors, felonies, offenses, treason and espionage**, and **inchoate offenses**.

Finally, Chapter 4 discusses the general features of crime. Let's walk through a situation in view of the features discussed.

Facts: Joan killed her husband by stabbing him with a kitchen knife. Joan had been frequently subjected to beatings, some resulting in hospitalization, from her husband. Moreover, her husband had threatened to kill Joan on at least four prior occasions.

1. *Actus reus*: The first general feature of crime is that there has to be an act in violation of the law. Here, the act is murder. If Joan stabbed her husband and he survived, she could be charged with attempted murder. If Joan took steps to complete the murder but was unable to carry out her attempt, she could be charged with conspiracy to commit murder. If she approached an undercover police officer and asked him to commit a murder, she could be charged with solicitation to commit a murder.

2. *Mens rea*: A guilty mind is the second general feature that has to be established and is probably the most complex because it involves subjective evaluation of the mind. Should Joan be held to blame for this crime? Did Joan intend the consequences of her action?

3. **Concurrence:** The third element is the concurrence of the act and the intent. Joan's actions have to be linked with her intent.

4. Harm: The harm in this case, the death of another human being, is easily identified.

5. Causation: There has to be a link between the act and the harm. If Joan shot her husband and he survived for a month but then died of complications related to a cancerous brain tumor, it would be difficult to convict Joan of murder because the act (the shooting) would not be linked to the harm (the death).

6. Legality: There has to be a law on the books to punish someone for his or her behavior. Murder is well defined in our law books.

7. Punishment: Not only must there be a law on the books, but that law must provide a punishment for the crime. Statutory punishments for murder are among the severest punishments available to judges.

Even if each of the statutory elements can be established, a defendant has the opportunity to raise defenses that could excuse his or her actions. For example, Joan might argue that she committed the act in self-defense as a battered woman who thought her life was in danger.

The last part of Chapter 4 discusses several types of defenses, including alibi, justifications, excuses, procedural, and innovative. The **alibi defense** is very straightforward in that the defendant argues that he or she was nowhere near the crime when it happened. **Justification defenses** are used when the defendant admits to committing the act but claims it was necessary to avoid a greater evil. Examples include self-defense, necessity, and defense of home. **Excuse defenses** are used when a defendant claims that some personal condition or circumstance was such that he or she should not be held accountable. Examples include age, insanity, involuntary intoxication, and unconsciousness. **Procedural defenses** are defenses based on procedure, such as double jeopardy, collateral estoppel, selective prosecution, denial of speedy trial, and prosecutorial misconduct. Innovative defenses are similar to personal defenses but are unique and emerging defenses. Examples include black rage, urban survival syndrome, the abuse defense, premenstrual stress syndrome, and cultural defenses.

Teaching Outline

    I. Introduction (p. 120)
- Define law.

Law   A rule of conduct, generally found enacted in the form of a statute, that proscribes or mandates certain forms of behavior. (p. 120)

    II. The Nature and Purpose of Law (p. 120)
- Explain and highlight the difference in the various types of law.

Statutory Law   Written or codified laws, the "law on the books," as enacted by a government body or agency having the power to make laws. (p. 121)

Penal Code   The written, organized, and compiled form of the criminal laws of a jurisdiction. (p. 121)

Case Law   The body of judicial precedent, historically built upon legal reasoning and past interpretations of statutory laws, that serves as a guide to decision making, especially in the courts. (p. 121)

Common Law   Law originating from usage and custom rather than from written statutes. The term refers to an unwritten body of judicial opinion, originally developed by English courts, that is based upon nonstatutory customs, traditions, and precedent that help guide judicial decision making. (p. 121)

    III. The Rule of Law (p. 121)
- Explain the rule of law and how society must be governed by established principles and codes.

Rule of Law   The maxim that an orderly society must be governed by established principles and known codes that are applied uniformly and fairly to all of its members. (p. 121)

Jurisprudence   The philosophy of law. Also, the science and study of the law. (p. 122)

    IV. Types of Law (p. 122)
       A. Criminal Law (p. 122)

Criminal Law   The branch of modern law that concerns itself with offenses committed against society, its members, their property, and the social order. (p. 122)

- Describe the two types of written law.

Substantive Criminal Law   The part of the law that defines crimes and specifies punishments. (p. 122)

Procedural Law   The part of the law that specifies the methods to be used in enforcing the substantive law. (p. 123)

    B. Civil Law (p. 123)

Civil Law   The branch of modern law that governs relationships between parties. (p. 123)

- Contrast civil with criminal law.
- Examples of concern in civil law include divorce, child custody, the creation of wills, libel, unfair hiring practices, and property transfers.
- Civil law seeks compensation, not punishment.
- Civil law is concerned with assessing liability, not intent.

INSTRUCTIONAL CUE

Use several of the civil case examples in the textbook to illustrate the increases in the number of civil law cases filed in court, and discuss issues of compensatory damages, punitive damages, and gross negligence.

Tort   A wrongful act, damage, or injury not involving a breach of contract. Also, a private or civil wrong or injury. (p. 123)

Class-Action Lawsuit   A lawsuit filed by one or more people on behalf of themselves and a larger group of people "who are similarly situated." *Source*: Gerald and Kathleen Hill, *The Real Life Dictionary of the Law* (Santa Monica, CA: General Publishing Group, 2000). Online version Web posted at http://dictionary.law.com/lookup2.asp. Accessed February 21, 2002. (pp. 124–125)

Compensatory Damages   Damages recovered in payment for an actual injury or economic loss. (p. 124)

Punitive Damages   Damages requested or awarded in a civil lawsuit when the defendant's willful acts were malicious, violent, oppressive, fraudulent, wanton, or grossly reckless. *Source*: Gerald and Kathleen Hill, *The Real Life Dictionary of the Law*. Accessed February 21, 2002. (p. 125)

Gross Negligence   The intentional failure to perform a manifest duty in reckless disregard of the consequences as affecting the life or property of another. *Source*: Henry Campbell Black, Joseph R. Nolan, and Jacqueline M. Nolan-Haley, *Black's Law Dictionary*, 6th ed. (St. Paul, MN: West, 1990), p. 1003. (p. 125)

    C. Administrative Law (p. 126)
- Refers to the body of regulations that have been created by governments to control the activities of industry, business, and individuals
    D. Case Law (p. 126)

Precedent   A legal principle that ensures that previous judicial decisions are authoritatively considered and incorporated into future cases. (p. 126)

Stare Decisis   The legal principle that requires that in subsequent cases on similar issues of law and fact courts be bound by their own earlier decisions and by those of higher courts having jurisdiction over them. The term literally means "standing by decided matters." (p. 126)

    E. Procedural Law (p. 126)
- Refers to the part of the law that specifies the methods to be used in enforcing substantive law
  V. General Categories of Crime (p. 128)
    A. Felonies (p. 128)

Felonies   A criminal offense punishable by death or by incarceration in a prison facility for at least one year. (p. 128)

      B. Misdemeanors (p. 128)

Misdemeanors   An offense punishable by incarceration, usually in a local confinement facility, for a period of which the upper limit is prescribed by statute in a given jurisdiction, typically one year or less. (p. 128)

      C. Offenses (p. 129)

Offense   A violation of the criminal law. Also, in some jurisdictions, a minor crime, such as jaywalking, sometimes described as *ticketable*. (p. 129)

Infraction   A minor violation of state statute or local ordinance punishable by a fine or other penalty or by a specified, usually limited, term of incarceration. (p. 129)

      D. Treason and Espionage (p. 129)

Treason   A U.S. citizen's actions to help a foreign government overthrow, make war against, or seriously injure the United States. Also, the attempt to overthrow the government of the society of which one is a member. *Source*: Daniel Oran, *Oran's Dictionary of the Law* (St. Paul, MN: West, 1983), p. 306. (p. 129)

Espionage   The "gathering, transmitting, or losing" of information related to the national defense in such a manner that the information becomes available to enemies of the United States and may be used to their advantage. *Source*: Henry Campbell Black, Joseph R. Nolan, and Jacqueline M. Nolan-Haley, *Black's Law Dictionary*, 6th ed. (St. Paul, MN: West, 1990), p. 24. (p. 129)

      E. Inchoate Offenses (p. 130)

Inchoate Offense   An offense not yet completed. Also, an offense that consists of actions or conduct that is a step toward the intended commission of another offense. (p. 130)

INSTRUCTIONAL CUE

Discuss how the seriousness of a particular crime, as determined by the degree of punishment, can change over time. Drunk driving is a good example. Changes in the seriousness of drug crimes are another good example.

    VI. General Features of Crime (p. 130)

      A. The Criminal Act (*Actus Reus*) (p. 130)

Actus Reus   An act in violation of the law. Also, a guilty act. (p. 130)

      B. Guilty Mind (*Mens Rea*) (p. 131)

Mens Rea   The state of mind that accompanies a criminal act. Also, a guilty mind. (p. 131)

     • Discuss negligence and reckless behavior.

Reckless Behavior   Activity that increases the risk of harm. (p. 131)

Criminal Negligence   Behavior in which a person fails to reasonably perceive substantial and unjustifiable risks of dangerous consequences. (p. 132)

     • Emphasize that *mens rea* is not the same as motive.

Motive   A person's reason for committing a crime. (p. 132)

      1. Strict Liability and *Mens Rea*

Strict Liability   Liability without fault or intention. Strict liability offenses do not require *mens rea*. (p. 132)

        C. Concurrence (p. 132)

Concurrence   The coexistence of (1) an act in violation of the law and (2) a culpable mental state. (p. 132)

        D. Other Features of Crime (p. 132)
            1. Causation
- The concurrence of a guilty mind and a criminal act may produce or cause harm.

Legal Cause   A legally recognizable cause. A legal cause must be demonstrated in court in order to hold an individual criminally liable for causing harm. (p. 133)

            2. Harm
- Review the concept of victimless crime.

            3. Legality
- Refers to the existence of a law that prohibits or mandates an action.

Ex post facto   Latin for "after the fact." The Constitution prohibits the enactment of *ex post facto* laws, which make acts committed before the laws in question were passed punishable as crimes. (p. 133)

            4. Punishment
            5. Necessary Attendant Circumstances

Attendant Circumstances   The facts surrounding an event. (p. 134)

INSTRUCTIONAL CUE

After describing the various features of crime, you can help students understand that there can be no crime unless all the features are present by describing to them a courtroom situation in which a prosecutor proves each element.

    VII. Elements of a Specific Criminal Offense (p. 134)

Element (of a crime)   In a specific crime, one of the essential features of that crime, as specified by law or statute. (p. 134)

        A. The Example of Murder (p. 134)
- Review the elements of the crime of murder.

        B. The *Corpus Delicti* of a Crime (p. 136)

Corpus Delicti   The facts that show that a crime has occurred. The term literally means "the body of the crime." (p. 136)

    VIII. Types of Defenses to a Criminal Charge

Defense (to a criminal charge)   Evidence and arguments offered by a defendant and his or her attorney(s) to show why that person should not be held liable for a criminal charge. (p. 137)

Alibi   A statement or contention by an individual charged with a crime that he or she was so distant when the crime was committed, or so engaged in other provable activities, that his or her participation in commission of that crime was impossible. (p. 137)

Justification   A legal defense in which the defendant admits to committing the act in question but claims it was necessary in order to avoid some greater evil. (p. 137)

Excuse   A legal defense in which the defendant claims that some personal condition or circumstance at the time of the act was such that he or she should not be held accountable under the criminal law. (pp. 137–138)

Procedural Defense   A defense that claims that the defendant was in some significant way discriminated against in the justice process or that some important aspect of official procedure was not properly followed in the investigation or prosecution of the crime charged. (pp. 137–138)

INSTRUCTIONAL CUE

Describe the defense attorney's role in proving the existence of a criminal defense. Explain that a defense to a criminal charge does not necessarily mean that a person denies committing the act in question. Use self-defense as an example of how one person can kill another and still be found not guilty.

   A. Alibi (p. 138)
   B. Justifications (p. 138)
       1. Self-Defense

Self-Defense   The protection of oneself or of one's property from unlawful injury or from the immediate risk of unlawful injury. Also, the justification that the person who committed an act that would otherwise constitute an offense reasonably believed that the act was necessary to protect self or property from immediate danger. (p. 138)

Reasonable Force   A degree of force that is appropriate in a given situation and is not excessive. Also, the minimum degree of force necessary to protect oneself, one's property, a third party, or the property of another in the face of a substantial threat. (p. 138)

       2. Defense of Others

Alter Ego Rule   In some jurisdictions, a rule of law that holds that a person can only defend a third party under circumstances and only to the degree that the third party could act on his or her own behalf. (p. 138)

       3. Defense of Home and Property
           • Justifiable use of reasonable force by a property owner
       4. Necessity
           • Illegal action needed to prevent greater harm
       5. Consent
           • Harm that occurs after the injured person gave consent
       6. Resisting Unlawful Arrest
           • Justifiable if the arresting officer uses excessive force
   C. Excuses
       1. Duress
       2. Age

Cultural Defense   A defense to a criminal charge in which the defendant's culture is taken into account in judging his or her culpability. (pp. 140–141)

       3. Mistake
       4. Involuntary Intoxication
       5. Unconsciousness
       6. Provocation
       7. Insanity

Insanity Defense   A legal defense based on claims of mental illness or mental incapacity. (p. 144)

INSTRUCTIONAL CUE LINKED TO THE STUDENT STUDY GUIDE

Use Student Activity 2 of the Student Study Guide to help explain the insanity defense. After discussing this activity and the case included in it, provide to students the facts of the John Hinkley case. Remember that he was found not guilty of attempting to murder then President Reagan because of a successful insanity defense. Be sure to highlight the public outrage in response to this decision and that it was a contributing factor in states' adopting guilty but mentally ill statutes.

---

    a. The M'Naghten Rule

M'Naghten Rule   A rule for determining insanity that asks whether the defendant knew what he or she was doing or whether the defendant knew that what he or she was doing was wrong. (p. 144)

    b. Irresistible Impulse

    c. The Durham Rule

    d. The Substantial Capacity Test

    e. The Brawner Rule

    f. The Insanity Defense and Social Reaction

    g. Guilty But Mentally Ill

Guilty But Mentally Ill (GBMI)   A verdict, equivalent to a finding of "guilty," that establishes that the defendant, although mentally ill, was in sufficient possession of his or her faculties to be morally blameworthy for his or her acts. (p. 146)

    h. Temporary Insanity

    i. The Insanity Defense under Federal Law

    j. Consequences of an Insanity Ruling

  8. Diminished Capacity

Diminished Capacity   A defense based upon claims of a mental condition that may be insufficient to exonerate the defendant of guilt but that may be relevant to specific mental elements of certain crimes or degrees of crime. (p. 147)

  9. Mental Incompetence

Incompetent to Stand Trial   In criminal proceedings, a finding by a court that, as a result of mental illness, defect, or disability, a defendant is incapable of understanding the nature of the charges and proceedings against him or her, of consulting with an attorney, or of aiding in his or her own defense. (p. 148)

  D. Procedural Defenses (p. 149)

    1. Entrapment

Entrapment   An improper or illegal inducement to crime by agents of law enforcement. Also, a defense that may be raised when such inducements have occurred. (p. 149)

    2. Double Jeopardy

Double Jeopardy   A common law and constitutional prohibition against a second trial for the same offense. (p. 150)

    3. Collateral Estoppel

    4. Selective Prosecution

    5. Denial of a Speedy Trial

    6. Prosecutorial Misconduct

    7. Police Fraud

Learner Activities

Activity 1

Visit the links at **Library Extra 4–1, 4–2, 4–3, and 4–4**. Try to find an article relevant to ethics and law. Read the article and summarize the content of the article below.

LIBRARY EXTRA

_____

_____

_____

_____

_____

_____

Activity 2

It would be helpful to refer to the text's discussion of the insanity defense before tackling this activity.

The insanity defense is one of the more controversial and complex defenses available to defendants. It is controversial because the public thinks that defendants are excused from punishment when found not guilty as the result of this defense. The complexity lies in the link it makes between the medical and legal professions.

Consider the legal implications of the following case: Tom Smith had recently escaped from a mental hospital when he was picked up by a concerned motorist. At a highway rest area, Tom killed the motorist by strangulation. He was charged with murder. On two prior occasions, Tom had been found not guilty by reason of insanity.

The medical implications are as follows: Tom has the IQ of about a 10-year-old child. He has a 30-year history of mental illness, dating back to his return from the Vietnam War. Tom suffers from posttraumatic stress disorder and is unable to recover from the horrors he experienced in war. He is delusional and strangled the motorist because the motorist listened to Grateful Dead rock music, which caused Tom to think he was the Antichrist.

The prosecution had no trouble establishing the elements of crime. The defense attorneys used an insanity defense (irresistible-impulse test), claiming that Tom belongs in a mental hospital, not a maximum-security prison. If you were the judge in this case, what would you decide? Should Tom be punished as a criminal or treated as a person with a mental illness? Be sure to explain your answer.

_____

_____

_____

_____

_____

Activity 3

An effective way for you to understand domestic violence and battered women's syndrome is to interview a domestic violence expert or a provider of victims' services. This activity requires you to contact such a professional in your community to discuss domestic violence and battered women's defense. Look in the telephone book for a shelter for abused or battered women, or contact the prosecutor's office for information on how to contact a provider of victims' services. A mental health facility is also a good resource. Complete an informational interview with this person to learn about domestic violence in your community. Ask about the extent of the problem and the types of resources available to domestic violence victims, and ask the person to comment on battered women's syndrome.

When you complete this interview, discuss what you discovered in the space below.

_____

_____

_____

_____

_____

_____

_____

_____

Activity 4

Presented below are several case descriptions. If you were a defense attorney asked to take each of these cases, what would you recommend as the best defense? (Refer to Table 4–2 in the book for assistance.)

1. Art Kapser and John Gelbor were good friends and coworkers. After work, Art and John went bowling. After John picked up a spare in the seventh frame, the two got into an argument on proper scoring of a spare. John punched Art in the face, knocking him to the floor and screaming, "If you don't shut up, I will kill you." Art left the bowling alley but returned with a .38-caliber revolver and shot John in the back, killing him instantly. Art was charged with murder. What could Art use as a defense?

2. Kellie Koser attended a college party. One of the partygoers handed her a beer. She drank it, although she did not know that the beer contained a sedative. She got tired quickly and decided to drive home. She fell asleep at the wheel and killed a bicyclist. She was charged with manslaughter. What could Kellie use as a defense?

3. Shelly Morrison and Todd Rutlow both drive the same model of pickup truck. Both trucks are black with white pinstripes, both have red fuzzy dice hanging from the rearview mirror, and both have a bumper sticker with the slogan "Peace is Possible." Moreover, both leave their keys in the ignition when they park. Shelly, after completing a long day of Christmas shopping, got into a black truck and drove away. She did not know it was Todd's truck. Police quickly apprehended Shelly and charged her with motor vehicle theft. What would you recommend as a defense?

4. Charles Shuter was charged with raping his 14-year-old daughter. The prosecutor also charged the mother with conspiracy to commit rape because she knew about the rape and bought condoms for her husband to use when committing the crime. The mother claims she did not contact the police because the husband threatened to kill her. What would you recommend as a defense for the mother?

5. When Marnee Diaz lost her job, she couldn't keep up with her bills. In order to put food on the table, she began robbing banks. What would you recommend as a defense?

6. Carol Smith is addicted to crack but enrolled herself in a drug-treatment program to control her addiction. An undercover police officer joined the same program to get information about drug suppliers. He got friendly with Ms.

Smith and asked her to buy him some crack. She refused on four occasions. On the fifth occasion, however, she brought him one rock of crack cocaine. She was arrested for drug possession. What defense would you recommend?

7. Jason Jenser was a heavy drinker. Whenever he drank, he beat his lover, Bill. He frequently put a gun to Bill's head, threatened to kill him, and caused him numerous physical injuries. Bill wanted to leave, but Jason threatened him with physical violence, so he stayed. That same evening, while Jason was sleeping, Bill picked up a shotgun and killed him. What defense would you recommend?

_____

_____

_____

_____

_____

_____

Internet Activity

Visit law.com (http://www.law.com) and find the law dictionary that the site provides. (*Hint:* Click on Look Up Legal Terms.) Enter each of the key terms (one at a time) at the start of Chapter 4 into the dictionary, and compare the definitions there with the definitions in the textbook (see the glossary). Write the definitions from the two sources side by side and compare them. What differences exist? What terms are in the textbook that are not in the online dictionary?

_____

_____

_____

_____

_____

Distance Learning Activity

Visit the website for the *National Law Journal* or some other major industry legal publication. (National Law Journal page is at http://www.nlj.com, and Court TV On-Line is at http://www.courttv.com.) Submit a summary of one of the articles or cases posted on the website. If your instructor asks you to do so, share your summary with the other students in your class and participate in an online discussion about the issues that students wrote about.

_____

_____

_____

_____

_____

_____

Learning Activities Utilizing the World Wide Web

There are student-based activities in the Student Study Guide (Internet Activity, Distance Learning Activity, CJ Today on the World Wide Web) that are similar in focus to those that follow. However, the following are presented as instructor-led activities, to be used in a classroom with online access.

Prior to class, visit http://www.law.com and find the law dictionary that the site provides. Enter each of the key terms at the start of Chapter 4 into the dictionary. Prepare slides for classroom projection that show the definitions from law.com and the textbook side by side. Ask your students to discuss what differences exist in the two definitions.

Visit the website for the *National Law Journal* or one other major industry legal publication. (National Law Journal page is at http://www.nlj.com, and Court TV On-Line is at http://www.courttv.com.) Display for class each site. Discuss with your students the various issues that are highlighted on each site.

Other websites for organizations and agencies related to the material in Chapter 4 include:

Rule of Law	http://www.users.bigpond.com/smartboard/btof/index18.htm
WashLaw Web	http://www.washlaw.edu
International Center for Criminal Law	http://www.icclr.law.ubc.ca
U.S. Attorney Office	http://www.usdoj.gov/ag
American Bar Association	http://www.abanet.org/crimjust/home.html
American Prosecutor's Research	http://www.ndaa-apri.org
Legal Law Help	http://www.legallawhelp.com

Suggested Answers to Chapter Discussion Questions

1. **What is common law? What impact does common law have on contemporary American criminal justice?**

Common law is a body of unwritten judicial opinion that is based on customary social practices of Anglo-Saxon society during the Middle Ages. It forms the basis of much of our modern statutory and case law and has often been called *the* major source of modern criminal law. Although largely supplanted in all U.S. jurisdictions by statutory (written) law, common law principles still serve as powerful interpreters of legal issues that arise in state codes and the dictates of state law.

2. **What is the rule of law? What is its purpose in Western democracies? What does it mean to say that "nobody is above the law"?**

The rule of law is essentially the belief that an orderly society must be governed by established principles and codes that are applied uniformly and fairly to all of its members. The rule of law is central to Western democracies. It allows people to speak their mind, stand up for what they think is right, organize to protest government, and live free without the threat of lawlessness. The rule of law established limits to all types of behavior, and it is a way to communicate expectations about how one should behave in a democracy. What it means to say "nobody is above the law" is that everybody, including those who write laws (politicians) and those who enforce it (police officers and the like), must abide by the rule of law.

3. **What types of law does this chapter discuss? What purpose does each serve?**

   - **Criminal law** is the rules and regulations that define what behaviors are criminal and specifies punishments. Such offenses are committed against society.

   - **Civil law** focuses on regulating relationships between parties. The focus of civil law is on noncriminal relationships.

   - **Administrative law** focuses on the regulations created by government to control businesses, industries, and individuals.

   - **Case law** provides a guide to court decision making because it includes the body of judicial precedent.

   - **Procedural law** regulates the behavior of individuals (that is, police officers, prosecutors, and the like) responsible for enforcing the substantive law.

4. **What five categories of criminal law violations does this chapter discuss? Describe each, and rank the categories in terms of seriousness.**

   - **Felonies** are serious crimes, such as murder and rape. Offenders convicted of felonies can be incarcerated or sentenced to death and will lose certain privileges.

   - **Misdemeanors** are relatively minor crimes, such as petty theft. Generally, misdemeanors are punishable by a year or less in prison.

   - **Offenses** are minor violations of the law, such as spitting on the sidewalk and littering. Offenders are usually ticketed.

   - **Treason** and **espionage** are considered among the most serious felonies. Treason occurs when a U.S. citizen helps a foreign government overthrow, make war against, or injure the United States. Espionage focuses on the gathering, transmitting, and losing of information related to national defense.

   - **Inchoate offenses** are offenses not yet completed, such as conspiracy or an attempt. Inchoate offenses can still be serious (attempted murder), but they are less serious because the offense was not completed.

5. **List and describe the eight general features of crime that this chapter discusses. What are the "three conjoined elements" that comprise the legal essence of the concept of crime?**

   (1) *Actus Reus*—The guilty act.

   (2) *Mens Rea*—The guilty mind.

   (3) **Concurrence**—The coexistence of (1) an act in violation of the law and (2) a culpable mental state.

   (4) **Causation**—The concurrence of mind and act must produce harm.

   (5) **Harm**—The harm caused by the crime.

   (6) **Legality**—Refers to the existence of a law that prohibits or mandates an action.

   (7) **Punishment**—The sanctions imposed for violating the law.

   (8) **Necessary Attendant Circumstances**—The facts surrounding an event.

   The three conjoined elements that comprise the legal essence of the concept of crime are (1) the criminal act, (2) a culpable mental state, and (3) a concurrence of the two.

6. **What is meant by the *corpus delicti* of a crime?**

   Corpus delicti, a Latin term that means "body of the crime," is the set of facts that show that a crime has occurred. The term does not refer to the human remains of the victim of a homicide.

   How does the *corpus delicti* of a crime differ from the statutory elements that must be proved to convict a particular defendant of committing that crime?

The *corpus delicti* of an offense consists of two aspects: (1) that a certain result has been produced and (2) that a person is criminally responsible for its production. Elements of the crime are the essential features of that crime as established by law or statute. Those elements specify exactly what conditions are necessary for a person to be charged in a given instance of criminal activity.

7. **What four broad categories of criminal defenses does our legal system recognize? Under what circumstances might each be employed?**

The four categories of criminal defense recognized include **alibi, justification, excuse,** and **procedural defense**. An alibi means that the defendant was somewhere else at the time of the crime. When a defendant offers a justification, he or she admits to the wrong but argues that it was necessary to avoid a greater evil. A defendant offering an excuse claims that a personal condition or circumstance was such that he or she should not be held accountable under the law. A defendant who makes a procedural defense claims that he or she was discriminated against in some way or appropriate procedures were not followed.

8. **How does the legal concept of insanity differ from psychiatric explanations of mental illness? Does the insanity defense serve a useful function today?**

Legal insanity meets the needs of the judiciary and is used to determine guilt and innocence. Psychiatry is concerned with the diagnosis and treatment of mental illness. Medical conceptions do not always fit into the legal categories to handle cases involving the mentally ill.

Arguments supporting the insanity defense often cite the need to protect those who cannot protect themselves. Proponents often liken the mentally disabled to a child because, like a child, they lack the capacity for making sound, rational decisions or for controlling their actions. Because the behavior of such persons does not result from reasoned choice, they say, it is behavior for which they simply cannot be held culpable.

Opponents of the insanity defense discount the notion that anyone can be relieved of responsibility for his or her actions on the basis of an inability to make "right" choices. They often argue that, right choice or not, the actions of the mentally disabled are based on choices they themselves made and for which they should be held responsible. Opponents sometimes present the dubious argument that since the mentally disabled realize benefits from their right choices, it is only fair that they be held responsible for their wrong choices as well.

If you could create your own rule for determining insanity in criminal trials, what would it be? How would it differ from existing rules?

Many believe that the mechanisms by which insanity is determined are flawed. There is a sense of frustration engendered when one set of psychiatrists (the prosecution's) evaluates an offender as mentally competent while another set (the defense's) finds the same offender mentally impaired. The uncertainty caused by such conflicts leads to overwhelming mistrust of the process itself.

Additional mistrust results from the fact that the process of evaluating an individual's mental state is an inexact science that can be manipulated. The fact that practitioners can be—and have been—fooled into making incorrect diagnoses further diminishes public confidence in the system's ability to achieve a just solution.

Any modification of the rules for determining an offender's mental state would have to meet due process requirements. Given that due process affords the opportunity to challenge any claims made against the accused, any new rules would have to include comparable provisions. Consequently, the form of such rules would likely be similar to the existing forms.

Key—Student Study Guide Questions

True or False

_____ 4-1. A basic distinction between criminal and civil law is that criminal acts injure individuals and society as a whole. **(True, p. 122)**

_____ 4-2. Misdemeanors are generally less serious than felonies. **(True, p. 129)**

_____ 4-3. Procedural law defines behaviors as criminal and specifies punishment. **(False, p. 126)**

_____ 4-4. The rule of law is also referred to as the supremacy of law. **(True, p. 121)**

_____ 4-5. Civil law is primarily concerned with assessing intent. **(False, p. 123)**

_____ 4-6. The Durham insanity rule states that a person is not guilty of a crime if, at the time of the crime, he or she didn't know what he or she was doing or didn't know that it was wrong. **(False, p. 146)**

_____ 4-7. Treason is the act of a U.S. citizen that helps a foreign government overthrow, make war against, or seriously injure the United States. **(True, p. 129)**

_____ 4-8. Procedural defense is based on discrimination by the justice system. **(True, p. 149)**

_____ 4-9. Contract law is the body of regulations created by governments to control the economic activities of industry, business, and individuals. **(False, p. 126)**

_____ 4-10. Insanity is a legal definition and not a psychiatric one. **(True, p. 143)**

Multiple Choice

4-11. Which of the following is generally considered the most serious?
   a. felonies (p. 129)
   b. misdemeanors
   c. offenses
   d. infractions

4-12. Which of the following is a procedural defense?
   a. duress
   b. mistake of fact
   c. double jeopardy (p. 149)
   d. infancy

4-13. Which type of law refers to a traditional body of unwritten legal precedents created through everyday practice and supported by court decisions?
   a. civil
   b. conflict
   c. common (p. 121)
   d. administrative

4-14. Murder, robbery, and drug offenses would all be defined as crimes under
   a. civil law.
   b. criminal law. (p. 122)
   c. common law.
   d. administrative law.

4-15. What type of law results from legislative action and is thought of as the "law on the books"?
   a. procedural
   b. administrative
   c. statutory (p. 121)
   d. substantive

4-16. Tax laws, health codes, and restrictions on pollution are examples of
    a. administrative law. (p. 126)
    b. procedural law.
    c. civil law.
    d. criminal law.

4-17. What is the Latin term that means "the body of the crime"?
    a. *actus reus*
    b. *mens rea*
    c. *stare decisis*
    d. *corpus delicti* (p. 136)

4-18. Which of the following is not an excuse defense?
    a. involuntary intoxication
    b. self-defense (p. 138)
    c. infancy
    d. insanity

4-19. Which of the following elements of crime means "guilty mind"?
    a. concurrence
    b. harm
    c. *actus reus*
    d. *mens rea* (p. 131)

4-20. A woman breaks into a home and, once inside, is cornered by the family dog, Spike, a Rottweiler. When the homeowner gets home and sees what Spike has in his control, she calls the police, who arrest the suspect. Based on these facts, the woman who broke into the home could be charged with
    a. conspiracy to commit burglary.
    b. nothing; she did not commit a crime.
    c. burglary.
    d. attempted burglary. (p. 131)

Fill-In

4-21. _____ governs relationships between parties. **(Civil law, p. 123)**

4-22. A(n) _____ is an offense punishable by incarceration, usually in a local confinement facility, for a period of which the upper limit is prescribed by statute in a given jurisdiction, typically limited to a year or less. **(misdemeanor, p. 129)**

4-23. The _____ holds that a person is not guilty of a crime if, at the time of the crime, he or she either didn't know what he or she was doing or didn't know that it was wrong. **(M'Naghten rule, p. 144)**

4-24. A(n) _____ consists of an action or conduct that is a step toward the intended commission of another crime. **(inchoate offense, p. 130)**

4-25. The _____ states that a person is not criminally responsible for his or her behavior if his or her illegal actions were the result of some mental disease or defect. **(Durham rule, p. 146)**

4-26. _____ is a procedural defense similar to double jeopardy. **(*Collateral estoppel*, p. 150)**

4-27. _____ is the science and study of law. **(Jurisprudence, p. 122)**

4-28. A(n) _____ is an offense punishable by death or by incarceration for at least a year. **(felony, p. 128)**

4-29. _____ literally means "guilty mind." **(*Mens rea*, p. 131)**

4-30. _____ is the part of the law that defines crimes and specifies punishments. **(Substantive criminal law, p. 122)**

Key—Crossword Puzzle

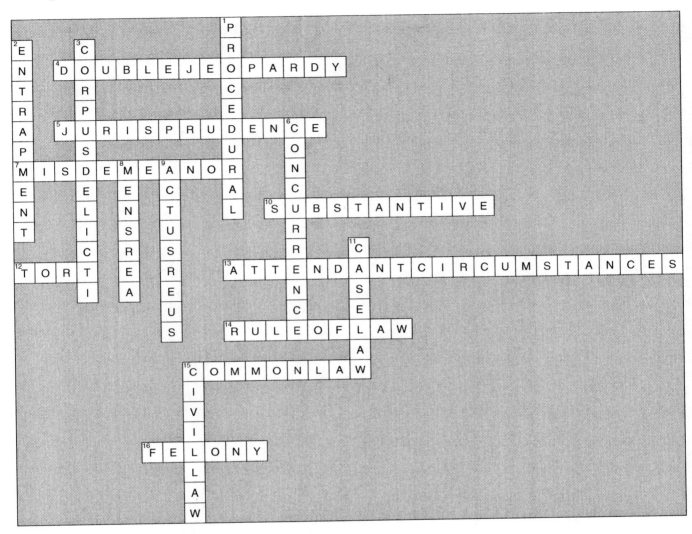

Across

4. Prohibition against a second trial for the same offense.
5. Science and study of the law.
7. Less serious than a felony and more serious than an infraction.
10. Type of criminal law that describes what constitutes particular crimes and specifies appropriate punishment for each offense.
12. Private or civil wrong or injury.
13. Facts surrounding an event.
14. Also called supremacy of the law.
15. Law originating from custom.
16. Offense punishable by incarceration in a prison facility for at least one year.

Down

1. Type of criminal law that specifies the rules that determine how those accused of a crime are dealt with in the judicial system.
2. Improper or illegal inducement to crime by agents of enforcement.
3. Body of the crime.
6. Coexistence of an act in violation of the law and a culpable mental state.
8. Guilty mind.
9. Guilty act.
11. Judicial precedent.
15. Branch of modern law that governs relationships between parties.

Key—Word Search Puzzle

```
H O H V H R J T W Q U D F S W R O C I W E S P I O N A G E C
V B W V A I P Z O V W V H W W J J F H F Z C O S F H X S M X
L V K I G A Y K U R L S N J Y A T D W E D E A G I D H W B P
Z P E N A L C O D E U A T U L X Y L Z O N D D S C N Z O C U
I P C G I V C U W M Q F Y M D U P D G Z W T Q Q E K G P Q L
D D Q N D L A U N M H S E I M C L S E R Q O R G Y L H Z Q T
E C U L T U R A L D E F E N S E R F F D I K L A Z V A B B M
Z X L P Y P U N I T I V E D A M A G E S Q E N M P I D W B G
W S P B J H H V Y Y Q Z W T G E Y V K Q H T W Z E M T L R B
H S P O N Z T L B C U I D J U R I S P R U D E N C E E D C F
Y P V M S C F Z R C N W L H G C Q M L X Y X F W Q N O N B I
P W Q Y S T I N F R A C T I O N M Y Q I Q N W C Q U C C T X
Y O B T H B F N D O W C C X J I S N A K M Q O I S U O C R G
T A I S I D V A C I C M E Y J D V K E K T I V U L K N Y R X I
R L K N D B V C H M H W U S N D S L E G W N I A I C S A S I
E A R A K Y X U T O I R N R N H D X O V K A O W F U R I S N
A D U K V D O X P O A N Y W X I B M D N Y E O T M R J O N R E
S P W J F A O B H E E T I F M I S D E M E A N O R R C N A B C
N E D J A R W L U A Z P V E S M W I O K K K V K X V E R A B O
S G H W R U G V M B E K V L O H T H W T R W F J A P N P Y L M
G R B F L N I S N L Y R W X F E G B D O X K S V R C E Q E F P
J U T E D K B H S E A I X A F D R S N R M S N E E C Z R O E E
F L Q L K X P S H L J P N F P E C T K S T B B C W E O R C N N
P E S N L Y H J L U R E Y Q F I N A L I J M K E W E O C E S S
P X O Y M C I B W B Q O M G E G S P A P A G D J S C R V C A A
H C V T R Y W E I F K I T X M Y J A T S C J N C G F N M W E T
T O L R M K C D H E A A W B V I W R I B U W P I Z T F M M O O
W L F V E J B M I E P U W Q H I R P D V E S E S T B J H N R R
C C W M N W M M M B A S D X A I G E U L Y E X E I K Y G X J Y
```

Alibi

Alter Ego Rule

Case Law

Civil Law

Compensatory

Concurrence

Cultural Defense

Diminished Capacity

Double Jeopardy

Entrapment

Espionage

Excuse

Ex Post Facto

Felony

Inchoate Offense

Infraction

Jurisprudence

Law

Misdemeanor

Motive

Penal Code

Precedent

Punitive Damages

Reasonable Force

Rule of Law

Tort

Treason

CHAPTER 5

Policing: History and Structure

OUTLINE

- Introduction
- Historical Development of the Police
- American Law Enforcement Today: From the Federal to the Local Level
- Federal Agencies
- State Agencies
- Local Agencies
- Private Protective Services

LEARNING OBJECTIVES

After reading this chapter, you should be able to:

- Summarize the historical development of policing in America, including the impact of the Prohibition era on American policing
- Describe the nature of scientific police studies, and explain the significance they hold for law enforcement practice today
- Describe the three major levels of public law enforcement in the United States today
- Describe the nature and extent of private protective services in the United States today, and describe the role these services might play in the future
- Explain the relationship between private security and public policing in America today

Chapter Summary

Chapter 5 begins with a discussion of the historical development of police departments in England and America. The text covers the historical evolution of policing in England because of similarities in its development to historical changes in American policing. An organized police response to social problems in England did not occur until the 1700s. Prior to that time, a posse, led by a shire reeve or *comes stabuli*, would respond to assist victims. The English police started to evolve in the 1700s when **Henry Fielding** became the magistrate of the Bow Street region of London. In 1829, under the guidance of **Sir Robert Peel**, the **New Police** (or the **Metropolitan Police**) was formed; it has been acknowledged as the world's first modern police force. Characteristics of the New Police force can still be found in English and American police forces. For example, the New Police operated under the belief that it was possible to discourage crime by patrolling the streets; the New Police wore uniforms to make themselves accessible to the public; and they structured their departments much the same as a military organization.

American policing evolved similarly, and early police departments, such as those organized in New York City, Boston, and Cincinnati, studied Peel's New Police when deciding structure and police response. However, police departments in the United States also addressed the special and unique concerns of the country, such as managing the Western frontier.

American police departments have evolved considerably over the years, relying recently on scientific research when deciding how to respond to crime most effectively. The text discusses important research studies, such as the **Kansas City Preventive Patrol Experiment**, that have had a tremendous impact on the current structure and philosophy of police departments. This experiment, conducted in the mid-1970s, tested (among other things) the effectiveness of preventive patrol in deterring crime and making citizens feel safe. The results from this study indicate that the number of officers on preventive patrol does not have a deterrent effect on preventable crimes and does not make citizens feel safe. These findings have forced police departments to alter how they use police officers on patrol and employ such innovative police strategies as directed patrol and split-force patrol.

Chapter 5 also provides a discussion of the decentralized structure of policing in the United States, highlighting differences among federal, state, local, and privately owned law enforcement agencies. Federal law enforcement agencies are responsible for enforcing federal laws. Although many agencies enforce federal law, the text describes in detail the best known: the Federal Bureau of Investigation.

Chapter 5 also discusses the responsibilities of state and local law enforcement agencies. State police agencies, whether centralized or decentralized, are responsible for patrolling state highways and conducting statewide criminal investigations. Officers who work for local law enforcement agencies have a more diverse job description than federal and state officers do. For example, the text discusses the diverse responsibilities of officers who work for the New York City Police Department. It also discusses the wide diversity in size and structure of local law enforcement agencies.

Chapter 5 concludes with a discussion of the growing private law enforcement industry. Indeed, the number of individuals employed in private security is higher than that in the other levels combined. Although the primary concern of the textbook is how local, state, and federal police respond to crime, discussion of private policing is important because of the growing influence of private security in criminal justice and the overlap of public and private security agencies.

Teaching Outline

I. Introduction (p. 160)

II. Historical Development of the Police (p. 161)

    A. English Roots (p. 161)

- Early American policing was based on the British model.
- Introduce law enforcement in Great Britain and early efforts focused on the activities of the posse.

Comes Stabuli A nonuniformed mounted law enforcement officer of medieval England. Early police forces were small and relatively unorganized but made effective use of local resources in the formation of posses, the pursuit of offenders, and the like. (p. 161)

Night Watch An early form of police patrol in English cities and towns. (p. 161)

Statute of Winchester A law, written in 1285, that created a watch and ward system in English cities and towns and that codified early police practices. (p. 161)

    1. The Bow Street Runners
- Emerged in early 1700s in response to Jonathan Wild's criminal organization

Bow Street Runners An early English police unit formed under the leadership of Henry Fielding, magistrate of the Bow Street region of London. (p. 162)

    2. The New Police

New Police A police force formed in 1829 under the command of Sir Robert Peel. It became the model for modern-day police forces throughout the Western world. (p. 162)

Bobbies The popular British name given to members of Sir Robert (Bob) Peel's Metropolitan Police Force. (p. 162)

- Considered the first modern police force
- Also known as the Metropolitan Police

  B. The Early American Experience (p. 163)
    1. The Frontier
- Vigilantism was common.

Vigilantism The act of taking the law into one's own hands. (p. 163)

    2. Policing America's Early Cities
- Police reform was intense in the early 1900s.
    3. Prohibition and Police Corruption

Wickersham Commission The National Commission on Law Observance and Enforcement. In 1931, the commission issued a report stating that Prohibition was unenforceable and carried a great potential for police corruption. (p. 165)

  C. The Last Half of the Twentieth Century (p. 165)
- Significant police reforms occurred in the 1960s and 1970s, influenced in part by the President's Commission reports and the National Advisory Commission on Criminal Justice Standards and Goals.

INSTRUCTIONAL CUE LINKED TO THE STUDENT STUDY GUIDE

Use Student Activity 1 to illustrate the historical changes of law enforcement in the United States.

- Highlight the increasing focus on scientific police management and the influence of the Law Enforcement Assistance Administration (LEAA).

Law Enforcement Assistance Administration (LEAA) A now-defunct federal agency established under Title I of the Omnibus Crime Control and Safe Streets Act of 1967 to funnel federal funding to state and local law enforcement agencies. (p. 165)

  D. Scientific Police Management (p. 166)

Scientific Police Management The application of social scientific techniques to the study of police administration for the purpose of increasing effectiveness, reducing the frequency of citizen complaints, and enhancing the efficient use of available resources. (p. 166)

    1. Exemplary Projects

Exemplary Projects Program An initiative, sponsored by the Law Enforcement Assistance Administration, designed to recognize outstanding innovative efforts to combat crime and to provide assistance to crime victims. (p. 166)

    2. The Kansas City Experiment

- This experiment showed that preventive patrol had little influence on crime and did not make citizens feel safe.

Kansas City Experiment The first large-scale scientific study of law enforcement practices. Sponsored by the Police Foundation, it focused on the practice of preventive patrol. (p. 167)

INSTRUCTIONAL CUE

Discuss response time findings. The research in this area indicates that improving police response time does not increase the likelihood of apprehending suspects. Why is this so? The problem is that most citizens wait a considerable amount of time before calling the police.

INSTRUCTIONAL CUE

Revisit the research issues discussed in Chapter 3. Discuss research methodology with the students. They probably have not had much exposure to a controlled experiment. Use the Kansas City Preventive Patrol Experiment to illustrate this type of research design.

---

    3. Effects of the Kansas City Studies (p. 167)

- Findings led to the development of directed patrol activities and prioritizing calls for service.

Directed Patrol A police management strategy designed to increase the productivity of patrol officers through the application of scientific analysis and evaluation of patrol techniques. (p. 167)

    4. Recent Studies

- Indianapolis Directed Patrol Experiment—directed patrols focused on reducing gun crime
- Boston's Operation Ceasefire—an initiative targeting homicide victimization
- National Evaluation of Weed and Seed—community-based anti-crime initiative
- Kansas City Gun Experiment—vigorous enforcement of existing gun laws
- Minneapolis Domestic Violence Experiment—tested the impact of arrest on crime
- Problem-Oriented Policing in Newport News—compared incident-driven policing to problem-oriented policing

---

INSTRUCTIONAL CUE

Break the class into small groups of four or five students. Assign each group one of the studies mentioned in the text. You might want to request that they get copies of the studies. Have each group discern the design of the study and its important findings; then have groups share information with the rest of the class.

Sworn Officer   A law enforcement officer who is trained and empowered to perform full police duties, such as making arrests, conducting investigations, and carrying firearms. *Source*: Adapted from Darl H. Champion and Michael K. Hooper, *Introduction to American Policing* (New York: McGraw-Hill, 2003), p. 166. (p. 170)

>   5. Evidence-Based Policing

Evidence-Based Policing   The use of best available research on the outcomes of police work to implement guidelines and evaluate agencies, units, and officers. *Source*: Lawrence W. Sherman, *Evidence-Based Policing* (Washington, D.C.: The Police Foundation, 1998), p. 3. (p. 170)

INSTRUCTIONAL CUE LINKED TO THE STUDENT STUDY GUIDE

Use Student Activity 2 to discuss the usefulness of social science to police agencies. This may be a difficult assignment for students. Be sure that students understand the Kansas City research design before asking them to complete this assignment.

>   III. American Law Enforcement Today: From the Federal to the Local Level (p. 170)
>   IV. Federal Agencies (p. 170)

Federal Law Enforcement Agency   A U.S. government agency or office whose primary functional responsibility is the enforcement of federal criminal laws.

>   A. The Federal Bureau of Investigation (p. 170)
>   • Review the history of the FBI.
>   • Describe the FBI today.
>   B. The FBI and Counterterrorism (p. 174)
>   • After 9/11/2001, the FBI and other federal agencies underwent a major "reorganization and mobilization."

INSTRUCTIONAL CUE LINKED TO THE STUDENT STUDY GUIDE

Use Student Activity 3 to discuss federal law enforcement activities in the United States. Ask the class about the agencies they researched. It is likely that students will choose several of the agencies listed on the CJ Today website or on the Web, which will give you the opportunity to highlight federal law enforcement activities and the efforts of many different law enforcement agencies.

>   V. State Agencies (p. 175)
>   • Created in the late 1900s in response to specific state needs
>   • Centralized versus decentralized models
>   VI. Local Agencies (p. 179)
>   • Include a wide variety of police agencies, including sheriffs' departments and municipal police departments

Municipal Police Department   A city- or town-based law enforcement agency; also known as *local police*. (p. 179)

Sheriff   The elected chief officer of a county law enforcement agency. The sheriff is usually responsible for enforcement in unincorporated areas and for the operation of the county jail. (p. 179)

INSTRUCTIONAL CUE

Gather information about the agencies in the jurisdiction of your college or university and present it to the class. Discuss the number and types of law enforcement agencies within your jurisdiction.

VII. Private Protective Services (p. 181)

Private Protective Services   Independent or proprietary commercial organizations that provide protective services on a contractual basis. (p. 181)

- Discuss the activities of the Pinkerton and Brinks companies.
- Stress the differences in priorities of the private and public law enforcement agencies.
- Describe the major findings about private policing from the Hallcrest Report.

A. Integrating Public and Private Security (p. 185)

- The relationship between public and private law enforcement continues to evolve.

INSTRUCTIONAL CUE

This is a good place to revisit the goal conflicts discussed in Chapter 1. Highlight the primary concerns of public and private agencies, and explain why these agencies focus on different priorities.

INSTRUCTIONAL CUE LINKED TO THE STUDENT STUDY GUIDE

Use Student Activity 4 to highlight the levels of law enforcement. This exercise highlights the fragmentation of policing in law enforcement. A good way to illustrate such problems is to discuss overlapping investigations that often occur. For example, the local police and the sheriff's agency might be investigating an individual for drug dealing. The DEA, as well as the FBI, might also be investigating that drug dealer. You can discuss the fact that although agencies often try to cooperate and share information, "turf battles" often arise between agencies.

Learner Activities

Activity 1

The text discusses the 1931 Wickersham Commission. The recommendations of this commission have had an incredible impact on the criminal justice system. First, go to the library to find one of the commission reports (much of this report is available as a Library Extra). You will see that the report is a large volume, but each report has a smaller section on the police. Review the section on policing, and then answer the following discussion questions.

Which commission report did you examine? What types of law enforcement problems are identified in that report? Are the problems similar to or different from problems experienced by law enforcement today? What are some of the ethical dilemmas faced by police officers in the 1930s? What recommendations are made in that report to reform policing?

Activity 2

Assume that you have just been hired as the police chief of a small (about 45 officers) department. You were hired because you promised the mayor and city council that you could reduce the number of street crimes by using more officers on directed patrol. The city council has agreed to provide the department with funds to hire 16 more police officers to be used for this purpose. However, this money will be provided to the department only after you discuss how you will document whether directed patrol deters crime. Specifically, the city council wants you to design a research study, not unlike the Kansas City Preventive Patrol Experiment, to evaluate the effectiveness of directed patrol. In the space provided below, discuss your research design, including how you would use the new officers in the study, length of time of the study, and beat selection. Be sure to read the discussion on the Kansas City Preventive Patrol Experiment in the book. In addition, it might be helpful to read publications about other research studies to get some ideas on how to design a study. You can read more about the National Weed and Seed Evaluation and the Kansas City Gun Experiment discussed in Chapter 5 at **Library Extra 5–2** and **Library Extra 5–4**.

LIBRARY EXTRA

Activity 3

In Chapter 5 the text discusses the important role that federal agencies play in law enforcement. The text highlights the activities of the Federal Bureau of Investigation but mentions that there are dozens of federal law enforcement agencies. This activity requires that you learn about the activities of a federal law enforcement agency other than the FBI. You can do this by visiting the website of a federal agency. Choose an agency. In the space provided below, compare and contrast the activities of the Federal Bureau of Investigation and the agency that you selected. In what ways are the law enforcement activities of that agency similar to the activities of the FBI? In what ways are they different?

Activity 4

Find out which law enforcement agencies have law enforcement responsibilities and duties in the county where the university you attend is located. List these agencies, their law enforcement responsibilities, and the level of policing they represent (for example, federal, state, local, or private). Do these agencies have responsibilities that overlap? What changes would you suggest to use their personnel resources more effectively?

_____

_____

_____

_____

_____

_____

Internet Activity

Visit a number of private security agency sites on the Web. (You can find such sites listed in the Cybrary, at http://www.cybrary.info.) Gather information on each agency, including things such as services offered, requirements for hiring, employment opportunities, and table of organization. Assemble a notebook (or disk) containing the information you have gathered, organized by agency. Your instructor may request that you submit the material.

_____

_____

_____

_____

_____

_____

Distance Learning Activity

Find the code of ethics for at least three law enforcement agencies. Compare and contrast the behaviors that are included in each code of ethics.

_____

_____

_____

_____

_____

_____

Learning Activities Utilizing the World Wide Web

There are student-based activities in the Student Study Guide (Internet Activity, Distance Learning Activity, CJ Today on the World Wide Web) that are similar in focus to those that follow. However, the following are presented as instructor-led activities, to be used in a classroom with online access.

Prior to class, visit a number of private security agency sites on the Web. (You can find such sites listed in the Cybrary, at http://www.cybrary.info.) Gather information on each agency, including services offered, requirements for hiring, employment opportunities, and table of organization. Prepare a presentation for class containing the information you have gathered, organized by agency. Present and review in class.

Visit the websites of three different law enforcement agencies: one federal, one state, and one local. Use any search engine to gather information on these agencies. Summarize the characteristics of the different agencies. In class, have students view the information and assess the amount and type of information posted on the World Wide Web for each type of department.

Other websites for organizations and agencies related to the material in Chapter 5 include:

Alcohol, Tobacco, and Firearms	http://www.atf.treas.gov
Drug Enforcement Administration	http://www.usdoj.gov/dea
Central Intelligence Agency	http://www.odci.gov
U.S. Marshals Service	http://www.usdoj.gov/marshals
U.S. Secret Service	http://www.treas.gov/usss
U.S. Postal Inspection Service	http://www.usps.gov/websites/ depart/inspect
U.S. Customs Service	http://www.customs.ustreas.gov
U.S. Coast Guard	http://www.uscg.mil
Citizenship and Immigration Services	http://www.uscis.gov
Law Enforcement Links	http://www.leolinks.com
Homeland Security	http://www.dhs.gov/dhspublic

Suggested Answers to Chapter Discussion Questions

1. **Describe the historical development of policing in America. What impact did the Prohibition era have on the development of American policing?**

   The rise of policing in America was shaped by many unique factors, including the huge expanse of unchartered Western territory, wealth, and a widely dispersed population. One of the major factors shaping American policing was the frontier. Since it was unsettled and wild, law and order was enforced primarily by citizen posses and vigilante groups. More structured law enforcement occurred in larger cities. Policing in these cities closely resembled the British model, paramilitary organizational structure, wearing police uniforms, and focusing on the prevention of crime. As society changed culturally and technologically, so did American policing. America's experiment with Prohibition was a complete failure, and it impacted policing by creating opportunities for corruption and graft. The Wickersham Commission, after reviewing problems with law enforcement, established guidelines that have since impacted many aspects of law enforcement.

2. **What is scientific police management? What assumptions about police work have scientific studies of law enforcement called into question?**

   Scientific police management is the use of social scientific techniques to study policing for the purpose of increasing effectiveness, reducing the frequency of citizen complaints, and enhancing the efficient use of available resources. Police work is replete with assumptions about what works effectively and what doesn't. Classic scientific studies designed to validate or invalidate those assumptions include the 1974 Kansas City Preventive Patrol Experiment, which questioned the effectiveness of routine police patrol; the 1994 Kansas City Gun Experiment, which sought to determine if vigorous gun law enforcement would reduce gun-related crime; the 1984 Minneapolis study of domestic violence, which attempted to show the impact of arrest, versus other dispositions, on the reduction of crime; and the Newport News, Virginia, test, conducted during the 1980s, that compared traditional incident-driven policing to a new approach called problem-oriented policing.

What other assumptions made about police work today might be similarly questioned or studied?

Potential assumptions about police work worth examining include the effects of higher minimum education standards on police violence, the effects of higher minimum education standards on police corruption, and studies related to the effectiveness of female officers.

3. **What are the three levels of law enforcement described in this chapter? Why do we have so many different types of enforcement agencies in the United States?**

Law enforcement in the United States exists at the federal, state, and local levels. Legislative and jurisdictional limitations on the investigatory responsibilities of particular agencies, and the technical investigatory specialization of other agencies, serve to explain the existence of the widely varied types of law enforcement agencies.

What problems, if any, do you think are created by such a diversity of agencies?

American law enforcement professionals, functioning in what some call the most complex organization in the world, are rightfully proud of their performance in accomplishing an extraordinarily difficult task. Their achievements are attributable to the routinely competent performance of mundane, often thankless, and sometimes dangerous duties by a core group of dedicated and courageous men and women. In an environment of high stress, swirling emotions, and ever-changing legal, tactical, and administrative rules, they protect us with selflessness and commitment of the highest order.

But it is an undeniable reality that the complex organization in which they, on the whole, perform so admirably can also be a confusing miasma of jurisdictional disputes, competition for limited funding, political maneuvering and manipulation, stifling personal and organizational ego contests, impenetrable bureaucracy, administrative inertia, and duplicated effort resulting in extraordinary inefficiency. Hence, some suggest that a unified national police force, which would take the place of existing multilevel agencies, would solve many of the problems that exist in American policing today.

4. **Describe the nature and extent of private protective services in the United States today. Contrast the current deployment of private security personnel with the number of public law enforcement personnel.**

Private protective services have had an incredible impact on law enforcement and safety in America. More people are employed in private security than in all local, state, and federal law enforcement agencies combined. It is estimated that there are nearly 2 million people working in private security and probably about 1 million working in public law enforcement. This gap will increase, as it is anticipated that the number of people employed in private security will increase at a faster rate compared to the number in public law enforcement.

What do you think will be the future role of private protective services in the United States? How can the quality of such services be ensured?

Private police services will likely continue to expand as organizations and citizens seek to increase their sense of security in what they perceive to be an increasingly dangerous world. Factors that can ensure high-quality delivery of private police services include thorough screening of applicants, standardized training in essential technical skills, professional certification processes, and state licensure.

5. **What is the relationship between private security and public policing in America today? How might the nature of that relationship be expected to change over time? Why?**

The growth of the private security industry has certainly caused friction with public law enforcement. Sources of friction include the erosion of public law enforcement's turf, moonlighting by public officers in private security, and different relationships and case priorities when interacting with a prosecutor's office. This relationship is constantly evolving, with some scholars noting that the distinction is "increasingly meaningless," and there is a general recognition that both can benefit from cooperation.

Key—Student Study Guide Questions

True or False

____ 5-1. A centralized state law enforcement agency combines the tasks of major criminal investigations with highway patrol. **(True, pp. 175-176)**

____ 5-2. More people are employed in private security than in all local, state, and federal police agencies combined. **(True, p. 184)**

____ 5-3. Early American police departments were structured according to the British model. **(True, p. 161)**

____ 5-4. *Comes stabuli* is a Latin term that means "a uniformed leader of the county." **(False, p. 161)**

____ 5-5. Congress created the Federal Bureau of Investigation in 1980 because crime rates had increased dramatically in the previous decade. **(False, p. 171)**

____ 5-6. Early in his career, J. Edgar Hoover was personally responsible for apprehending the infamous criminal Jonathan Wild. **(False, p. 162)**

____ 5-7. Results from the Kansas City Preventive Patrol Experiment indicate that officers on preventive patrol deter crimes such as burglary and robbery; therefore, citizens feel safe. **(False, p. 167)**

____ 5-8. Robert Peel is famous for his law enforcement activities on the Western frontier. **(False, p. 162)**

____ 5-9. The scientific police study undertaken in Newport News, Virginia, examined whether mandatory arrests can deter domestic violence batteries. **(False, p. 169)**

____ 5-10. Directed patrol is a police management strategy designed to increase the productivity of patrol officers through the application of scientific analysis and evaluation of patrol techniques. **(True, p. 167)**

Multiple Choice

5-11. Which of the following aspects of police work is the "backbone of policing"?
   a. management
   b. administration
   c. patrol (p. 168)
   d. investigation

5-12. Who is most closely associated with London's Bow Street Runners?
   a. Jonathan Wild
   b. Henry Fielding (p. 162)
   c. Sir Robert Peel
   d. Patrick Murphy

5-13. Which of the following was not characteristic of the "New Police"?
   a. They adopted a military administrative style.
   b. They occupied fixed posts throughout the city awaiting a public outcry. (p. 162)
   c. They believed that it was possible to discourage crime.
   d. They were uniformed.

5-14. Which of the following studies found that offenders who were arrested were less likely to commit repeat offenses than those handled in some other fashion?
   a. Newport News Problem-Oriented Policing Experiment
   b. Newark Foot Patrol Experiment
   c. Kansas City Preventive Patrol Experiment
   d. Minneapolis Domestic Violence Experiment (p. 169)

5-15. Which federal law enforcement agency has responsibility for maintaining the Combined DNA Index System (CODIS)?
   a. U.S. Marshals Service
   b. U.S. Customs Service
   c. Federal Bureau of Investigation (p. 173)
   d. Drug Enforcement Administration

5-16. Shire reeve means
   a. police chief.
   b. attorney general.
   c. mounted officer.
   d. leader of the county. (p. 161)

5-17. The mission statement of which federal law enforcement agency includes protecting and defending the United States against terrorist and foreign intelligence threats?
   a. U.S. Marshals Service
   b. U.S. Customs Service
   c. Federal Bureau of Investigation (p. 174)
   d. Drug Enforcement Administration

5-18. A _____ is responsible for the operation of a county jail.
   a. sheriff (p. 179)
   b. uniformed patrol officer
   c. U.S. marshal
   d. state highway patrol officer

5-19. Who was responsible for starting the world's first modern police force?
   a. "Wild Bill" Hickok
   b. Richard Mayne
   c. Henry Fielding
   d. Sir Robert Peel (p. 162)

5-20. All of the following are reasons for the growth of private security in America except
   a. the fiscal crisis of the states.
   b. public police agencies requesting assistance from private agencies. (p. 185)
   c. an increase in fear of crime.
   d. an increase in crimes in the workplace.

Fill-In

5-21. The _____ was the study credited with beginning the tradition of scientific police evaluation. **(Kansas City Preventive Patrol Experiment, p. 167)**

5-22. The _____ is responsible for maintaining the "Ten Most Wanted" list. **(Federal Bureau of Investigation, p. 173)**

5-23. The _____ was written in 1285, and it created a watch and ward system in cities and towns and codified early British police practices. **(Statute of Winchester, p. 161)**

5-24. _____ means "leader of the county." **(Shire reeve, p. 161)**

5-25. The first scientifically engineered social experiment to test the impact of the use of arrest on crime was the _____. **(Minneapolis Domestic Violence Experiment, p. 169)**

5-26. The _____ were also known as the Metropolitan Police. **(New Police, p. 162)**

5-27. _____ is a police management strategy designed to increase the productivity of patrol officers through the application of scientific analysis and evaluation of patrol techniques. **(Directed patrol, p. 167)**

5-28. _____ means "mounted officer." **(*Comes stabuli*, p. 161)**

5-29. The study that found that vigorous enforcement of gun laws could reduce crime was the _____. **(Kansas City Gun Experiment, p. 169)**

5-30. The federal law enforcement agency that compiles DNA profiles is the _____. **(Federal Bureau of Investigation, p. 173)**

Key—Crossword Puzzle

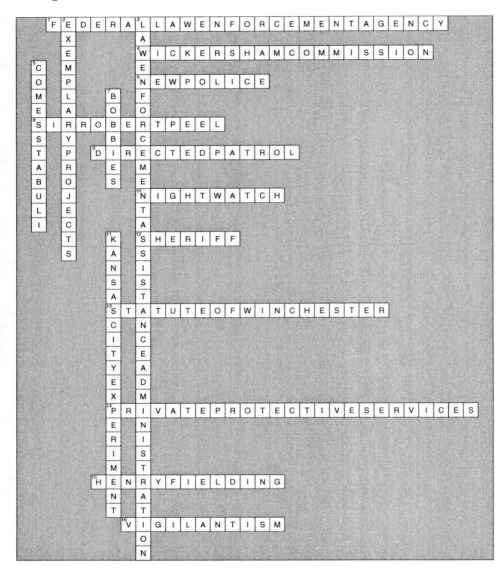

Across

1. Example includes the FBI, DEA, or ATF.
4. Officially called the National Commission on Law Observance and Enforcement.
6. Also known as the Metropolitan Police Force.
8. Leader of the Metropolitan Police Force.
9. Police management strategy designed to increase the productivity of patrol officers through the scientific analysis and evaluation of patrol techniques.
10. Early form of police patrol in English cities and towns.
12. Person responsible for the operation of the jail.
13. Law that created the watch and ward system in 1285.
14. Independent or proprietary commercial organizations that provide protective services to employers on a contractual basis.
15. Leader of the Bow Street Runners.
16. Act of taking the law into one's own hands.

Down

2. Hidden cameras project in Seattle is one example.
3. Sponsor of the Exemplary Projects Program.
5. Nonuniformed mounted early law enforcement officers in medieval England.
7. Nickname for Metropolitan Police Officers.
11. First large-scale scientific study of law enforcement practices.

Key—Word Search Puzzle

Bobbies
Bow Street Runners
Comes Stabuli
Directed Patrol
Evidence-based policing
Exemplary Projects Program
Henry Fielding
Kansas City Experiment
Law Enforcement Assistance Administration
New Police

Night Watch
Police History
Private Protective Services
Scientific Police Management
Sheriff
Sir Robert Peel
Statute of Winchester
Sworn Officer
Vigilantism
Wickersham Commission

CHAPTER 6

Policing: Purpose and Organization

OUTLINE

LEARNING OBJECTIVES

After reading this chapter, you should be able to:

- Explain the basic purposes of policing in democratic societies
- List and discuss the five core operational strategies of today's police departments
- Define the term *police management*, and describe the different types of organizational structures typical of American police departments
- Identify the three styles of policing, and discuss differences in these approaches
- Describe community policing, and explain how it differs from traditional policing
- Describe the changed role of American police in the post–9/11 environment
- Explain police discretion and how it affects the practice of contemporary law enforcement
- Demonstrate why professionalism is important in policing today
- Identify some of the issues related to ethnic and gender diversity in policing, and suggest ways of addressing them

Chapter Summary

Chapter 6 discusses several areas of concern to the police organization. These areas include the police mission, operational strategies, managing police departments, policing styles, discretion and the officer, professionalism and ethics, and ethnic and gender diversity in policing.

Chapter 6 begins with a discussion of the police mission. In general, the basic purposes of policing include enforcing the law, apprehending offenders, preventing crime, preserving the peace, and providing services. This section also discusses how terrorism has impacted the police mission of federal, state, and local law enforcement agencies.

The mission of policing directly shapes the operational strategies departments use to accomplish their goals. Chapter 6 discusses the five core operational strategies of police departments: preventive patrol, routine incident response, emergency response, **criminal investigation**, and **problem solving**. These operational strategies highlight how police work in a democratic society. Importantly, this section also highlights the objectives, performance standards, and processes involved for each operational strategy.

Chapter 6 also discusses **police management**. Police management focuses on the administrative activities that control, direct, and coordinate police personnel, resources, and activities. This section discusses the general structure of police organizations and highlights the **chain of command**.

Police departments have unique policing styles formed in response to community and organizational factors. Three types of policing styles, developed by James Q. Wilson, are discussed in Chapter 6. First, police officers employed in **watchman style** departments are most concerned with maintaining order. These officers possess a considerable amount of discretion to resolve situations. Second, police officers in **legalistic style** departments are expected to enforce the letter of the law, meaning that their discretion to use a nonenforcement response is limited. Moreover, these officers are likely to ignore other disruptive behaviors. Third, officers in a **service style** department are most concerned with helping citizens rather than strictly applying the letter of the law. These officers would be familiar with community resources and use these resources to help solve community and individual problems.

Many police departments are moving to the service style, using what are popularly known as community policing strategies. **Community policing** is a strategy that calls for police departments to develop community relationships and solicit citizen assistance in solving problems. The current movement toward community policing has its roots in the **police–community relations** programs advocated in the 1960s, as well as in the **team policing** ideas of the 1970s. This chapter in the text discusses several examples of community-policing programs, such as Houston's DART program, Chicago's Alternative Policing Strategy, and Baltimore's Project Cope.

Chapter 6 also introduces the idea of **police discretion**. Despite the influence of departmental styles, individual officers possess an opportunity to make choices when enforcing the law. When "working the streets," officers are not directly supervised by superiors, providing them with discretion to informally or formally resolve incidents. The text describes potential factors that might influence the ways officers use discretion, such as the background of the officer, characteristics of the suspect, community interest, and pressures from the victim.

The author discusses key issues related to resolving many of the issues facing police departments in the section on **professionalism** and **ethics**. Doing accreditation of police departments, raising educational standards, and improving the recruitment and selection of officers are changes being made to address problem areas of policing.

The author concludes by discussing issues of ethnic and gender diversity in policing. Statistics show that the number of police from minority groups has dramatically increased, but employment of women still lags significantly behind.

Teaching Outline

    I. Introduction (p. 192)

    II. The Police Mission (p. 192)

        A. Enforcing the Law (p. 192)

- Police agencies are the primary enforcers of federal, state, and local criminal laws.
- Research shows that only 10% to 20% of all calls require a law enforcement response.

        B. Apprehending Offenders (p. 193)

        C. Preventing Crime (p. 194)

Crime Prevention   The anticipation, recognition, and appraisal of a crime risk and the initiation of action to eliminate or reduce it. (p. 194)

- Review the history of prevention efforts.
- Provide examples of crime prevention techniques and programs.
  1. Predicting Crime

CompStat   A crime-analysis and police-management process built on crime mapping that was developed by the New York City Police Department in the mid-1990s. (p. 195)

        D. Preserving the Peace (p. 195)

Quality-of-Life Offense   A minor violation of the law (sometimes called a *petty crime*) that demoralizes community residents and businesspeople. Quality-of-life offenses involve acts that create physical disorder (for example, excessive noise or vandalism) or that reflect social decay (for example, panhandling and prostitution). (p. 195)

- Peacekeeping is a virtually limitless police activity.
- Discuss the broken windows thesis.

        E. Providing Services (p. 198)

        F. Terrorism's Impact on Policing (p. 198)

- Law enforcement agencies at all levels consider terrorism a priority issue.
- The role of local law enforcement in responding to terrorism has changed significantly since the World Trade Center and Pentagon attacks of September 11.

    III. Operational Strategies (p. 198)

        A. Preventive Patrol (p. 198)

- Today's dominant policing strategy—consumes most of the resources of local and state agencies.
- The purpose of patrol is to deter crimes, to interrupt crimes, to position officers for quick response, and to increase the public's feeling of safety and security.

        B. Routine Incident Response (p. 198)

Response Time   A measure of the time that it takes for police officers to respond to calls for service. (p. 200)

        C. Emergency Response (p. 200)

- Probably the most important aspect of what police do

        D. Criminal Investigation (p. 200)

Criminal Investigation   "The process of discovering, collecting, preparing, identifying, and presenting evidence to determine *what happened and who is responsible*" when a crime has occurred. *Source*: Wayne W. Bennett and Karen M. Hess, *Criminal Investigation*, 6th ed. (Belmont, CA: Wadsworth, 2001), p. 3. Italics in original. (p. 200)

Crime Scene   The physical area in which a crime is thought to have occurred and in which evidence of the crime is thought to reside. (p. 201)

Preliminary Investigation   All of the activities undertaken by a police officer who responds to the scene of a crime, including determining whether a crime has occurred, securing the crime scene, and preserving evidence. (p. 202)

- Review the activities involved in a preliminary investigation.

Crime-Scene Investigator   An expert trained in the use of forensics techniques, such as gathering DNA evidence, collecting fingerprints, photography, sketching, and interviewing witnesses. (p. 202)

Solvability Factor   Information about a crime that forms the basis for determining the perpetrator's identity. (p. 202)

  E. Problem Solving (p. 202)
  F. Support Services (p. 203)

INSTRUCTIONAL CUE

Divide the class into six groups, each assuming one of the six operational strategies. After small-group discussion on each strategy, a spokesman from each group can be part of a panel discussion on police operational strategies.

 IV. Managing Police Departments (p. 203)

Police Management   The administrative activities of controlling, directing, and coordinating police personnel, resources, and activities in the service of crime prevention, the apprehension of criminals, the recovery of stolen property, and the performance of a variety of regulatory and helping services. *Source*: This definition draws on the classic work by O. W. Wilson, *Police Administration* (New York: McGraw-Hill, 1950), pp. 2–3. (p. 203)

  A. Police Organization and Structure (p. 203)

Line Operations   In police organizations, field activities or supervisory activities directly related to day-to-day police work. (p. 203)

Staff Operations   In police organizations, activities (like administration and training) that provide support for line operations. (p. 203)

  B. Chain of Command (p. 203)

Chain of Command   The unbroken line of authority that extends through all levels of an organization, from the highest to the lowest. (p. 203)

Span of Control   The number of police personnel or the number of units supervised by a particular commander. (p. 204)

 V. Policing Styles (p. 204)
  A. The Watchman Style of Policing (p. 207)

Watchman Style   A style of policing marked by a concern for order maintenance. Watchman policing is characteristic of lower-class communities where police intervene informally into the lives of residents to keep the peace. (p. 207)

  B. The Legalistic Style of Policing (p. 207)

Legalistic Style   A style of policing marked by a strict concern with enforcing the precise letter of the law. Legalistic departments, however, may take a hands-off approach to otherwise disruptive or problematic behavior that does not violate the criminal law. (p. 207)

C. The Service Style of Policing (p. 207)

Service Style   A style of policing marked by a concern with helping rather than strict enforcement. Service-oriented police agencies are more likely to take advantage of community resources, such as drug-treatment programs, than are other types of agencies. (p. 207)

D. Police–Community Relations (p. 208)

Police–Community Relations (PCR)   An area of emerging police activity that recognizes the need for the community and the police to work together effectively and that is based on the notion that the police derive their legitimacy from the community they serve. PCR began to be of concern to many police agencies in the 1960s and 1970s. (p. 208)

1. Team Policing

- One outgrowth of this focus on community is the emphasis on team policing.

Team Policing   The reorganization of conventional patrol strategies into "an integrated and versatile police team assigned to a fixed district." *Source*: Sam S. Souryal, *Police Administration and Management* (St. Paul, MN: West Publishing Co., 1977), p. 261. (p. 209)

2. Community Policing

- Three "corporate strategies" guide American policing.
- Strategic policing uses innovative enforcement techniques to target nontraditional types of criminals.

Strategic Policing   A type of policing that retains the traditional police goal of professional crime fighting but enlarges the enforcement target to include nontraditional kinds of criminals, such as serial offenders, gangs and criminal associations, drug-distribution networks, and sophisticated white-collar and computer criminals. Strategic policing generally makes use of innovative enforcement techniques, including intelligence operations, undercover stings, electronic surveillance, and sophisticated forensics methods. (p. 210)

- Problem-solving policing focuses on addressing underlying social problems.

Problem-Solving Policing   A type of policing that assumes that crimes can be controlled by uncovering and effectively addressing the underlying social problems that cause crime. Problem-solving policing makes use of community resources, such as counseling centers, welfare programs, and job-training facilities. It also attempts to involve citizens in crime prevention through education, negotiation, and conflict management. (p. 210)

- Community policing addresses the causes of crime and aims to reduce the fear of crime.

Community Policing   "A collaborative effort between the police and the community that identifies problems of crime and disorder and involves all elements of the community in the search for solutions to these problems." *Source*: Community Policing Consortium, *What Is Community Policing?* (Washington, D.C.: The Consortium, 1995). (p. 210)

INSTRUCTIONAL CUE

The underlying premise of these three corporate strategies is that police organizations are similar to businesses. The police are expected to respond to crime but also be accountable to the public. Police administrators have different approaches to balancing these issues effectively. Discuss some of these approaches in class.

- Review Chicago's community policing initiative.

E. Critiques of Community Policing (p. 212)

- Problems include police managers unwilling to accept this new philosophy, additional goal conflict caused by involving the community in decision making, resistance from the police subculture, and unsupportive public officials.

Police Subculture   A particular set of values, beliefs, and acceptable forms of behavior characteristic of American police. Socialization into the police subculture begins with recruit training and continues thereafter. (p. 213)

INSTRUCTIONAL CUE LINKED TO THE STUDENT STUDY GUIDE

Use Student Activity 1 to help students understand community policing.

VI. Terrorism's Impact on Policing (p. 214)
- The police role in America began a new era because of 9/11/2001.
- Budget sometimes dictates the amount of engagement in antiterrorism activities at the local level.
- Review the preliminary results of the Taking Command Initiative to assess the current state of Homeland Security.
  A. Intelligence-Led Policing and Antiterrorism (p. 216)
   - Information has been analyzed and integrated into a useful perspective.

Intelligence-Led Policing   The collection and analysis of information to produce an intelliegence end product designed to inform police decision making at both the tactical and strategic levels. *Source*: Angus Smith, ed., Intelligence-Led Policing (Richmond, VA: International Association of Law Enforcement Intelligence Analysts, 1997), p. 1. (p. 216)

Criminal Intelligence   Information compiled, analyzed, and/or disseminated in an effort to anticipate, prevent, or monitor criminal activity. *Source*: Office of Justice Programs, *The National Criminal Intelligence Sharing Plan* (Washington, DC: U.S. Department of Justice, 2005), p. 27. (p. 216)

  B. Community Policing and Antiterrorism (p. 219)
   - Community policing is a natural conduit for information gathering and the development of counterterrorism intelligence.
   - The Office for Domestic Preparedness has described the roles community policing can play in the intelligence process.
  C. Information Sharing and Antiterrorism (p. 219)
   - A fully integrated national criminal justice information system does not yet exist.

MATRIX   The Multistate Anti-Terrorism Information Exchange (p. 221)

VII. Discretion and the Individual Officer (p. 221)

Police Discretion   The opportunity that individual law enforcement officers have for the exercise of choice in their daily activities. (p. 221)

- Factors That Influence the Discretionary Decisions of Individual Officers
  - Background of the officer
  - Characteristics of the suspect
  - Department policy
  - Community interest
  - Pressures from victims
  - Disagreement with the law
  - Available alternatives
  - Personal practices of the officer

INSTRUCTIONAL CUE

Relate issues of police discretion with the policing styles discussed earlier. How would police officers in legalistic departments exercise discretion? Watchman? Service?

INSTRUCTIONAL CUE LINKED TO THE STUDENT STUDY GUIDE

Use Student Activity 2 to help students understand police use of discretion.

　　VIII.　Professionalism and Ethics (p. 223)

Police Professionalism　The increasing formalization of police work and the accompanying rise in public acceptance of the police. (p. 223)

Police Ethics　The special responsibility for adherence to moral duty and obligation that is inherent in police work. (p. 223)

　　　　A.　Education and Training (p. 224)

Peace Officer Standards and Training (POST) Program　The official program of a state or legislative jurisdiction that sets standards for the training of law enforcement officers. All states set such standards, although not all use the term *POST*. (p. 224)

INSTRUCTIONAL CUE

Choose a few professions (doctor, lawyer teacher), and compare the entry-level requirments to those of a peace officer. After someone is hired, what are the continuing training requirements for each profession? Discuss the differences.

　　IX.　Ethnic and Gender Diversity in Policing (p. 228)
　　　　• Although ethnic minorities are employed in policing in numbers that approach their representation in the American population, women are still significantly underrepresented.
　　　　A.　Women as Effective Police Officers (p. 230)
　　　　B.　Increasing the Number of Minorities and Women in Police Work (p. 230)

INSTRUCTIONAL CUE

Brainstorm a list of strategies that would stimulate more interest in law enforcement from women and minorities. After hiring and training them, how can departments work to retain these valuable employees?

Learner Activities

Activity 1

The text describes the Chicago Police Department's community policing program. Before beginning this assignment, read that section of the text again. This activity requires you to find information about one other police department's community policing program. There are several ways to do this. First, you could interview officers from the department you select. Second, you can visit the department's website. Most police departments have websites, and if they have a community-policing program, information will be posted on it. Third, there is a large body of research on community policing. You should be able to retrieve books or articles describing various community-policing programs from the library. A good book describing a few different approaches to community policing is *The New Blue Line* by David Bayley and Jerome Skolnick. Finally, you can learn from the community policing studies posted on the National Criminal Justice Reference Service page at http://www.ncjrs.org.

In the space provided below, compare and contrast what you found with the textbook's discussion of community policing in Chicago.

_____

_____

_____

_____

_____

_____

Activity 2

Answer the following questions on police discretion in the space provided below. Should police officers enforce the law equally in all situations? In what types of situations should police officers be allowed to not enforce the law? In what types of situations should they be required to fully enforce the law? Why does police discretion exist? What are its strengths and weaknesses? What is the relationship between discretion and police ethics?

_____

_____

_____

_____

_____

_____

Activity 3

In Chapter 6 the text describes individual police officer discretion as an important aspect of policing but also notes the dangers of having limited oversight of officers in most situations. Below are a number of examples in which police officers have to exercise discretion; this is not uncommon in police work. After each example, discuss how you, as a police officer, would respond to the situation. There are no right answers, but be certain to justify your response with an explanation.

1. You are dispatched to a low-income apartment complex. A man (his name is Arnold), who is homeless and addicted to crack, refuses to leave the entrance area to the building. He allows those living in the building to enter and does not bother most of them; however, a tenant has called to complain and would like him removed. It is midwinter and the temperature is below freezing. As the responding officer, how would you use your discretion to respond to this situation? Why?

2. While on random preventive patrol in a high-crime neighborhood, you notice two young children (you think they are about eight or nine years old) hanging around outside a drugstore. When you approach them, they start acting very nervous (it is about eight o'clock at night). As you talk to them, a third kid, same age, comes out of the store followed by the cashier, who tells you that he has just tried to steal three candy bars. How would you respond to this situation? Justify your action.

3. While randomly patrolling a neighborhood, you observe a vehicle run a red light. While in pursuit, you also notice that the person is driving in a haphazard manner. After the person stops his vehicle, you discover that he is drunk. The person driving the car, however, is also your favorite uncle. How would you respond to this situation? How does your response differ from your responses to the previous two situations?

4. Your department has received a call from a citizen complaining that his next-door neighbors have been fighting for the last two hours (it is 3:30 A.M.). When you knock on the door and announce that you are the police, the fighting abruptly stops. A male, about 24 years old, opens the door, apologizes for the disturbance, and promises that they will be quiet. However, he will not allow you into the home to talk with the person he was fighting with. How would you resolve this situation?

_____

_____

_____

_____

_____

_____

Activity 4

LIBRARY EXTRA

For this activity, first read the executive summary of the report on intelligence-led policing at **Library Extra 6–8**. This report discusses how criminal intelligence is being used to guide policing. After reading some of the report, summarize what you have learned in the space below.

_____

_____

_____

_____

_____

Internet Activity

Use the Cybrary (http://www.cybrary.info) to find descriptions of terrorism and policing studies on the Web. What kinds of studies did you find? What do they deal with? What were the findings or results of each of these studies? (*Hint:* You might want to first check the National Criminal Justice Reference Service at http://www.ncjrs.org.)

_____

_____

_____

_____

_____

Distance Learning Activity

In the space below, highlight the pros and cons of community policing. Some of the strengths and weaknesses are discussed in the textbook, but you should also visit additional websites containing community policing information. For example, see **Library Extra 6–5**.

LIBRARY EXTRA

_____

_____

_____

_____

_____

Learning Activities Utilizing the World Wide Web

There are student-based activities in the Student Study Guide (Internet Activity, Distance Learning Activity, CJ Today on the World Wide Web) that are similar in focus to those that follow. However, the following are presented as instructor-led activities, to be used in a classroom with online access.

Prior to class, check out the Cybrary (http://www.cybrary.info) to find descriptions of terrorism and policing studies on the Web. Prepare a list (for presentation) and short description of each piece of research with a link to the website. Ask the following questions to stimulate discussion: What were the findings or results of each of these studies? How will the results be utilized?

Other websites for organizations and agencies related to the material in Chapter 6 include:

California Peace Officer Standards and Training	http://www.post.ca.gov
Community Oriented Policing Services (COPS)	http://www.cops.usdoj.gov
Community Policing Consortium (CPC)	http://www.communitypolicing.org
Copsonline	http://www.copsonline.com
Federal Law Enforcement Training Center	http://www.treas.gov/fletc
New York City Police Department (NYPD)	http://www.ci.nyc.ny.us/html/nypd
Singapore Police Force	http://www.spinet.gov.sg/pollink
Treasury of Police Humor	http://www.policehumor.com

Suggested Answers to Chapter Discussion Questions

1. **What are the basic purposes of policing in democratic societies? How are they consistent with one another? In what ways might they be inconsistent?**

   The basic purposes of policing are to enforce and support laws, investigate crimes and apprehend offenders, prevent crime, help ensure domestic peace and tranquility, and provide the community with needed enforcement-related services. These purposes overlap in several ways. For example, police officers investigate crimes and apprehend offenders, which enforces and supports the laws of a society. However, these purposes can be inconsistent as well. In an effort to prevent crime, police officers might use overly aggressive patrol strategies, which could push the community away from the police, and the end result might be less domestic peace.

2. **What are the five core operational strategies that police departments use today?**
   - Preventive patrol
   - Routine incident response
   - Emergency response
   - Criminal investigation
   - Problem solving

3. **Define the term** *police management*, **and describe the different types of organizational structures typical of American police departments.**

   Police management includes the administrative activities of controlling, directing, and coordinating police personnel, resources, and activities in the service of preventing crime, apprehending criminals, recovering stolen property, and performing regulatory and helping services. The two basic organizational types associated with police agencies are line and staff. Line operations focus on field and supervisory activities related to daily police work. Staff operations include support roles, such as police administration.

4. **What are the three styles of policing described in this chapter? How do they differ? Which one characterizes the community in which you live?**

   The three styles of policing are: watchman, legalistic, and service. The watchman style is typical of lower-class communities, and the primary concern is maintaining order. Officers working in such departments have considerable discretion in deciding when and how to enforce the law. The legalistic style is marked by enforcing the precise letter of the law. Officers in these departments have limited discretion and generally ignore order maintenance situations unless the criminal law was broken. The service style focuses on a concern with helping rather than enforcing the law.

5. **What is community policing? How does it differ from traditional policing?**

   Community policing focuses on a collaborative effort between the police and all elements of the community to identify problems and solutions in responding to crime and disorder. There are many ways that community policing differs from traditional policing. First, community-policing agencies are willing to work with the public and other community agencies to solve problems. In contrast, the relationship between citizens and other community agencies and the police may involve conflict in traditional policing. Second, community policing focuses on solving problems and traditional policing focuses on solving crimes. Third, community policing focuses on all types of problems, even minor incidents, and traditional policing tends to consider non-crime-related calls for service as low-priority items. Finally, community policing is accountable to the community, and traditional policing is accountable to the law.

   Does community policing offer an opportunity to improve policing services in the United States? Why or why not?

   Community policing certainly has the potential to improve policing services in the United States, but police organizations are very resistant to change. The philosophy that underlies community policing is promising. Police agencies should work with the community and community agencies, coordinating priorities and sharing responsibilities for community safety. If a department fully commits to community policing, and the community commits to the collaboration, policing services would certainly improve.

6. **What new responsibilities have American police agencies assumed since the 9/11 terrorist attacks? What new challenges are they facing?**

   American police agencies have assumed new responsibilities since the 9/11 attacks in the areas of terrorism prevention and response. While the core mission of American police departments has not changed, law enforcement agencies at all levels now devote an increased amount of time and other resources to preparing for possible terrorist attacks and to gathering the intelligence necessary to thwart them. In particular, local police departments play an especially important role in responding to the challenges of terrorism. Not only must they help prevent attacks, but they must respond quickly when attacks occur, offering critical evacuation, emergency medical, and security services to help stabilize communities following an incident. Community-policing programs have been adapted to the needs of terrorism prevention because community policing provides a natural conduit for information gathering and the development of counterterrorism intelligence.

7. **What is meant by police discretion? How does the practice of discretion by today's officers affect their departments and the policing profession as a whole?**

   Police discretion is the opportunity for law enforcement officers to exercise choice in their daily activities. Discretion is essential to policing in America. Because police agencies receive too many calls and departmental priorities are influenced by a number of external factors, flexibility in police response is critical to police legitimacy. If, however, police discretion results in unpredictable and discriminatory practices, such as racial profiling, then the reputation of police departments and the policing profession is damaged.

8. **What is police professionalism? How can you tell when police action is professional? Why is professionalism important in policing today?**

   Police professionalism is the increasing formalization of police work and the accompanying rise in public acceptance of the police. Police action is generally professional when it is rational, fair, and unbiased. Professionalism is important in policing because it legitimizes the police role in society. A commitment to ethical guidelines, professional associations, and accreditation sends a clear message about the quality of a profession.

9. **What issues related to gender and ethnicity are important in American policing? How can existing problems be addressed?**

   The two critical issues are recruiting of women and minorities to policing and increasing the number of women and minorities in leadership positions. These problems can be addressed by involving underrepresented groups in departmental affirmative action and long-term planning programs, encouraging an open promotion system, and conducting periodic audits to ensure that female officers are not being underutilized.

Key—Student Study Guide Questions

True or False

____ 6-1. Legalistic police agencies are more likely to take advantage of community resources, such as drug-treatment programs, than are other types of departments. **(False, p. 207)**

____ 6-2. Scholars argue that American policing has just started the political era of policing. **(False, p. 206)**

____ 6-3. Span of control refers to the crime priorities of a police department. **(False, p. 204)**

____ 6-4. A watchman style of policing is characteristic of lower-class communities where informal police intervention into the lives of residents is used to help keep the peace. **(True, p. 207)**

____ 6-5. Today, increasing numbers of law enforcement agencies embrace the role of service provider. **(True, p. 209)**

____ 6-6. Police subculture generally refers to a group of corrupt officers working to undermine the goals of a police organization. **(False, p. 213)**

_____ 6-7. Quality-of-life offenses are generally minor law violations that demoralize citizens by creating disorder. **(True, p. 195)**

_____ 6-8. The policing reform era that lasted from the 1930s until the 1970s was characterized by pride in professional crime fighting. **(True, p. 206)**

_____ 6-9. Although many police departments have dramatically increased recruitment of ethnic minorities, females are still substantially underrepresented. **(True, pp. 229–230)**

_____ 6-10. CompStat is a process that originally was developed by the New York City Police Department. **(True, p. 196)**

Multiple Choice

6-11. Which of the following aspects of the police mission focuses on responding to quality-of-life offenses?
a. providing services
b. apprehending offenders
c. preventing crime
d. preserving the peace (p. 195)

6-12. Which historical era of policing is characterized by close ties between police and public officials?
a. community problem-solving era
b. renaissance era
c. political era (p. 206)
d. reform era

6-13. Which of the following is not a criticism of community policing strategies?
a. Efforts to promote community policing can demoralize a department.
b. Not all public officials are ready to accept community policing.
c. Not all police officers accept this new image of police work.
d. Goals of community policing are too narrowly defined. (pp. 212–213)

6-14. Which of Wilson's policing styles is becoming increasingly popular today?
a. service (p. 207)
b. paternalistic
c. watchman
d. legalistic

6-15. Of the three corporate strategies that guide American policing, which one emphasizes an increased capacity to deal with crimes that are not well controlled by traditional methods?
a. community policing
b. corporation policing
c. strategic policing (p. 210)
d. problem-solving policing

6-16. Which factor does not influence the discretionary decisions of individual officers?
a. background of the officer
b. pressures from crime victims
c. departmental policy
d. All are factors that might influence police discretion. (p. 221)

6-17. Officer Sally Kainer works in a department she describes as being concerned with community problems. She has been encouraged by the department to develop ties with other community agencies, such as the local chapter of Big Brothers/Big Sisters, and to rely on them for assistance. Which of Wilson's policing styles does Sally's department represent?
a. service style (pp. 207–208)
b. paternalistic style
c. watchman style
d. legalistic style

6-18. What two factors determine the extent that a police department will be engaged in terrorism prevention activities?
   a. media pressure; number of officers
   b. budget; assessed likelihood of attack (p. 214)
   c. community pressure; legislative policy
   d. size of the police department; public concern about terrorism

6-19. Neighborhood watch programs and drug awareness workshops are examples of
   a. police–community relations programs. (p. 208)
   b. team policing programs.
   c. police crime-fighting activities.
   d. innovative police strategies.

6-20. Enforcing the strict letter of the law characterizes the _____ style of policing.
   a. service
   b. paternalistic
   c. legalistic (p. 207)
   d. watchman

Fill-In

6-21. The _____ style of policing is marked by a concern for order maintenance. **(watchman, p. 207)**

6-22. The _____ era of policing is characterized by pride in professional crime fighting. **(reform, p. 206)**

6-23. _____ retains the traditional police goal of professional crime fighting but enlarges the enforcement target to include nontraditional types of criminals. **(Strategic policing, p. 210)**

6-24. A department using the _____ style of policing may take a hands-off approach to otherwise disruptive or problematic forms of behavior that are not violations of the criminal law. **(legalistic, p. 207)**

6-25. _____ is the number of police personnel or the number of units supervised by a particular commander. **(Span of control, p. 204)**

6-26. _____ assumes that many crimes are caused by existing social conditions and that crimes can be controlled by uncovering and effectively addressing underlying social problems. **(Problem-solving policing, p. 210)**

6-27. _____ are activities (such as administration and training) that provide support for line operations. **(Staff operations, p. 203)**

6-28. _____ is a collaborative effort between the police and the community that identifies problems of crime and disorder and involves all elements of the community in the search for solutions to these problems. **(Community policing, p. 209)**

6-29. The _____ style of policing is marked by a concern with helping rather than strict enforcement. **(service, p. 207)**

6-30. _____ is the increasing formalization of police work and the rise in public acceptance of the police that accompanies it. **(Police professionalism, p. 223)**

Key—Crossword Puzzle

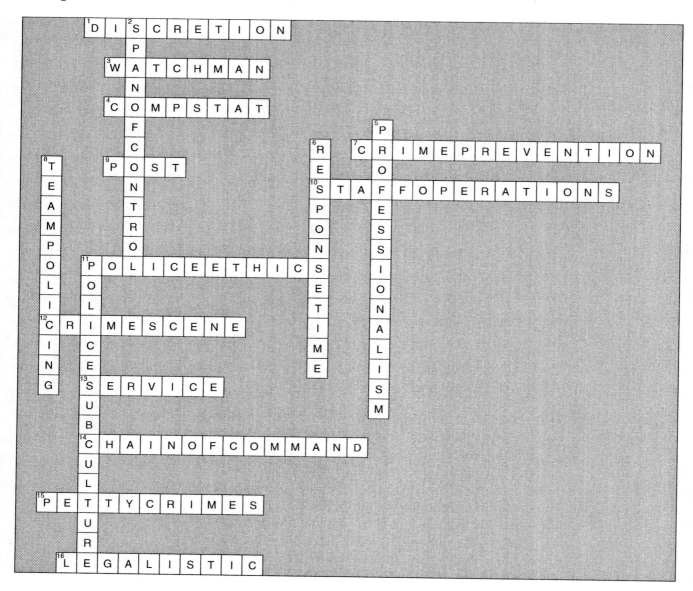

Across

1. Exercise in choice.
3. Departments in Wilson's typology concerned with order maintenance.
4. Crime-analysis process developed by the NYPD in the 1990s.
7. Term that represents a proactive approach to the problem of crime.
9. Set training standards for law enforcement agencies.
10. Support police line operations.
11. Special responsibility to adhere to moral duty and obligation that is inherent in police work.
12. Physical area in which police collect evidence.
13. Style of police department likely to use community policing.
14. Unbroken line of authority.
15. Also called quality-of-life offenses.
16. Departments in Wilson's typology concerned with strict enforcement of the law.

Down

2. Number of units supervised by a particular commander.
5. Increasing formalization of police work.
6. Time it takes to respond to a call for service.
8. Versatile police team assigned to a fixed district.
11. Also called police culture.

Key—Word Search Puzzle

```
R H S U H U P L Y I Y O T C L D W A I D E C X I D S H J O O
Z J K T X D C R X R V U P A D C J V V N S V J O L V I O J P
W J B I W W C A O N T U G R S V C E F Y Z Z Y O K W N O C R
W S P T B P T R H F Z J D R I A V L K T U F R Z O U T X L H E
C O L J M X B Q I W E H N Y D H Q P Q O I T H W C W E T H N L
M L S Q A C V L S M H S G Y G X U K H I N M Z Q H K L P N O I
M V T L Q K R C T H I W S Z Y J Y I B O D X H P U G L I C U M
U A A E F B Z I A V B N F I M N B I C M Y B R M S L I H J I N
N B F G O D N E M G T L A N O M U F T W N W O Q E L N A N F A
I I O A M Q Q M P E S G B L F N O T X C T U H B B N E C O R R
T L P L I D U G F S S C G U I N A J Q U F Z K G W E O C F C Y
Y I I X M A H Z W X C K F A N D L N P N F M Y K O P L E C O I
P T R T K Y H R H K A B E P B U V F I Y G N D O B P E L P M N
O Y R S J N Q Z G U L S X F W C E N S C K Q U L E L C P M V
L F A I K E F Q X X W B M W E H T N S S M W I N W R A D A E S
I A T C O M R E B M F N Q E W N E V T T K D X D X A M P N S T
C C I S W K W V J P O W V V Y J I A B A Q I I X H D T P M E I
I T O Y U D A A I U R N N N R M D Z Q P G H X I I O A I I G
N O N Y V T B N T C K U K Q B E P C O N P S A Y I O N L I D A
G R S L B T R E W C E C S N A X O N P E H K L T O N I C U M T
E I V E C S R F E U H S K O Z K L V I O E P X X I S D M I
W L O P S U H B U A H V A Y M N C U H V B O D Q N S N N S K T
J X J I U X U K L A Z I N L O I O U S A S M X I Y G D I I O
T J D H G L L G E P U Z C J S E N X O O N N Q P P J Y P R O N
O G H B L G H Q L X A E B S S T G D S S L M G O S Y C K S
T U V E T S A X G I B D O O W M Y W D T Z T D P O T P A H S
V C R I M E P R E V E N T I O N G L H D F D V L K T A X P O
G K P O L I C E C O M M U N I T Y R E L A T I O N S T T R Z
F X P O L I C E S U B C U L T U R E Y U P S T K G O G K Q R
```

Chain of Command

Community Policing

CompStat

Crime Prevention

Crime Scene

Criminal Investigation

Discretion

Ethics

Intelligence-Led Policing

Legalistic Style

Line Operations

Police-Community Relations

Police Subculture

Preliminary Investigation

Professionalism

Response Time

Service Style

Solvability Factor

Span of Control

Staff Operations

Team Policing

Watchman Style

CHAPTER 7

Policing: Legal Aspects

LEARNING OBJECTIVES

After reading this chapter, you should be able to:

- Explain how the Bill of Rights and democratically inspired legal restraints on the police help ensure personal freedoms in our society

- Describe the nature of due process and the specific constitutional amendments on which due process guarantees are based

- Explain the importance of the exclusionary rule and the fruit of the poisoned tree doctrine

- Define *arrest*, and describe how popular depictions of the arrest process by the police may not be consistent with legal understandings of the term

- Describe the circumstances under which police officers may search vehicles and the extent to which such searches are permissible

- Explain how the need to ensure public safety justifies certain suspicionless searches

- Recite the *Miranda* warnings, and describe in detail recent U.S. Supreme Court cases that have affected *Miranda* warning requirements

- Describe the nature of electronic evidence, and explain how first-on-the-scene law enforcement personnel should handle it

Chapter Summary

Chapter 7 examines the legal constraints on police behavior. It discusses how law enforcement agents are constrained by procedural law, highlighting the legal rules that affect the search and seizure of evidence, **arrest**, and **interrogation.**

When conducting investigations, law enforcement officers rely heavily on physical evidence to substantiate criminal charges. The legal constraints on evidence collection are found in the **Fourth Amendment**. In general, law enforcement agents get a **warrant** to search for and seize evidence when they can demonstrate **probable cause** to a neutral magistrate (a judge). If probable cause were later found to have been lacking, any items seized would be excluded as evidence. *Weeks* v. *United States* established the **exclusionary rule** for federal cases; *Mapp* v. *Ohio* made this rule applicable to the states.

There are many exceptions to the requirement that law enforcement agents obtain a warrant before collecting evidence, although most of them require that the agents establish probable cause. For example, if a police officer is in a place where he or she is legally allowed to be, then that officer can seize as evidence any contraband *in plain view*, although he or she could not move an object to put it into plain view. Another exception is a search incident to an arrest. When arresting a suspect, law enforcement agents can search the person and the area in the immediate control of that person (*Chimel* v. *California*) without a warrant. Other exceptions include emergencies, stop-and-frisk situations, concern for public safety, vehicle searches, and consent searches (see Table 7–3 for a complete list of established exceptions to the exclusionary rule).

The probable cause standard also applies to the law of **arrest**. Law enforcement agents arrest, or obtain a warrant to arrest, a suspect when the facts cause a reasonable person to believe that a specific individual has committed a crime. There are, however, instances in which police officers might question someone they suspect of committing a crime but may not make an arrest. For example, a police officer might stop to question a suspicious-looking individual and do a quick pat-down search for weapons (*Terry* v. *Ohio*). If the citizen is able to dispel the concerns of the officer, then that person is free to leave.

Chapter 7 concludes with a discussion of **interrogation**. Law enforcement agents can, and do, question citizens suspected of committing crime, but they cannot conduct an interrogation before ensuring that the suspect is protected against self-incrimination. Courts have prohibited physically coercive techniques when questioning suspects (*Brown* v. *Mississippi*). The privilege against self-incrimination does not prevent officers from using psychologically coercive techniques to elicit confessions as long as the suspect is informed of his or her rights prior to custodial interrogation (*Miranda* v. *Arizona*). This rights include:

1. You have the right to remain silent.
2. Anything you say can be used against you in a court of law.
3. You have the right to talk to an attorney and have a lawyer present when you are being questioned.
4. If you want a lawyer and cannot afford one, one will be appointed to you.
5. If you answer questions with a lawyer, you have the right to stop answering questions at any time.

The Fourth and Fifth Amendments mandate the two most significant and controversial procedural constraints on police behavior. These constraints have evolved considerably over the last 40 years because of changes in the ideological makeup of the Supreme Court. For example, evidence obtained based on an invalid warrant can still be used when the officer was acting in "**good faith**" (*United States* v. *Leon*). Law enforcement agents can question suspects without reading them their *Miranda* rights when public safety is at risk (*New York* v. *Quarles*).

Legal issues have evolved in response to technological changes in society. For example, police officers can monitor telephone conversations but must make every effort to monitor only those conversations related to the criminal activity under investigation. The book also discusses how the USA Patriot Act of 2001 made it easier for law enforcement to intercept many forms of electronic communication.

Teaching Outline

   I. Introduction (p. 240)

  II. The Abuse of Police Power (p. 240)

     • Introduce the cases of Amadou Diallo, Abner Louima, and Rodney King.

    A. A Changing Legal Climate (p. 242)

       • Explain how Supreme Court decision making has changed from the Warren Court's expansion of individual rights to the new conservative philosophy.

Bill of Rights   The popular name given to the first ten amendments to the U.S. Constitution, which are considered especially important in the processing of criminal defendants. (p. 242)

INSTRUCTIONAL CUE

Recall that one of the important issues discussed in Chapter 1 was the tension between individual-rights advocates and public-order advocates. During the Warren Court era, the Court was stacked with individual-rights advocates, but it became increasingly conservative during the Rehnquist era. Some say that the recent appointments of Justices John G. Roberts, Jr. and Samuel Alito, Jr. will lead the court to become significantly more focused on public order.

  III. Individual Rights (p. 243)

    A. Due Process Requirements (p. 244)

       • Define, and then discuss, the impact of landmark cases.

Landmark Case   A precedent-setting court decision that produces substantial changes in both the understanding of the requirements of due process and the practical day-to-day operations of the justice system. (p. 244)

       • The focus of this chapter is due process requirements for evidence and investigation, arrest, and interrogation.

  IV. Search and Seizure (p. 244)

Illegally Seized Evidence   Evidence seized without regard to the principles of due process as described by the Bill of Rights. Most illegally seized evidence is the result of police searches conducted without a proper warrant or of improperly conducted interrogations. (p. 244)

    A. The Exclusionary Rule (p. 244)

       • *Weeks* v. *U.S.*: Formed the basis for the exclusionary rule.

Exclusionary Rule   The understanding, based on Supreme Court precedent, that incriminating information must be seized according to constitutional specifications of due process or it will not be allowed as evidence in criminal trials. (p. 245)

INSTRUCTIONAL CUE

Help students visualize the process of obtaining a warrant by walking them through the steps. For example, a narcotics detective receives information from a reliable informant that a student is selling cocaine from his residence hall. The detective does three undercover buys over a two-week period, gets a warrant by demonstrating these facts to a magistrate, and executes the warrant. Link this situation to the checks on police behavior. First, require the police to get the warrant before searching and seizing evidence. Second, if the arrested suspect's case gets into the court system, his attorney would probably make a motion to suppress the evidence, arguing that the evidence was obtained in an unreasonable search and seizure. Be sure to explain such a motion.

---

1. Problems with Precedent
   - Explain the important influence that the Supreme Court can have on criminal justice policy.

Writ of *Certiorari*   A writ issued from an appellate court for the purpose of obtaining from a lower court the record of its proceedings in a particular case. In some states, this writ is the mechanism for discretionary review. A request for review is made by petitioning for a writ of *certiorari*, and the granting of review is indicated by the issuance of the writ. (p. 245)

2. The Fruit of the Poisoned Tree Doctrine
   - Established by *Silverthorne Lumber Co. v. U.S.*

Fruit of the Poisoned Tree Doctrine   A legal principle that excludes from introduction at trial any evidence later developed as a result of an illegal search or seizure. (p. 246)

B. The Warren Court (1953–1969) (p. 246)
   1. Application of the Exclusionary Rule to the States
      - *Mapp* v. *Ohio*: The Fourth Amendment's exclusionary rule is applicable to the states through the due process clause of the Fourteenth Amendment.
   2. Searches Incident to Arrest
      - *Chimel* v. *California*: A search, incident to a lawful arrest, is limited to the area in the immediate control or grabbing area of the suspect.
      - *Minnesota* v. *Olson:* It extends the protection against warrantless searches to overnight guests.
      - *Minnesota* v. *Carter:* A defendant has to establish that he or she has a reasonable expectation of privacy in the place searched.
C. The Burger Court (1969–1986) and Rehnquist Court (1986–2005) (p. 248)
   1. Good-Faith Exceptions to the Exclusionary Rule
      - *United States* v. *Leon* found that an original affidavit had not been sufficient to establish probable cause.

Good-Faith Exception   An exception to the exclusionary rule. Law enforcement officers who conduct a search, or seize evidence, on the basis of good faith (that is, where they believe they are operating according to the dictates of the law) and who later discover that a mistake was made (perhaps in the format of the application for a search warrant) may still use the seized evidence in court. (p. 249)

Probable Cause   A set of facts and circumstances that would induce a reasonably intelligent and prudent person to believe that a particular other person has committed a specific crime. Also, reasonable grounds to make or believe an accusation. Probable cause refers to the necessary level of belief that would allow for police seizures (arrests) of individuals and full searches of dwellings, vehicles, and possessions. (p. 249)

   - *Massachusetts* v. *Sheppard, Illinois* v. *Krull, Maryland* v. *Garrison,* and *Illinois* v. *Rodriguez* all represent additional efforts by the Court to diminish the scope of the exclusionary rule.

INSTRUCTIONAL CUE LINKED TO THE STUDENT STUDY GUIDE

Use Student Activity 1 to help students think about the balance between crime control and individual rights.

---

2. The Plain-View Doctrine

- *Harris* v. *U.S.* found that objects in plain view of an officer who is rightfully in that position may be taken into evidence.

Plain View   A legal term describing the ready visibility of objects that might be seized as evidence during a search by police in the absence of a search warrant specifying the seizure of those objects. To lawfully seize evidence in plain view, officers must have a legal right to be in the viewing area and must have cause to believe that the evidence is somehow associated with criminal activity. (p. 250)

- *U.S.* v. *Irizarry* and *Arizona* v. *Hicks* both limit the scope of the plain-view search.
- *Horton* v. *California* states inadvertence is not a necessary condition to justify a plain-view search.

3. Emergency Searches of Property

Emergency Search   A search conducted by the police without a warrant that is justified on the basis of some immediate and overriding need, such as public safety, the likely escape of a dangerous suspect, or the removal or destruction of evidence. (p. 253)

- *Warden* v. *Hayden* first recognized the need for emergency searches.
- Other emergency search cases include *Mincey* v. *Arizona*, *Maryland* v. *Buie*, *Wilson* v. *Arkansas* (the U.S. Supreme Court ruled that police officers must knock and announce their identity before entering a dwelling, even when they have a search warrant), *Richards* v. *Wisconsin* (the U.S. Supreme Court ruled that police can make "no-knock" entries if announcing their presence might inhibit the investigation of the crime), and *Illinois* v. *McArthur* (the U.S. Supreme Court ruled that police officers with probable cause to believe that a home contains contraband or evidence of criminal activity may reasonably prevent a suspect found outside the home from reentering it while they apply for a search warrant).

V. Arrest (p. 253)

Arrest   The act of taking an adult or juvenile into physical custody by authority of law for the purpose of charging the person with a criminal offense, a delinquent act, or a status offense, terminating with the recording of a specific offense. Technically, an arrest occurs whenever a law enforcement officer curtails a person's freedom to leave. (p. 253)

INSTRUCTIONAL CUE

It will be difficult for students to memorize the important holdings of the cases presented in Chapter 7. There are two strategies you can use to help students learn these cases. First, limit the number of cases that they are expected to know. Have them focus on those cases that you think are most important, and provide them the list of cases in advance of reading the chapter. Second, if you would like them to know all of the cases, then construct a study sheet with them. One side of the study sheet might be for Fourth Amendment cases. You can provide subcategories (such as search incident to arrest cases and emergency circumstance cases) to organize the cases presented in this chapter. Do the same for the Fifth Amendment cases. Construct three- or four-word descriptions of each ruling. For example, *Mapp* v. *Ohio* could be the "exclusionary rule for state cases." *Warden* v. *Hayden* could be the "emergency search of property" case.

A. Searches Incident to Arrest (p. 256)

Search Incident to an Arrest   A warrantless search of an arrested individual conducted to ensure the safety of the arresting officer. Because individuals placed under arrest may be in possession of weapons, courts have recognized the need for arresting officers to protect themselves by conducting an immediate search of arrestees without obtaining a warrant. (p. 256)

- *U.S.* v. *Robinson* established that a search incident to a lawful arrest does not violate Fourth Amendment protections.
- *Terry* v. *Ohio* established the stop-and-frisk exception. A citizen can be briefly detained by law enforcement agents without probable cause when they have reasonable suspicion to believe the person has committed or is about to commit a crime.

Reasonable Suspicion   The level of suspicion that would justify an officer in making further inquiry or in conducting further investigation. Reasonable suspicion may permit stopping a person for questioning or for a simple pat-down search. Also, a belief, based on a consideration of the facts at hand and on reasonable inferences drawn from those facts, that would induce an ordinarily prudent and cautious person under the same circumstances to conclude that criminal activity is taking place or that criminal activity has recently occurred. Reasonable suspicion is a *general* and reasonable belief that a crime is in progress or has occurred, whereas probable cause is a reasonable belief that a *particular* person has committed a *specific* crime. (p. 256)

- *U.S.* v. *Sokolow*: The court held that the validity of a *Terry* stop will be based on the "totality of the circumstances."
- *Minnesota* v. *Dickerson*: Established that the search subsequent to a *Terry* stop must be to identify a weapon.
- *Brown* v. *Texas*: The Supreme Court case that held that officers may not stop and question an unwilling citizen whom they don't suspect of breaking the law.
- *Smith* v. *Ohio*: The court held that a citizen has the right to protect his or her belongings from police inspection.
- *California* v. *Hodari D.*: The court held that if a suspect runs from the police and discards incriminating evidence, the suspect can be arrested based upon that evidence.

B. Emergency Searches of Persons (p. 258)

- *Arkansas* v. *Sanders*: The Court recognized the need for emergency searches of persons.
- *U.S.* v. *Borchardt*: This is a decision from the Fifth Circuit Court of Appeals that held that a defendant could be prosecuted for the drugs found during medical treatment. It did not matter that he objected to the treatment.

C. Vehicle Searches (p. 259)

- *Carroll* v. *U.S.*: The Court held that a warrantless search of a vehicle is valid based on a reasonable belief that contraband is present.
- *Preston* v. *U.S.*: The limit of a warrantless search of a vehicle is defined. Officers should get a warrant when time and circumstances allow it.
- *South Dakota* v. *Opperman*: The Court held that a warrantless inventory search is not unconstitutional, and in *Colorado* v. *Bertine*, the Court held that officers may open closed containers found during an inventory search.
- *Florida* v. *Wells*: The court held that for evidence found during an inventory search to be used against the suspect, "standardized criteria" must be in place.
- *Ornelas* v. *U.S.*: It found that reasonable suspicion can expand into probable cause if the situations warrents.

Fleeting-Targets Exception   An exception to the exclusionary rule that permits law enforcement officers to search a motor vehicle based upon probable cause but without a warrant. The fleeting-targets exception is predicated upon the fact that vehicles can quickly leave the jurisdiction of a law enforcement agency. (p. 261)

- *Florida* v. *Jimeno*: Once a suspect consents to a search, officers can assume that consent applies to containers within the vehicle.

- *United States* v. *Ross*: The Court held that once probable cause exists, officers can search the entire vehicle.
   1. Roadblocks and Motor Vehicle Checkpoints
      - *Michigan Department of State Police* v. *Sitz*: The case involved the legality of highway sobriety checkpoints. The Court ruled that such stops are reasonable insofar as they are essential to the welfare of the community as a whole.
   2. Watercraft and Motor Homes
      - *U.S.* v. *Villamonte-Marquez*: Applied the *Carroll* decision to watercrafts.
      - *California* v. *Carney*: Applied the *Carroll* decision to motor homes.
   D. Suspicionless Searches (p. 263)
      - *National Treasury Employees Union* v. *Von Raab* and *Skinner* v. *Railway Labor Executives' Association*: The key to these cases is the compelling interest concept.

Compelling Interest   A legal concept that provides a basis for suspicionless searches when public safety is at issue. (Urinalysis tests of train engineers are an example.) It is the concept upon which the Supreme Court cases of *Skinner* v. *Railway Labor Executives' Association* (1989) and *National Treasury Employees Union* v. *Von Raab* (1989) turned. In those cases, the Court held that public safety may sometimes provide a sufficiently compelling interest to justify limiting an individual's right to privacy. (p. 263)

Suspicionless Search   A search conducted by law enforcement personnel without a warrant and without suspicion. Suspicionless searches are permissible only if based on an overriding concern for public safety. (p. 263)

INSTRUCTIONAL CUE LINKED TO THE STUDENT STUDY GUIDE

Use Student Activity 2 to help students apply the legal aspects of the Fourth Amendment. For scenario 1, the *Terry* stop, plain-view, and emergency cases apply. For scenario 2, the plain-view cases are relevant. You could also discuss the automobile consent cases as being applicable (*Florida* v. *Jimeno*). For scenario 3, again the plain-view cases are relevant. For scenario 4, the nontestimonial cases are relevant. Finally, the search incident to arrest, plain-view, and emergency search of property cases are relevant to scenario 5.

- *Florida* v. *Bostick*: Permits warrantless "sweeps" of intercity buses.
   E. High-Technology Searches (p. 266)
VI. The Intelligence Function (p. 267)
   A. Informants (p. 267)
      - *Aguilar* v. *Texas*: Clarifies the use of informants and established the two-pronged test to decide if informant information establishes probable cause.
      - Exceptions to the two-pronged test are identified in the *Harris* v. *U.S.* and *Spinelli* v. *U.S.* decisions.
      - *Illinois* v. *Gates*: The Court established the totality of the circumstances test for establishing probable cause for a warrant based on information from an informant.
      - *Alabama* v. *White*: The Court ruled that an anonymous tip could form the basis for a stop when the informant accurately predicts the behavior of the suspect.
      - *U.S. Department of Justice* v. *Landano*: The U.S. Supreme Court required that an informant's identity be revealed through a federal Freedom of Information Act request.

B. Police Interrogation (p. 268)

Interrogation The information-gathering activities of police officers that involve the direct questioning of suspects. (p. 269)

    1. Physical Abuse
- Law enforcement agents cannot use physically coercive interrogation techniques to elicit confessions. (*Brown* v. *Mississippi*)

    2. Inherent Coercion
- *Ashcraft* v. *Tennessee*

Inherent Coercion The tactics used by police interviewers that fall short of physical abuse but that nonetheless pressure suspects to divulge information. (p. 269)

    3. Psychological Manipulation

Psychological Manipulation Manipulative actions by police interviewers, designed to pressure suspects to divulge information, that are based on subtle forms of intimidation and control. (p. 369)

- *Leyra* v. *Denno*: Police cannot use professionals skilled in psychological manipulation.
- *Arizona* v. *Fulminante*: The Court ruled that a confession was coerced in this specific case but also found that a coerced confession can be a harmless trial error if other evidence still proves guilt.

C. The Right to a Lawyer at Interrogation (p. 270)
- *Escobedo* v. *Illinois*: The case recognized the right to have legal counsel present during police interrogation.

D. Suspects' Rights: The *Miranda* decision (p. 271)
- *Miranda* v. *Arizona*: A person in custody must be advised of various warnings and his or her legal rights prior to being subjected to custodial interrogation.

Miranda Warnings The advisement of rights due criminal suspects by the police before questioning begins. *Miranda* warnings were first set forth by the Supreme Court in the 1966 case of *Miranda* v. *Arizona*. (p. 271)

    1. Waiver of *Miranda* Rights by Suspects
- *Miranda* rights can be waived through a voluntary "knowing and intelligent" waiver (see *Moran* v. *Burbine* and *Colorado* v. *Spring*).

INSTRUCTIONAL CUE LINKED TO THE STUDENT STUDY GUIDE

Use Student Activity 3 to help students see the current application of *Miranda*. Ask the class whether they think it is still necessary to require the *Miranda* warnings.

---

    2. Inevitable-Discovery Exception to *Miranda*
- *Nix* v. *Williams*

    3. Public-Safety Exception to *Miranda*
- *New York* v. *Quarles*
- See also *Kuhlmann* v. *Wilson* and *Illinois* v. *Perkins*

    4. *Miranda* and the Meaning of Interrogation

Miranda Trigger The dual principles of custody and interrogation, both of which are necessary before an advisement of rights is required. (p. 275)

E. Gathering Special Kinds of Nontestimonial Evidence (p. 275)

1. The Right to Privacy
   - *Hayes* v. *Florida* and *Winston* v. *Lee* placed limits on seizure of personal forms of nontestimonial evidence.
   - *Schmerber* v. *California* held that warrants must be obtained for bodily intrusions unless fast action is necessary to prevent the destruction of evidence.
2. Body Cavity Searches
   - *U.S.* v. *Montoya de Hernandez*

F. Electronic Eavesdropping (p. 277)
   - *Olmstead* v. *U.S.*: Holds that telephone lines are not an extension of defendants' homes.
   - *Lee* v. *U.S.* and *Lopez* v. *U.S.*: States that recording devices carried on the body of an undercover agent or informant produce admissible evidence.
   - *Katz* v. *U.S.*: The Court held that seizing conversations when a person makes an effort to keep conversations private, even in a public place, requires a warrant.
   - *Lee* v. *Florida*: The Court applied the Federal Communications Act to telephone conversations.
   - *U.S.* v. *White*: The Court held that law enforcement may intercept electronic information when one of the parties involved in the communication gives his or her consent.
   - *U.S.* v. *Karo*

1. Minimization Requirements for Electronic Surveillance
   - Established in *U.S.* v. *Scott*.
2. The Electronic Communications Privacy Act of 1986
   - ECPA requires that investigating officers obtain wiretap-type court orders to eavesdrop on ongoing communications.

Electronic Communications Privacy Act (ECPA)   A law passed by Congress in 1986 establishing the due process requirements that law enforcement officers must meet in order to legally intercept wire communications. (p. 278)

   - Messages stored for fewer than 180 days are protected like U.S. mail.
   - Messages stored in excess of 180 days can be accessed with a court order.

3. The Telecommunications Act of 1996
4. The USA PATRIOT Act of 2001
   - Makes it easier for law enforcement to intercept many forms of electronic communication
   - Added felony violations of the Computer Fraud and Abuse Act to Section 2516(1) of Title 18 of the U.S. Code
   - Modified several aspects of the ECPA

Sneak and Peek Search   A search that occurs in the suspect's absence and without his or her prior knowledge. (pp. 280, 282)

5. Gathering Electronic Evidence

Electronic Evidence   Information and data of investigative value that are stored in or transmitted by an electronic device. *Source*: Adapted from: Technical Working Group for Electronic Crime Scene Investigation, *Electronic Crime Scene Investigation: A Guide for First Responders* (Washington, D.C.: National Institute of Justice, 2001), p. 2. (p. 282)

Latent Evidence   Evidence of relevance to a criminal investigation that is not readily seen by the unaided eye. (p. 282)

Digital Criminal Forensics   The lawful seizure, acquisition, analysis, reporting, and safeguarding of data from digital devices that may contain information of evidentiary value to the trier of fact in criminal events. *Source:* Adapted from Larry R. Leibrock, "Overview and Impact on 21st Century Legal Practice: Digital Forensics and Electronic Discovery," no date. Web posted at http://www.courtroom 21.net/FDIC.pps (accessed July 5, 2005). (p. 282)

INSTRUCTIONAL CUE LINKED TO THE STUDENT STUDY GUIDE

Use Student Activity 4 to help students learn more about the important cases discussed in Chapter 7.

Learner Activities

Activity 1

Recall from the discussion in Chapter 1 that justice requires a fair balance between individual and community interests. The Supreme Court's interpretation of the Fourth Amendment provides an effective illustration of the difficulties in finding a fair balance. A public-order advocate might argue that the exclusionary rule has handcuffed the abilities of the police to effectively protect the community. An individual-rights advocate, on the other hand, might argue that such changes have resulted in positive reform of the police and such rights need to be expanded. What is your opinion? If the president appointed you to the Supreme Court, would you be willing to overturn *Mapp* v. *Ohio* and eliminate the exclusionary rule? Why or why not?

Activity 2

In the following search-and-seizure situations, note whether you think the evidence seized would be excluded in a court of law. In addition, try to note cases that apply to each circumstance.

1. Police Officer A observed an automobile going the wrong way on a one-way street. When the officer tried to stop the automobile, the driver fled, resulting in a high-speed chase. The chase ended when the driver's car crashed into a telephone pole. Concerned that the car might ignite from a gas leak, the officer pulled the unconscious woman from the car. After he had pulled the woman a safe distance from the car, he went back into the car to locate her purse for identification, at which time he found a knife covered in blood on the front seat. It was later discovered that the knife was used in a murder of another police officer. Should the knife be excluded? What court case(s) justify your decision?

2. While off duty and at a party, Police Officer A was asked by the home owner to get some ice from his basement. Since the ice machine was not immediately apparent, the officer opened two doors. Behind door number two were six marijuana plants. The officer arrested the home owner. Would you exclude the marijuana plants? What court case(s) justify your decision?

3. Defendant A was suspected of selling stolen property from his dorm room. An undercover campus police officer knocked on Defendant A's door, and when Defendant A answered, the officer asked for an affordable radar detector. In response, Defendant A said that he just got two new ones last night. While in the room, the officer noticed various other items she suspected as being stolen. She bought one of the radar detectors and then used it to convince a judge to issue a search warrant of the room. Among the items confiscated in the search with the warrant were four radar detectors, three television sets, two air-conditioning units, and 1,500 compact discs. Should this evidence be excluded? What court case(s) justify your decision?

4. Police Officer A and Police Officer B were observing a street corner for drug activity and noticed Defendant A selling drugs to Defendant B. These officers quickly arrived at the scene but were only able to arrest Defendant B. Before they could handcuff him, Defendant B swallowed what appeared to them to be one balloon of heroin. Police Officer B forced his finger down Defendant B's throat, causing him to vomit. Among the expelled material was one balloon of heroin. Would this evidence be excluded? What court case(s) justify your decision?

5. When executing a valid arrest warrant for an assault charge in Defendant A's home, Police Officer A seized a handgun in the search incident to the arrest. Alarmed that her life was in danger, Police Officer A made Defendant A lie with his face down on the floor and quickly perused three adjoining rooms. While walking through the kitchen, she noticed a pile of semiautomatic weapons on the table and seized them as evidence. Should these weapons be excluded? What case(s) justify your decision?

_____

_____

_____

_____

_____

_____

Activity 3

One of the important policy issues being debated in courts and among politicians is whether the *Miranda* decision should be overturned. Visit the Cybrary at http://www.cybrary.info. Use the search function to find websites about the application of the *Miranda* rule. After you peruse several sites, answer the following questions in the space provided below. Should police officers be required to read a *Miranda*-type warning prior to custodial interrogation, or should *Miranda* be overturned? Explain your answer.

_____

_____

_____

_____

_____

Activity 4

Chapter 7 provides an analysis of many landmark cases. The full texts of several of these Supreme Court decisions are posted as Library Extras. For example, included is the full text of the *Weeks* v. *U.S.*, *Silverthorne Lumber Company* v. *U.S.*, *Mapp* v. *Ohio*, *Harris* v. *U.S.*, *Terry* v. *Ohio*, *Brown* v. *Mississippi*, and *Miranda* v. *Arizona* decisions. Read the full text of one of these cases. Then, in the space provided below, provide a complete summary of the case. Be sure to discuss the facts of the case and the Court's decision, and then provide the reason(s) for the Court's decision in the case.

_____

_____

_____

_____

_____

_____

Internet Activity

Use the Cybrary (http://www.cybrary.info) to find information about legal issues, ethics, and policing. Use the search function available to locate information about the exclusionary rule. What kinds of information did you find?

_____

_____

_____

_____

_____

Distance Learning Activity

Write a case scenario that raises a Fourth Amendment concern. Submit the case or cases relevant to resolving this concern. Here is an example of what this exercise asks you to do: Defendant Sally Smith was watching television when a police officer knocked at her door. Sally opened the door and said, "What do you want?" The officer responded, "I just wanted to talk to you about a robbery that occurred over on 8th and Vine." Sally responded, "Sure, come on into my home; I don't have anything to hide." While sitting at the kitchen table, the officer noticed a marijuana plant on a window ledge. The officer then placed her in handcuffs, arresting her for possession of a controlled substance. The officer then searched Sally and found a small bag of cocaine in her right front pocket. The relevant cases are tied to consent issues, plain view, and search incident to arrest.

If your instructor asks you to do so, submit your scenario to the other students in your class and see whether they can identify the key procedural issues and cases.

_____

_____

_____

_____

_____

_____

Learning Activities Utilizing the World Wide Web

There are student-based activities in the Student Study Guide (Internet Activity, Distance Learning Activity, CJ Today on the World Wide Web) that are similar in focus to those that follow. However, the following are presented as instructor-led activities, to be used in a classroom with online access.

Prior to class, go to the Cybrary (http://www.cybrary.info) to find information about legal issues and policing. Use the search function available to locate information about the exclusionary rule. Display the information you found.

Other websites for organizations and agencies related to the material in Chapter 7 include:

Police Guide	http://www.policeguide.com
Law Enforcement Links	http://www.leolinks.com
American Bar Association	http://www.abanet.org
American Civil Liberties Union (ACLU)	http://www.aclu.org
American Prosecutors Research Institute	http://www.ndaa.org
U.S. Evidence Law	http://www.law.cornell.edu/topics/evidence.html
Justice Denied	http://www.justicedenied.org
Stanford Law and Policy Review	http://www.stanford.edu/group/SLPR
Kuglick's Forensic Resource and Criminal Law	http://www.kruglaw.com

Suggested Answers to Chapter Discussion Questions

1. **How do the Bill of Rights and democratically inspired legal restraints on the police help ensure personal freedoms in our society?**

   The Bill of Rights and legal restraints show that the police are not above the law. Police officers have to collect evidence to arrest suspects, but they must do so within the boundaries of the Fourth Amendment. Suspects may have to be released if police officers do not follow the law. Officers cannot arrest suspects without cause, thus limiting the likelihood that police use arrest to coerce innocent citizens. The Fifth Amendment constrains police interrogation procedures. Police are not able to use physical force, and the use of other types of coercion is also limited. These rights are central to democracy, and without them personal freedoms would suffer greatly.

2. **What is due process? On what constitutional amendments are due process guarantees based? Can we ensure due process in our legal system without substantially increasing the risk of criminal activity?**

   Due process generally focuses on the processes in place to protect individual rights. These rights are guaranteed by the Fifth, Sixth, and Fourteenth Amendments of the U.S. Constitution. It is difficult to fairly balance due process with the risk of criminal activity. If due process rights are increased, and additional procedural constraints are put in place limiting police investigation procedures, then it is likely that criminal activity will increase. If due process rights are limited, then criminal activity might decrease. The attempt to balance these positions provides an explanation for the constant state of flux of due process guarantees.

3. **What is the exclusionary rule? What is the fruit of the poisoned tree doctrine? What is their importance in American criminal justice?**

The exclusionary rule is the understanding, based on Supreme Court precedent, that incriminating information must be seized according to constitutional specifications of due process or it will not be allowed as evidence in a criminal trial. The fruit of the poisoned tree doctrine is a legal principle that excludes from introduction at trial later any evidence developed as a result of an illegal search or seizure. The exclusionary rule and the fruit of the poisoned tree doctrine are important because they essentially punish the police for violating due process guarantees. If police officers violate the Fourth Amendment in the processing of evidence, the exclusionary rule prevents the use of this evidence to obtain a conviction. Any evidence collected following an illegal search is also lost because of the fruit of the poisoned tree doctrine.

4. **What is arrest, and when does it occur? How do legal understandings of the term differ from popular depictions of the arrest process?**

An arrest is the act of taking an adult or juvenile into physical custody by authority of law for the purpose of charging the person with a criminal offense, a delinquent act, or a status offense, terminating with the recording of a specific offense. Technically, an arrest occurs whenever a law enforcement officer curtails a person's freedom to leave. Popular depictions of arrest differ significantly from legal understandings. When an arrest occurs in popular culture (often arrest is not necessary because deadly force was used by the police officer), it is usually after a high-speed chase or pursuit, the suspect resists the arrest, and then the officer reads the suspect his or her *Miranda* rights. In practice, such situations rarely occur, and a person is usually arrested after agreeing to be questioned by police officers.

5. **Under what circumstances may police officers search vehicles? What limits, if any, are there on such searches? What determines such limits?**

Vehicle searches are problematic for police officers. The U.S. Supreme Court, however, has given officers some freedom because of the mobility of automobiles. In general, an investigatory stop is permissible if supported by reasonable suspicion, and a warrantless search of the vehicle is valid if based on probable cause. Warrantless searches may extend to any area of the vehicle, including the glove compartment, the trunk, and packages in the vehicle and trunk. Officers can also request that the motorist and passengers get out of the vehicle. There are some limits on the extent of such searches, determined by case precedent. Officers must have a reason to stop a vehicle. If conducting an inventory search, officers must follow standardized criteria authorizing the search. Finally, full search of a vehicle incident to the issuance of a citation is not permitted.

6. **What are suspicionless searches? How does the need to ensure public safety justify certain suspicionless searches?**

A suspicionless search is a search conducted by law enforcement personnel without a warrant and without suspicion. Suspicionless searches are only permissible if based on an overriding concern for public safety. The court essentially ruled that the need to ensure public safety provided a compelling interest that negated the rights of individual privacy. The court has used several drug cases to define and expand this right, arguing that the public-safety interests furthered by mandatory drug testing of employees outweighed privacy interests.

7. **List each of the *Miranda* warnings. Which recent U.S. Supreme Court cases have affected *Miranda* warning requirements?**

   - You have the right to remain silent.
   - Anything you say can and will be used against you in a court of law.
   - You have the right to talk to a lawyer and to have a lawyer present while you are being questioned.

- If you want a lawyer before or during questioning but cannot afford to hire a lawyer, one will be appointed to represent you at no cost before any questioning.

Moran v. *Burbine* and *Colorado* v. *Spring* describe the waiver of *Miranda* rights by suspects. *Nix* v. *Williams* created the inevitable-discovery exception to the *Miranda* requirements. *New York* v. *Quarles* established the public-safety exception to the *Miranda* rule.

8. **What is electronic evidence?**

Information and data of investigative value that are stored in or transmitted by an electronic device are called electronic evidence.

How should first-on-the-scene law enforcement personnel handle such evidence?

In addition to following general forensic and procedural principles, first responders should use special precautions when confronted with potential sources of electronic evidence. Experts emphasize five key points:

- Don't turn any electronic device on or off. Leave such devices as found, and let specially trained technicians handle them.
- Immediately secure, document, and/or photograph perishable data such as found on pagers, cell phones, and similar devices.
- Identify and label telephone lines attached to modems and caller ID boxes.
- Preserve latent fingerprints on keyboards and other components for collection after completing the recovery of electronic evidence, to prevent data loss from the effects of chemicals used to process latent prints.
- Secure and preserve items that may assist in the examination of electronic evidence. Calendars or software manuals, for example, may contain handwritten notes showing passwords or other crucial information.

Key—Student Study Guide Questions

True or False

____ 7-1. Most jurisdictions allow arrest for a felony without a warrant as long as probable cause is established. **(False, p. 254)**

____ 7-2. Officers may not stop and question an unwilling citizen when they have no reason to suspect him or her of a crime. **(True, p. 257)**

____ 7-3. *Arizona* v. *Hicks* established the exclusionary rule for the states. **(False, p. 252)**

____ 7-4. Public safety may provide a sufficiently compelling interest such that an individual's right to privacy can be limited under certain circumstances. **(True, p. 264)**

____ 7-5. If the police initiate an arrest in a person's home, because of the law regarding search incident to arrest, they could search the entire residence, including opening drawers, closets, and trunks. **(False, p. 257)**

____ 7-6. A writ of *certiorari* is the warrant federal agents need to make an arrest. **(False, p. 245)**

____ 7-7. Probable cause must be satisfactorily demonstrated by police officers in a written affidavit to a magistrate before a search warrant can be issued. **(True, p. 249)**

____ 7-8. Certain emergencies permit police to search premises without a warrant. **(True, p. 253)**

_____ 7-9. Nontestimonial evidence, such as blood, cannot be seized as evidence. **(False, p. 275)**

_____ 7-10. The Electronic Communications Privacy Act prohibits law enforcement officers from seizing electronic communications under any circumstances. **(False, p. 278)**

Multiple Choice

7-11. Which of these statements about the search and seizure of evidence is false?

    a. A warrantless search of an automobile is valid if it is based on probable cause that contraband is present.

    b. Evidence viewed by an officer in plain view, when legally in a place where the officer is allowed to be, will not be excluded.

    c. Evidence illegally seized by the police cannot be used in a trial under most circumstances.

    d. In all circumstances, police officers must get a warrant in order to seize evidence. (p. 244)

7-12. Which constitutional amendment establishes legal boundaries for the search and seizure of evidence?

    a. Fourth (p. 243)

    b. Fifth

    c. First

    d. Second

7-13. Which constitutional amendment establishes legal boundaries for the interrogation of suspects?

    a. Fourth

    b. Fifth (p. 243)

    c. First

    d. Second

7-14. Which of the following legal principles excludes from introduction at trial any evidence obtained as a result of an illegal search or seizure?

    a. plain-view doctrine

    b. public-safety exception

    c. good-faith exception

    d. fruit of the poisoned tree doctrine (p. 246)

7-15. Which U.S. Supreme Court case established the public-safety exception to the _Miranda_ rule?

    a. _Brown_ v. _Mississippi_

    b. _New York_ v. _Quarles_ (p. 274)

    c. _Mapp_ v. _Ohio_

    d. _Weeks_ v. _United States_

7-16. Which of the following U.S. Supreme Court cases does not involve police interrogation of suspects?

    a. _Brown_ v. _Mississippi_

    b. _Chimel_ v. _California_ (p. 247)

    c. _Miranda_ v. _Arizona_

    d. _Escobedo_ v. _Illinois_

7-17. Which U.S. Supreme Court case made the exclusionary rule applicable to the states?

    a. _Brown_ v. _Mississippi_

    b. _New York_ v. _Quarles_

    c. _Mapp_ v. _Ohio_ (p. 246)

    d. _Weeks_ v. _United States_

7-18. Which of the following U.S. Supreme Court cases does not involve the search of a vehicle?
   a. *United States* v. *Ross*
   b. *United States* v. *Leon* (p. 249)
   c. *Carroll* v. *United States*
   d. *South Dakota* v. *Opperman*

7-19. In which of the following situations would a law enforcement agent not be required to read a suspect the *Miranda* warnings?
   a. A suspect makes a spontaneous statement, such as stating "I just killed my wife," to officers when arriving at the scene. (p. 275)
   b. A police officer arrests a person for robbery and assault. When traveling to the police station for booking purposes, she asks the suspect, "What do you know about this robbery?"
   c. An off-duty police officer apprehends a purse snatcher. As the officer waits for a police car to transport the suspect, he asks, "How many purses have you stolen in the last month?"
   d. Jason Melo, convicted of rape and burglary, was serving time in a maximum-security prison. He was also a suspect in a murder investigation. In the visiting room of the prison, the detective asked Jason, "Did you murder your brother-in-law?"

7-20. In which of the following situations would a law enforcement officer be able to conduct a search if he or she did not have probable cause to do so?
   a. vehicle search
   b. search incident to an arrest
   c. suspicionless search (pp. 263–264)
   d. none of the above

Fill-In

7-21. The case that established the good-faith exception to the exclusionary rule is _____. **(*U.S.* v. *Leon*, p. 249)**

7-22. The case that articulated the fruit of the poisoned tree doctrine is _____. **(*Silverthorne Lumber Co.* v. *U.S.*, pp. 245–246)**

7-23. The case that established a two-pronged test to the effect that informant information could establish probable cause if both criteria were met is _____. **(*Aguilar* v. *Texas*, p. 268)**

7-24. The case that established the famous requirement of police to advise a suspect of his or her rights is _____. **(*Miranda* v. *Arizona*, p. 271)**

7-25. The case that first recognized the need for emergency searches is _____. **(*Warden* v. *Hayden*, p. 253)**

7-26. The case that held a search incident to an arrest invalid when it goes beyond the person arrested and the area subject to that person's "immediate control" is _____. **(*Chimel* v. *California*, p. 247)**

7-27. The case that established the stop-and-frisk exception to the exclusionary rule is _____. **(*Terry* v. *Ohio*, p. 256)**

7-28. The case that placed limits on an officer's ability to seize evidence discovered during a pat-down search is _____. **(*Minnesota* v. *Dickerson*, p. 257)**

7-29. The case that made the exclusionary rule applicable to the states is _____. **(*Mapp* v. *Ohio*, p. 246)**

7-30. The case that established the exclusionary rule in federal cases is _____. **(*Weeks* v. *U.S.*, pp. 244–245)**

Key—Crossword Puzzle

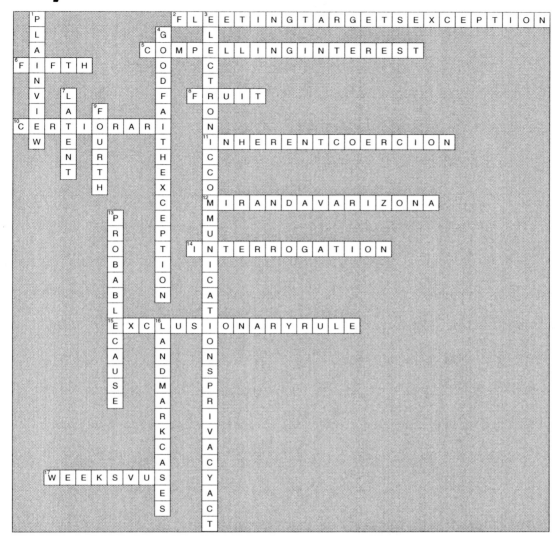

Across

2. Exception predicated on the fact that vehicles can quickly leave the jurisdiction.

5. Concept central to *National Treasury Employees Union* v. *Von Raab*.

6. Amendment providing protection against self-incrimination.

8. _____ of the poisoned tree doctrine.

10. Writ of _____.

11. Tactic used by police interviewers that falls short of physical abuse but that nonetheless pressures suspects to divulge information.

12. Case establishing the famous requirement of a police rights advisement of suspects.

14. Police activity regulated by *Brown* v. *Mississippi*.

15. Rule that means evidence illegally seized by the police cannot be used in a trial.

17. First landmark case on search and seizure.

Down

1. *Arizona* v. *Hicks* focuses on this exclusionary rule exception.

3. ECPA.

4. Exception established in *U.S.* v. *Leon*.

7. Evidence of relevance to a criminal investigation that is not readily seen by the unaided eye.

9. Amendment concerned with unreasonable searches and seizures.

13. Required standard for a search warrant.

16. Cases that produce substantial changes in the understanding of the requirements of due process.

Key—Word Search Puzzle

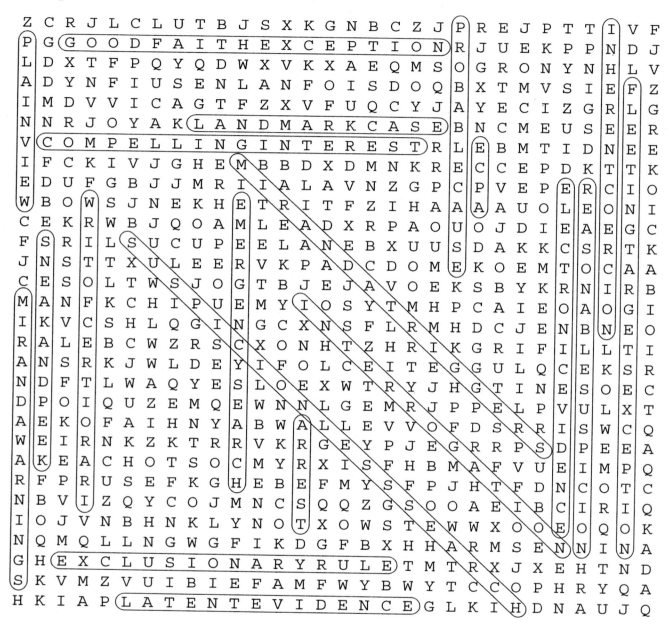

Arrest
Compelling Interest
ECPA
Electronic Evidence
Emergency Search
Exclusionary Rule
Fleeting-Targets Exception
Good-Faith Exception
Inherent Coercion
Interrogation

Landmark Case
Latent Evidence
Miranda Triggers
Miranda Warnings
Plain View
Probable Cause
Reasonable Suspicion
Sneak and Peek
Suspicionless Search
Writ of *Certiorari*

CHAPTER 8

Policing: Issues and Challenges

LEARNING OBJECTIVES

After reading this chapter, you should be able to:

- Describe the police working personality, and relate it to police culture
- List and describe different types of police corruption, and discuss possible methods for building police integrity
- Explain the dangers of police work, and discuss what can be done to reduce those dangers
- Describe the situations in which police officers are most likely to use force, and provide some guidelines for determining when too much force has been used
- Describe racial profiling, and explain why it has become a significant issue in policing today
- Describe the civil liability issues associated with policing, and identify common sources of civil suits against the police

Chapter Summary

Chapter 8 discusses several important police issues, including **police working personality** and culture, **corruption**, the dangers of police work, **police use of force**, **racial profiling** and biased policing, and police civil liability.

One powerful influence on law enforcement officers is the police culture. New recruits are molded by the police culture as supervisors and other officers teach rookie officers the informal policies of the department. Thus, there are two sets of rules that new police officers must learn and follow. The first set of rules includes those formal departmental policies and legal constraints that the officer learns in the training academy. The second set of rules involves the informal socialization that takes place as officers interact with older, experienced officers who teach how formal rules are interpreted. For example, experienced officers might explain to a new recruit that accepting free meals or bribes is expected, despite departmental policy clearly forbidding such behavior. The text discusses such activities in the section on police **corruption**, noting its historical pervasiveness. Chapter 8 also discusses how police departments have attempted to respond to police corruption.

Chapter 8 also discusses the dangers of police work. Police work is dangerous, and officers are killed in the line of duty. For example, approximately 146 American law enforcement officers were killed in 2003. The rate of violent death of law enforcement officers, however, is relatively small. There are several other dangers discussed in this chapter. Law enforcement officers are exposed to disease and infected evidence and must take necessary precautions or risk being infected with the agents that cause AIDS, hepatitis B, or tuberculosis. Other dangers include the stress and fatigue of police work. Stress is probably the least visible of police dangers, but its impact on officers is enormous.

Police use of force is also examined in Chapter 8. The use of force by police officers is very rare. When used, force is typically applied in an arrest situation when the suspect resists or is under the influence of drugs or alcohol. Deadly force is defined as the force likely to cause death or great bodily harm. The use of deadly force is a significant issue for law enforcement because of the potential civil liability, and *Tennessee* v. *Garner* is an important case, as it specifies the conditions under which deadly force can be used in the apprehension of suspected felons.

Another area of civil liability discussed in Chapter 8 is racial profiling. Called "driving while black" or "driving while brown," racial profiling comprises those police-initiated actions that are based on race, ethnicity, or national origin rather than the behavior of the individual or crime-specific information.

There are several common sources of civil suits brought against police departments. These sources include failure to protect property, failure to render proper medical assistance, false arrest, false imprisonment, and inappropriate use of deadly force. Important considerations for civil suits are **1983 Lawsuits**, which are civil suits brought under Title 42, Section 1983, of the U.S. Code against anyone who denies others their constitutional rights to life, liberty, or property without due process of law, and **Bivens actions**, which are civil suits, based on the case of *Bivens* v. *Six Unknown Named Defendants*, brought against federal government officials for denying the constitutional rights of others.

Teaching Outline

   I. Introduction (p. 290)
  II. Police Personality and Culture (p. 290)
    • Introduce the characteristics of Skolnick's working personality.

Police Working Personality   All aspects of the traditional values and patterns of behavior evidenced by police officers who have been effectively socialized into the police subculture. Characteristics of the police personality often extend to the personal lives of law enforcement personnel. (p. 290)

  III. Corruption and Integrity (p. 291)

- Highlight examples of corruption, and introduce the differences between "grass eating" and "meat eating" and the findings of the Knapp Commission.

Police Corruption   The abuse of police authority for personal or organizational gain. *Source*: Carl B. Klockers et al., "The Measurement of Police Integrity," *National Institute of Justice Research in Brief* (Washington, D.C.: NIJ, 2000), p. 1. (p. 293)

Knapp Commission   A committee that investigated police corruption in New York City in the early 1970s. (p. 294)

    A. Money—The Root of Police Evil? (p. 295)
- Discuss the influence of monetary pressures on police corruption.

    B. Building Police Integrity (p. 296)
- Introduce police practices that have been found to promote integrity
- High moral standards
- Training
- Peer group socialization

Internal Affairs   The branch of a police organization tasked with investigating charges of wrongdoing against other members of the department. (p. 297)

    C. Drug Testing of Police Employees (p. 297)
- Introduce the Model Drug Testing Policy.
- Discuss the cases *Turner* v. *Fraternal Order of Police* (drug testing can occur based on reasonable suspicion) and *Caruso* v. *Ward* (random drug testing is not allowed).

  IV. The Dangers of Police Work (p. 298)

    A. Violence in the Line of Duty (p. 299)
- There were 152 officers killed in the line of duty in 2002.
- The World Trade Center attacks produced a greater number of deaths in the 2001 statistics.

    B. Risk of Disease and Infected Evidence (p. 300)
- Stress concerns about AIDS, hepatitis, tuberculosis, and other diseases.
- Highlight the efforts to minimize the risk faced by police officers.

Biological Weapon   A biological agent used to threaten human life (for example, anthrax, smallpox, or any other infectious disease). *Source*: Technical Working Group on Crime Scene Investigation, *Crime Scene Investigation: A Guide for Law Enforcement* (Washington, D.C.: National Institute of Justice, 2000), p. 12. (p. 300)

    C. Stress and Fatigue among Police Officers (p. 302)
- Police work is one of the most stressful jobs in the country.
- Stress is caused by external, organizational, personal, and operational stressors.

    1. Stress Reduction
- Discuss efforts to reduce stress.

    2. Officer Fatigue
- Discuss officer fatigue.

  V. Police Use of Force (p. 303)

Police Use of Force   The use of physical restraint by a police officer when dealing with a member of the public. *Source*: National Institute of Justice, *Use of Force by Police: Overview of National and Local Data* (Washington, D.C.: NIJ, 1999) (p. 303)

Excessive Force The application of an amount and/or frequency of force greater than that required to compel compliance from a willing or unwilling subject. *Source*: International Association of Chiefs of Police, *Police Use of Force in America 2001* (Alexandria, VA: IACP, 2001), p. 1. (p. 304)

Problem Police Officer A law enforcement officer who exhibits problem behavior, as indicated by high rates of citizen complaints and use-of-force incidents and by other evidence. *Source*: Samuel Walker, Geoffrey P. Alpert, and Dennis J. Kenney, *Responding to the Problem Police Officer: A National Study of Early Warning Systems* (Washington, D.C.: NIJ, 2000). (p. 305)

    A. Deadly Force (p. 306)

Deadly Force Force likely to cause death or great bodily harm. Also, "the intentional use of a firearm or other instrument resulting in a high probability of death." *Source*: Sam W. Lathrop, "Reviewing Use of Force: A Systematic Approach," *FBI Law Enforcement Bulletin*, October 2000, p. 18. (p. 306)

- *Tennessee* v. *Garner*: Deadly force can be used when the suspect is thought to pose a significant threat of serious injury or death to the public or the officer.
- *Graham* v. *Connor*: The Court established the standard of "objective reasonableness" by which an officer's use of deadly force could be assessed in terms of "reasonableness at the moment."

    B. Less-Lethal Weapons (p. 309)

Less-Lethal Weapon A weapon that is designed to disable, capture, or immobilize—but not kill—a suspect. Occasional deaths do result from the use of such weapons, however. (p. 309)

    VI. Racial Profiling and Biased Policing (p. 309)

Racial Profiling "Any police-initiated action that relies on the race, ethnicity, or national origin rather than (1) the behavior of an individual or (2) on information that leads the police to a particular individual who has been identified as being, or having been, engaged in criminal activity." *Source*: Deborah Ramierz, Jack McDevitt, and Amy Farrell, *A Resource Guide on Racial Profiling Data Collection Systems: Promising Practices and Lessons Learned* (Washington, D.C.: USDOJ, 2000), p. 3. (p. 309)

- Discuss recent media, political, and research attention to this issue.
- A. Racially Biased Policing (p. 313)
  - Introduce the findings from the Racially Biased Policing Study by PERF.
  - Most law enforcement officers are dedicated to serving with fairness and dignity.
  - Most police officers share an intolerance for racially biased policing.
  - This report also describes the qualities of an unbiased police officer.

    VII. Police Civil Liability (p. 314)

Civil Liability Potential responsibility for payment of damages or other court-ordered enforcement as a result of a ruling in a lawsuit. Civil liability is not the same as criminal liability, which means "open to punishment for a crime." *Source*: Adapted from Gerald and Kathleen Hill, *The Real Life Dictionary of the Law*, Web posted at law.com. Accessed June 11, 2003. (p. 315)

    A. Common Sources of Civil Suits

- *Malley* v. *Briggs*: A police officer who effects an arrest or conducts a search on the basis of an improperly issued warrant can be liable for monetary damages.
- Examples include false arrest, assault, and negligent actions.

B. Federal Lawsuits

1983 Lawsuit   A civil suit brought under Title 42, Section 1983, of the U.S. Code against anyone who denies others their constitutional rights to life, liberty, or property without due process of law. (p. 317)

Bivens Action   A civil suit based upon the case of *Bivens* v. *Six Unknown Named Defendants*, brought against federal government officials for denying the constitutional rights of others. (p. 318)

Learner Activities

Activity 1

Read **Library Extra 8–1** on promoting police integrity. What does the author suggest are the key principles for promoting police integrity?

LIBRARY EXTRA

_____

_____

_____

_____

_____

_____

Activity 2

For this activity, first read the short research report on police use of deadly force posted at **Library Extra 8–6**. This report presents findings from a study on the use of force by and against Phoenix police officers. After reading the report, summarize the findings in the space provided below. In your synopsis, be sure to answer the following questions: How often do the police use force? How often do suspects use force against the police? What type of force is used in arrest situations? What factors predict police use of force?

LIBRARY EXTRA

_____

_____

_____

_____

_____

_____

Activity 3

Compile a list of the police civil liability cases discussed in this chapter. What are the major findings of each case?

_____

_____

_____

_____

_____

_____

Activity 4

Use the Cybrary (http://www.cybrary.info) to find articles about racial profiling and police ethics. Describe these studies and their findings.

_____

_____

_____

_____

_____

_____

Internet Activity

Use the Cybrary (http://www.cybrary.info) to find articles about police stress. What kinds of studies did you find? What do they deal with? What were the findings or results of each of these studies?

_____

_____

_____

_____

_____

_____

Distance Learning Activity

Visit a number of police memorial websites. What type of information is included at these websites? Assemble a notebook (or disk) containing the information you have gathered. Your instructor may request that you submit the material.

_____

_____

_____

_____

_____

Learning Activities Utilizing the World Wide Web

There are student-based activities in the Student Study Guide (Internet Activity, Distance Learning Activity, CJ Today on the World Wide Web) that are similar in focus to those that follow. However, the following are presented as instructor-led activities, to be used in a classroom with online access.

Prior to class, go to the Cybrary (http://www.cybrary.info) to find articles about police stress. Prepare for class display the studies you found. Lead a class discussion by asking these questions: What do these websites deal with? What were the findings or results of each of these studies?

Visit a number of police memorial websites. What type of information is included at these websites? Prepare for inclass display the information you have gathered. Discuss.

Other websites for organizations and agencies related to the material in Chapter 8 include:

Police Stress	http://stressline.com
Abner Louima Torture Case	http://www.thesmokinggun.com/torture/torture.htm
AJAX	http://www.sagal.com/ajax.ajax.htm
American Police Hall of Fame and Museum	http://www.aphf.org
Beside the Badge	http://my.dmci.net/~lmcpub
California Law Enforcement Basic	http://www.clew.org/Tm/TmCtrs/BasicAcad.html
California Law Enforcement Image	http://www.calpoliceimage.com
Campus Law Enforcement	http://dpsw.usc.edu/UnivPD Web.html
Heavy Badge	http://www.heavybadge.com
Ira Wilsker's Law Enforcement Sites	http://www.ih2000.net/ira

Suggested Answers to Chapter Discussion Questions

1. **What is the police working personality? What are its central features?**

   The working personality includes all aspects of the traditional values and patterns of behavior evidenced by police officers who have been effectively socialized into the police subculture. Characteristics of the police personality often extend to the personal lives of law enforcement personnel. Characteristics of the police working personality include authoritarianism, cynicism, conservatism, suspicion, hostility, individualism, insecurity, loyalty, efficiency, honor, secretiveness, and prejudice.

   How does the police working personality develop?

   American police officers develop a working personality through an informal socialization process wherein officers learn "appropriate" police behavior (that is, acceptable to fellow officers) from veteran members of the department. Once acquired, it creates a "streetwise" view of the world shared by members of the police ranks.

   How does it relate to police culture?

   The police working personality is a central component of police culture. Rookie officers are socialized into the police culture. Hiring practices, training, and interactions with supervisors, other officers, and citizens are all issues that impact this socialization process. The working personality is one by-product of this socialization process.

2. **What are the different types of police corruption?**

Police corruption ranges from minor violations to serious violations of the law. Examples might include accepting gratuities, playing favorites, taking minor or major bribes, committing criminal acts, denying civil rights, or committing violent crime. Researchers have also provided more specific categories of police corruption. Barker and Carter, for example, distinguish between occupational deviance and abuse of authority, and the Knapp Commission report distinguished between grass eaters and meat eaters.

What themes run through the findings of the Knapp Commission and the Wickersham Commission?

Both the Knapp and Wickersham Commissions found existence of the infamous "blue wall," a contributing factor in police corruption. The willingness of police officers to tolerate corrupt behavior known to them rather than to report it (characterized as "ratting" on a fellow officer) baffles most observers.

Another important theme is that when huge sums of money are available with which to tempt police officers, some yield. That is less a function of their status as police officers and more the result of their status as human beings. The kingpins of the illegal liquor trade during Prohibition amassed such sums. Even greater wealth is in the hands of present-day drug lords. It is no surprise that some of that money is put to use to corrupt some members of the law enforcement community.

What innovative steps might police departments take to reduce or eliminate corruption among their officers?

Like crime, corruption will never be eliminated. Human beings, by nature, are flawed; they will, on occasion, behave beneath expectations. Departmental leaders, however, can establish programs to minimize corruption. Ethics training must be emphasized. Additionally, formal and informal leaders within police ranks must create a culture wherein intolerance of behavior that diminishes the group is valued above misplaced loyalty toward a corrupt fellow officer.

3. **What are the dangers of police work? What can be done to reduce those dangers?**

The dangers of police work include violence in the line of duty, risk of disease and infected evidence, and stress and fatigue among police officers. Many police departments have taken proactive steps to reduce these dangers, improving training, developing support programs, and making organizational adjustments. The most important step that has been taken is that departments have acknowledged that these dangers exist and are starting to take proactive steps to reduce these dangers.

4. **In what kinds of situations are police officers most likely to use force? When has too much force been used?**

It is important to note that the use of force is a relatively rare occurrence. Police use force in less than 20% of all adult custodial arrests. A report by the National Institute of Justice indicates that use of force typically occurs when making an arrest, the suspect resists, and the suspect is under the influence of alcohol or drugs or is mentally ill. The use of excessive force is more problematic. Force is excessive when it exceeds the level considered justifiable under the circumstances.

5. **What is racial profiling? Why has it become a significant issue in policing today?**

Racial profiling is any police-initiated action that is based on the race, ethnicity, or national origin rather than (1) on the behavior of an individual, or (2) on information that leads the police to a particular individual who has been identified as being, or having been, engaged in criminal activity. It has become a significant issue in policing today. First, several research reports were published that indicated that racial profiling is a significant problem. Second, media coverage of these reports and the publicity of specific profiling incidents increased public awareness and concern about this problem.

6. **What are some of the civil liability issues associated with policing? What are some of the common sources of civil suits against the police? How can civil liability be reduced?**

There are several civil liability issues associated with policing. First, there have been an increasing number of suits brought in federal courts against police departments. Second, such cases generate a good deal of media publicity and criticism directed at the police department. Third, in general, the U.S. Supreme Court has supported a type of qualified immunity for individual officers.

Some of the common sources of civil suits include failure to protect property, false imprisonment, inappropriate use of force or deadly force, racial profiling, false arrest, failure to prevent a foreseeable crime, and violations of constitutional rights. The most common sources of lawsuits include assault, battery, false imprisonment, and malicious prosecutions.

Most police departments have started to carry liability insurance to protect themselves against the financial damages from losing a large civil suit.

Key—Student Study Guide Questions

True or False

____ 8-1. Most large law enforcement agencies have their own internal affairs division. **(True, p. 297)**

____ 8-2. Barker and Carter describe acts of occupational deviance as those that further the goals of law enforcement. **(False, p. 293)**

____ 8-3. Meat-eating police corruption is the most common form of police deviance, involving mostly small bribes or relatively small services. **(False, p. 294)**

____ 8-4. Police officers who have adopted a "working personality" are primarily concerned with fairness. **(False, p. 290)**

____ 8-5. The Knapp Commission investigated police use of deadly force in the late 1990s. **(False, p. 294)**

____ 8-6. In *Malley* v. *Briggs*, the Supreme Court banned random drug testing of police officers. **(False, p. 316)**

____ 8-7. According to research by Alpert and Dunham, the force factor is a key element to consider in attempting to reduce injuries to both police and suspects. **(True, p. 305)**

____ 8-8. Currently, the fleeing felon rule guides police decision making in deadly force situations. **(False, p. 306)**

____ 8-9. Less-lethal weapons are designed to disable but not kill a suspect. **(True, p. 309)**

____ 8-10. A federal lawsuit against the police is often called a 2003 lawsuit. **(False, p. 317)**

Multiple Choice

8-11. Which type of police corruption occurs in order to further the organizational goals of law enforcement?
   a. meat-eating
   b. grass-eating
   c. occupational deviance
   d. abuse of authority (p. 295)

8-12. Which type of police corruption is motivated by the desire for personal benefit?
   a. meat-eating
   b. grass-eating
   c. occupational deviance (p. 293)
   d. abuse of authority

8-13. Which Supreme Court case is not directly relevant to police civil liability issues?
   a. *Malley* v. *Briggs*
   b. *City of Canton, Ohio* v. *Harris*
   c. *Tennessee* v. *Garner* (p. 306)
   d. *Board of County Commission of Bryan County, Oklahoma* v. *Brown*

8-14. What division in a police department investigates charges that officers are guilty of wrongdoing?
   a. strategic investigations
   b. intelligence
   c. internal affairs (p. 297)
   d. officer supervision

8-15. Historically, officers were allowed to use deadly force to prevent the escape of a suspected felon. This was known as the
   a. deadly force statute.
   b. "shoot to kill" policy.
   c. escaping suspect doctrine.
   d. fleeing felon rule. (p. 306)

8-16. A police officer can be sued for
   a. false arrest.
   b. failure to prevent a foreseeable crime.
   c. negligence in the care of persons in police custody.
   d. all of the above. (p. 315)

8-17. Officers who have adopted the police working personality are often
   a. cynical.
   b. authoritarian.
   c. prejudiced.
   d. all of the above. (p. 291)

8-18. What standard for deadly force was established in *Graham* v. *Connor*?
   a. objective reasonableness (p. 306)
   b. probable cause
   c. clear and present danger
   d. best guess

8-19. What commission provided the grass-easting and meat-eating distinctions to describe types of police corruption?
   a. Johnson Commission
   b. Nixon Commission
   c. Knapp Commission (p. 294)
   d. Burger Commission

8-20. What area of police civil liability received a significant amount of media attention in the late 1990s?
   a. deadly force
   b. drug testing
   c. racial profiling (p. 309)
   d. false arrest

Fill-In

8-21. A(n) _____ is likely to have high rates of citizen complaints. **(problem police officer, p. 305)**

8-22. The _____ encompasses all aspects of the traditional values and patterns of behavior evidenced by police officers who have been effectively socialized into the police subculture. **(police working personality, p. 290)**

8-23. _____ is the use of physical restraint by a police officer. **(Use of force, p. 303)**

8-24. Who developed the term police working personality? _____ **(Jerome Skolnick, p. 290)**

8-25. A(n) _____ is an agent used to threaten human life, such as anthrax. **(biological weapon, p. 300)**

8-26. _____ is the branch of the police department that investigates wrongdoing among members of the department. **(Internal affairs, p. 297)**

8-27. _____ is the abuse of police authority for personal or organizational gain. **(Police corruption, p. 293)**

8-28. Civil suits brought under Title 42, Section 1983, of the U.S. Code are called _____. **(1983 Lawsuits, p. 317)**

8-29. _____ is the name given to civil suits brought against federal government officials for denial of the constitutional rights of others. **(*Bivens* action, p. 318)**

8-30. _____ is the application of an amount and/or frequency of force greater than that required to compel compliance from a willing or unwilling suspect. **(Excessive force, p. 304)**

Key—Crossword Puzzle

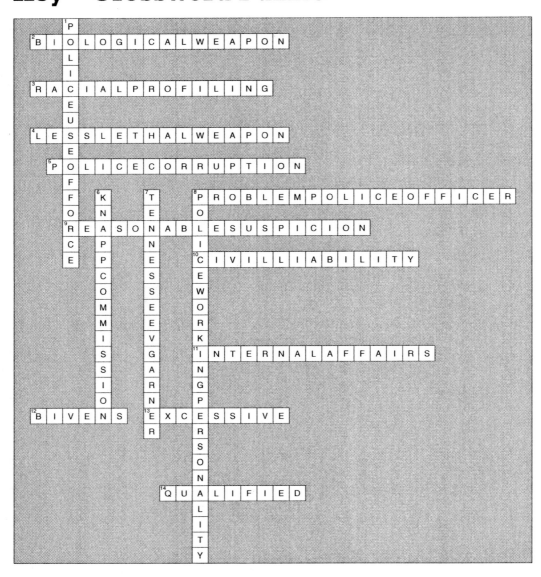

Across

2. Anthrax or smallpox.
3. Any police-initiated action that relies on the person's race, ethnicity, or national origin.
4. Weapon designed to disable but not kill.
5. Abuse of police authority for personal or organizational gain.
8. Police officer with high rate of citizen complaints.
9. When drug testing of police officers can occur.
10. Payment for a ruling in a lawsuit.
11. Department that polices the police.
12. _____ v. *Six Unknown Federal Agents.*
13. Use of force greater than is required for compliance.

14. Type of immunity given to police officers generally.

Down

1. Use of physical restraint by a police officer.
6. Famous police corruption commission.
7. Case that specified the conditions under which deadly force could be used in the apprehension of suspected felons.
8. All aspects of the traditional values and patterns of behavior evidenced by police officers who have been effectively socialized into the police subculture.

Key—Word Search Puzzle

```
C J G F L I R T R M G D K J A G B B K F B J M B A M G E X L
L J O R U I N T E R N A L A F F A I R S J J J F A D M J I B
F N U H I C X E R G D O M T J C M Q J I F F I V J S I C F A
Y A G Y O M P H W S V M W G L D A Q U Z H X V V N O F Q L P
B F R Z L Y V M O D F G P H U L Z B L J O G J O E P W X L O
F G A O S J G F B X N I Q U W Q U U I F B U P J Q O F V B L
D L S Y V U Y A P W C M F V U M I Y N N W A J W P L D H W I
V J S E J A S J V U X T A V L Y R D N N E A R R P I X T G C
V V E B P W A E H L Y N J Q K S Y H Z W P D A S R C Z U K E
Y W A A N S L B F K I H X Y J O G E L Q J Q G F O E S A A U
P A T S T R E S S F Q Z O K Q K Q A X B A M G K B W D H D S
P C E J O D E A D L Y F O R C E H R R Q J J A N L O R C G E
H M R Q C K I U D P M A D V Q T H A T X Y Q O A E R K I S O
W Y S U D L A J B J Q T D S E K X C E O R S I P M K R O A F
S U B O P O H C L B F X A L Q E C I U A X R X P P I R R U T F
N Q P Q B T O K Q F W I S J C K I A J Y U M M C O L G P W Q R
L B X Q P D M N P H X S B R I A V L P S H N C O L G P W Q R
O I Y T P B K E P C E E O U G Q I P Z S K U O M I P T F D C
F V I N T H D N A L F F W N S T L R F P V N N M C E I U W E
K E V D P L P T O T E X I H Q N L O U O E F S I E R O G X Q
R N Q H I W W J C V E L V C I Q I F A K D S P S O S N H V X
M S C Q N Z T W I D I A E C J O A I E W T C Q S F O G F K T
K A C K S D V S O F P Z T G H K B L H D P W M I F N O J A Q
J C E U S M S Y O E B N B E F D I I Z A G G G O I A K C F X
D T U M C E Y R G Q W N G C R F L N B P K W Y N C L R T E O
J I M J C I P Z A X R Q Q I B S I G F V W U C M E I I P H U
D O N X R P X L G C X R V O K T T L T D M W N Z R T A G J W
L N E M I T R N G G G Q B P K Z Y G T E J Q A N X Y Z B C A
R K M Q T Y P S I C I P A Q B H E S L C F J J V S A H J A S
W N P L I T F R D B I O L O G I C A L W E A P O N M T B X Y
```

Biological Weapon

Bivens Action

Civil Liability

Corruption

Deadly Force

Excessive Force

Grass Eaters

Internal Affairs

Knapp Commission

Less-Lethal Weapons

Meat Eaters

Police Use of Force

Police Working Personality

Problem Police Officer

Profiling

Racial Profiling

Stress

The Courts: Structure and Participants

CHAPTER 9

LEARNING OBJECTIVES

After reading this chapter, you should be able to:

- Describe the development of the American court system
- Explain the concept of the dual-court system in America
- Identify some of the differences between the state and federal court systems
- Identify and explain the roles of the professional members of the courtroom work group
- Discuss indigent defense, and know what forms it takes in the United States
- Identify and explain the roles of the nonprofessional courtroom participants
- Explain the roles of expert and lay witnesses in a criminal trial, and describe how their testimony might differ
- Explain how professional and nonprofessional courtroom participants work together to bring most criminal trials to a successful close

Chapter Summary

Chapter 9 provides an introduction to the American court system. It discusses the history of the dual-court structure in America, highlighting the decisions made at the various state and federal court levels. The text also describes the roles and responsibilities of "professional" and "nonprofessional" members of the **courtroom work group**.

The American court system is unique in many ways. One of its distinctive characteristics is that it is a dual-court system of state and federal courts. The founding fathers thought an essential feature of the new republic would be the power of individual states to retain authority and autonomy separate from federal control. However, the nation's founders also created a federal court system to mediate violations of federal law and resolve violations of due process guarantees.

Most states have a three-level court structure. Trial courts are at the lowest level. Trial courts of limited or special jurisdiction hear only cases involving very minor crimes, such as misdemeanors and traffic violations. A judge, rather than a jury, usually resolves these cases. **Trial courts of general jurisdiction**, however, hear any criminal case and also provide the first level of appeal for cases decided in a court of limited jurisdiction. These decisions can then be appealed to the state intermediate appellate court. Appellate courts are concerned with reviewing the case on the record and will not conduct a new trial. Finally, all states have supreme courts, generally referred to as **courts of last resort**. The text provides a discussion of the Florida system to illustrate the various levels of a state court system.

The text also describes the **federal court system**. There are 94 district courts in the federal system. These courts are considered the trial courts of the federal system. The U.S. courts of appeal provide the first level of appeal in the federal system. These courts, often referred to as circuit courts, are responsible for reviewing decisions from the federal district courts. The federal Supreme Court is the most powerful court in the United States. This Court reviews circuit court and state supreme court decisions.

Chapter 9 describes the courtroom work group. The first professional courtroom work group member discussed in Chapter 9 is the **judge**. The primary responsibility of the judge is to ensure that justice prevails. The judge is probably the most powerful individual in the courtroom, able to influence the outcome of a case by ruling on matters of law, procedure, and sentence. The text describes the qualifications necessary to be a judge and the selection of judges. Some judges are elected officials, others are appointed, and others are selected by the Missouri Plan. Although judges are generally well respected and highly ethical, the text describes several examples of judicial misconduct.

The prosecuting attorney is responsible for representing the public and thus presents the state's case against the defendant. **Prosecutors**, typically with the help of several assistants, are responsible for deciding the appropriate charges for a defendant, preparing a case for each step of the court process, introducing evidence and witnesses to support the charges at trial, and perhaps advising the police. If the defendant is convicted, prosecutors make sentencing recommendations. The text also describes the significant amount of discretion possessed by prosecutors. Their discretion is limited, however, by a series of court decisions discussed in the text. For example, prosecutors are required to disclose any evidence that the defense requests.

The prosecutor's main adversary is the **defense attorney**. While the prosecutor is responsible for case and trial preparation on behalf of the state, the defense attorney does the same for the defendant. The text describes the types of attorneys who provide criminal defense in the criminal justice system. In addition, it explains many of the important right-to-counsel cases. According to the Supreme Court's interpretation of the Sixth Amendment, defendants who face imprisonment if convicted and who are too poor to pay for an attorney are appointed counsel. These court decisions have forced states to provide counsel to indigent defendants using an assigned counsel, public defense, or contract arrangement system.

There are various other professional members discussed in Chapter 9. The **bailiff**, for example, keeps order in the courtroom and maintains physical custody of the jury. The local court administrator is responsible for managing the local court. The court reporter creates the record of all that occurs at trial. The clerk of courts maintains court records, swears in witnesses, and marks for identification all physical evidence introduced at trial. Finally, **expert witnesses** have special knowledge and skills recognized by the court as relevant to the determination of guilt or innocence.

Finally, Chapter 9 discusses the various "nonprofessional courtroom participants. Although not considered members of the courtroom work group, these outsiders can have a significant impact on the trial process. Lay witnesses provide testimony relevant to a specific case. Jurors hear the evidence presented and then make a determination regarding guilt. Crime victims have historically been considered the forgotten members of the criminal justice process, but their standing is changing. The defendant is also considered an outsider, but he or she has to be present at trial and can try to defend himself or herself. Finally, the press is often present in the courtroom, especially in celebrated cases, and may influence trial processes by publicizing facts about the case prior to trial or being present to record and publish trial testimony.

Teaching Outline

    I. Introduction (p. 328)

    II. History and Structure of the American Court System (p. 328)

Federal Court System   The three-tiered structure of federal courts, comprising U.S. district courts, U.S. courts of appeal, and the U.S. Supreme Court. (p. 329)

State Court System   A state judicial structure. Most states have at least three court levels: generally, trial courts, appellate courts, and a state supreme court. (p. 329)

Jurisdiction   The territory, subject matter, or people over which a court or other justice agency may exercise lawful authority, as determined by statute or constitution. (p. 329)

    III. The State Court System (p. 330)

        A. The Development of State Courts (p. 330)

           • Massachusetts Bay Colony "General Court"

           • Pennsylvania Referee System

           • Difference between original and appellate jurisdiction

Original Jurisdiction   The lawful authority of a court to hear or act on a case from its beginning and to pass judgment on the law and the facts. The authority may be over a specific geographic area or over particular types of cases. (p. 331)

Appellate Jurisdiction   The lawful authority of a court to review a decision made by a lower court. (p. 331)

        B. State Court Systems Today (p. 332)

           1. State Trial Courts

               • Lower courts are trial courts of limited or special jurisdiction.

               • Trial courts are trial courts of general jurisdiction.

Trial *de Novo*   Literally, "new trial." The term is applied to cases that are retried on appeal, as opposed to those that are simply reviewed on the record. (p. 333)

           2. State Appellate Courts

               • States have appellate divisions to review actions of a lower court.

Court of Last Resort   The court authorized by law to hear the final appeal on a matter. (p. 333)

Appeal   Generally, the request that a court with appellate jurisdiction review the judgment, decision, or order of a lower court and set it aside (reverse it) or modify it. (p. 333)

               • Intermediate appellate court (court of appeals)

- High-level appellate courts (courts of last resort)
- May appeal from court of last resort to federal system
- Several court decisions, however, limit such access
- *Keeney* v. *Tamayo-Reyes*: The U.S. Supreme Court ruled that a federal evidentiary hearing will occur only if the defendant can demonstrate some reason for not developing those facts at the state level or if he or she can show a fundamental miscarriage of justice from failure to hold such a hearing.
- *Herrera* v. *Collins*: New evidence of innocence is no reason for a federal court to order a new state trial.

INSTRUCTIONAL CUE

Locate examples of state court systems to show the various models used.

INSTRUCTIONAL CUE LINKED TO THE STUDENT STUDY GUIDE

Use Student Activity 1 to help students understand state court systems.

3. State Court Administration

State Court Administrator A coordinator who assists with case-flow management, operating funds budgeting, and court docket administration. (p. 334)

- Introduce the common tasks of state court administrators.

INSTRUCTIONAL CUE

Web Extra 9–1 provides a link to the National Center for State Courts, and **Web Extra 9–2** provides a link to the Administrative Office of the United States Court, which is responsible for administering the federal court system. Use these resources to begin a class discussion on court administration.

WEB EXTRA

INSTRUCTIONAL CUE LINKED TO THE STUDENT STUDY GUIDE

Use Student Activity 2 to help students understand the functions of dispute-resolution and mediation centers.

4. Dispute-Resolution Centers and Community Courts

Dispute-Resolution Center An informal hearing place designed to mediate interpersonal disputes without resorting to the more formal arrangements of a criminal trial court. (p. 335)

Community Court A low-level court that focuses on quality-of-life crimes that erode a neighborhood's morale, that emphasizes problem solving rather than punishment, and that builds upon restorative principles such as community service and restitution. (p. 336)

INSTRUCTIONAL CUE

Web Extra 9–3 has more information about dispute-resolution centers and community courts.

WEB EXTRA

IV. The Federal Court System (p. 336)
   A. U.S. District Courts (p. 336)
      - Lowest level of the federal court system

- Made up of 94 district courts
- Considered the trial courts of the federal system

B. U.S. Courts of Appeal (p. 337)
   - The intermediate appellate courts
   - Made up of 13 circuit courts (U.S. Court of Appeals for the federal circuit and 12 regional courts of appeal)
   - Have mandatory jurisdiction over the decisions of district courts within their circuit

C. The U.S. Supreme Court (p. 338)
   - Describe the immense power of this Court because it has power of judicial review.

Judicial Review   The power of a court to review actions and decisions made by other agencies of government. (p. 339)

- *Marbury* v. *Madison*: Establishes the Court's authority as final interpreter of the U.S. Constitution.
1. Increasing Complexity and the Supreme Court
2. The Supreme Court Today
   - Court may review any case it believes is worthy of review but typically only reviews cases involving a substantial federal question.

INSTRUCTIONAL CUE LINKED TO THE STUDENT STUDY GUIDE

Students will have a better understanding of the U.S. Supreme Court after completing Student Activity 3. After students complete this exercise, have them present what they learned to the class. This exercise is intended to help students see the types of individuals who had an incredible impact on legal processes.

INSTRUCTIONAL CUE

Students may have a difficult time understanding how the state and federal court systems interact in practice. One way to illustrate state and federal court decision-making processes is to walk a case through the various levels. For example, you can discuss a felony murder trial that receives a significant amount of pretrial publicity. Discuss how the defendant would be tried first in a state court of general jurisdiction. Then explain the process of appeal from the state intermediate appellate court to the court of last resort. Also, since there may have been a Sixth Amendment due process issue, describe how the case could be appealed directly to the U.S. Supreme Court or to a federal district court.

V. The Courtroom Work Group (p. 340)

Courtroom Work Group   The professional courtroom actors, including judges, prosecuting attorneys, defense attorneys, public defenders, and others who earn a living serving the court.

VI. Professional Courtroom Participants (p. 341)
   A. The Judge (p. 341)

Judge   An elected or appointed public official who presides over a court of law and who is authorized to hear and sometimes to decide cases and to conduct trials. (p. 341)

- A judge's primary duty is to ensure justice.
- A judge holds ultimate authority on matters of law, evidence, and court decorum.

1. Judicial Selection
   - Federal judges are nominated by the U.S. president and confirmed by the Senate.
   - State judges are generally selected through popular election, political appointment, or the Missouri Plan.
   - Judges elected via popular election must campaign, run along party lines, and generate campaign funding.
   - Politicians, usually the governor, appoint political appointees.
   - The Missouri Plan (also called merit selection) combines election and appointment. Candidates are first chosen by a nonpartisan nominating committee. The governor then selects the final candidates. After a period of time in office, these judges run unopposed and will be reappointed based on their records.

2. Judicial Qualifications
   - Today, judges in all states (appellate and general jurisdiction courts) must hold a law degree, be licensed attorneys, and be members of the bar association.
   - Many states require professional training as well.

3. Judicial Misconduct
   - Occasionally a judge oversteps his or her authority or exhibits unprofessional behavior.

   B. The Prosecuting Attorney (p. 343)

Prosecutor   An attorney whose official duty is to conduct criminal proceedings on behalf of the state or the people against those accused of having committed criminal offenses. (p. 343)

1. Prosecutorial Discretion
   - Prosecutors have incredible influence on a case because they decide the charges to file, can accept a plea bargain, appear before a grand jury, decide what witnesses should appear, and make sentencing recommendations to the judge.

Prosecutorial Discretion   The decision-making power of prosecutors, based upon the wide range of choices available to them, in the handling of criminal defendants, the scheduling of cases for trial, the acceptance of negotiated pleas, and so on. The most important form of prosecutorial discretion lies in the power to charge, or not to charge, a person with an offense. (p. 345)

   - Prosecutors must assist the defense in preparing a case for trial by providing evidence in their possession.
   - *Brady* v. *Maryland*: The Supreme Court held that the prosecution is required to disclose exculpatory evidence that relates to the guilt or innocence of a defendant.
   - *U.S.* v. *Bagley*: The Supreme Court ruled that the prosecution must disclose any evidence that the defense requests.
   - Prosecutors are generally immune from civil liability (*Ambler* v. *Pachtman*) but are not completely immune when giving legal advice to the police (*Burns* v. *Reed*).

2. The Abuse of Discretion
3. The Prosecutor's Professional Responsibility

   C. The Defense Counsel (p. 346)

Defense Counsel   A licensed trial lawyer, hired or appointed to conduct the legal defense of an individual accused of a crime and to represent him or her before a court of law. (p. 346)

- Defense attorneys represent the accused after arrest and ensure that the civil rights of the defendant are not violated.
- The defense attorney is involved in all stages of the court process.

1. The Criminal Lawyer
   - Includes private attorneys, court-appointed counsel, and public defenders
2. Criminal Defense of the Poor
   - *Powell* v. *Alabama*: This 1932 case held that if state defendants charged with a capital crime are unable to afford counsel, the court would appoint one for them.
   - *Johnson* v. *Zerbst*: This 1938 case held that all defendants unable to afford counsel would be appointed one in federal criminal proceedings.
   - *Gideon* v. *Wainwright*: This 1963 case held that all *felony* defendants unable to afford counsel would be appointed one in state criminal proceedings.
   - *Argersinger* v. *Hamlin*: This 1972 case requires legal representation for anyone facing imprisonment.
   - *In re Gault*: This 1967 case granted juveniles the right to appointed counsel.

INSTRUCTIONAL CUE

Be sure to explain to students why defendants need the assistance of counsel. Discuss the complexity of court proceedings. Point out that the majority of defendants are poor and uneducated. In the same way we rely on doctors when we need medical treatment, defendants need attorneys, as educated and trained professionals, to cut through legal complexities on their behalf.

- Describe the different types of indigent defense systems.
- The most widely used system of indigent defense is assigned counsel. Assigned counsel are court-appointed defense attorneys whom the state pays at a set rate.

Public Defender   An attorney employed by a government agency or subagency, or by a private organization under contract to a government body, for the purpose of providing defense services to indigents; or an attorney who has volunteered such service. (p. 348)

- *Contractual arrangement* refers to a system through which individual attorneys, local bar associations, or law firms are paid to provide defense services to indigent defendants on a contractual basis.
- Defendants can also waive their right to an attorney and undertake their own defense (*Faretta* v. *California*).

3. The Ethics of Defense
   - Describe the ethical standards applicable to defense attorneys.
   - *Nix* v. *Whiteside*: Lawyers have a duty to reveal known instances of client perjury.

INSTRUCTIONAL CUE LINKED TO THE STUDENT STUDY GUIDE

Student Activity 4 will give students an appreciation for the moral and ethical dilemmas faced by courtroom work group actors.

D. The Bailiff (p. 352)

Bailiff The court officer whose duties are to keep order in the courtroom and to maintain physical custody of the jury. (p. 353)

- The bailiff ensures order, announces the judge's entry, calls witnesses, and prevents the escape of the accused. The bailiff also supervises the jury.

E. Local Court Administrators (p. 353)
- Provide uniform court management

F. The Court Reporter (p. 353)
- Creates the record of all that occurs at trial

G. The Clerk of Court (p. 354)
- Maintains all court records, prepares a jury pool, marks physical evidence for identification, and swears in witnesses

H. Expert Witnesses (p. 355)

Expert Witness A person who has special knowledge and skills recognized by the court as relevant to the determination of guilt or innocence. Unlike lay witnesses, expert witnesses may express opinions or draw conclusions in their testimony. (p. 355)

VII. Nonprofessional Courtroom Participants (p. 356)

A. Lay Witnesses (p. 356)
- Explain that sometimes lay witnesses are ordered to court by subpoenas.

Lay Witness An eyewitness, character witness, or any other person called upon to testify who is not considered an expert. Lay witnesses must testify to facts only and may not draw conclusions or express opinions. (p. 356)

Subpoena A written order issued by a judicial officer or grand jury requiring an individual to appear in court and to give testimony or to bring material to be used as evidence. Some subpoenas mandate that books, papers, and other items be surrendered to the court. (p. 357)

- These witnesses are paid even if they are federal prisoners (*Demarest v. Manspeaker*).
- An increasing number of states have instituted guidelines to protect victims and witnesses. Victim-assistance programs protect the rights of these witnesses.

Victim-Assistance Program An organized program that offers services to victims of crime in the areas of crisis intervention and follow-up counseling and that helps victims secure their rights under the law. (p. 357)

B. Jurors (p. 357)

Juror A member of a trial or grand jury who has been selected for jury duty and is required to serve as an arbiter of the facts in a court of law. Jurors are expected to render verdicts of "guilty" or "not guilty" as to the charges brought against the accused, although they may sometimes fail to do so (as in the case of a hung jury). (p. 357)

- Most states use 12-person juries, but juries can have as few as six people.
- Ideally, the jury is a microcosm of society, representing diversity in race, economic class, age, education, background, and so on.

INSTRUCTIONAL CUE

Stress that juries can be unpredictable. Even in cases in which there is overwhelming evidence in support of a conviction, jurors have been known to return "not guilty" verdicts, reacting more to emotional testimony than facts. One of the best movie portrayals of jury decision making is *12 Angry Men*.

C. The Victim (p. 360)

- Discuss the hardships experienced by victims in the criminal court process.

INSTRUCTIONAL CUE

Have your students imagine what it would be like for a victim to testify at trial. Explain that many victims have to sit outside the courtroom waiting to be called as witnesses. Explain that the process is intimidating, frightening, and overwhelming for victims. Remind students that it is the responsibility of the defense attorney to raise some doubt in the minds of jurors about the suspect's guilt. This can often result in a very painful cross-examination for the victim.

D. The Defendant (p. 361)

- Defendants must be present at trial (*Crosby* v. *U.S.*).
- Defendants have the right to represent themselves, but most choose to use attorneys.

E. Spectators and the Press (p. 361)

- Pretrial publicity may make it difficult to find jurors who have yet to form an opinion on innocence or guilt.

Change of Venue   The movement of a suit or trial from one jurisdiction to another or from one location to another within the same jurisdiction. A change of venue may be made in a criminal case to ensure that the defendant receives a fair trial. (p. 362)

- Cameras in the courtroom can also disrupt proceedings.

Learner Activities

Activity 1

Choose a state and see if you can determine the court structure and jurisdiction of courts in that state. Search for information on the court system on the World Wide Web. In the space provided below, discuss these issues.

_____

_____

_____

_____

_____

Activity 2

Determine whether there is a dispute-resolution center near you. If so, visit that center to learn more about it. Interview professionals and volunteers who work for the center to determine the types of cases handled, the caseload, and how the center supports or replaces traditional court processes. If you are unable to locate a dispute-resolution center, then visit three websites that deal with dispute-resolution and mediation issues. Discuss what you learned about dispute-resolution centers in the space provided below.

_____

_____

_____

_____

_____

_____

Activity 3

The Supreme Court is one of the most powerful institutions in America. The decisions of this Court have had significant impact on both social and criminal justice issues. Some of the greatest legal minds of American history served as justices of the Supreme Court. Through this activity, you will learn more about a justice who served on the Supreme Court. You can choose a current member of the Court or any other historic justice. Use the Web and media databases to identify and gather information about the justice you selected. Use your university library to find additional information. In the space provided below, write a description of the justice you selected, and include a discussion of some of the important cases that he or she helped decide.

_____

_____

_____

_____

_____

_____

Activity 4

Ethical issues for the courtroom work group: Put yourself in the place of each courtroom work group participant listed below and explain how you would handle each ethical dilemma.

THE PROSECUTOR

1. While preparing the case against an accused arson defendant, you discover a witness who provides an alibi for the defendant. Do you tell the defense attorney about your discovery? Would it make any difference if the defendant were involved in organized crime? What if the defendant were charged with murder and arson?

2. After you have successfully prosecuted a rapist, you uncover evidence that indicates that the victim in the case created the story to avenge a love affair that went sour. What do you do? What would you do if you knew that the suspect was charged with rape on two other occasions but was not convicted due to legal technicalities?

THE DEFENSE ATTORNEY

1. You are asked to represent a defendant who cannot afford to pay your full fee at the present time. Should you work out an arrangement so that your client pays you a $1,000 retainer now and pays the rest of the fee if and when she is acquitted (recognizing that conviction would result in incarceration and no real opportunity to earn the money for your fee)?

2. Your client informs you that she did in fact murder her mom. Should you inform the court of this information? Possessing such knowledge, should you allow your client to take the stand and deny her guilt?

THE JUDGE

1. At arraignment, you ask a defendant if he has yet obtained counsel. He replies that he wants to defend himself. He has a fifth-grade education and works as a day laborer for a local construction firm. He is charged with armed robbery and faces ten years in prison. Should you let him defend himself?

2. You are assigned to preside over a jury trial in a gruesome homicide case that has been widely publicized in the area. Although the defense does not request it, should you order a change of venue?

Internet Activity

Use the Cybrary (http://www.cybrary.info) to locate a detailed description of a state court system (perhaps the court system in your home state). Describe the various courts that comprise the system, the staff roles, and the administrative agencies (for example, the administrative office of state courts). Outline the functions of each.

Distance Learning Activity

This distance learning assignment is designed to help you learn more about the U.S. Supreme Court. Visit the Supreme Court's website at http://www.supremecourtus.gov. Explore the various links from this page. List ten facts that you learned about the Supreme Court from this exercise. Submit these facts if your instructor asks you to do so.

Learning Activities Utilizing the World Wide Web

There are student-based activities in the Student Study Guide (Internet Activity, Distance Learning Activity, CJ Today on the World Wide Web) that are similar in focus to those that follow. However, the following are presented as instructor-led activities, to be used in a classroom with online access.

Use the Cybrary (http://www.cybrary.info) to locate a detailed description of a state court system, perhaps the court system in your home stat). Describe the various courts that comprise the system, the staff roles, and the administrative agencies (for example, the administrative office of state courts). Outline the functions of each.

This distance learning assignment is designed to help you learn more about the U.S. Supreme Court. Visit the Supreme Court's website at http://www.supremecourtus.gov. Explore the various links from this page. List ten facts that you learned about the Supreme Court from this exercise. Submit these facts if your instructor asks you to do so.

Other websites for organizations and agencies related to the material in Chapter 9 include:

Supreme Court of the United States	http://www.supremecourtus.gov
U.S. Federal Judiciary	http://www.uscourts.gov
Federal Courts	http://www.law.emory.edu/FEDCTS
National Center for State Courts	http://www.ncsconline.org
Professional Bail Agents of the United States	http://www.pbus.com
CourtTV On-Line	http://www.courttv.com
Courts.Net	http://www.courts.net
Florida CyberCourt Home Page	http://www.flcourts.org
International Court of Justice	http://www.icj-cij.org

Suggested Answers to Chapter Discussion Questions

1. **How did the American court system develop? What are some of the unique features of American court history?**

   The dual-court system is the result of compromise. The nation's founders stressed a need for individual states to retain significant legislative authority and judicial autonomy separate from federal control. States, when joining the union, were assured of limited federal intervention into their affairs. States were free to create laws and create a court system to interpret such laws. Unique features include the fact that state courts do not hear cases of federal law and the federal courts only decide issues of state law when there is a conflict between state statutes and constitutional guarantees.

2. **What is the dual-court system? Why do we have a dual-court system in America?**

   The dual-court system in America is comprised of courts on two levels—the federal and the state. The dual-court system results from America's adoption of the federal system of governance. The federal government holds to itself power over matters that are national in scope while relinquishing power to the states over other matters. This structure necessitates the existence of court systems in each resulting jurisdiction that are empowered to rule on matters from the unique perspective of that jurisdiction's constitution.

3. **What are some of the differences between the state and federal court systems?**

   There are several differences that can be discussed. First, the two court systems have different jurisdiction over various issues of law. Second, the number of cases processed by the two systems is very different. Far more cases are processed through state court than the federal court system. Third, the types of cases processed by the two systems are different, as many more misdemeanors and offenses are processed in state court systems. Finally, state court systems are much more likely to have instituted some informal type of court, such as dispute-resolution centers, to handle some cases.

4. **Who are the professional members of the courtroom work group, and what are their roles?**

- Judge—Ensures justice (balancing rights of accused and the interests of society). Holds ultimate authority.
- Prosecutor—Responsible for presenting the state's case against the defendant; also is a quasi-legal adviser to police departments.
- Defense Counsel—Responsible for representing the accused as soon as possible after arrest and through all stages of the court process.
- Bailiff—Responsible for ensuring order in the court.
- Local Court Administrators—Responsible for facilitating the smooth functioning of courts.
- Court Reporter—Responsible for creating a record of all that occurs during a trial.
- Clerk of Court—Maintains all records of criminal cases, prepares a jury pool, and marks physical evidence during trial.
- Expert Witnesses—Testifies at trial about scientific evidence.

5. **What are the three forms of indigent defense used in the United States?**

The three forms of indigent defense are court-assigned counsel, public defenders, and contractual arrangements.

Why might defendants prefer private attorneys over public counsel?

Attorneys who serve as public counsel often carry notoriously large caseloads and have limited funding for conducting a defense. They often focus on plea bargaining as a means of expediting cases through the system. Defendants believe that the degree of effort they receive from assigned counsel is less than they would receive from paid counsel.

6. **Who are the nonprofessional courtroom participants, and what are their roles?**

- Lay Witnesses—Provide nonexpert testimony, such as eyewitness testimony.
- Jurors—Are the arbiters of facts presented at trial.
- Victim—Works with the prosecutor to obtain a conviction.
- Defendant—Obviously wants to defend himself against the charges.
- Press—Provides an unbiased overview of courtroom proceedings.

7. **What is an expert witness? What is a lay witness? How might their testimony differ?**

An expert witness possesses special knowledge and skills that are recognized by the court as being relevant to the determination of guilt or innocence. A lay witness is anyone called as an eyewitness or character witness or for some other explanatory purpose who is not an expert on relevant topics.

An expert witness's testimony may include opinions or drawn conclusions. A lay witness, on the other hand, must testify to facts alone and is precluded from offering opinions or conclusions on the possible meaning of those facts relevant to the case at trial.

What are some of the issues involved in deciding whether a person is an expert for purposes of testimony?

Expert witnesses can opine and conclude based on their interpretation of the evidentiary material. Conflicting interpretations can lead to opposing opinions and conclusions. The testimony of a single expert witness might give those who hear it a greater degree of understanding. But when two expert witnesses testify with strongly held and convincingly expressed opinions that disagree, it tends to confuse the typical listener. The resulting lack of clarity most often translates to doubt in the minds of the jurors.

8. **How do the professional and nonprofessional courtroom participants work together to bring most criminal trials to a successful close? What do you think a "successful close" might mean to the judge? To the defense attorney? To the prosecutor? To the jury? To the defendant? To the victim?**

Both the professional and nonprofessional courtroom participants work together to bring cases to a successful close by understanding their respective roles. Each party has responsibilities that must be met so that cases can be processed in a way that is in accordance with the law.

A judge might define success as the closure of a trial with all legal requirements met and a verdict rendered. Understandably, the defense attorney and his or her client (the defendant) might define success as an acquittal, while both the prosecutor and the victim would consider a conviction a successful conclusion. For the jury, success might mean arriving at a verdict that left each jury member feeling as if he or she had contributed to the achievement of justice for all parties involved.

Key—Student Study Guide Questions

True or False

_____ 9-1. The prosecution must disclose any evidence related to a case that the defense requests. **(True, p. 345)**

_____ 9-2. The federal court system consists of three tiers, including the U.S. district courts, U.S. courts of appeal, and the U.S. Supreme Court. **(True, p. 336)**

_____ 9-3. Federal judges are usually elected officials who then serve life terms on the bench. **(False, p. 342)**

_____ 9-4. The case of *Marbury* v. *Madison*, decided in 1803, was the first instance in which the U.S. Supreme Court declared its authority to review the actions of Congress to determine whether they comply or conflict with the Constitution. **(True, p. 339)**

_____ 9-5. In the 1993 case of *Herrera* v. *Collins*, the U.S. Supreme Court ruled that new evidence of innocence is not a sufficient reason for a federal court to order a new state trial if there are no constitutional grounds for appeal. **(True, p. 334)**

_____ 9-6. The phrase "courtroom work group" refers to all persons who are licensed to practice law and who earn their living primarily in the courtroom. **(True, p. 340)**

_____ 9-7. The jurisdiction of a court can refer to the territory, subject matter, or persons over which a court may lawfully exercise its authority. **(True, p. 329)**

_____ 9-8. A defense attorney who is aware that her client is about to commit perjury on the stand is obligated to inform the court of this fact, even if it violates the attorney–client privilege. **(True, p. 352)**

_____ 9-9. The Missouri Plan is a method typically used to select state prosecutors. **(False, p. 342)**

_____ 9-10. Dispute-resolution centers are generally not allowed to mediate disputes when criminal charges are pending against either of the disputants. **(False, p. 335)**

Multiple Choice

9-11. Which Supreme Court case decided that state prosecuting attorneys are immune from liability for damages for participating in a probable cause hearing, but not for giving legal advice to the police?
   a. *Imbler* v. *Pachtman* (p. 345)
   b. *Burns* v. *Reed*
   c. *Argersinger* v. *Hamlin*
   d. *Johnson* v. *Zerbt*

9-12. State courts are generally divided into three levels, with _____ at the top of the hierarchy.
   a. courts of limited jurisdiction
   b. intermediate appellate courts
   c. courts of last resort (p. 333)
   d. trial courts

9-13. When the U.S. Supreme Court orders the lower court to "forward up the record" of a case that has been tried so the high court can review it, it issues a
   a. writ of trial *de novo*.
   b. *nolo contendere*.
   c. writ of *mandamus*.
   d. writ of *certiorari*. (p. 340)

9-14. The Missouri Plan is a mechanism suggested by the American Bar Association for
   a. limiting judicial discretion during sentencing.
   b. using the merit plan for selection of judges. (p. 342)
   c. reducing endless appeals by defendants.
   d. speeding the flow of cases through the courts.

9-15. The *jurisdiction* of a court is
   a. the geographic area it covers.
   b. the subject matter it deals with.
   c. its place in the hierarchy of the court system.
   d. all of the above. (p. 329)

9-16. State court administrators are responsible for all of the following except
   a. training support personnel.
   b. ruling on issues of law. (p. 334)
   c. managing court case flow.
   d. coordinating between state court levels and jurisdiction.

9-17. As discussed in the text, criminal law is a field that
   a. attracts many prestigious lawyers.
   b. is a high-status segment of the legal profession.
   c. few law students actively choose to pursue. (p. 346)
   d. has high financial rewards for most practitioners.

9-18. Under the _____ system, legal services for defendants are provided by private practice attorneys paid for by the court and selected from a roster of all practicing criminal attorneys within the jurisdiction of the court.
   a. retained counsel
   b. contract
   c. public defender
   d. court-appointed counsel (p. 347)

9-19. In *Gideon* v. *Wainwright* (1963), the U.S. Supreme Court held that
   a. in federal cases, the right to counsel becomes applicable as soon as a defendant is arrested.
   b. the right to counsel applies not only to state trials of defendants charged with felonies but in all trials of defendants that might result in a jail sentence.
   c. a defendant has a right to counsel when submitting a guilty plea to the court for any offense.
   d. the right to appointed counsel applies to all indigent defendants in state court who are charged with a felony. (p. 347)

9-20. The 1803 case of _____ established the U.S. Supreme Court's authority as final interpreter of the U.S. Constitution.
 a. ***Marbury v. Madison* (p. 339)**
 b. *Herrera* v. *Collins*
 c. *McNabb* v. *U.S.*
 d. *Brady* v. *U.S.*

Fill-In

9-21. The court officer who keeps order in the courtroom and maintains custody of the jury is the _____. **(bailiff, p. 352)**

9-22. _____ of general jurisdiction are the first level of appeal from trial courts of limited jurisdiction. **(Trial courts, p. 331)**

9-23. _____ involves moving a trial from one jurisdiction to another. **(Change of venue, p. 362)**

9-24. The _____ assists with the management of cases, budgeting, and docket administration. **(state court administrator, p. 334)**

9-25. _____ means, literally, "new trial." **(Trial *de novo*, p. 333)**

9-26. The highest-level appellate court in a state system is often referred to as the _____ because no legal recourse remains available to the defendant within the state system. **(court of last resort, p. 333)**

9-27. The lawful authority of a court to review a decision made by a lower court is called _____. **(appellate jurisdiction, p. 331)**

9-28. A(n) _____ is issued when an appellate court agrees to hear a case. It orders the lower court to forward up the records of the case. **(writ of *certiorari*, p. 340)**

9-29. A(n) _____ is a person who has special knowledge recognized by the court as relevant to the determination of the guilt or innocence of the accused. **(expert witness, p. 355)**

9-30. A(n) _____ is a written order requiring someone to appear in court to testify. **(subpoena, p. 357)**

Key—Crossword Puzzle

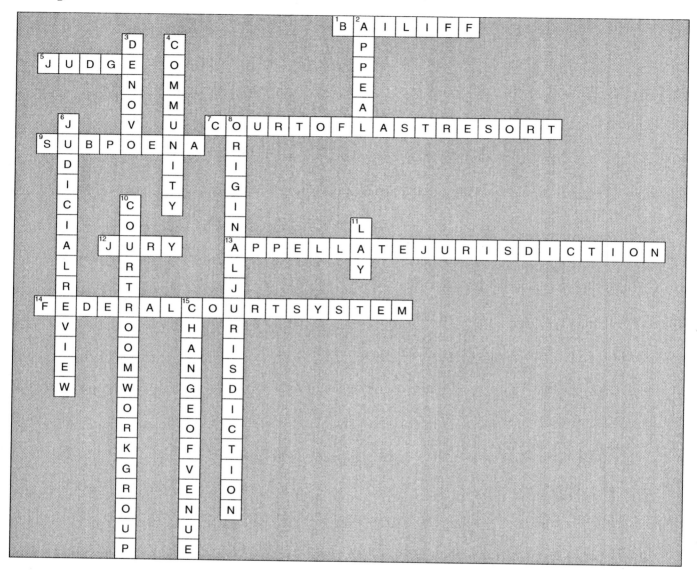

Across

1. Person who tries to maintain order in the court.
5. Elected or appointed public official who presides over a court of law and who is authorized to hear and sometimes to decide cases and to conduct trials.
7. Court authorized by law to hear the final appeal on a matter.
9. Written order that requires a person to appear at a designated court.
12. Group of 6 or 12 persons makes up this.
13. Authority of a court to review a decision made by a lower court.
14. U.S. district courts, U.S. courts of appeal, and U.S. Supreme Court.

Down

2. Review of the judgment, decision, or order of a lower court.
3. New trial.
4. Court that focuses on quality-of-life crimes.
6. Power of a court to review actions and decisions made by other agencies of government.
8. Authority of a court to hear a case from its beginning and to pass judgment.
10. All who earn a living serving the court.
11. Eyewitness is this type of witness.
15. Motion used in a high-profile case.

Key—Word Search Puzzle

Appeal

Appellate Jurisdiction

Bailiff

Change of Venue

Community Court

Courtroom Work Group

Defense Counsel

Expert Witness

Federal Court System

Judge

Judicial Review

Jurisdiction

Juror

Lay Witness

Prosecutor

Prosecutorial Discretion

Public Defender

State Court System

Subpoena

Trial *de Novo*

Victim-Assistance Program

Pretrial Activities and the Criminal Trial

OUTLINE

- Introduction
- Pretrial Activities
- The Criminal Trial
- Stages of a Criminal Trial
- Improving the Adjudication Process

LEARNING OBJECTIVES

After reading this chapter, you should be able to:

- **List and explain the steps typically taken during pretrial activities**
- **Explain plea bargaining, and discuss its impact on the criminal justice system**
- **Describe the various stages of a criminal trial**
- **Explain the hearsay rule, and identify recognized exceptions to it**
- **Explain the possible benefits of a professional jury system**
- **Describe methods that have been suggested for improving the adjudication process**

Chapter Summary

A fundamental concept of criminal justice in the United States is that the criminal justice system is an adversarial system. Justice is achieved when a talented adversary is able to convince a judge or jury that his or her perspective is the correct one. Chapter 10 focuses on two issues central to understanding this adversarial system. First, the text describes pretrial activities. Second, the text describes the trial process.

Chapter 10 describes the early steps of the long and arduous court process. Usually within 48 hours after arrest, a suspect appears before a judge for his or her **first appearance**. During this stage, the legality of the arrest is assessed, the defendant is informed of the charges, and the decision on whether to release or detain pending trial is made. Judges have several bail options as well as a number of alternatives. Some alternative bail programs include **release on recognizance (ROR); property bonds;** deposit bail; **conditional release;** third-party custody; unsecured bond; and signature bond. Some states have enacted danger laws, limiting the right to bail for certain types of offenders. Suspects then experience either a grand jury hearing or a preliminary hearing. There are significant differences between these two types of hearings, but the purpose of both is to filter cases out of the system if there is insufficient evidence to pursue the charges. Finally, the defendant is again informed of the charges and asked to make a plea at the arraignment stage. Defendants will plead either guilty, not guilty, or *nolo contendere* (no contest).

This chapter also provides a discussion of **plea bargaining**. Think of plea bargaining as a negotiation process that involves the defendant, defense counsel, and the prosecutor. Defendants frequently waive their right to a trial and plead guilty, hoping to get something in return, such as a reduced sentence or a reduction in the number of charges. Prosecutors and defense attorneys also benefit from the plea-bargaining process because it helps keep cases moving through the court system. Defendants do have the right to withdraw a plea.

Chapter 10 concludes with a discussion of the trial process. Defendants have the right to a speedy trial, which generally means within 70 days after indictment. Once the trial process is initiated, the first step is **jury selection**. Attorneys, and in some jurisdictions the judge, select members of the jury through the *voir dire* process. Potential jurors can be dismissed by using challenges for cause and **peremptory challenges**. If a case is high profile, the jury will be sequestered for the length of the trial. After the jury is selected, the prosecution and defense will make **opening statements**. After these statements are completed, then the prosecution and the defense present various types of evidence, such as **real, circumstantial**, and **direct. Closing arguments** provide a review and a summation of the evidence. The judge then charges the jury and provides instructions on deliberation. Finally, the jury deliberates on the evidence presented during the trial and returns to the court with a verdict.

Teaching Outline

I. Introduction (p. 370)

II. Pretrial Activities (p. 371)

    A. The First Appearance (p. 371)

First Appearance   An appearance before a magistrate during which the legality of a defendant's arrest is initially assessed and the defendant is informed of the charges on which he or she is being held. At this stage in the criminal justice process, bail may be set or pretrial release may be arranged. Also called *initial appearance*. (p. 371)

- *McNabb* v. *U.S.*: This case is responsible for creating the notion that a suspect should have his or her first appearance within 48 hours of arrest.
- A suspect does not have a right to present evidence but is entitled to representation by counsel at this stage.

1. Pretrial Release
   - Release versus Pretrial Detention

Pretrial Release   The release of an accused person from custody, for all or part of the time before or during prosecution, upon his or her promise to appear in court when required. (p. 372)

   - Most defendants are released after posting bail.

2. Bail

Bail Bond   A document guaranteeing the appearance of the defendant in court as required and recording the pledge of money or property to be paid to the court if he or she does not appear, which is signed by the person to be released and any other persons acting in his or her behalf. (p. 373)

   - Bail helps ensure reappearance of the accused, and it prevents people who have not been convicted from suffering imprisonment.

3. Alternatives to Bail
   - Release on Recognizance (ROR)

Release on Recognizance (ROR)   The pretrial release of a criminal defendant on his or her written promise to appear in court as required. No cash or property bond is required. (p. 374)

   - Property Bonds

Property Bond   The setting of bail in the form of land, houses, stocks, or other tangible property. In the event that the defendant absconds prior to trial, the bond becomes the property of the court. (p. 374)

   - Deposit Bail
     - The court acts as the bail bondsman in some jursidictions.
   - Conditional Release

Conditional Release   The release by executive decision of a prisoner from a federal or state correctional facility who has not served his or her full sentence and whose freedom is contingent on obeying specified rules of behavior. (p. 375)

   - Release with conditions, such as participation in a drug-treatment program
   - Third-Party Custody
     - Release to another individual or agency
   - Unsecured Bond
     - Release with no monetary deposit
   - Signature Bond
     - Release upon the defendant's written promise to appear
     - Limiting the right to bail for some types of offenders

4. Pretrial Release and Public Safety

Danger Law   A law intended to prevent the pretrial release of criminal defendants judged to represent a danger to others in the community. (p. 375)

   - *U.S. v. Hazzard*: This case held that Congress was justified in providing for denial of bail to offenders who represent a danger to the community.

INSTRUCTIONAL CUE LINKED TO THE STUDENT STUDY GUIDE

Student Activity 1 is an exercise in bail decision making.

    B. The Grand Jury (p. 376)
- The federal government and about half the states use a grand jury as part of the pretrial process.
- Grand juries serve primarily as filters.
- Grand jury hearings are secret; the defendant does not have the opportunity to appear before the grand jury and has no right to cross-examine witnesses.

    C. The Preliminary Hearing (p. 376)
- If a state does not use a grand jury, then it will use a preliminary hearing.
- The purpose is to challenge the legal basis of the detention.

Competent to Stand Trial   A finding by a court, when the defendant's sanity at the time of trial is at issue, that the defendant has sufficient present ability to consult with his or her attorney with a reasonable degree of rational understanding and that the defendant has a rational as well as factual understanding of the proceedings against him or her. (p. 377)

- *Sell* v. *U.S.*: The court placed strict limits on the government's power to forcibly medicate some mentally ill defendants to make them competent to stand trial.

    D. Arraignment and the Plea (p. 378)
- Once indicted, the accused will be formally arraigned.
- Here the defendant is again informed of the charges against him or her and is asked to make a plea (for example, guilty, not guilty, or *nolo contendere*).

Plea   In criminal proceedings, a defendant's formal answer in court to the charge contained in a complaint, information, or indictment that he or she is guilty of the offense charged, is not guilty of the offense charged, or does not contest the charge. (p. 378)

Nolo Contendere   A plea of "no contest." A no-contest plea may be used when the defendant does not wish to contest conviction. Because the plea does not admit guilt, however, it cannot provide the basis for later civil suits that might follow a criminal conviction. (p. 378)

    E. Plea Bargaining (p. 378)

Plea Bargaining   The process of negotiating an agreement among the defendant, the prosecutor, and the court as to an appropriate plea and associated sentence in a given case. Plea bargaining circumvents the trial process and dramatically reduces the time required for the resolution of a criminal case. (p. 378)

- *Henderson* v. *Morgan*: The U.S. Supreme Court held that a defendant can withdraw a plea after it has been given.

    III. The Criminal Trial (p. 380)

Rules of Evidence   Rules of court that govern the admissibility of evidence at a criminal hearing and trial. (p. 380)

    A. Nature and Purpose of the Criminal Trial (p. 380)

Adversarial System   The two-sided structure under which American criminal trial courts operate that pits the prosecution against the defense. In theory, justice is done when the most effective adversary is able to convince the judge or jury that his or her perspective on the case is the correct one. (p. 381)

IV. Stages of a Criminal Trial (p. 381)

    A. Trial Initiation: The Speedy Trial Act (p. 382)

Speedy Trial Act   A 1974 federal law requiring that proceedings in a federal criminal case against a defendant begin within a specified period of time, such as 70 working days after indictment. Some states also have speedy trial requirements. (p. 382)

- Discuss the important cases that deal with trial delay.
- *Klopfer* v. *North Carolina*: The Court held that the right to a speedy trial is a fundamental guarantee of the Constitution.
- *Barker* v. *Wingo*: The right to a speedy trial can be violated even in cases where the defendant does not object to the delays.
- *Strunk* v. *United States*: Denial of a speedy trial could result in the dismissal of all charges.
- *U.S.* v. *Taylor*: When the defendant willfully delays the trial, such delays do not apply to the 70-day period (of the Speedy Trial Act) to bring a case to trial.
- *Fex* v. *Michigan*: The 180-day period begins when the prisoner's disposition has been delivered to the court.
- *Doggett* v. *United States*: A delay, resulting from governmental negligence, of nearly nine years violated speedy trial provisions.

    B. Jury Selection (p. 383)

- The court recognizes three types of challenges.
- Challenge to the array is a challenge of the entire jury pool.
- Challenge for cause argues that a juror cannot be fair or impartial.
- Peremptory challenge is a challenge to a juror without giving a reason.

Premptory Challenge   The right to challenge a potential juror without disclosing the reason for the challenge. Prosecutors and defense attorneys routinely use peremptory challenges to eliminate from juries individuals who, although they express no obvious bias, are thought to be capable of swaying the jury in an undesirable direction. (p. 383)

Jury Selection   The process whereby, according to law and precedent, members of a particular trial jury are chosen. (p. 383)

- The key to the jury selection process is *voir dire*.
- Through the *voir dire* process, both the prosecution and defense attorneys question potential jurors.
- *Witherspoon* v. *Illinois*: A person opposed to the death penalty can be excluded from a jury when a death sentence is a possibility.
- *Mu'Min* v. *Virginia*: Pretrial publicity of a case in the news media influences potential jury members. But if a prospective juror can be shown to be unbiased by the publicity, he or she can serve.

Scientific Jury Selection   The use of correlational techniques from the social sciences to gauge the likelihood that potential jurors will vote for conviction or acquittal. (p. 384)

Sequestered Jury   A jury that is isolated from the public during the course of a trial and throughout the deliberation process. (p. 385)

    1. Jury Selection and Race

- *Batson* v. *Kentucky*: The use of peremptory challenges for purposeful discrimination is a violation of the defendant's right to an impartial jury.
- The text discusses several other important Supreme Court decisions on jury selection and race.

- *Powers* v. *Ohio*: The Supreme Court ruled in favor of a white defendant who claimed his rights were violated by excluding blacks through the use of peremptory challenges.
- *Edmonson* v. *Leesville Concrete Co.*: Peremptory challenges in civil trial are not acceptable if based on race.
- *Georgia* v. *McCollum*: Defendants cannot use their peremptory challenges to exclude jurors based on race.
- *Campbell* v. *Louisiana*: The court held that a white criminal defendant can raise equal protection and due process objections to discrimination against blacks in the selection of grand jurors.

INSTRUCTIONAL CUE LINKED TO THE STUDENT STUDY GUIDE

Student Activity 3 will help students understand the early stages of the trial process.

    C. Opening Statements (p. 387)

Opening Statement The initial statement of an attorney or the defense, made in a court of law to a judge, or to a judge and jury, describing the facts that he or she intends to present during trial to prove the case. (p. 387)

- The purpose of opening statements is to advise the jury of what the attorneys intend to prove and to describe how proof will be offered.

    D. The Presentation of Evidence (p. 387)

        1. Types of Evidence

Evidence Anything useful to a judge or jury in deciding the facts of a case. Evidence may take the form of witness testimony, written documents, videotapes, magnetic media, photographs, physical objects, and so on. (p. 387)

Direct Evidence Evidence that, if believed, directly proves a fact. Eyewitness testimony and videotaped documentation account for the majority of all direct evidence heard in the criminal courtroom. (p. 387)

Circumstantial Evidence Evidence that requires interpretation or that requires a judge or jury to reach a conclusion based upon what the evidence indicates. From the close proximity of a smoking gun to the defendant, for example, the jury might conclude that she pulled the trigger. (p. 387)

Real Evidence Evidence that consists of physical material or traces of physical activity. (p. 388)

        2. The Evaluation of Evidence
- *Michigan* v. *Lucas*: The U.S. Supreme Court ruled that the Sixth Amendment right to confront witnesses may not extend to evidence of a prior sexual relationship between a rape victim and criminal defendant.

Probative Value The degree to which a particular item of evidence is useful in, and relevant to, providing something important in a trial. (p. 389)

        3. The Testimony of Witnesses

Testimony Oral evidence offered by a sworn witness on the witness stand during a criminal trial. (p. 390)

- Defendants do not have to take the stand, and if they do not, prosecutors and judges cannot comment on this fact (*Griffin* v. *California*).
- Direct examination
- Cross-examination

Perjury   The intentional making of a false statement as part of the testimony by a sworn witness in a judicial proceeding on a matter relevant to the case at hand. (p. 390)

    4. Children as Witnesses
- *Coy* v. *Iowa*: The Court decided that a courtroom screen used to shield a child witness from the defendant violated the confrontation clause of the Sixth Amendment.
- *Maryland* v. *Craig*: In this case, however, the Court held that allowing a child to testify using closed-circuit television does not violate the confrontation clause.
- *White* v. *Illinois*: This case allowed testimony by a medical provider and a babysitter, who repeated what a child had said, to be heard.

    5. The Hearsay Rule

Hearsay   Something that is not based upon the personal knowledge of a witness. Witnesses who testify about something they have heard, for example, are offering hearsay by repeating information about a matter of which they have no direct knowledge. (p. 391)

Hearsay Rule   The long-standing precedent that hearsay cannot be used in American courtrooms. Rather than accepting testimony based upon hearsay, the court will ask that the person who was the original source of the hearsay information be brought into court to be questioned and cross-examined. Exceptions to the hearsay rule may occur when the person with direct knowledge is dead or is otherwise unable to testify. (p. 391)

- Exceptions to the hearsay rule
- Dying declaration
- Spontaneous statement
- Out-of-court statements

    E. Closing Arguments (p. 391)

Closing Argument   An oral summation of a case presented to a judge, or to a judge and jury, by the prosecution or by the defense in a criminal trial. (p. 391)

INSTRUCTIONAL CUE LINKED TO THE STUDENT STUDY GUIDE

Student Activity 4 illustrates various aspects of the trial process to students.

    F. The Judge's Charge to the Jury (p. 392)
    G. Jury Deliberations and the Verdict (p. 392)

Verdict   The decision of the jury in a jury trial or of a judicial officer in a nonjury trial. (p. 392)

    1. Problems with the Jury System
- Problems include emotions being confused with fact, confusion over legal technicalities, and inattention during long trials.
- Professional Jurors

INSTRUCTIONAL CUE

Compile the facts and witness information for one specific case. Ask students to decide which witnesses could support the prosecution's case and which witnesses would support the defense's case. With the help of the class, walk the case through the trial process, giving examples of opening and closing statements and the types of questions asked on direct, and highlight important points for cross-examination.

    V. Improving the Adjudication Process (p. 393)

Learner Activities

Activity 1

BAIL OR NO BAIL?

1. Salvadore Lopez is a 52-year-old farm worker who cannot read. He has a wife and two children. Lopez was charged with smuggling guns, marijuana, and other narcotics across the Mexican border. The prosecutor, when discussing the case with the news media, says that he suspects Lopez was involved with guns and drugs for years but, until now, has avoided being arrested by authorities. Lopez claims that he is completely innocent and wouldn't know what marijuana looked like if he saw it. Should he be detained or released? How much bail would you set in order to release? What other information would you need to know?

2. Roger A. Kooney is a 27-year-old electrical engineer. Kooney is charged with vehicular homicide stemming from the death of Chris Pariano. Pariano was stepping out of his pickup truck when Kooney sped down the wrong side of the street. Kooney was drunk at the time, according to police. The police also learned that he had eight previous convictions for drunken driving and 19 other serious vehicular offenses. Should he be detained or released? How much bail would you set in order to release? What other information would you need to know?

3. Edward Savitz is a 50-year-old single man who has a good-paying full-time job and lives in an expensive high-rise apartment. He is charged with the statutory rape of a 16-year-old, sexual abuse of two others, and corrupting the morals of a minor. It is alleged that he paid to have sex with hundreds of boys, but on all occasions the young men agreed to participate. The maximum sentence that he can receive for his crimes is five to ten years. Savitz has tested positive for HIV, the virus that causes AIDS. Should he be detained or released? How much bail would you set in order to release? What other information would you need to know?

4. At the age of 19, Frank Anderson was convicted of rape and sentenced to prison for three years. Approximately one year after his release, he became a suspect in a number of robberies of women. He threatened a number of the victims with bodily harm if they filed complaints. One 21-year-old victim nevertheless agreed to cooperate with the authorities, and Anderson was arrested and charged with robbery. Shortly after his initial appearance, he was released on bail. Anderson then broke into the 21-year-old woman's house, beat her, kicked her numerous times, and stole $3,000 and a gun. The victim suffered a concussion and needed seven stitches. Anderson was identified and again apprehended and was charged with an additional count of robbery. Should he be detained or released? How much bail would you set in order to release? What other factors would you need to know?

5. An 18-year-old girl, Kim Walak, was arrested for shoplifting. She claimed to be indigent (poor), with no steady source of income; she lived with an unemployed boyfriend; and she had dropped out of school in the eleventh grade. She had one prior arrest for shoplifting, but those charges were dismissed for unknown reasons. Should she be detained or released? How much bail would you set in order to release? What other factors would you need to know?

_____

_____

_____

_____

_____

_____

Activity 2

Historically, courts have resisted allowing cameras in our nation's courtrooms out of a fear that it would adversely impact a defendant's right to a fair trial. Courts were concerned that the media's search for the sensational would turn our courtrooms into sideshows. For example, when Bruno Hauptmann was accused of kidnapping the Lindbergh baby, he was convicted in an atmosphere of circus sensationalism that degraded the entire judicial process. Among other things, the prosecutor gave newspaper interviews constantly; although the judge prohibited cameras from taking pictures, a reporter brought a camera into the courtroom and took pictures; and during the trial, the public applauded state witnesses. Hauptmann was convicted, and appellate courts ruled that the publicity did not bias the final decision. Recently the U.S. Supreme Court decided that it was not unconstitutional for cameras to be in our nation's courtrooms. As discussed in the text, the majority of states now permit such coverage.

Do you think cameras should be allowed in trial courts of general jurisdiction? Be sure to discuss the pros and cons of having cameras in the courtroom. Do you think cameras influence jury verdicts? Why or why not?

Activity 3

Go to the CourtTV website at http://www.courttv.com. This website provides a discussion of many current and famous cases that have received publicity across the country. Choose one of the cases presented on the website, and read the facts of the case. In the space provided below, write an opening statement for the prosecutor and an opening statement for the defense attorney. Be sure to use the facts of the case in your statement.

Activity 4

Attend a trial at a local courthouse. In the space provided below, describe the case and the steps of the trial you saw. Were you able to see the complete trial? What was the verdict? Was a jury present? What trial stages did you see? What types of witnesses were called to present evidence? What types of evidence were presented? Was the victim present? What was the defendant's demeanor during testimony? Did the jury appear to be attentive?

_____

_____

_____

_____

Internet Activity

Visit Cornell University Law School's Legal Information Institute at http://www.law.cornell.edu. Describe each of the site's features, paying special attention to the resources available in the sections entitled "Court Opinions," "Law by Source or Jurisdiction," and "Constitutions and Codes." After exploring each feature, describe in detail those that you find most useful. Why do you especially like those features?

_____

_____

_____

_____

_____

_____

Distance Learning Activity

This distance learning exercise will be challenging and time-consuming, but it is an effective way to highlight the stages of the criminal trial. Search the World Wide Web for information about a specific criminal trial. In the space below, highlight the key facts of the case. What facts do you think the prosecutor will emphasize? What facts will the defense attorney emphasize?

_____

_____

_____

_____

_____

Learning Activities Utilizing the World Wide Web

There are student-based activities in the Student Study Guide (Internet Activity, Distance Learning Activity, CJ Today on the World Wide Web) that are similar in focus to those that follow. However, the following are presented as instructor-led activities, to be used in a classroom with online access.

Visit Cornell University Law School's Legal Information Institute at http://www.law.cornell.edu. In class, display each of the site's features, paying special attention to the resources available in the sections entitled "Court Opinions," "Law by Source or Jurisdiction," and "Constitutions and Codes." After exploring each feature, lead a discussion of those the class finds most useful. Why are these features most useful as compared to the others?

This distance learning exercise will be challenging and time-consuming, but it is an effective way to highlight the stages of the criminal trial. Search the World Wide Web for information about a specific criminal trial. For class display, highlight the key facts of the case. To begin a class discussion, ask: What facts do you think the prosecutor will emphasize? What facts will the defense attorney emphasize?

Other websites for organizations and agencies related to the material in Chapter 10 include:

Office of the U.S. Attorney General	http://www.usdoj.gov/ag
American Bar Foundation	http://www.abf-sociolegal.org
Prosecuting Attorneys, District Attorneys, Attorneys General and U.S. Attorneys	http://www.co.eaton.mi.us/ecpa /proslist.htm
Delaware Public Defender Home Page	http://www.state.de.us/govern/ agencies/pubdefen/indexpd.htm
Federal Magistrate Judges' Association	http://www.fedjudge.org
Illinois Office of the State Appellate Defender	http://www.state.il.us/defender
National Jurist Online for Future Lawyers	http://www.natjurist.com
New York State Defenders Association	http://www.nysda.org
Citizens for Effective Justice	http://www.reducecrime.org
Trial Lawyers for Public Justice	http://www.tlpj.org

Suggested Answers to Chapter Discussion Questions

1. **What steps are typically taken during pretrial activities (that is, before the start of a criminal trial)?**
   - First appearance (which includes the bail decision)
   - Grand jury or preliminary hearing
   - Arraignment and the plea
   - Plea bargaining

2. **What is plea bargaining, and what is its purpose? What impact does plea bargaining have on the criminal justice system? Given the issues associated with plea-bargaining, do you believe that it is an acceptable practice? Explain.**

   Plea bargaining is the negotiation process that occurs among defendant, prosecutor, and defense counsel. Its purpose is to provide a mutual agreement of these parties and the disposition of the case.

   Plea bargaining is essential to case processing. Prosecutors are able to get convictions, even if they have weak evidence, because of plea bargaining. The adversarial standard of proof beyond a reasonable doubt is difficult to achieve, and thus plea bargaining provides a sure thing. It also is beneficial to the entire court process, as the process saves time and resources of all parties since case preparation for trial is not completed. The existence of plea bargaining has also created an informal system in courthouses, as parties agree to common going rates, allowing for the smooth processing of cases.

   Detractors of the plea bargaining process point to the public's perception that offenders manipulate the process to escape just punishment. They see this as the strongest argument against plea bargaining. Such people cite denial of society's sense of justice when an offender receives a lesser degree of punishment than his or her actions might otherwise deserve.

Its supporters contend that plea bargaining is an essential and effective means of moving cases through an expensive and overburdened system. In the absence of plea bargaining, they say, the sheer volume of cases would overwhelm the system, causing it to grind to a halt.

Most people find plea bargaining acceptable simply because the alternative—significant expansion of the criminal justice system at extraordinary expense—is just not economically feasible.

3. **What are the various stages of a criminal trial? Describe each one.**

- Trial initiation. It is important to note that there are time limitations on the processing of cases.
- Jury selection. Jury members are selected from the public for jury duty. Prosecuting and defense attorneys question (*voir dire*) prospective jury members and eliminate them by making peremptory and for-cause challenges.
- Opening statements. Opening statements begin the presentation of information to the jury. Opening statements provide an opportunity for the prosecution and defense to describe what they intend to prove.
- Presentation of evidence. The state presents its evidence, and then the defense follows. Evidence presented includes direct, circumstantial, real, and hearsay.
- Closing arguments. Closing arguments are an oral summation of the case.
- Judge's charge to the jury. The judge instructs the jury about the evidence presented and matters of law and describes the deliberation process.
- Jury deliberations and the verdict. The jury discusses the case, takes votes, and ultimately reaches a verdict.

4. **What is the hearsay rule? Under what circumstances might a dying declaration be a valid exception to the hearsay rule? What other exceptions to the hearsay rule have courts recognized?**

The hearsay rule is the long-standing precedent that hearsay cannot be used in American courtrooms. Rather than accepting testimony based upon hearsay, the court will ask that the person who was the original source of the hearsay information be brought into court to be questioned and cross-examined.

A dying declaration is a statement made by a person who is about to die. When such statements relate to the cause and circumstances of the impending death, they may usually be repeated at trial (by those who heard them) as an exception to the hearsay rule. Most courts accept the truth of such statements on grounds that in the face of impending death, the dying individual would be unlikely to lie because he or she wishes to have a clear conscience.

Spontaneous statements and out-of-court statements are other exceptions.

5. **Do you think the present jury system is outmoded? Why?**

Some think the present jury system is not so much outmoded as it is overmanipulated. The tailoring of juries during *voir dire* to achieve a desired racial, ethnic, or gender balance is disconcerting to many. Their simplistic view of the requirement for a trial before a randomly selected jury means just that—pick 12 people at random, put them in the jury box, hold the trial.

Others, however, believe changes to the jury process are essential. An oft-heard recommendation is for reduction of the size requirement from 12 members to six. Some advocate elimination of the current random selection process as being too expensive and time-consuming. They suggest establishment of a professional jury system to improve efficiency.

How might a professional jury system be more effective than the present system of peer jurors?

Proponents of the professional jury concept suggest such a system would provide greater dependability, would provide a jury pool with greater understanding of the law and legal processes, and would enhance equity by reducing the impact of emotionalism.

Opponents say the notion of professional jurors is an idea whose time should never come. They suggest jurors might vote based not on the evidence presented but on the fact that the accused "fits the type" for a ruling of guilt or innocence, an opinion based on the jurors' previous trial experiences.

6. How might the adjudication process be improved?

There have been several proposals for improvement: first, court unification to eliminate the overlapping and fragmented jurisdictions of court decision making; second, court-watch citizen groups; third, statistical measurement of court performance.

Key—Student Study Guide Questions

True or False

_____ 10-1. The process by which a potential juror is interviewed by the prosecutor and defense counsel is *voir dire*. **(True, p. 383)**

_____ 10-2. If a defendant chooses not to testify at his or her trial, the prosecutor is allowed to point out to the jury that an innocent person would want to take the stand in an effort to clear his or her name. **(False, p. 390)**

_____ 10-3. In a challenge for cause, a juror can be excused by either the defense or prosecution, and no reason for doing so needs to be stated. **(False, p. 383)**

_____ 10-4. Grand juries meet in secret, and a person under investigation has no legal right to be present or even notified of a grand jury investigation. **(True, p. 376)**

_____ 10-5. The U.S. Supreme Court has ruled that plea bargaining is an important and necessary component of the American system of justice. **(True, p. 379)**

_____ 10-6. A witness's statement that she didn't see the defendant commit the crime but did see him arguing with and threatening the victim shortly before the crime occurred is an example of circumstantial evidence. **(True, p. 387)**

_____ 10-7. A sequestered jury is isolated from the public during the course of a trial and throughout the deliberation process. **(True, p. 385)**

_____ 10-8. A challenge to the array indicates that the defense attorney does not believe that the pool from which the jury is being selected is representative of the community at large. **(True, p. 383)**

_____ 10-9. According to the decision in *McNabb* v. *United States*, a person in custody must have an appearance in court within 48 hours of his or her arrest. **(True, p. 371)**

_____ 10-10. Hearsay evidence is automatically excluded from the courtroom, regardless of the circumstances. **(False, p. 391)**

Multiple Choice

10-11. The _____ is a sort of "mini-trial" that allows the defendant to challenge the legal basis for his or her detention by examining the evidence in the case and attempting to have it disallowed or refuted.
   a. grand jury
   b. arraignment
   c. preliminary hearing (p. 376)
   d. first appearance

10-12. A purpose of bail is to
   a. examine the sufficiency of the evidence against the accused.
   b. ensure the appearance of the accused individual at trial. (p. 373)
   c. deter future offenses.
   d. protect the community from criminals.

10-13. _____ programs release defendants on their own after a promise to appear at court, with no requirement for posting a cash or property bond.
   a. Voluntary community release
   b. Signature bond
   c. Preventive detention
   d. Release on recognizance (p. 374)

10-14. A grand jury has all of the following characteristics and duties except that it does not
   a. determine if an accused individual should be held over for an actual trial.
   b. meet in secret, with no opportunity for the accused to cross-examine witnesses.
   c. have the option to initiate prosecution independent of the prosecutor.
   d. deliver a verdict of guilty or not guilty in criminal trials. (p. 376)

10-15. The advantage of a plea of *nolo contendere* over a guilty plea is that it
   a. usually results in a lighter sentence for the offender.
   b. protects the accused in the event of a subsequent civil suit. (p. 378)
   c. limits the judge's sentencing alternatives.
   d. allows the defendant to use a legal loophole to avoid responsibility.

10-16. In what year did Congress pass the federal Speedy Trial Act?
   a. 2000
   b. 1985
   c. 1980
   d. 1974 (p. 382)

10-17. In jury selection, challenges for cause
   a. are only made by the defense.
   b. are not required to be justified by the attorney requesting the challenge.
   c. deal with sound legal reasons for removing potential jurors. (p. 383)
   d. are ruled upon by the prosecuting attorney.

10-18. Which constitutional amendment guarantees a right to an impartial jury?
   a. Fourth
   b. Sixth (p. 383)
   c. Fifth
   d. Eighth

10-19. *Voir dire* is used to determine
   a. judicial bias.
   b. if prospective jurors are biased or hold preconceived notions of guilt or innocence. (p. 383)
   c. the validity of a claim of prosecutorial misconduct.
   d. whether the racial makeup of an impaneled jury violates Supreme Court guidelines.

10-20. The murder weapon would primarily be considered _____ evidence.
   a. direct
   b. real (p. 388)
   c. testimonial
   d. damning

Fill-In

10-21. _____ is that which requires interpretation or that which requires the judge or jury to reach a conclusion based upon what the evidence indicates. **(Circumstantial evidence, p. 387)**

10-22. _____ consists of physical material or traces of physical activity such as tire tracks. **(Real evidence, p. 388)**

10-23. Removing an unwanted potential juror without the need to disclose a reason for the removal is accomplished by means of a(n) _____. **(peremptory challenge, p. 383)**

10-24. _____ is the pretrial release of a defendant based on a written promise to appear at future hearings. **(Release on recognizance, p. 374)**

10-25. An appearance before a magistrate at which the legality of the defendant's arrest is reviewed and the defendant is informed of the charges is called the _____. **(first appearance, p. 371)**

10-26. A(n) _____ is a sort of "mini-trial" in which the defendant has the opportunity to challenge the legal basis for his or her detention by examining the evidence in the case and attempting to refute it. **(preliminary hearing, p. 376)**

10-27. _____ is a false statement made by a sworn witness during a judicial proceeding. **(Perjury, p. 390)**

10-28. _____ is a plea of "no contest." ***(Nolo contendere*, p. 378)**

10-29. Court rules that govern the admissibility of evidence at criminal hearings and trials are called _____. **(rules of evidence, p. 380)**

10-30. _____ is a statement that is not based upon the personal knowledge of a witness. **(Hearsay, p. 391)**

Key—Crossword Puzzle

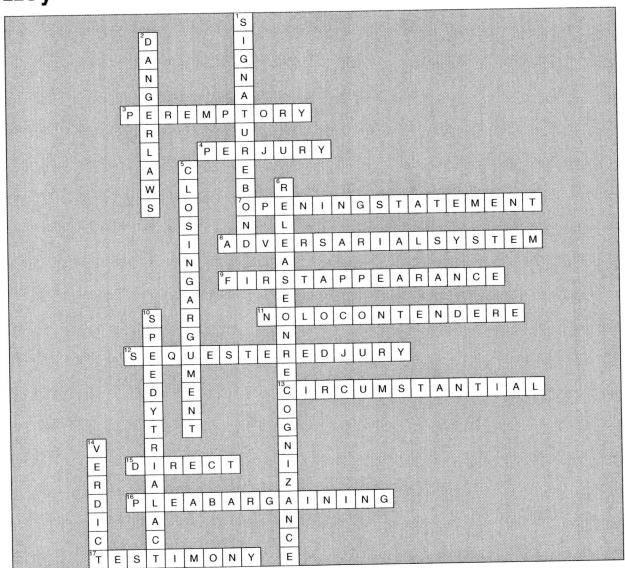

Across

3. Limited number of these types of challenges.
4. What people commit when they lie on the witness stand.
7. Initial statement of an attorney.
8. Two-sided structure under which American criminal trial courts operate that pits the prosecution against the defense.
9. Court stage at which bail is typically set.
11. No contest.
12. Jury isolated from the public.
13. Evidence that requires interpretation.
15. Eyewitness testimony is this type of evidence.
16. Process of negotiating an agreement among the defendant, the prosecutor, and the court as to an appropriate plea and associated sentence in a given case.
17. Oral evidence offered by a sworn witness.

Down

1. It allows release based on the defendant's written promise to appear.
2. Laws that limit the right to bail for certain kinds of offenders.
5. Oral summation of a case.
6. Release by promise.
10. Act that establishes the time periods required for a case to be processed by the court system.
14. Decision of the jury.

Key—Word Search Puzzle

```
M G Q G O R D C L O S I N G A R G U M E N T C U S B K I V O
G U V P Q T X Y A D V E R S A R I A L S Y S T E M U L T W B
Y V W F N O L O C O N T E N D E R E U O V O F K T Y Y E B H
O W B D Y Y M I U D L D R W I R V J P H R Y H C I O G X T N
D W E H T G T Z J V M P R S D R X B I E D I L Z Z T Z P G U
A Z F M P R E T R I A L R E L E A S E N R M Q A E U J S N J
F J H E A R S A Y S M W Q Z L G Y B H M M J J L W E N C G Z
C Z D R V O E A T U Z T Q Q J Q E W O C Z U E I T C I R R
O S D B D H O C Q I X I I C B O K Q D S I K J R C S Q E U E
N Y I Y P S C S I U F T E V I D E N C E S T P A Y P U N L L
D Q Z V V E T W O R E Y N W F G G S F L E N L B K Y I T E E
I S Y B F P R K T S C S N Y J I M P U G J A O I Y M K I S A
T Q Z D A B Z E D H V U T O V W R F G W I G L Q F T O F O S
I T P R A I O Y M U P A M E V Y R S W R Q I R X T Y O I F E
O E Z Q E N L P O P N R G S R J Y I T S U A N J E N B C E O
N S D A X A G B E I T L O F T E E Y E A N X A J S T S J V N
A T J I I E L E O N U O V P W A D A V P P N I W S Y P U I R
L I U H R J P E R N I B R U E E N J W Y L P P R O M Z R D E
R M R C F E G P V L D N Y Y E R Z T U K A E E X C G M Y E C
E O Y Q R F C R Q I A K G P C E T A I R T V A A Y O K S N O
L N S D V O N T K Z D W S S D H O Y I A Y S Q F R S M E E G
E C L W G E R G R V G K N F A A T L X O A E M E W L N E X N
A Y E F J V P D N O I L X C O A T S L A N R V G C U L C P I
S E H C F C P E D I S H D Q I E I R E W E A D E I O O D T E A
O I T U A F C D F C W N E M J G K M M T N I V P D I V I S N C
J P I N B C S U I R T L E N V I H H S E F G R A E A O B C
X E O Q A L I J Z K B Y T H C H G D G D N L E J P S N N J E
I M N A V V Z L Y F A Q O C E E O P Z J T K S L X P C L E
C O M P E T E N T T O S T A N D T R I A L S I Q V Z I G E N
```

Adversarial System

Bail Bond

Circumstantial Evidence

Closing Argument

Competent to Stand Trial

Conditional Release

Danger Law

Direct Evidence

Evidence

First Appearance

Hearsay

Jury Selection

Nolo Contendere

Opening Statement

Peremptory Challenge

Perjury

Plea

Pretrial Release

Property Bond

Real Evidence

Release on Recognizance

Rules of Evidence

Scientific Jury Selection

Sequestered Jury

Speedy Trial Act

Testimony

Verdict

CHAPTER 11

Sentencing

LEARNING OBJECTIVES

After reading this chapter, you should be able to:

- Describe the five goals of contemporary criminal sentencing
- Illustrate the difference between indeterminate and structured sentencing
- Describe the different types of structured sentencing models in use today
- Define mandatory sentencing, and explain how it came about
- Describe truth in sentencing
- Explain the importance of federal sentencing guidelines
- Describe the nature and importance of the presentence investigation report
- Describe the history of victims' rights and services, and discuss the growing role of the victim in criminal justice proceedings today
- List the four traditional sentencing options
- Outline the arguments for and against capital punishment

Chapter Summary

Duane Harris, having recently pleaded guilty to one count of armed robbery, stood before Judge Joe Marist waiting to hear his sentence. The judge, known by his peers as "Hanging Joe," sentenced Duane to the maximum possible sentence under the law: ten to 25 years in a maximum-security prison. Why did the judge decide to sentence Harris to the longest prison term possible? What factors did he consider to arrive at his sentence? What other options did he have? Could he have sentenced him to a longer term? Could he have sentenced him to death for the crime?

The text discusses several important aspects of sentencing in Chapter 11. The text describes five goals of contemporary sentencing: retribution, incapacitation, deterrence, rehabilitation, and restoration. **Retribution** corresponds to the just deserts model of sentencing and is best understood from the biblical reference to "eye for an eye, tooth for a tooth." **Incapacitation** seeks to isolate offenders from society. **Deterrence**, both **specific** and **general**, focuses on preventing crimes. **Rehabilitation** seeks to change the offender, and **restoration** seeks to make the victim "whole again."

Chapter 11 also describes types of sentencing practices. Harris was convicted in a state that uses an **indeterminate sentencing** model. Judges have the most discretion in states adhering to this model. A judge is expected to assess the differences among cases, situations, and offenders in an attempt to tailor the sentence to be appropriate and proportionate. It is also believed that offenders will be more likely to participate in rehabilitation programs if they can reduce the amount of time served.

The text highlights several problems with the indeterminate sentencing model. The most significant criticism is the inequality of sentences. Harris received the maximum possible sentence under the law. It is possible that another offender, sentenced by another judge in an adjacent courtroom, could receive a probation sentence or significantly fewer years in prison. The personalities of different judges, race of the offender, race of the victim, and social class have all been shown to be factors contributing to disparities in sentences.

In response to the various problems of indeterminate sentencing systems, states and the federal government have revised sentencing practices in order to structure sentencing more precisely. For example, some states have adopted a **determinate sentencing model** that requires offenders to be sentenced to a fixed term. Other states have developed **voluntary/advisory sentencing guidelines**, and some have adopted **presumptive sentencing guidelines**. Guideline jurisdictions specify a presumptive sentence for an offense but also allow the judge to consider **aggravating** and **mitigating** factors. Another type of structured sentencing discussed in the text is **mandatory sentencing**.

In general, judges try to make informed and fair sentencing decisions. The **presentence investigation report** assists judges with their decisions. Provided as a detailed report, as an abbreviated report, or as an oral report to the court, the presentence investigation report provides information about the defendant and the offense. It may also include a recommendation from the probation officer. Another factor that judges may consider when deciding the sentence is the impact of the crime on the victim. **Victim-impact statements** provide an opportunity for crime victims, or surviving family members of a victim, to describe the suffering caused by the crime.

Finally, the text discusses the typical sentencing options available to the judge. Imprisonment and probation are mentioned but are discussed in more detail in later chapters of the text. The frequent use of fines as a criminal sanction is also discussed. Chapter 11 concludes with a discussion of capital punishment.

There are currently nearly 3,500 offenders on death row. The number of offenders executed in a year is relatively small, but those numbers will probably increase because of Supreme Court rulings on *habeas corpus* review. **Capital punishment** is one issue that generates considerable debate. Many people oppose the death penalty because they believe it is not an effective deterrent to crime, is not applied fairly, or is costly and because there is always a risk of killing an innocent person. However, most of the public supports capital punishment. Revenge, just deserts, and protection are the key supporting arguments of retentionists.

Teaching Outline

  I. Introduction (p. 402)

Sentencing The imposition of a criminal sanction by a judicial authority. (p. 402)

  II. The Philosophy and Goals of Criminal Sentencing (p. 403)

     A. Retribution (p. 403)

Retribution The act of taking revenge upon a criminal perpetrator. (p. 403)

- Corresponds to the just deserts model of sentencing

Just Deserts A model of criminal sentencing that holds that criminal offenders deserve the punishment they receive at the hands of the law and that punishments should be appropriate to the type and severity of the crime committed. (p. 403)

- The primary sentencing tools of the just deserts model are prison and death.

     B. Incapacitation (p. 404)

Incapacitation The use of imprisonment or other means to reduce the likelihood that an offender will be capable of committing future offenses. (p. 404)

- The "lock 'em up" approach

     C. Deterrence (p. 404)

Deterrence A goal of criminal sentencing that seeks to inhibit criminal behavior through the fear of punishment. (p. 404)

Specific Deterrence A goal of criminal sentencing that seeks to prevent a particular offender from engaging in repeat criminality. (p. 404)

General Deterrence A goal of criminal sentencing that seeks to prevent others from committing crimes similar to the one for which a particular offender is being sentenced by making an example of the person sentenced. (p. 404)

- Contrast deterrence and retribution: Retribution focuses on the past; deterrence focuses on the future.

     D. Rehabilitation (p. 404)

Rehabilitation The attempt to reform a criminal offender. Also, the state in which a reformed offender is said to be. (p. 404)

- This approach first became popular in the 1930s, but the emphasis on this philosophy declined dramatically after Martinson published his research stating that "nothing works" to reduce recidivism.

     E. Restoration (p. 405)

Restoration A goal of criminal sentencing that attempts to make the victim "whole again." (p. 405)

Restorative Justice A sentencing model that builds upon restitution and community participation in an attempt to make the victim "whole again." (p. 405)

- Stress that the dominant philosophies guiding sentencing decisions today are incapacitation and deterrence. An effective way to demonstrate the predominance of these philosophies is to show a graph illustrating the number of incarcerated prisoners over time. Even with declining crime rates, the number of defendants sentenced to incarceration continues to grow.

  III. Indeterminate Sentencing (p. 406)

Indeterminate Sentencing A model of criminal punishment that encourages reha-bilitation via the use of general and relatively unspecified sentences (such as a term of imprisonment of from one to ten years). (p. 406)

- It relies heavily on judges' discretion.
- Parole is an important aspect of the indeterminate model.
- The primary determinant of the amount of time actually served is the inmate's behavior while incarcerated.

INSTRUCTIONAL CUE

Provide students with the sentencing options when operating under an indeterminate sentencing model. For example, a defendant convicted of burglary could be sentenced to a fine, probation, five to ten years in prison, or ten to 25 years, depending on the judge's decision. Use examples like this to highlight the problems with the indetermi-nate sentencing model.

A. Critiques of Indeterminate Sentencing (p. 407)
- It contributes to inequality in sentencing, and decisions are influ-enced by judicial personality and social characteristics of the defen-dant.
- Defense attorneys manipulate the system to appear before the "right" judge.
- It produces dishonesty in sentencing.
- Time served is generally far less than what is indicated on the books.

Gain Time The amount of time deducted from time to be served in prison on a given sentence for participation in special projects or programs. (p. 407)

Good Time The amount of time deducted from time to be served in prison on a given sentence as a consequence of good behavior. (p. 407)

IV. Structured Sentencing (p. 408)
- The problems with indeterminate sentencing led many states to revise their sentencing codes. States were concerned that three fundamental sentenc-ing principles were being ignored.

Proportionality A sentencing principle that holds that the severity of sanctions should bear a direct relationship to the seriousness of the crime committed. (p. 408)

Equity A sentencing principle, based upon concerns with social equality, that holds that similar crimes should be punished with the same degree of severity, regardless of the social or personal characteristics of the offenders. (p. 408)

Social Debt A sentencing principle that holds that an offender's criminal history should objectively be taken into account in sentencing decisions. (p. 408)

INSTRUCTIONAL CUE LINKED TO THE STUDENT STUDY GUIDE

Use Student Activity 1 to help students evaluate issues of equity, proportionality, and social debt.

- These concerns were addressed by adopting variously structured sentenc-ing models.

Structured Sentencing A model of criminal punishment that includes determinate and commission-created presumptive sentencing schemes, as well as voluntary/advi-sory sentencing guidelines. (p. 408)

Determinate Sentencing A model of criminal punishment in which an offender is given a fixed term that may be reduced by good time or gain time. Under the model, for example, all offenders convicted of the same degree of burglary would be sentenced to the same length of time behind bars. (p. 408)

Voluntary/Advisory Sentencing Guidelines Recommended sentencing policies that are not required by law. (pp. 408–409)

Presumptive Sentencing A model of criminal punishment that meets the following conditions: (1) The appropriate sentence for an offender convicted of a specific charge is presumed to fall within a range of sentences authorized by sentencing guidelines that are adopted by a legislatively created sentencing body, usually a sentencing commission, (2) sentencing judges are expected to sentence within the range or to provide written justification for departure, (3) the guidelines provide for some review, usually appellate, of the departure from the guidelines. (pp. 408–409)

- Allows for the consideration of aggravating and mitigating circumstances.

Aggravating Circumstances Circumstances relating to the commission of a crime that make it more grave than the average instance of that crime. (p. 409)

Mitigating Circumstances Circumstances relating to the commission of a crime that may be considered to reduce the blameworthiness of the defendant. (p. 409)

INSTRUCTIONAL CUE

Death penalty legislation provides an effective illustration of the differences between aggravating and mitigating circumstances. For example, the aggravating circumstances that might be considered during the sentencing phase of a death penalty trial include the number of victims murdered, whether the murder occurred during the commission of another crime (felony murder), the heinousness of the murder, and whether the victim was a law enforcement officer. Mitigating factors include the age of the defendant, his or her mental state at the time of the offense, prior record, and whether drugs or alcohol contributed to the offense.

   A. Federal Sentencing Guidelines (p. 409)

Truth in Sentencing A close correspondence between the sentence imposed upon those sent to prison and the time actually served prior to release from prison. *Source:* Lawrence A. Greenfeld, *"Prison Sentences and Time Served for Violence,"* Bureau of Justice Statistics Selected Findings, No. 4, April 1995. (p. 409)

- The Sentencing Reform Act
- Limited the discretion of federal judges by mandating the creation of federal sentencing guidelines.
- Specified the purposes of sentencing to include deterring criminals, incapacitating or rehabilitating offenders, and providing just deserts in punishing criminals.
- Key court decision on the federal sentencing guidelines:
- *Mistretta* v. *U.S.*: The Court held that Congress acted appropriately in the creation of the federal sentencing guidelines, and the guidelines could be applied in federal cases nationwide.
   1. Federal Guideline Provisions
       - A sentencing range is specified, and judges are allowed to depart from the guidelines if a case has atypical features (aggravating or mitigating circumstances).
       - *Deal* v. *U.S.*: It is possible to try and to convict a defendant for six separate offenses in a single proceeding and use the federal sentencing guidelines to convict and sentence the defendant as a career offender as a consequence.

2. Plea Bargaining under the Guidelines
    *   Plea bargaining continues under the guidelines, but the plea has to be fully disclosed in the record of the court and detail the actual conduct of the offense.

B. The Legal Environment of Structured Sentencing (p. 413)
    *   *Apprendi* v. *New Jersey*: Requiring sentencing judges to consider facts not proven to a jury violates the federal Constitution.
    *   *Harris* v. *U.S.*: The sentence imposed did not extend beyond the statutory minimum.
    *   *U.S.* v. *Cotton*: The finding was based on overwhelming and uncontroverted evidence and was not improper.
    *   *Blakely* v. *Washington*: Invalidated any sentencing schema that allow judges rather than juries to determine any factor that increases a criminal sentence, except for prior convictions.
    *   *U.S.* v. *Booker* and *U.S.* v. *Fanfan*: Focused on the constitutionality of federal sentencing practices that relied on determination of facts by a judge rather than a jury in the application of sentencing guidelines.

C. Mandatory Sentencing

Mandatory Sentencing   A structured sentencing scheme that allows no leeway in the nature of the sentence required and under which clearly enumerated punishments are mandated for specific offenses or for habitual offenders convicted of a series of crimes. (p. 414)

*   Introduce the concept of three-strikes laws.
*   Discuss their impact on crime and the criminal justice system.

Diversion   The official suspension of criminal or juvenile proceedings against an alleged offender at any point after a recorded justice system intake, but before the entering of a judgment, and referral of that person to a treatment or care program administered by a nonjustice or private agency. Also, release without referral. (p. 415)

V. Innovations in Sentencing (p. 418)
    A. Questions about Alternative Sanctions (p. 418)
VI. The Presentence Investigation (p. 418)

Presentence Investigation   The examination of a convicted offender's background prior to sentencing. Presentence examinations are generally conducted by probation or parole officers and are submitted to sentencing authorities. (p. 418)

*   The purpose is to give the judge information about a defendant's background.
*   Can be a detailed written report, an abbreviated written report, or a verbal report.
*   Information includes personal information, prior record, current offense information, health history, work history, social history, and education.

INSTRUCTIONAL CUE LINKED TO THE STUDENT STUDY GUIDE

Student Activity 2 illustrates the various factors that can influence sentencing decisions.

INSTRUCTIONAL CUE

Have the students brainstorm to identify the factors that they think are relevant for a judge to know to make an accurate sentencing decision.

VII. The Victim—Forgotten No Longer (p. 422)

- The Crime Victims' Rights Act, part of the Justice for All Act of 2004, establishes statutory rights for victims of federal crimes and gives them the necessary legal authority to assert those rights in federal court.

A. Victim-Impact Statements (p. 423)

Victim-Impact Statement   The in-court use of victim- or survivor-supplied information by sentencing authorities wishing to make an informed sentencing decision. (p. 423)

- These statements usually describe the loss, suffering, and trauma experienced by the crime victim or the victim's survivors.
- This information should be considered by the judge; however, research indicates that these statements rarely affect sentencing decisions.

VIII. Modern Sentencing Options (p. 423)

INSTRUCTIONAL CUE LINKED TO THE STUDENT STUDY GUIDE

Use Student Activity 3 to demonstrate the changing status of crime victims in the criminal justice system.

B. Fines (p. 425)

- One of the oldest forms of punishment
- Use of day fines (fines should be proportionate to the severity of the offense and the financial resources of the offender)

IX. Death: The Ultimate Sanction (p. 426)

Capital Punishment   The death penalty. Capital punishment is the most extreme of all sentencing options. (p. 426)

Capital Offense   A criminal offense punishable by death. (p. 426)

- Discuss the history of capital punishment.
  - Since 1608, 18,800 legal executions have occurred.
  - The numbers have declined this century.
  - The federal government and 38 states have capital punishment laws.
  - About 60 offenses are eligible for the death penalty.
  - As of April 1, 2005, 3,452 persons were under the sentence of death.

INSTRUCTIONAL CUE LINKED TO THE STUDENT STUDY GUIDE

Student Activity 4 will expose students to a variety of death penalty issues. After students complete this assignment, have them present what they learned to the class.

A. *Habeas Corpus* Review (p. 427)

Writ of *Habeas Corpus*   A writ that directs the person detaining a prisoner to bring him or her before a judicial officer to determine the lawfulness of the imprisonment. (p. 427)

- *McClesky* v. *Zant*: Limits the number of appeals available to a condemned person. After the first appeal, the defendant must show (1) why the subsequent appeal wasn't included in the first appeal and (2) how the defendant was harmed by the absence of the claim.
- *Coleman* v. *Thompson*: State prisoners condemned to die cannot cite "procedural default" (such as a defense attorney's failure to meet a filing deadline for appeals in state court) as the sole reason for an appeal to federal court.

- *Schlup* v. *Delo*: An appeal based upon new evidence can be heard if it is "more likely than not that no reasonable juror" would have found the defendant guilty.
- Appeals are also limited by the Antiterrorism and Effective Death Penalty Act.

B. Opposition to Capital Punishment (p. 429)
- There is a risk that innocent people will be executed.

INSTRUCTIONAL CUE

Discuss the decision by the governor of Illinois in February 2000 to conduct an investigation of the death penalty system in that state. One factor that motivated the governor was the fact that 13 individuals have had to be released from death row because they were wrongfully convicted.

- It is not an effective deterrent.
- It is arbitrary and discriminatory.
- It is far too expensive.
- Killing at the hands of the state is not a righteous act.

C. Justifications for Capital Punishment (p. 434)
- Retentionist position
  - Revenge
  - Just deserts
  - Protection

D. The Courts and the Death Penalty (p. 434)
- Key Supreme Court decisions:
  - *Wilkerson* v. *Utah*: Upheld the use of the firing squad as a method of execution.
  - *In re Kemmler*: "Punishments are cruel when they involve torture or a lingering death; but the punishment of death is not cruel, within the meaning of that word as used in the Constitution." Also, this case upheld the use of electrocution as a method of execution.
  - *Furman* v. *Georgia*: "Evolving standards of decency" might necessitate a reconsideration of the constitutionality of capital punishment. Allowing the jury to decide guilt and the punishment of death at the same time allowed for an arbitrary and capricious application of the death penalty.
  - *Gregg* v. *Georgia*: The two-step process of a judge or jury deciding guilt and then undertaking a separate sentencing phase was specifically upheld by the Supreme Court.
  - *Coker* v. *Georgia*: The death penalty is not an acceptable punishment for the crime of rape, concluding that execution would be "grossly disproportionate" to the crime.
  - *Ring* v. *Arizona*: Attorneys for an Arizona death row inmate successfully challenged that state's practice of allowing judges, sitting without a jury, to make factual determinations on imposition of the death penalty.
  - *Summerlin* v. *Stewart*: Vacated the death sentences in 100 cases in three states. *Schiro* v. *Summerlin* reinstated the same sentences.
  - *Woodson* v. *North Carolina*: Laws requiring the mandatory application of the death penalty for specific crimes are prohibited.
  - *Penry* v. *Johnson*: The U.S. Supreme Court found that a state trial court in Texas failed to consider the defendant's mental retardation.

- *Atkins* v. *Virginia*: The U.S. Supreme Court ruled that executing mentally retarded people violated the Constitution's ban on cruel and unusual punishment.
- *Thompson* v. *Oklahoma*: Death penalty cannot be used as a punishment for a defendant who was younger than 16 at the time of the offense.
- *Roper* v. *Simmons*: Held that anyone who committed the crime when younger than 18 could not be sentenced to death.

E. The Future of the Death Penalty (p. 437)

Learner Activities

Activity 1

In the space provided, answer the questions at the end of each scenario.

1. Darryl Jackson is a 20-year-old unemployed male. He is addicted to cocaine, has no family, and is homeless. He has three prior felony convictions (all drug possession). He has recently been convicted of his fourth felony (a burglary), and you are the judge deciding his fate. The sentencing statute allows you to sentence Darryl with anywhere from a minor fine to life imprisonment (or any combination of punishments). The specific facts of the case:

   On October 18, Darryl Jackson entered the apartment of Angela Starter. He entered by picking the lock on her back door. He stole her stereo ($1,500), jewelry ($3,500), and Matchbox car collection ($800). When Darryl was leaving her apartment, a security officer stopped and apprehended him for the Starter burglary. Darryl claimed he needed to sell the goods so that he would have money for food.

   What sentence would you give Darryl?

2. Ron Kuzak is a 20-year-old male. He is a college student with a 3.6 grade point average, works part-time at McDonald's, and goes to church on Sunday (he sings in the choir). He is also addicted to cocaine. He has three prior felony convictions (all drug possession). He has recently been convicted of his fourth felony (a burglary), and you are the judge deciding his fate. The sentencing statute allows you to sentence Ron with anywhere from a minor fine to life imprisonment (or any combination of punishments). The specific facts of the case:

   On October 18, Ron Kuzak entered the apartment of Joni McDougal. He entered by picking the lock on her back door. He stole her watch ($1,500), diamond ring ($3,500), and Beanie Baby collection ($800). When Ron was leaving her apartment, a security officer stopped and apprehended him for the burglary. Ron claimed he needed to sell the goods so that he would have money for college tuition.

   What sentence would you give Ron?

Activity 2

What sentence would you give each of the following defendants? What factors would be most important to you? What other types of information would you want to know to make a more informed sentencing decision?

1. Miss Colby, a 32-year-old single mother, was convicted of reckless driving. On January 23, she was driving while intoxicated along State Street and hit a parked fire truck. The fire department was responding to an emergency medical call, attempting to transport an elderly man who had suffered a heart attack to the hospital. Because of the accident, the man could not be transported until another transport vehicle arrived. Colby was originally charged with driving while intoxicated, but the prosecutor allowed her to plead guilty to reckless driving.

2. Daniel Driver, 35 years old, was convicted on felony child molestation charges. He was on parole for similar charges at the time of the current offense. Driver is divorced, works as a computer consultant for an electronics firm, and has been described as an "active churchgoer."

3. Maria Campo, 40, pleaded guilty to two counts of passing bad checks. Campo had been purchasing new furniture for her apartment, paying with checks for which she had no funds. She has two previous convictions for forgery.

4. Thomas "Ziggy" Petruzzelli, 16, was convicted on involuntary manslaughter charges. The fight that led to the stabbing happened on July 4 outside a convenience store. Ziggy was standing outside the store asking adults to buy him a pack of cigarettes—something he could not do as a minor. Bruce Pearl, 33, agreed to buy the cigarettes, but when Pearl came back outside the store, the two began arguing. Ultimately, Ziggy's father got involved, intervening with a two-by-four. His father is currently awaiting trial on an assault with a deadly weapon charge.

Activity 3

Robert Jones, son of Debbie and Tom Jones, was murdered on his way home from work. Darrin Alexander was quickly apprehended near the scene of the crime, was identified by multiple eyewitnesses, and confessed to the crime. At trial, the jury took only 48 minutes to reach a guilty verdict in this death penalty case.

Robert Jones's parents had completed a written victim-impact statement and had prepared oral statements. However, the judge did not allow them to speak. Despite their objections, the sentencing phase of the trial occurred without their input. Alexander had 12 witnesses speak on his behalf. The jury, after considering the aggravating and mitigating factors in the case, decided to sentence Alexander to life imprisonment rather than to death.

Some victim advocates would argue that this would not have occurred if there existed a federal constitutional amendment that protected crime victims. Victim advocates believe that such an amendment would give victims complete protection of their rights.

Lawyers are split on their support for such an amendment. Some argue against it because it might put a halt to plea bargaining, it would overburden the system, courts are ill-equipped to handle such a radical change, and it would give victims too much veto power. Others, however, support the amendment, arguing that it would protect victims from such harm as described above, would give victims a voice in all court proceedings, would lessen the traumatizing impacts of crime, and would make the system more balanced. There are many additional arguments both for and against the amendment.

What do you think? This student activity requires you to take a position in support of or against this constitutional amendment. Make a strong argument for your position.

_____

_____

_____

_____

_____

_____

Activity 4

Visit **Library Extra 11–6**. This link will take you to the report "A Broken System: Error Rates in Capital Cases, 1973–1995." Write a summary of the information provided in the report in the space below.

LIBRARY EXTRA

_____

_____

_____

_____

_____

_____

Internet Activity

Visit the Death Penalty Information Center at http://www.deathpenaltyinfo.org. Review the various subjects in the "Issues" area provided by the site. Provide a brief description of the kinds of material at least five subareas contain. Which of these subareas do you find the most interesting? Why? Your instructor may request that you submit your findings.

_____

_____

_____

_____

_____

Distance Learning Activity

In the space below, take a position on the death penalty. Visit three or four websites to search for evidentiary support for your position. The following pages will be helpful: (1) ACLU's Death Penalty page: http://www.aclu.org/death-penalty; (2) Amnesty International Death Penalty Campaign: http://www.web.amnesty.org/rmp/dplibrary.nsf/index?openview; (3) Death Penalty Focus: http://www.deathpenalty.org; (4) Death Penalty Information Center: http://www.deathpenaltyinfo.org. If your instructor asks you to do so, participate in a class debate on the issue.

Learning Activities Utilizing the World Wide Web

There are student-based activities in the Student Study Guide (Internet Activity, Distance Learning Activity, CJ Today on the World Wide Web) that are similar in focus to those that follow. However, the following are presented as instructor-led activities, to be used in a classroom with online access.

Visit the Death Penalty Information Center at http://www.deathpenaltyinfo.org. Review the various "Information Topics" provided by the site. Look at each of the subareas (under Information Topics), including those under "General," "Issues," "Special Topics," and "In-Depth Reports." Provide a brief description of the kinds of material each subarea contains for display in class. Ask the class which of these subareas seems the most interesting and why.

Divide the class into groups, each taking a position on the death penalty. In class, display three or four websites for evidentiary support for your position. The following pages will be helpful: (1) ACLU's Death Penalty page: http://www.aclu.org/death-penalty; (2) Amnesty International Death Penalty Campaign: http://www.web.amnesty.org/rmp/dplibrary.nsf/index?openview; (3) Death Penalty Focus: http://www.deathpenalty.org; (4) Death Penalty Information Center: http://www.deathpenaltyinfo.org. After preparation, allow the class to participate in a debate on the issue.

Other websites for organizations and agencies related to the material in Chapter 11 include:

National Association of Sentencing Advocates (NASA)	http://www.sentencingproject.org/nasa
State Sentencing Commissions	http://www.ussc.gov/states/nascaddr.htm
Coalition for Federal Sentencing Reform	http://www.sentencing.org
U.S. Sentencing Commission	http://www.ussc.gov
ACLU's Death Penalty Page	http://www.aclu.org/death-penalty
Amnesty International Death Penalty Campaign	http://www.web.amnesty.org/rmp/dplibrary.nsf/index?openview
Death Penalty Focus	http://www.deathpenalty.org
Death Penalty Information Center (DPIC)	http://www.deathpenaltyinfo.org
Death Penalty Resources	http://sun.soci.niu.edu/~critcrim/dp/dp.html

Suggested Answers to Chapter Discussion Questions

1. **Describe the five goals of contemporary criminal sentencing discussed in this chapter. Which of these goals do you think ought to be the primary goal of sentencing? How might your choice vary with the type of offense? In what circumstances might your choice be less acceptable?**

   Retribution is the taking of revenge upon an offender for his or her criminal act(s). Incapacitation seeks to deny a criminal the opportunity to commit an offense. Deterrence is the effort to prevent others from committing a criminal act similar to the one for which an offender is being sentenced. Rehabilitation is the effort to reform an offender. Restoration attempts to make the victim of a criminal act "whole again."

   Many factors must be considered in determining the primary goal of sentencing. Among them are the prevailing public attitude toward crime and punishment and the severity of the crime for which the offender is being punished. Sentencing goals must be individualized for the crime and the offender. For example, it would be unjust to focus on retribution with a first offender convicted of committing a relatively minor property offense while emphasizing rehabilitation for a repeat offender convicted of a violent crime.

2. **Illustrate the difference between indeterminate and structured sentencing. What led some states to abandon indeterminate sentencing?**

   Indeterminate sentencing seeks to rehabilitate by affording the offender an opportunity to reduce his or her sentence. Under indeterminate sentencing, offenders receive unspecified sentences (e.g., one to ten years of imprisonment). The offender's performance while incarcerated determines the point at which she or he is paroled. In addition to good time, the offender can accelerate his or her release through participation in various rehabilitation programs. Critics of the indeterminate model called for the recognition of the basic sentencing principles of proportionality, equity, and social debt. These criticisms led many states to adopt some form of structured sentencing, such as determinate sentencing (convicted offenders are sentenced to a fixed term reduced by good time), or sentencing guidelines (general guidelines based on past sentencing practices).

3. **What structured sentencing models are in use today? Which model holds the best promise for long-term crime reduction? Why?**

   Structured sentencing models include determinate sentencing, voluntary/advisory sentencing guidelines, and presumptive sentencing. Although each structured sentencing model has some advantages in better accomplishing proportionality, equity, and social debt when compared to indeterminate sentencing, these models are not without criticism, and there is little evidence to indicate that any of these models will be effective long-term crime-reduction strategies.

   In your opinion, is the return to just deserts consistent with structured sentencing? Explain.

   In determining appropriate sentences under the structured sentencing model, sentencing commissions typically consider the degree of deserved punishment as a factor in the equation. It would seem, therefore, that the notion of just deserts is inherently consistent with this model.

4. **What is mandatory sentencing? How does it differ from indeterminate sentencing? Why was mandatory sentencing created?**

   Mandatory sentencing is a structured sentencing scheme that allows no leeway in the nature of the sentence required and under which clearly enumerated punishments are mandated for specific offenses or for habitual offenders convicted of a series of crimes. Mandatory sentencing eliminates judicial discretion. In contrast, judges have the most discretion under indeterminate sentencing schemes. Mandatory sentencing laws are generally reactionary measures, usually created during periods of emphasis on a specific type of crime, such as drugs or violent crime. The media, politicians, and the public create and react to this emphasis, and a common policy outcome is sentencing enhancements or mandatory sentences.

5. **What is truth in sentencing? How have states attempted to meet federal truth-in-sentencing requirements?**

Truth in sentencing occurs when there is a close correspondence between the sentence imposed upon an offender and the time actually served prior to release from prison. Many states have replicated the federal truth-in-sentencing model because the federal government has made funds available to states for prison construction.

6. **Explain the development of federal sentencing guidelines. What have recent court decisions said about the applicability of those guidelines?**

The Sentencing Reform Act of 1984 created the nine-member U.S. Sentencing Commission. This commission was provided general guidelines to follow during its deliberations and then analyzed thousands of cases, eventually creating a punishment scale in the form of a sentencing table. Punishments within the table were regarded as typical for specific offenses. The commission also considered federal law, parole guidelines, and the impact of particular kinds of sentences on federal prison populations. The key factors that judges are to consider when deciding sentences under the guidelines are the seriousness of the offense and the prior record of the offender. Recently, however, the U.S. Supreme Court has called into question the fact-finding authority of federal (and state) judges in making sentencing decisions, ruling that other than the fact of a prior conviction, any fact that increases the penalty for a crime beyond the prescribed statutory maximum is, in effect, an element of the crime, which must be submitted to a jury and proved beyond a reasonable doubt. Consequently, federal sentencing guidelines have become merely advisory and federal judges are now given wide latitude in imposing punishments. While federal judges must still take the guidelines into consideration in reaching sentencing decisions, they do not have to follow them.

7. **What is a presentence investigation? How do presentence investigations contribute to the contents of presentence reports? How are presentence reports used?**

Presentence investigations include the examination of a convicted offender's background prior to sentencing. Presentence examinations are generally conducted by probation or parole officers and are submitted to sentencing authorities. The investigation is critical to the quality of the report, as probation officers rely on official records and information provided by the offender and victim. The more thorough the investigation is, the better the report. Presentence reports are used by judges to make more informed sentencing decisions, and generally a judge follows the report writer's recommendation.

8. **Describe the history of victims' rights and services in this country. What role does the victim play in criminal justice proceedings today?**

Victims have historically been considered outsiders to the criminal justice process. The role of the crime victim in the criminal justice process started to change in the 1970s as grassroots organizations worked to inform the public and politicians about the plight of crime victims. One result of this pressure was the 1982 President's Task Force on Victims of Crime. The task force opened a floodgate of legislative changes that have since been implemented to assist crime victims. Among the changes is an expansion of the role of the victim in criminal justice proceedings. Victims, for example, are able to provide victim-impact statements, and the constitutional amendments being considered will increase their involvement in the process even further.

9. **What are the four traditional sentencing options that this chapter discusses? Under what circumstances might each be appropriate?**

The four traditional sentencing options are fines, probation, imprisonment, and death. The option selected depends usually on the severity of the offense and background characteristics of the defendant. Often two or more of these options are combined.

10. **Do you support or oppose capital punishment? Outline the arguments on both sides of the issue.**

Few issues inflame Americans' passions as intensely as capital punishment. The views of both sides, often expressed through references to biblical passages they believe support their respective positions, typically reflect only the religious convictions of supporters and opponents alike, without regard for legal factors. While the "eye for an eye" cry of proponents and the "vengeance is mine, sayeth the Lord" chant of dissenters might play well on the six o'clock news, such visceral responses do little to advance reasoned discourse on the issue. Rather, they simply illustrate the sheer emotionalism surrounding the states' authority to take a human life.

One criminal justice professor offered three anecdotal examples, drawn from actual exchanges between students in his classes, that depict the degree to which this emotionalism inhibits reasonable discussion of capital punishment.

In the first instance, supporters argued that execution serves to deter crime. When opponents countered with statistical evidence disproving that position, the supporters rejected their opposition with the emotion-based argument that "It sure will deter the guy who was just executed!"

The second example involved a discussion of more than 300 cases of allegedly mistaken executions that have occurred since 1901. In each case, authorities reportedly discovered that the individual whose life they had taken was, in fact, not guilty of the crime for which he was executed. Not surprisingly, students opposed to capital punishment cited these events as proof that the law was wrong and called for immediate revocation of all capital punishment laws. They remained adamant even when it was pointed out that most claims of mistaken execution could not be supported with evidence.

In the third illustration, opponents cited the disproportionate rates at which minority offenders are sentenced to death. Death penalty supporters responded that there are simply more of "them" committing crimes that warrant execution—"them" being the supporters' word choice, not the professor's. This is a shining example of the discussants' tendency to dismiss findings supported by the data in favor of gut responses driven by blind commitment to their emotional positions.

Reasoned intellectual debate focused on the legal issues of capital punishment is needed in our society, but unless participants control their emotions, reasoned intellectual debate will be a rare event, indeed.

Key—Student Study Guide Questions

True or False

_____ 11-1. Deterrence is based on the idea of "an eye for an eye." **(False, p. 404)**

_____ 11-2. Mitigating circumstances result in harsher sentences under the determinate model. **(False, p. 409)**

_____ 11-3. Sentencing philosophies are manifestly intertwined with issues of religion, morals, values, and emotions. **(True, p. 402)**

_____ 11-4. The overall goal of deterrence is crime prevention. **(True, p. 404)**

_____ 11-5. Presumptive sentencing guidelines eliminate judicial discretion. **(False, p. 409)**

_____ 11-6. Most judges ignore the presentence investigation report writer's recommendations. **(False, pp. 419–420)**

_____ 11-7. Very few states currently use capital punishment as a sentencing option. **(False, p. 430)**

_____ 11-8. Justifications for the death penalty are collectively referred to as the retentionist position. **(True, p. 434)**

____ 11-9. Truth in sentencing means that before sentencing, probation officers present their investigation reports based on the truths they uncovered. **(False, p. 409)**

____ 11-10. General deterrence is a goal of criminal sentencing that seeks to prevent a particular offender from engaging in repeat criminality. **(False, p. 404)**

Multiple Choice

11-11. Modern sentencing practices are influenced by which of the following goals?
   a. retribution
   b. incapacitation
   c. deterrence
   d. rehabilitation
   e. all of the above (p. 403)

11-12. Which official is responsible for conducting presentence investigations in most jurisdictions?
   a. judge
   b. defense attorney
   c. prosecutor
   d. probation or parole officer (p. 419)

11-13. What philosophy of sentencing seeks to prevent others from committing crimes similar to the one for which an offender is being sentenced?
   a. rehabilitation
   b. retribution
   c. deterrence (p. 404)
   d. incapacitation

11-14. The retribution goal of sentencing corresponds to what model of sentencing?
   a. just deserts model (p. 403)
   b. medical model
   c. restoration model
   d. psychological healing model

11-15. _____ sentencing relies heavily upon a judge's discretion to choose among types of sanctions and set upper and lower limits on the length of prison stays.
   a. Intermediate
   b. Indeterminate (p. 406)
   c. Determinate
   d. Deterrent

11-16. Much of the philosophical basis of today's victims' movement can be found in the _____ model.
   a. restorative justice (p. 405)
   b. retribution
   c. restitution
   d. none of the above

11-17. The future of the death penalty rests primarily with
   a. the president.
   b. state legislatures. (p. 440)
   c. Congress.
   d. all of the above.

11-18. A study of the efficacy of victim-impact statements found that judicial sentencing decisions were _____ affected by them.
   a. greatly
   b. rarely (p. 423)
   c. modestly
   d. never

11-19. Which of the following is not one of the retentionist justifications for the death penalty?
   a. deterrence (p. 434)
   b. revenge
   c. just deserts
   d. protection

11-20. Which U.S. Supreme Court case created the two-step trial procedure that separated the determination of guilt and sentencing stages?
   a. *Gregg* v. *Georgia* (p. 435)
   b. *Poyner* v. *Murray*
   c. *Furman* v. *Georgia*
   d. none of the above

Fill-In

11-21. A(n) _____ is an examination of a convicted offender's background prior to sentencing. **(presentence investigation, p. 419)**

11-22. _____ is an attempt to have a close correspondence between the sentence imposed and the actual time served. **(Truth in sentencing, p. 409)**

11-23. The attempt to reform a criminal offender is called _____. **(rehabilitation, p. 404)**

11-24. _____ is a goal of criminal sentencing that attempts to prevent a particular offender from engaging in repeat criminal behavior. **(Specific deterrence, p. 404)**

11-25. A sentence of two to 12 years is an example of _____. **(indeterminate sentencing, p. 406)**

11-26. _____ is the act of taking revenge upon a criminal perpetrator. **(Retribution, p. 403)**

11-27. _____ is a model for criminal punishment that sets one particular punishment, or length of sentence, for each specific type of crime. **(Determinate sentencing, p. 408)**

11-28. The amount of time deducted from time to be served in prison on a given sentence based upon good behavior while in prison is called _____. **(good time, p. 407)**

11-29. _____ are factors surrounding an offense that could result in a harsher sentence. **(Aggravating circumstances, pp. 409–410)**

11-30. A(n) _____ is a criminal offense punishable by death. **(capital offense, p. 426)**

Key—Crossword Puzzle

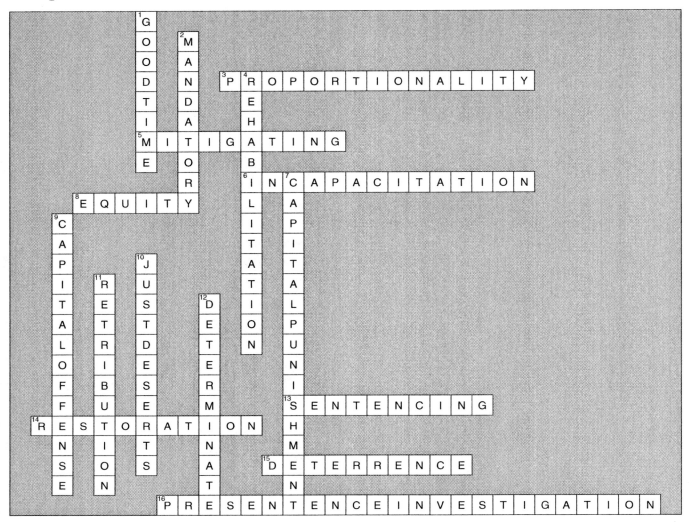

Across

3. Sentencing principle that holds that the severity of sanctions should bear a direct relationship to the seriousness of the crime committed.

5. Not aggravating but _____ circumstances.

6. Use of imprisonment or other means to reduce the likelihood that an offender will be capable of committing future offenses.

8. Sentencing principle based on concerns for social equality.

13. Imposition of a criminal sanction by a judicial authority.

14. Act of making the victim "whole again."

15. Goal of criminal sentencing that seeks to inhibit criminal behavior through the fear of punishment.

16. Prior to sentencing, a probation officer usually conducts one of these.

Down

1. Amount of time deducted from time to be served in prison on a given sentence for good behavior.

2. Sentencing scheme that allows no leeway in the nature of the sentence.

4. Attempt to change the offender.

7. Also called the death penalty.

9. Offense that is punishable by death.

10. Retribution corresponds to this model of sentencing.

11. "An eye for an eye."

12. Also called fixed sentencing.

Key—Word Search Puzzle

```
G P R E S U M P T I V E S E N T E N C I N G Z G K F O J N X
A Y B E U I N D E T E R M I N A T E S E N T E N C I N G G A
G I N A C A P I T A L P U N I S H M E N T J N J K T O Y L B
G L K T V I C T I M I M P A C T S T A T E M E N T H F D E D
R J Y Z K I L H G A N F E N O F H J F X Z O Z P S G S U K E
A U Y P R O P O R T I O N A L I T Y F N U H T R X M R H O T
V K U X C A P I T A L O F F E N S E E T U B Y E N X V A E E
A B G E N E R A L D E T E R R E N C E Z E B Q S J N A B C R
T W R I T O F H A B E A S C O R P U S D Z S T E T Z F C S M
I I Z T R R X H Y M D U S K M E Z H L N S Q R N T G B T I I
N B A F T E C U F O E R P J I L S A O S Y O U T A Z P H R N
G W L F H S S X X G O J N P K C I I G T K Q T E G Z E K U A
C Y I Z F T K T X E Q K F I B C T S Q W Y G H N M I C I C T
I P R W B O V M O U K M F Z O A S N U E N K I C O P I N T E
R H O V M R M R Q R G P Q S T X V L A I R C N E A Q F C U S
C H J C W A N P R S A A M I E T I B C A N J S I X E I A R E
U G A I N T I M E H A T L V O D S N U E H T E N V N C P E N
M E J S J I D G F J X I I G J G E F T A E Z N V D A C I T T
S W D C P V E U Y C B A L O H T L N E G N P T E W J U E I E
T H Y O E E T Q J A T V T A N Y E M A O Y I E S R U S T A N
A X O C Q J E B H Z S F V E N S M A I A V A N T Y T E N T C
N D P V U U R E V I N L S N Y H V T X D Z F C I U D R A T I
C J O I I S R C L U F T Y R B H U Y P B H L I G Q E R T E N
E Z X W T T E Z Z W F O O H J B R F I J X Q N A H S E N C G
S O H U Y I N W Q G C T L Z I Q S R N M I A G T B E N C I M
I P D C D C C D W N A T D R U Y P P V F R P G I B R C N I A
J L B F V E E G G D K W T J E A C C N M X D E O O T E T N N
G O O D T I M E N W F E V Q R X J Y X D A L Z N H S A V G T
R H Z E J D F A V T R R V B Z U Y L Z W T H J U T A E W D T
S K B P I Q M I T I G A T I N G C I R C U M S T A N C E S S
```

Aggravating Circumstances
Capital Offense
Capital Punishment
Determinate Sentencing
Deterrence
Equity
Gain Time
General Deterrence
Good Time
Incapacitation
Indeterminate Sentencing
Just Deserts
Mandatory Sentencing
Mitigating Circumstances

Presentence Investigation
Presumptive Sentencing
Proportionality
Rehabilitation
Restoration
Restorative Justice
Retribution
Sentencing
Social Debt
Specific Deterrence
Structured Sentencing
Truth in Sentencing
Victim-Impact Statement
Writ of *Habeas Corpus*

Probation, Parole, and Community Corrections

OUTLINE

LEARNING OBJECTIVES

After reading this chapter, you should be able to:

- Explain the differences between probation and parole, and describe the advantages and disadvantages of each
- Describe in detail the legal environment surrounding the use of probation and parole, and know the names of significant court cases
- Describe the federal probation system
- Explain the nature of the job of probation and parole officers
- List the advantages of intermediate sanctions over more traditional forms of sentencing
- Describe the likely future of probation and parole

Chapter Summary

Chapter 12 discusses many issues important to understanding **community corrections**. This chapter focuses primarily on probation and parole. However, there is also a discussion of intermediate sanctions.

Probation is a sentence of imprisonment that is suspended. Offenders, if they abide by the specific and general conditions of probation, will serve their entire sentences in the community. This provides them with the opportunity to continue to work or remain in school, maintain family and social ties, and use the treatment programs available in the community. Chapter 12 discusses the history of probation in the United States and describes it as the most common form of criminal sentencing today. There are close to four million offenders currently on probation, and even offenders convicted of serious crimes are eligible for probation.

Parole is often mistaken for probation, but the two sentences are different. When sentencing an offender to probation, a judge makes the decision that a prison sentence should be suspended and the offender should serve his or her sentence in the community. An offender is on parole when he or she first serves time in prison and then is conditionally released by the paroling authority. However, similar to the constraints put on the probationer, the parolee must abide by general and specific conditions or face **revocation** of parole.

The text then describes the advantages and disadvantages of probation and parole. Advantages include lower cost than imprisonment, increased employment opportunities, opportunity to pay **restitution**, opportunity to receive community support, the reduced risk of criminal socialization, and the increased use of community services and opportunities for rehabilitation. Disadvantages include concerns about the lack of punishment, increased risk to the community, and increased social costs.

The legal environment of probation and parole is interesting because convicted offenders have fewer legal protections than someone accused of a crime. For example, the Supreme Court has decided that probation officers may conduct searches without a warrant or without probable cause (*Griffin* v. *Wisconsin*). Parole boards do not have to specify the evidence used in denying parole (*Greenholtz* v. *Nebraska*), and incriminating statements to a probation officer may be used as evidence if the probationer does not specify a right against self-incrimination (*Minnesota* v. *Murphy*). It is important to note, however, that probationers and parolees have some legal protections. The important *Gagnon* v. *Scarpelli* and *Morrissey* v. *Brewer* decisions declared that probationers and parolees deserve procedural safeguards when their probation or parole is being revoked.

The last section of Chapter 12 describes intermediate and innovative sentences. Judges have a wide variety of intermediate sanctions at their disposal. A **split sentence** requires the convicted person to serve a period of confinement in a facility followed by a period of probation. Similar to this type of sentence, **shock probation** (or **shock parole**) involves sentencing an offender to prison but then allowing him or her to be released early to probation. The first part of a split sentence is typically spent in a jail, and the first part of a shock probation sentence is spent in prison. **Shock incarceration** is a sentence to a military-style "boot camp" prison. **Intensive supervision** involves frequent face-to-face contacts between the probationary client and probation officer. Other intermediate sanctions discussed in Chapter 12 include **mixed sentences, community service**, and **home confinement**.

Teaching Outline

I. Introduction (p. 452)

Community Corrections The use of a variety of officially ordered program-based sanctions that permit convicted offenders to remain in the community under conditional supervision as an alternative to an active prison sentence. (p. 452)

INSTRUCTIONAL CUE

Although all of the sentencing options discussed in Chapter 12 can be considered community-based sentences, stress that the type of restriction varies depending on the sentence. For example, house arrest is more restrictive than straight probation, electronic monitoring is more restrictive than house arrest, and shock incarceration is more restrictive than electronic monitoring.

II.   What Is Probation? (p. 453)

Probation   A sentence of imprisonment that is suspended. Also, the conditional freedom granted by a judicial officer to an adjudicated adult or juvenile offender, as long as the person meets certain conditions of behavior. (p. 453)

- Explain that probation is a court-ordered sanction combining control with opportunities for rehabilitation.
- Briefly describe the history of probation in the United States.

A.   The Extent of Probation (p. 453)

- Probation is the most common form of criminal sentencing in the United States.
- Between 20% and 60% of convicted offenders are sentenced to probation, and these numbers are increasing.
- Even violent offenders receive probationary terms.
- Close to four million offenders are currently on probation.

INSTRUCTIONAL CUE LINKED TO THE STUDENT STUDY GUIDE

Student Activity 1 will help students understand some of the problems with probation as a sentencing option.

B.   Probation Conditions (p. 456)

Probation Revocation   A court order taking away a convicted offender's probationary status and usually withdrawing the conditional freedom associated with that status in response to a violation of the conditions of probation. (p. 456)

- General conditions include "obey all laws," "possess no firearm," and "maintain employment."
- Specific conditions depend on the nature of the offense. An example might be requiring the offender to surrender his or her driver's license.

C.   The Federal Probation System (p. 457)

- The system is 80 years old, authorized by the National Probation Act of 1925.
- Federal probation officers may arrest probationers for violations; however, they are encouraged to obtain a warrant, even though they have statutory authority.

INSTRUCTIONAL CUE

The following example can help describe the general and specific conditions of probation. Alice Meyer was convicted of drunk driving (her second offense). The judge sentenced her to probation. Thus, she had to abide by the general conditions of probation in that jurisdiction, including meeting with her probation officer once a month, obeying all laws, and maintaining employment. The judge added two specific conditions to her probation. First, she was required to attend Alcoholics Anonymous meetings once a week. Second, she had to attend a victim-impact panel. At these panels, offenders listen to survivors of drunk-driving accidents talk about the harm caused by the crime.

III. What Is Parole? (p. 458)

Parole   The status of a convicted offender who has been conditionally released from prison by a paroling authority before the expiration of his or her sentence, is placed under the supervision of a parole agency, and is required to observe conditions of parole. (p. 458)

Prisoner Rentry   The managed return to the community of individuals released from prison. Also called reentry. (p. 458)

Parole Board   A state paroling authority. Most states have parole boards that decide when an incarcerated offender is ready for conditional release. Some boards also function as revocation hearing panels. (pp. 458–459)

A. The Extent of Parole (p. 459)

- Discuss the movement to abolish parole.
- Just over 750,000 inmates are on parole.
- Discuss the considerable variation in the numbers of inmates on parole by state.
- About 42% of parolees successfully complete parole, and 26% are returned for violations.

Parole (Probation) Violation   An act or a failure to act by a parolee (or probationer) that does not conform to the conditions of his or her parole (or probation). (p. 460)

B. Parole Conditions (p. 460)

Conditions of Parole (Probation)   The general and special limits imposed upon an offender who is released on parole (or probation). General conditions tend to be fixed by state statute, while special conditions are mandated by the sentencing authority (court or board) and take into consideration the background of the offender and the circumstances of the offense. (p. 460)

Parole Revocation   The administrative action of a paroling authority to remove a person from parole status in response to a violation of lawfully required conditions of parole, including the prohibition against commission of a new offense, and usually resulting in a return to prison. (p. 460)

Restitution   A court requirement that an alleged or convicted offender pay money or provide services to the victim of the crime or provide services to the community. (p. 460)

C. Federal Parole (p. 460)

- Made by the U.S. Parole Commission
- Is slowly being phased out

INSTRUCTIONAL CUE LINKED TO THE STUDENT STUDY GUIDE STUDENT

Activity 2 demonstrates the relationship between imprisonment and community corrections programs. This activity provides an excellent opportunity to discuss the strengths and weaknesses of probation and parole. Stress that one way to reduce prison populations is to rely on probation/parole rather than incarceration. The problem, of course, is that the public believes that these sentences are lenient. Intermediate sanctions are one compromise instituted. They are a mechanism to reduce overcrowding but also satisfy the public's desire for harsher sanctions.

IV. Probation and Parole: The Pluses and Minuses (p. 460)

A. Advantages of Probation and Parole (p. 460)

- Lower cost
- Increased employment
- Restitution

- Community support
- Reduced risk of criminal socialization
- Increased use of community services
- Increased opportunity for rehabilitation

    B. Disadvantages of Probation and Parole (p. 461)
    - A relative lack of punishment
    - Increased risk to the community
    - Increased social costs

INSTRUCTIONAL CUE LINKED TO THE STUDENT STUDY GUIDE

Student Activity 3 can help demonstrate the trends in state parole.

    V. The Legal Environment (p. 462)
    - Probation officers may conduct a search of a probationer's residence without a warrant or without probable cause (*Griffin* v. *Wisconsin*). This holding applied to parolees in *Pennsylvania Board of Probation and Parole* v. *Scott*.

Revocation Hearing   A hearing held before a legally constituted hearing body (such as a parole board) to determine whether a parolee or probationer has violated the conditions and requirements of his or her parole or probation. (p. 462)

INSTRUCTIONAL CUE

Review the important legal aspects discussed in Chapter 7. Remind students about the purpose of the exclusionary rule and *Miranda* protections. You can also use this discussion as an opportunity to demonstrate how conviction changes an offender's legal status.

- *Escoe* v. *Zerbst* argued that the revocation of probation without notice or hearing was acceptable practice. (However, notice and hearing are required after *Mempa* v. *Rhay*.)
- *Gagnon* v. *Scarpelli* and *Morrissey* v. *Brewer* declared a need for procedural safeguards for probationers and parolees, respectively.
- *Greenholtz* v. *Nebraska* established that parole boards do not have to specify the evidence used in deciding to deny parole.
- *Bearden* v. *Georgia* established that probation cannot be revoked for failure to pay a fine and make restitution if it cannot be shown that the defendant is responsible for the failure.
- *Minnesota* v. *Murphy* states that incriminating statements to a probation officer may be used as evidence if the probationer does not specify a right against self-incrimination.

    VI. The Job of Probation and Parole Officers (p. 464)
    - The four functions of probation/parole work:
        - Presentence investigations
        - Intake procedures
        - Needs assessment and diagnosis
        - Supervision of clients

    A. The Challenges of the Job (p. 466)
    - Walking the fine line between conflicting duties (social work versus corrections)
    - High caseloads

Caseload   The number of probation or parole clients assigned to one probation or parole officer for supervision. (p. 466)

• Lack of opportunity for career mobility

VII. Intermediate Sanctions (p. 466)

Intermediate Sanctions   The use of split sentencing, shock probation or parole, shock incarceration, community service, intensive supervision, or home confinement in lieu of other, more traditional sanctions, such as imprisonment and fines. (p.466)

INSTRUCTIONAL CUE LINKED TO THE STUDENT STUDY GUIDE
Student Activity 4 will demonstrate the different types of intermediate sanctions.

A. Split Sentencing (p. 467)

Split Sentence   A sentence explicitly requiring the convicted offender to serve a period of confinement in a local, state, or federal facility followed by a period of probation. (p. 467)

B. Shock Probation and Shock Parole (p. 467)

Shock Probation   The practice of sentencing offenders to prison, allowing them to apply for probationary release, and enacting such release in surprise fashion. Offenders who receive shock probation may not be aware of the fact that they will be released on probation and may expect to spend a much longer time behind bars. (p. 467)

C. Shock Incarceration (p. 467)

Shock Incarceration   A sentencing option that makes use of "boot camp"–type prisons to impress on convicted offenders the realities of prison life. (p. 467)

D. Mixed Sentencing and Community Service (p. 468)

Mixed Sentence   A sentence that requires that a convicted offender serve weekends (or other specified periods of time) in a confinement facility (usually a jail) while undergoing probation supervision in the community. (p. 468)

Community Service   A sentencing alternative that requires offenders to spend at least part of their time working for a community agency. (p. 469)

E. Intensive Supervision (p. 469)

Intensive Probation Supervision (IPS)   A form of probation supervision involving frequent face-to-face contact between the probationer and the probation officer. (p. 469)

F. Home Confinement and Electronic Monitoring (p. 470)

Home Confinement   House arrest. Individuals ordered confined to their homes are sometimes monitored electronically to ensure they do not leave during the hours of confinement. Absence from the home during working hours is often permitted. (p. 470)

Remote Location Monitoring   A supervision strategy that uses electronic technology to track offenders sentenced to house arrest or those who have been ordered to limit their movements while completing a sentence involving probation or parole. (p. 470)

VIII. The Future of Probation and Parole (p. 472)

A. Reinventing Parole (p. 473)

• Two out of every three people released from prison are rearrested within three years.
• Recommendations from a 2004 report focused on creating a seamless continuum of services for offenders leaving jail.

B. Reinventing Probation (p. 474)

• Allows the resources of the community to focus on the rehabilitation of the offender.

Learner Activities

Activity 1

According to the Bureau of Justice Statistics study discussed at the beginning of Chapter 12, 5% of murderers and 21% of sexual offenders are sentenced to probation. Do you think that murderers and sexual offenders should be sentenced to probation? Why or why not? What factors contribute to courts relying on probation for these types of offenders? Are there any offenses for which you would exclude probation as a sentencing option? Explain your answer.

_____

_____

_____

_____

_____

_____

Activity 2

One of the significant pressures affecting the criminal justice system is overcrowding in the prison system. Most prisons operate above capacity, and some state systems are under court mandate to reduce overcrowding. At the same time, however, many states are considering abolishing parole. Parole has traditionally been one mechanism that can reduce overcrowding by allowing the early release of inmates. Do you think parole should be eliminated? Why or why not? Are there other mechanisms that states can use to reduce prison populations? Explain your answer.

_____

_____

_____

_____

_____

_____

Activity 3

LIBRARY EXTRA

Visit **Library Extra 12–2** and read the publication on trends in state parole. In the space below, describe the major trends identified. What trends do you think will influence parole in the next ten years? Explain your answer.

_____

_____

_____

_____

_____

_____

Activity 4

Locate a probation or parole agency in your state. Visit or call that agency, and interview an officer in each agency. Find out about the types of intermediate sanctions available in your state. In the space provided below, describe at least three of the intermediate sanction programs available.

_____

_____

_____

_____

_____

_____

Internet Activity

Visit the American Probation and Parole Association at http://www.appa-net.org. Use the site map on the home page to locate APPA position statements. What topics do these statements cover? Select three or four position statements, and read and summarize them. Your instructor may request that you submit your findings.

_____

_____

_____

_____

_____

Distance Learning Activity

Visit the Dispute Resolution Resources web page at http://adrr.com. This website provides essays on mediation and dispute resolution. Read one of the essays posted, and provide a summary of its key ideas. If your instructor asks you to do so, organize a class discussion that provides an opportunity to compare and contrast the findings from the different essays.

_____

_____

_____

_____

Learning Activities Utilizing the World Wide Web

There are student-based activities in the Student Study Guide (Internet Activity, Distance Learning Activity, CJ Today on the World Wide Web) that are similar in focus to those that follow. However, the following are presented as instructor-led activities, to be used in a classroom with online access.

Visit the American Probation and Parole Association at http://www.appa-net.org. Use the site map on the home page to locate APPA position statements. For classroom presentation, display the topics these statements cover. Use this information as a discussion starter.

Visit the Dispute Resolution Resources web page at http://adrr.com. This website provides essays on mediation and dispute resolution. Read and summarize some of the essays posted, and provide a summary of their key ideas to display and discuss in class. Lead the class in a discussion to compare and contrast the findings from the different essays.

Other websites for organizations and agencies related to the material in Chapter 12 include:

Alternative Dispute Resolution Resources, Mediation Essays, and Web Page Hosting for Mediators	http://adrr.com
Electronic monitoring	http://www.housearrest.com
Institute for Dispute Resolution	http://www.cpradr.org
Justice Concepts Incorporated	http://www.justiceconcepts.com
Mediation Works, Inc.	http://www.mwi.org
National Center on Institutions and Alternatives	http://www.igc.org/ncia
Sentencing Project	http://www.sentencingproject.org
Victim-Offender Reconciliation Program Resources	http://www.vorp.com
American Probation and Parole Association (APPA)	http://www.appa-net.org
International Community Corrections Association	http://www.iccaweb.org

Suggested Answers to Chapter Discussion Questions

1. **How do probation and parole differ? How are they alike? What are the advantages and disadvantages of each?**

   Probation is a sentence to prison that is suspended, and parole is early release after serving at least part of the sentence in prison. Both impose conditions on offenders, and if an offender fails to abide by the conditions, then the offender's probation or parole can be revoked. The advantages include saving money, providing opportunities for rehabilitation, and helping the offender to remain part of the community. The primary disadvantage is that there is an increased risk to the community because the offender has increased freedoms when on probation or parole.

2. **Describe the significant court cases that have had an impact on the practice of probation and parole.**

   - *Griffin* v. *Wisconsin*: The Supreme Court held that probation officers may conduct a search of a probationer's residence without a warrant or without probable cause.

- *Pennsylvania Board of Probation and Parole* v. *Scott*: The *Griffin* decision was applied to parolees.
- *Escoe* v. *Zerbst*: Argued that the revocation of probation without notice or hearing was acceptable practice.
- *Gagnon* v. *Scarpelli* and *Morrissey* v. *Brewer*: Declared a need for procedural safeguards for probationers and parolees, respectively.
- *Greenholtz* v. *Nebraska*: Established that parole boards do not have to specify the evidence used in deciding to deny parole.
- *Bearden* v. *Georgia*: Established that probation cannot be revoked for failure to pay a fine and make restitution if it cannot be shown that the defendant is responsible for the failure.
- *Minnesota* v. *Murphy*: States that incriminating statements to a probation officer may be used as evidence if the probationer does not specify a right against self-incrimination.

3. **What is the function of the federal probation system? How did it come into being?**

The federal probation system's primary function is to relieve overcrowding in the federal prison system. In an early Supreme Court case, the Court ruled that federal judges did not have the authority to suspend sentences and order probation. This outraged the National Probation Association, which campaigned vigorously to convince Congress to pass the National Probation Act of 1925.

4. **What do probation and parole officers do? What role do probation officers play in the sentencing of convicted offenders?**

The work of probation and parole officers consists generally of the following four functions: presentence investigation, other intake procedures, needs assessment and diagnosis, and client supervision. Probation officers play an important role in the sentencing of convicted offenders because after completing a presentence investigation, the probation officer makes a recommendation to the judge.

5. **What are intermediate sanctions? How do they differ from more traditional forms of sentencing? What advantages (if any) do they have over more traditional forms of sentencing?**

Intermediate sanctions include the use of split sentencing, shock probation or parole, shock incarceration, community service, intensive supervision, or home confinement in lieu of other, more traditional sanctions, such as imprisonment and fines. They differ from more traditional forms of sentencing options in that they are generally considered a compromise between the lack of punishment for some sentences (probation) and the excessive punishment of other sentences (such as imprisonment). The major advantage of intermediate sentences is that they give judges more options when deciding an appropriate sentence. Other advantages include that they are less expensive than imprisonment and also that they are socially cost-effective.

6. **How are probation and parole changing? What does the future hold for them? Do you agree with those who are trying to eliminate parole? Explain your position.**

Both probation and parole are frequently attacked for being ineffective and allowing offenders to get off easy for their crimes. These concerns are reflective of a broader social attitude that we must get tough with offenders. There has been significant pressure to abolish parole as well as significantly revise probation. Although the future is unclear, probation and parole will continue to play vital roles in the punishment of offenders. The reality of the imprisonment binge is that it is impossible for states to build prisons fast enough and many states' prison systems are overcrowded. Probation and parole are necessary to deal with this overcrowding issue. It is probably not wise to eliminate parole, but certainly the administration of parole can be improved.

Key—Student Study Guide Questions

True or False

____ 12-1. When using shock probation, the judge sentences an offender to a prison term and then suspends the sentence before the offender actually starts to serve the sentence in a jail or prison. **(False, p. 467)**

____ 12-2. Community service is a sentencing alternative that requires offenders to spend at least part of their time working for a community agency. **(True, p. 469)**

____ 12-3. A split sentence requires an offender to serve at least part of his or her sentence in a jail or prison, followed by a longer period on probation. **(True, p. 467)**

____ 12-4. Restitution is a court requirement that an offender pay money or provide services to the victim of the crime or provide services to the community. **(True, p. 460)**

____ 12-5. Parole is the status of an offender conditionally released from a prison by a paroling authority prior to the expiration of his or her sentence. **(True, p. 458)**

____ 12-6. Probation is the conditional freedom granted by a judicial officer to an adjudicated adult or juvenile offender after a period of incarceration. **(False, p. 453)**

____ 12-7. Few states use parole boards to decide when an incarcerated offender is ready for conditional release; most of that function has been taken over by prison wardens. **(False, pp. 458–459)**

____ 12-8. If a judge orders that a convicted offender's sentence be suspended and places the offender on probation, no further steps can be taken to reinstate the suspended prison time regardless of the offender's behavior while on probation. **(False, p. 456)**

____ 12-9. The number of probation and parole clients assigned to a probation or a parole officer for supervision is referred to as the officer's caseload. **(True, p. 466)**

____ 12-10. Any act or failure to act by a probationer (or parolee) that does not conform to the conditions of probation (or parole) is a violation. **(True, p. 464)**

Multiple Choice

12-11. Probation and parole
  a. are essentially the same and are terms that are used interchangeably.
  b. use different supervision techniques but are usually administered by the same office.
  c. are sentences handed down by the courts.
  d. are distinctly different forms of community corrections administered by different authorities. (p. 452)

12-12. The man known as the first probation officer, a Boston shoemaker, was
  a. John Howard.
  b. Ben Franklin.
  c. Thomas Mott Osborne.
  d. John Augustus. (p. 453)

12-13. In the 1973 case of *Gagnon* v. *Scarpelli*, the U.S. Supreme Court
a. affirmed the privilege against self-incrimination revocation hearings.
b. extended the holding in *Morrissey* v. *Brewer* to include probationers. (p. 462)
c. stressed the rehabilitative nature of probation.
d. ruled against the use of hearsay evidence in probation revocation hearings.

12-14. Parole boards grant _____ parole.
a. mandatory
b. conditional
c. discretionary (pp. 458–459)
d. limited

12-15. In what case did the court rule that the search authority of probation and parole officers might be extended to police officers in certain situations?
a. *U.S.* v. *Knights* (p. 462)
b. *Mempa* v. *Rhay*
c. *Griffin* v. *Wisconsin*
d. *Pennsylvania Board of Probation and Parole* v. *Scott*

12-16. In the event of a technical violation of probation, the _____ would be responsible for initiating violation proceedings.
a. police officer
b. probation officer (p. 456)
c. judge
d. prosecutor

12-17. In the 1983 case of *Bearden* v. *Georgia*, the U.S. Supreme Court determined that
a. a restitution order cannot be vacated through a filing of bankruptcy.
b. probation cannot be revoked for failure to pay a fine and make restitution if it can be shown that the defendant was not responsible for the failure. (p. 463)
c. a probationer's incriminating statements made to a probation officer may be used as evidence against him or her.
d. probation "comes as an act of grace to one convicted of a crime."

12-18. _____ allows for a three- to six-month regimen of military drill, drug treatment, exercise, and academic work in return for having several years removed from an inmate's sentence.
a. "Good time" law
b. Shock incarceration (p. 467)
c. Intensive parole
d. Intensive probation

12-19. All of the following are considered advantages of probation and parole except
a. relative lack of punishment. (pp. 460–461)
b. reduced risk of criminal socialization.
c. lower cost.
d. increased employment opportunities.

12-20. In the 1967 case of _____, the U.S. Supreme Court determined that both notice of the charges and a hearing are required in order to revoke an offender's probation.
a. *Gagnon* v. *Scarpelli*
b. *Morrissey* v. *Brewer*
c. *Mempa* v. *Rhay* (p. 462)
d. *Griffin* v. *Wisconsin*

Fill-In

12-21. _____ are state-ordered limits imposed on all offenders who are released on either probation or parole. **(General conditions, p. 456)**

12-22. _____ is the practice of sentencing offenders to prison, allowing them to apply for probationary release, and enacting such release in a surprise fashion. **(Shock probation, p. 467)**

12-23. A(n) _____ is used to decide if an offender has violated the terms of his or her probation or parole by committing a new offense or failing to live up to the conditions of probation or parole. **(revocation hearing, p. 456)**

12-24. Split sentencing, shock probation and parole, home confinement, shock incarceration, and community service are all examples of _____. **(intermediate sanctions, p. 466)**

12-25. _____ is also called house arrest. **(Home confinement, p. 470)**

12-26. A(n) _____ requires an offender to serve a period of confinement in a local, state, or federal facility followed by a period of probation. **(split sentence, p. 467)**

12-27. _____ makes use of "boot camp"-type prisons to impress upon convicted offenders the realities of prison life. **(Shock incarceration, p. 467)**

12-28. A(n) _____ requires that a convicted offender serve weekends in jail while on supervised probation in the community during the week. **(mixed sentence, p. 468)**

12-29. _____ is a sentencing alternative that requires offenders to spend at least part of their time working for a community agency. **(Community service, p. 469)**

12-30. _____ is a form of probation supervision involving frequent face-to-face contacts between the probationary client and probation officer. **(Intensive supervision, p. 469)**

Key—Crossword Puzzle

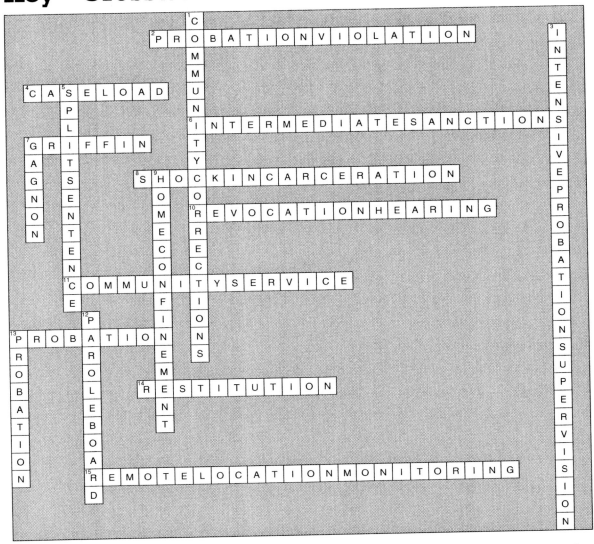

Across

2. Act or failure to act by a probationer that does not conform to the conditions of his or her probation.
4. Number of clients assigned to a probation officer.
6. Also called alternative sanctions.
7. _____ v. *Wisconsin*.
8. Like "boot camp."
10. Hearing to determine whether a probationer has violated probation.
11. Sentence that requires offenders to spend time working for a community agency.
13. Shock _____.
14. Court requirement that an alleged or convicted offender pay money or provide services to the victim.
15. Home confinement usually makes use of this system.

Down

1. Also called community-based corrections.
3. IPS.
5. Sentence explicitly requiring the convicted offender to serve a period of confinement in a local, state, or federal facility followed by a period of probation.
7. _____ v. *Scarpelli*.
9. Also called house arrest.
12. State paroling authority.
13. Suspended sentence.

Key—Word Search Puzzle

```
H L D O O E L X U P O Z J C I K R G F Y R V H C X F R T T O
L P E Y C O M M U N I T Y C O R R E C T I O N S F Z D A X R
G R H N M M R E J S S W B H Y C V F G X N U P L J C L R V H
F O L V L R G Z P R O B A T I O N R E V O C A T I O N X A S
G B W V Q E I O G D T C K P S D L A F F K E Z Z H Q F O C H
A A Q P Z M R A Q C C U N S X J D J L Y B S D L O S R U F O
J T S U D O D Q D S C O L V K V R H D N K G G Y M E L C E X C
J I R C D T B A M K U R N T Z L Z B N D S N S M E L S M A K
W O K D F E O C I W W W M J D X V Q E Q L I S M V C I C C B P
Y N M C B L Q V X L B T Z T I J X J I R X T N S O T J L E R
J T A B E O H T E Z Q V P A U Q T L Y A O R V U I N S Y A H O
C W K S C C H G D B V S C Q J E G Y P M W T F E G D I B B
N T A X C A P J S U F R Z F C R H O M T L U T E I N Z U F A
O C Z Y O T R A E I T O D B R N S F N W S G H X N T Y K U T
Z D D H M I W D N X W L D G O H C I C S M T C L E E W M P I
I H M F M O U S T O M E N I R B Z M Y X O C W X M N U P A O
U X P G U N D H E M Z A T G Y Z K M H D S F C N E C N E R N
P T F S N M W K N A H A Y Z E L D Z R W N E P N E T M O A
Y E U O I O A A C B C K F T S M L Q E V L M E A T X C I L
N L B L T N V Z E O A Z S U O A R S V Z Y V P R V I O E X
X W D U Y I O T V B L M F R H G L C T X Q B Z A E O M A B J
Y X K O S T M E R K H W Z P L B B Y I H J B K U W U L V O X
F Y C N E O R I I C G H Z F W C B E T U G G W U T Y Q E A E
L A C V R R M H E P D F Z C N L O C U X Z Z I B S Y P G R L
X C U X V I C J I E A R G M F V V O T A T O S H N U J U D D
G H F V I N O A S R Y C D N C B R S I K J I S Q C R P E K U
Y N Z D C G N G Q Q E V E U X M K B O E W C Y P U D A Y W T
F I N T E N S I V E P R O B A T I O N S U P E R V I S I O N
H L R C G B U R M Y K A X J K G S P H Z H H N M O W Q K R I
F F G T G F D Q U Y P Z V L G Q O O I J W S T T I D Z M I F
```

Caseload

Community Corrections

Community Service

Conditions of Parole

Home Confinement

Intensive Probation Supervision

Mixed Sentence

Parole

Parole Board

Probation

Probation Revocation

Remote Location Monitoring

Restitution

Revocation Hearing

Shock Probation

Split Sentence

Prisons and Jails

LEARNING OBJECTIVES

After reading this chapter, you should be able to:

- Describe the nature and history of early punishments and their impact on modern correctional philosophy
- Outline the historical development of prisons
- Discuss the major characteristics and purpose of today's prisons
- Describe the prison population in America today
- Describe the just deserts model, and explain how it has led to an increased use of imprisonment and to prison overcrowding
- Discuss how changes in the rate of criminal offending relate to changes in the rate of imprisonment during the last decade
- Explain the role that jails play in American corrections, and discuss the issues that jail administrators currently face
- Describe the role of private prisons today, and predict their future

Chapter Summary

Chapter 13 discusses five areas related to imprisonment in the United States: early punishments, the emergence of prisons, prisons today, jails, and private prisons.

The massive institutions that house many inmates today are a relatively new invention. Most early punishment was corporal punishment, attempting to satisfy the doctrine of **lex talionis**. Chapter 13 describes various types of corporal punishment, including flogging, mutilation, branding, public humiliation, workhouses, and exile.

Prisons first emerged in the early 1790s when Pennsylvania Quakers sought an alternative to corporal punishment. The **Pennsylvania system** made use of solitary confinement and also encouraged rehabilitation. The Pennsylvania system dominated prison construction until the 1820s. One of the first prisons to abandon the Pennsylvania model was Auburn prison in 1825, marking the beginning of the mass prison era. The Auburn style consisted of building mass prisons, where prisoners were held in congregate fashion and required to maintain silence.

The text describes several other historical eras in prison development. For example, it discusses how Captain Alexander Maconochie and Sir Walter Crofton influenced the practices at Elmira Reformatory. The reformatory era of prisons (1876–1890) gave way to the industrial prison era (1890–1935). During this era, prisons attempted to capitalize on convict labor. However, states had to limit the use of prison industries because of the **Ashurst-Sumners Act**. Punishment and security were the focus of the punitive era (1935–1945), but interest in reformation and rehabilitation of offenders grew in the era of treatment (1945–1967). Similarly, the community-based format era (1967–1980) attempted to decarcerate offenders and treat them in the community. This era was followed by the warehousing/overcrowding era (1980–1995)—a period during which the number of incarcerated inmates nearly tripled. Finally, the current era is referred to as the just deserts era (1995–present).

Today, there are almost 1,500 state and federal prisons in operation. The number of inmates is close to 1.5 million, and most prisons are operating above capacity. Most people sentenced to prison are convicted of violent crime, while property and drug crimes are nearly identical as the second most common types of offenses. There are more men than women in prison, and there are significant disparities by race. For example, the incarceration rate for African-Americans is ten times greater than the figure for whites. More than 350,000 people are employed in the maximum-, medium-, and minimum-security state prisons across the country. In contrast, the Federal Bureau of Prisons classifies its institution according to five security levels. Most states use a classification system to assign new prisoners to a custody level based on dangerousness, escape risk, and type of offense.

Jails are another type of confinement facility discussed in Chapter 13. Jails, the responsibility of local governments, generally house either pretrial detainees or offenders with a sentence of a year or less. There are approximately 700,000 persons in the 3,365 jails in the United States. This section of the text also discusses women as the largest growth group in jails nationwide. Women in jails pose unique challenges to jail administrators because most jurisdictions do not have separate housing for female inmates. The text also discusses the fact that many jurisdictions are using citizen volunteer programs, jail "boot camps," and regional jail systems.

The last section of Chapter 13 discusses private prisons. An increasing number of jurisdictions are contracting with private firms to provide their confinement responsibilities. Currently, there are more than 92,000 inmates housed in facilities run by private companies. Legal issues, and the relationship between the state-run and privately managed facilities, are interesting issues that have emerged since the privatization of prisons began.

Teaching Outline

I. Introduction (p. 482)

Prison A state or federal confinement facility that has custodial authority over adults sentenced to confinement. (p. 482)

II. Early Punishments (p. 482)
- Imprisonment is a relatively new punishment; most early punishments were corporal. This type of punishment is consistent with the doctrine of *lex talionis*.

Lex Talionis The law of retaliation, often expressed as "an eye for an eye" or "like for like." (p. 483)

A. Flogging (p. 483)
- Historically has been the most widely used physical punishment

---

INSTRUCTIONAL CUE

Discuss how schools, up until very recently, have relied on corporal punishment—especially whipping—to punish students for refusing to obey the rules.

B. Mutilation (p. 483)
- Considered a strategy of specific deterrence
C. Branding (p. 484)
- An example of branding is found in *The Scarlet Letter* by Nathaniel Hawthorne.
D. Public Humiliation (p. 484)
- Examples include the stocks, the pillory, the branks, and the ducking stool.
E. Workhouses (p. 484)

Workhouse An early form of imprisonment intended to instill habits of industry in the idle. (p. 484)

F. Exile (p. 484)

INSTRUCTIONAL CUE LINKED TO THE STUDENT STUDY GUIDE

Use Student Activity 1 to illustrate the use of the early punishments discussed in Chapter 13.

III. The Emergence of Prisons (p. 485)
A. The Penitentiary Era (1790–1825) (p. 485)
- Focus on the early influence of the Quakers, and describe characteristics of the Pennsylvania system.

Pennsylvania System A form of imprisonment developed by the Pennsylvania Quakers around 1790 as an alternative to corporal punishments. This style of imprisonment made use of solitary confinement and encouraged rehabilitation. (p. 487)

B. The Mass Prison Era (1825–1876) (p. 487)
- One of the first prisons to abandon the Pennsylvania model was Auburn prison in New York State.

Auburn System   A form of imprisonment developed in New York State around 1820 that depended upon mass prisons, where prisoners were held in congregate fashion requiring silence. This style of imprisonment was a primary competitor with the Pennsylvania system. (p. 487)

    C. The Reformatory Era (1876–1890) (p. 488)
- Grew out of practices of Captain Alexander Maconochie and Sir Walter Crofton

Reformatory Style   A late-nineteenth-century correctional model based upon the use of the indeterminate sentence and belief in the possibility of rehabilitation, especially for youthful offenders. The reformatory concept faded with the emergence of industrial prisons around the turn of the century. (p. 488)

    1. Captain Alexander Maconochie and Norfolk Island
- Maconochie reformed the prison at Norfolk Island, developing a system of marks and credits to earn early release. His mark system led to the recognition of the indeterminate sentence as a useful tool.

    2. Sir Walter Crofton and the Irish System
- Sir Walter Crofton adopted Maconochie's early-release idea, creating a four-stage system that helped the reintegration of offenders into the community.

    3. The Elmira Reformatory and the Birth of Parole in the United States
- These ideas influenced the practices at the Elmira Reformatory. Elmira, however, was considered a failure because of high rates of recidivism after release.

    D. The Industrial Era (1890–1935) (p. 490)

Industrial Prison   A correctional model intended to capitalize on the labor of convicts sentenced to confinement. (p. 490)

- With the failure of the reformatory style, prisons focused on the potential of inmate labor.
- Six systems of inmate labor were used in the early 1900s:
  - Contract system
  - Piece-price system
  - Lease system
  - Public-account system
  - State-use system
  - Public-works system

State-Use System   A system of inmate labor in which items produced by inmates may be sold only by or to state offices. Items that only the state can sell include such things as license plates and hunting licenses, whereas items sold only to state offices include furniture and cleaning supplies. (p. 490)

- Inmate labor was profitable, but prison industries dwindled in the early 1930s because of the Ashurst-Sumners Act.

Ashurst-Sumners Act   Federal legislation of 1935 that effectively ended the industrial prison era by restricting interstate commerce in prison-made goods. (p. 491)

- Prison industries are making somewhat of a comeback in some states and in the federal prison system under the state-use philosophy.
- Free-market prison industries are also staging a comeback.

    1. Prison Industries Today
    E. The Punitive Era (1935–1945) (p. 492)

- The focus during this era was on punishment and security.
   F. The Treatment Era (1945–1967) (p. 492)
- Interest grew in reformation and rehabilitation of offenders.
- The treatment era was based upon the medical model.

Medical Model A therapeutic perspective on correctional treatment that applies the diagnostic perspective of medical science to the handling of criminal offenders. (p. 492)

   G. The Community-Based Era (1967–1980) (p. 493)
- This era was based on the premise that rehabilitation could not occur in isolation from the community.
- Decarceration included halfway houses, work release, and open institutions.

Work Release A prison program through which inmates are temporarily released into the community in order to meet job responsibilities. (p. 494)

   H. The Warehousing Era (1980–1995) (p. 494)

Recidivism The repetition of criminal behavior. In statistical practice, a recidivism rate may be any of a number of possible counts or instances of arrest, conviction, correctional commitment, or correctional status change related to repetitions of these events within a given period of time. (p. 494)

Warehousing An imprisonment strategy that is based upon the desire to prevent recurrent crime but that has abandoned all hope of rehabilitation. (p. 495)

- Several factors contributed to the abandonment of community-based programs, including high rates of recidivism, public disappointment, high-profile news stories, and Martinson's research on the effectiveness of treatment programs.

Nothing-Works Doctrine The belief, popularized by Robert Martinson in the 1970s, that correctional treatment programs have had little success in rehabilitating offenders. (p. 495)

- Discuss how prison populations grew dramatically between 1980 and 2000.

INSTRUCTIONAL CUE

After collecting data on prison populations in your state, compare the growth of those inmate populations to the national trend, and discuss the issue of prison overcrowding as it pertains to your state system.

   I. The Just Deserts Era (1995–Present) (p. 496)

Justice Model A contemporary model of imprisonment based upon the principle of just deserts. (p. 495)

- Emphasis on Individual Responsibility
- Similar to the Punitive Era
- Examples of the move to this era include the use of chain gangs, hard labor, abolishment of parole, "three strikes and you're out" laws, and elimination of inmate "frills."
   IV. Prisons Today (p. 498)
- Approximately 1,500 state and 84 federal prisons are in operation today.
   - The prison population has quadrupled since 1980.
   - Highlight the disparities by race and by gender.

- Prisons are overcrowded.
- Most people who receive sentences are sentenced to state prisons for violent crimes.

A. Overcrowding (p. 499)

- Describe the definitions of prison capacity (rated, operational, and design).

Prison Capacity   The size of the correctional population an institution can effectively hold. There are three types of prison capacity: rated, operational, and design. *Source*: Bureau of Justice Statistics, *Prisoners in 1998* (Washington, D.C.: BJS, 1999), p. 7. (p. 500)

Rated Capacity   The number of inmates a prison can handle according to the judgment of experts. (p. 500)

Operational Capacity   The number of inmates a prison can effectively accommodate based upon management considerations. (p. 500)

Design Capacity   The number of inmates a prison was intended to hold when it was built or modified. (p. 500)

- *Rhodes* v. *Chapman* held that crowding is not cruel and unusual punishment.
1. Selective Incapacitation: A Strategy to Reduce Prison Populations
    - Collective incapacitation is a strategy that would imprison all serious offenders, and selective incapacitation seeks to identify the most dangerous and then remove them from society.

B. Security Levels (p. 502)

- Maximum
    - Older prisons with large inmate populations
    - High level of security
    - Frequent counts

INSTRUCTIONAL CUE

Organize a field trip to a nearby institution. Seeing the inside of a maximum-security prison is one of the most effective ways to highlight differences in the various types of prisons.

- Medium
    - Medium-security prisons are smaller than maximum-security and are more likely to have barbed-wire fences than thick walls.
    - Dormitory housing
- Minimum
    - Minimum-security prisons are like dormitories, and inmates are free to walk the yard.
    - Inmates may have private rooms.

C. Prison Classification Sustems (p. 503)

Classification System   A system used by prison administrators to assign inmates to custody levels based on offense history, assessed dangerousness, perceived risk of escape, and other factors. (p. 503)

D. The Federal Prison System (p. 504)
- The federal bureau of prisons was created in 1930.
- The federal system classifies prisons according to five custody levels.
- One of the most recent is the ultra-high-security prison (ADMAX).

ADMAX Administrative maximum. The term is used by the federal government to denote ultra-high-security prisons. (p. 505)

E. Recent Improvements (p. 507)
- Accreditation of prisons
- The National Academy of Corrections

V. Jails (p. 507)

Jail A confinement facility administered by an agency of local government, typically a law enforcement agency, intended for adults but sometimes also containing juveniles, which holds people detained pending adjudication or committed after adjudication, usually those sentenced to a year or less. (p. 507)

- There are 713,970 jail inmates; 12% are women.
- About 60% are pretrial detainees.
- A total of 3,365 jails are in operation today.
- Approximately 20 million people are admitted to jail each year.
- Sixty-one percent are members of minority groups.

A. Women and Jail (p. 508)
- Females are the largest growth group in jails nationwide.
- Pregnancy and drug abuse are significant sources of difficulty for jailed women.
- Many jurisdictions do not have separate jail facilities to house women.
- About 22% of correctional officers are women.

B. The Growth of Jails (p. 510)
- Crowding is caused by increasing crime rates and a punitive public attitude.
- Jails warehouse prisoners (when space is not available in prisons) and pretrial detainees.

C. Direct-Supervision Jails (p. 511)
- In response to many of the problems in jails, direct supervision emerged as a new jail strategy.

Direct-Supervision Jail A temporary confinement facility that eliminates many of the traditional barriers between inmates and correctional staff. Physical barriers in direct-supervision jails are far less common than in traditional jails, allowing staff members the opportunity for greater interaction with, and control over, residents. (p. 512)

- Attempts to reduce inmate dissatisfaction, deter rape and violence, and allow officers to maintain control of the institution

D. Jails and the Future (p. 513)
- Growth of jail industries
- Citizen volunteer programs
- Jail boot camps

 • Regional jails

Regional Jail   A jail that is built and run using the combined resources of a variety of local jurisdictions. (p. 513)

 • The emergence of state jail standards

VI. Private Prisons (p. 514)

Privatization   The movement toward the wider use of private prisons. (p. 514)

Private Prison   A correctional institution operated by a private firm on behalf of a local or state government. (p. 515)

INSTRUCTIONAL CUE LINKED TO THE STUDENT STUDY GUIDE

Student Activity 4 will help students understand private prisons in the United States.

Learner Activities

Activity 1

Consider the following case. Michael Faye was an 18-year-old American living with his parents in Singapore when he was arrested for spray-painting cars during ten days of vandalism. He confessed to these crimes but later said that his confession was coerced by police officials who severely beat him. He was convicted and sentenced to four strokes with a rattan cane—a punishment in which the prisoner is flogged, tearing open the skin and producing permanent scars. Was his punishment a violation of Michael Faye's rights? Remember that his crime took place in Singapore, a legal system that balances individual and community rights very differently from our own. Indeed, more than 1,000 prisoners are caned per year in Singapore. Do you think we should use similar types of punishment in the United States? Would you recommend the use of any of the other early punishments described in Chapter 13? Why?

_____

_____

_____

_____

_____

_____

Activity 2

LIBRARY EXTRA

Visit **Library Extra 13–3**. This link provides a discussion of internal prison classification systems. Summarize the major findings from this study.

_____

_____

_____

_____

_____

Activity 3

Collect data to answer the following questions about the prisons in the state where your campus is located. How many inmates are incarcerated in the state? How many prisons are there? How many maximum-security? Medium? Minimum? How has the number of prisoners changed over time? Present the data you collected in the space below, and then discuss how the data on your state system are similar to and different from the national data presented in Chapter 13.

_____
_____
_____
_____
_____
_____

Activity 4

Many private companies, such as Corrections Corporation of America and Corrections Concepts, have been able to convince legislators to turn over the operation of some prisons (or prison functions) to private companies. Do you think the use of private companies to run state prison systems is a good idea? What are some problems with using private companies? Do you think the prisons run by private companies will be more effective than state-run prisons? Explain your answer.

_____
_____
_____
_____
_____

Internet Activity

Visit the _Corrections Connection_ on the World Wide Web (http://www.corrections.com). View (and click on) the topics in the "Headlines" section. Write a brief summary of three different items. Your instructor may request that you submit these summaries.

_____
_____
_____
_____
_____

Distance Learning Activity

Visit the *Prison Legal News* (http://www.prisonlegalnews.org) website or some other corrections' news website. In the space below, summarize one of the articles or cases posted on the website. If your instructor asks you to do so, share your summary with other students in the class and participate in a class discussion about the issues that students wrote about.

_____

_____

_____

_____

_____

_____

Learning Activities Utilizing the World Wide Web

There are student-based activities in the Student Study Guide (Internet Activity, Distance Learning Activity, CJ Today on the World Wide Web) that are similar in focus to those that follow. However, the following are presented as instructor-led activities, to be used in a classroom with online access.

Visit the *Corrections Connection* on the World Wide Web (http://www.corrections. com). View the topics in the "Hot Topics" section. Display the highlights of each site and review them in class.

Visit the *Correctional News* website or some other major industry legal publication (see *Correctional News Online*: http://www.correctionalnews.com or *Prison Legal News*: http://www.prisonlegalnews.org). Display the sites in class, and ask students to summarize and discuss the articles in class.

Other websites for organizations and agencies related to the material in Chapter 13 include:

American Correctional Association	http://www.corrections.com/aca
American Jail Association	http://www.corrections.com/aja
Correctional News Online	http://www.correctionalnews.com
Corrections (NCJRS)	http://virlib.ncjrs.org/Corrections.asp
Federal Bureau of Prisons	http://www.bop.gov/bopmain.html
The Other Side of the Wall	http://www.prisonwall.org
Prison Diaries	http://www.npr.org/programs/atc/prisondiaries
Prison Industry Links	http://www.corrections.com/industries
National Juvenile Detention Association	http://www.njda.com
Prison Legal News	http://www.prisonlegalnews.org

Suggested Answers to Chapter Discussion Questions

1. **What types of criminal punishments were used before the advent of imprisonment as a criminal sanction? How have early punishments influenced modern correctional philosophy?**

   Most early punishments were cruel and inhumane. Types include flogging, mutilation, branding, public humiliation, workhouses, and exile. While it has been suggested that the United States return to physical punishments and public humiliation, most consider these options unacceptable. Opponents decry the deterrent effects, suggesting that such punishments would provoke rather than deter.

2. **Trace the historical development of prisons, beginning with the Pennsylvania system.**

   The Pennsylvania system, established by the Quakers around 1790, employed solitary confinement, penance, and Bible study to achieve rehabilitation.

   The Auburn style, also referred to as the congregate but silent system, was developed around 1820. In this form, massed prisoners were held in congregate fashion but required to maintain silence.

   Around 1876, the reformatory concept used indeterminate sentencing in an effort to rehabilitate inmates. It fell victim to the onset of the industrial prison age, in which states saw the opportunity to capitalize on inmate labor.

   Industrial prisons emerged around 1890. The demise of the industrial prison era was brought about by a moratorium on free-market prison industries imposed by the Ashurst-Sumners Act of 1935.

   The punitive era followed, characterized by an increased focus on custody and institutional security and an "out-of-sight, out-of-mind" philosophy in American attitudes toward inmates.

   In 1945, the treatment era evolved. Based upon a medical model of corrections, the philosophy implied that offenders were sick and could be rehabilitated through proper treatment.

   The community-based format, begun in the mid-1960s, represented a movement away from traditional confinement and an attempt to reform offenders' behavior within local communities.

   High recidivism rates, resulting in public disappointment, ultimately led to a warehousing strategy in the late 1970s. Warehousing seeks to prevent recurring crime but abandons any hope of rehabilitation. It has also resulted in high rates of overcrowding in prisons throughout the country.

   The mid-1990s saw the emergence of the just deserts era. Its emphasis is on individual responsibility for one's actions, with the imposition of deserved punishment as the logical consequence of wrongful actions. Just deserts continues to be the most influential perspective in the criminal justice field today, although there are some signs that it is beginning to wane.

   How has correctional practice in America changed over time?

   Clearly, each era has been based on dissatisfaction with the effects of the preceding philosophy, leading to a "try something different" approach. The eras' emphases seem to pass repetitively through a punishment-rehabilitation-punishment cycle, with the focus changing to accommodate social attitudes toward crime and criminal offenders.

   What changes do you predict for the future?

   The reemergence of prison industries, efforts to improve the quality of jail life, and the movement toward regional jails and private prisons typify ongoing efforts to find better ways to handle incarceration of convicted offenders.

3. **What are today's prisons like? What purposes do they serve?**

   Prisons have been influenced by a long history of using prisons to primarily punish. One goal of prisons is reform offenders—the hope that through isolation and treatment the offender will change. Such efforts to rehabilitate are adversely influenced by the bureaucratic realities of prison organizations as well as changing attitudes about crime and punishment in the United States. The public has come to expect that prisons are places of punishment, and there has been public and political pressure to remove various types of treatment programming. The number of prisons, and the size of prison populations, has grown dramatically in the last 25 years. Many prisons are overcrowded because of the emphasis on just deserts. Prisons certainly punish and isolate offenders from society, but they are not very effective at rehabilitating offenders.

4. **What are the social characteristics of today's prisoners? What gender and racial disparities, if any, exist in today's prison populations?**

Most people sentenced to state prisons have been convicted of violent crimes; most federal prisoners were convicted of drug crimes. Imprisonment varies considerably among states. There is a huge growing disparity between imprisonment rates for blacks and whites. Consider the following statistical difference: 1,229 white men are imprisoned for every 100,000 white men in their late 20s; 10,376 black men for every 100,000 black men of the same age are imprisoned. Many more men are sentenced to prison compared to women, but the incarceration rates for women are increasing at a greater rate.

5. **What is the just deserts model of corrections? Explain the pros and cons of this model. How has it led to an increased use of imprisonment and to prison overcrowding?**

The justice model emphasizes individual responsibility, and imprisonment is seen as a fully deserved and proper response for criminal behavior.

The just deserts model clearly achieves the sentencing goals of retribution, incapacitation, and deterrence. Society feels safer with so many of its predators locked away, and theoretically the pool of offenders available to commit crimes is reduced.

The downside, of course, is the high cost of housing, feeding, treating, training, and supervising an ever-growing prison population. And the pool of available offenders has not declined as anticipated, as new candidates move in to seize criminal opportunities vacated by incarcerated offenders.

6. **What is the relationship, if any, between changes in the rate of criminal offending and changes in the rate of imprisonment in America over the last decade? What is the reason for that relationship?**

It is difficult to evaluate the link between criminal offending and imprisonment rates. In general, crime rates have declined significantly over the last ten years and imprisonment rates have increased dramatically. Supporters of the just deserts philosophy argue that the increases in imprisonment rates have caused the decline in crime rates, although there are many other possible explanations for the decline in crime rates including demographic changes and increased effectiveness of other criminal justice strategies.

7. **What role do jails play in American corrections? What are some of the issues that jail administrators currently face?**

Jails have a variety of roles in American corrections. First, they receive individuals pending arraignment and hold them awaiting trial. Second, they readmit probation, parole, and bail-bond violators and absconders. Third, they temporarily detain juveniles, the mentally ill, and others pending transfer. Fourth, they hold individuals for the military, for protective custody, for contempt, and for the courts as witnesses. Fifth, they transfer inmates to federal, state, and local authorities. Sixth, they house inmates from federal and state prison institutions because of overcrowding. Seventh, they operate community-based programs. Finally, they hold inmates sentenced to short terms.

One issue for jail administrators is dealing with the growing population of women who are confined in jails. Jails were not designed to meet the unique needs of female offenders. Jails are also significantly overcrowded. Other issues include antiquated architectural design and organizational problems.

8. **What is the role of private prisons today? What will be the state of private prisons two or three decades from now?**

Private prisons present a viable option but raise difficult questions that will undoubtedly lead to legal challenges. For example, is the state ultimately responsible if an employee of a private prison firm harms an inmate? After all, the state incarcerated the inmate and then passed off responsibility for daily supervision of the inmate to a private entity by virtue of a contract with that entity. Does such passage of responsibility relieve the state of its overall responsibility?

To be successful, private prisons must be subject to aggressive oversight. States cannot adopt an "It's their problem now" attitude based on the belief that the existence of a contract shields the state from responsibility for conditions in the prisons.

Private prisons will likely flourish as governments seek to privatize many of the services and functions of government. The jury is still out on whether private prisons can consistently achieve correctional goals at predicted lower costs.

Key—Student Study Guide Questions

True or False

_____ 13-1. A state or federal confinement facility that has custodial authority over adults sentenced to confinement for less than one year is called a prison. **(False, p. 507)**

_____ 13-2. Under *lex talionis* the convicted offender was sentenced to a punishment that most closely approximated the original injury. **(True, p. 483)**

_____ 13-3. An overview of various approaches to correctional treatment suggests that programs focused on rehabilitation should be abolished. **(False, p. 493)**

_____ 13-4. Jails are often thought of as the "shame of the criminal justice system." **(True, p. 510)**

_____ 13-5. The movement toward the wider use of private prisons is called corporationalization. **(False, p. 514)**

_____ 13-6. Prisons that flourished during the industrial prison era, and whose intent was to capitalize on the labor of convicts sentenced to confinement, were part of the reformatory concept. **(False, p. 488)**

_____ 13-7. The just deserts model was a late-nineteenth-century correctional model based upon the use of the indeterminate sentence and belief in the possibility of rehabilitation of offenders. **(False, p. 496)**

_____ 13-8. At one time, England used hulks to house convicted offenders and send them into exile. **(True, p. 485)**

_____ 13-9. The 1935 Taft-Hartley Act effectively ended the industrial prison era by restricting interstate commerce in prison-made goods. **(False, p. 491)**

_____ 13-10. Direct-supervision jails are temporary confinement facilities that eliminate many of the traditional barriers between inmates and correctional staff. **(True, p. 512)**

Multiple Choice

13-11. The term used by the federal government to denote ultra-high-security prisons is
   a. ULTRAMAX.
   b. SUPERMAX.
   c. ADMAX. (p. 505)
   d. MAXIMAX.

13-12. The group that most influenced the beginnings of the American prison experience was the
   a. Pilgrims.
   b. Quakers. (p. 485)
   c. Catholic Church.
   d. Salvation Army.

13-13. The first American penitentiary, opened in the late 1700s in Philadelphia, was called
   a. Alcatraz.
   b. Huntsville Prison.
   c. Walnut Street Jail. (p. 485)
   d. Eastern Penitentiary.

13-14. One of the first attempts at parole, as practiced by Ireland's Sir Walter Crofton, allowed offenders to earn a conditional release by meeting certain objectives. Release was granted under a
   a. good behavior rule.
   b. Marx system.
   c. mark system.
   d. ticket of leave. (p. 489)

13-15. The feature of Eastern and Western penitentiaries that most clearly characterized the nineteenth-century Pennsylvania correctional philosophy was
   a. corporal punishment.
   b. solitary confinement. (p. 487)
   c. congregate cellblocks.
   d. the whipping post.

13-16. Auburn prison, established in 1823 in New York State, attempted to reform prisoners by
   a. enforcing the "codes of confinement."
   b. torturing them.
   c. using forced labor and the silent system. (p. 487)
   d. using the pleasure-pain principle.

13-17. *Lex talionis* is a Latin term that means
   a. "the law of the king."
   b. "the law of retaliation." (p. 483)
   c. "the law of the dead."
   d. "the law of the land."

13-18. The 1981 U.S. Supreme Court case of *Rhodes* v. *Chapman* dealt with the issue of prison overcrowding and held that
   a. placing two inmates in one cell is cruel and unusual punishment.
   b. placing two inmates in one cell is not cruel and unusual punishment. (p. 500)
   c. inmates must show that prison officials exhibited "deliberate indifference" by not dealing with overcrowding sooner.
   d. inmates have a reasonable expectation of privacy that is violated by having to share a cell with another inmate.

13-19. _____ house the most serious offenders and are characterized by double and triple security patterns.
   a. Maximum-security prisons (p. 502)
   b. Reformatories
   c. Medium-security prisons
   d. Minimum-security prisons

13-20. The number of inmates a prison was intended to hold when it was built or modified is its
   a. prison capacity.
   b. rated capacity.
   c. operational capacity.
   d. design capacity. (p. 500)

Fill-In

13-21. The _____ was a form of imprisonment developed by the Quakers that made use of solitary confinement and resulted in the nation's first penitentiary. **(Pennsylvania system, p. 487)**

13-22. _____ is the repetition of criminal behavior. **(Recidivism, p. 494)**

13-23. The _____ was a form of early imprisonment designed to instill a work ethic in the idle. **(workhouse, p. 484)**

13-24. The _____ held that treatment programs have little rehabilitative success. **(nothing-works doctrine, p. 495)**

13-25. The _____ is a form of inmate labor in which items produced by inmates are salable only to state agencies. **(state-use system, p. 490)**

13-26. _____ is a prison program through which inmates are temporarily released into the community in order to meet job responsibilities. **(Work release, p. 494)**

13-27. _____ is an imprisonment strategy that is based upon the desire to prevent recurrent crime but that has abandoned any hope of rehabilitation. **(Warehousing, p. 494)**

13-28. The _____ of imprisonment is characterized by a belief that offenders are sick and can be cured through behavioral and other forms of therapy. **(medical model, p. 492)**

13-29. The _____ is a contemporary model of imprisonment based on the social philosophy of just deserts. **(justice model, p. 496)**

13-30. A(n) _____ jail is built and run using the combined resources of a variety of local jurisdictions. **(regional, p. 513)**

Key—Crossword Puzzle

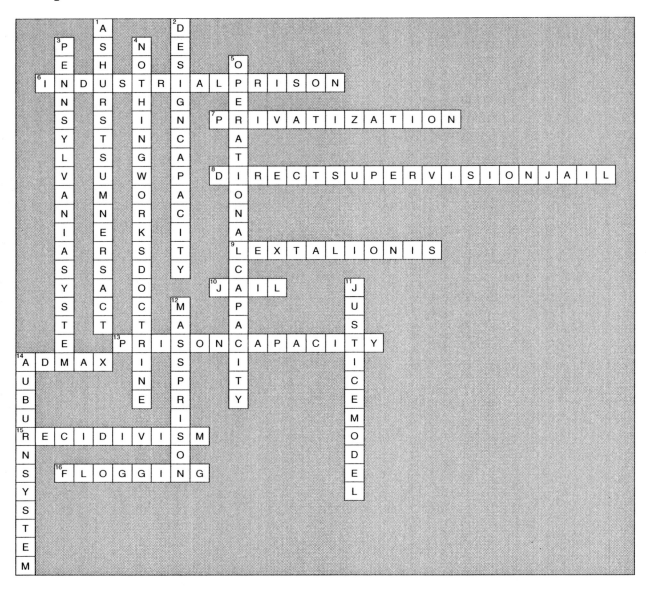

Across

6. Correctional model intended to capitalize on the labor of convicts.
7. Movement toward the wider use of private prisons.
8. Also called new-generation or podular jail.
9. Law of retaliation.
10. Short-term confinement facility.
13. Size of the correctional population an institution can effectively hold.
14. Administrative maximum.
15. Repetition of criminal behavior.
16. Historically, the most widely used of physical punishments.

Down

1. Act that ended the industrial prison era.
2. Number of inmates a prison was intended to hold when it was built or modified.
3. Form of imprisonment developed by the Quakers.
4. Belief popularized by Robert Martinson.
5. Number of inmates a prison can effectively accommodate based on management considerations.
11. Just deserts.
12. Auburn prison system emerged in this era.
14. Form of imprisonment developed in New York.

Key—Word Search Puzzle

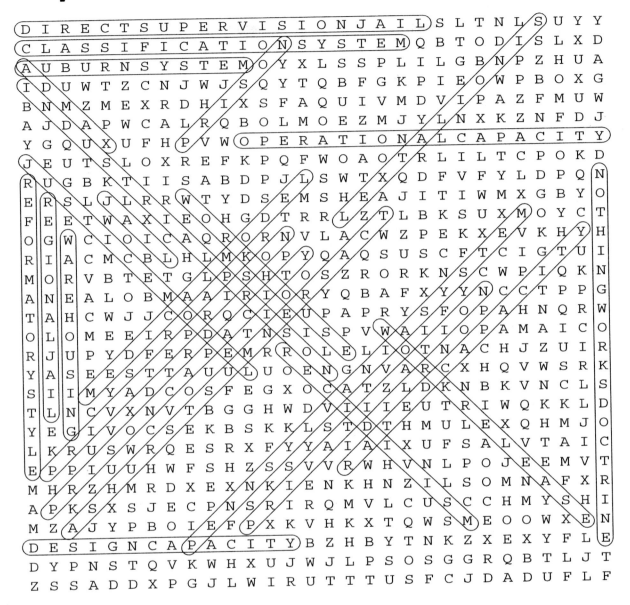

ADMAX
Ashurst-Sumners Act
Auburn System
Classification System
Design Capacity
Direct-Supervision Jail
Industrial Prison
Jail
Justice Model
Lex Talionis
Medical Model
Nothing-Works Doctrine
Operational Capacity

Pennsylvania System
Prison
Prison Capacity
Private Prison
Privatization
Rated Capacity
Recidivism
Reformatory Style
Regional Jail
Warehousing
Workhouse
Work Release

Prison Life

LEARNING OBJECTIVES

After reading this chapter, you should be able to:

- Describe the realities of prison life and subculture from the inmate's point of view
- Explain the concept of prisonization
- Illustrate the significant differences between men's prisons and women's prisons
- Describe the realities of prison life from the correctional officer's point of view
- Describe the causes of prison riots, and list the stages through which most riots progress
- Explain the nature of the hands-off doctrine, and discuss the status of that doctrine today
- Discuss the legal aspects of prisoners' rights, and explain the consequences of precedent-setting U.S. Supreme Court cases in the area of prisoners' rights
- Explain the balancing test established by the U.S. Supreme Court as it relates to the rights of prisoners
- Explain state-created rights within the context of corrections
- Describe the major problems and issues that prisons face today

Chapter Summary

Chapter 14 describes life in prison. The text focuses on the various social realities that coexist among correctional officers and inmates in male and female institutions, including prison riots, prisoners' rights, and other issues facing prisons today.

The discussion of the realities of the male inmate's world revolves around the discussion of **total institutions** and **prison subcultures**. Since inmates share all aspects of their lives on a daily basis, prison life is shaped by both the official structure and rules and the values and behavioral patterns of the inmates. New inmates undergo a process of **prisonization**, learning the values, language (**prison argot**), and rules of the institution. The text also describes nine inmate types who occupy various positions in the prison hierarchy.

Chapter 14 also describes the realities of life in prison for women. Although accounting for only 6.8% of the U.S. prison inmate population, the number of women in prison is growing rapidly. Two important factors contributing to this growth are female involvement in drug and drug-related offenses and the demise of the "chivalry factor." Although there is some disagreement among scholars attempting to describe the social structure of women's prisons, many researchers find that females are more likely to be involved in prison "families." Also, the amount and type of violence in female institutions is significantly different from what is found in male institutions. The text describes several types of female inmates, including the "square," the "cool," the "life," and "crack kids."

Correctional officers also undergo a socialization process into the prison culture. Due to overcrowded prisons and limitations in the number of staff, the primary mission of correctional officers is custody and control. The text describes six types of correctional officers and how they relate to inmates. The field of corrections is growing and is undergoing significant changes. Among the efforts to adapt to these changes is the professionalization of correctional officers.

Chapter 14 also discusses prison riots, emphasizing the explosive decade of prison riots. Several significant riots occurred between 1970 and 1980, beginning with the Attica riots and ending with the Santa Fe prison riots. Research indicates that the causes of prison riots include an insensitive prison administration and neglected inmates' demands, the lifestyles most inmates are familiar with on the streets, dehumanizing prison conditions, the way that riots regulate inmate society and redistribute power, and the power vacuums created by a variety of factors. The text also discusses the five typical stages of a riot and the control of riots.

Chapter 14 provides an examination of the legal rights of inmates. Historically, courts have adhered to a policy of nonintervention with regard to prison management. However, this **"hands-off doctrine"** was abandoned in the late 1960s. Courts have since provided precedent in many areas important to life in prison, including communications, religious practice, visitation, legal access to courts, privacy, medical care, and disciplinary proceedings. The **balancing test** is the important test applied to these areas of prison life. This test, articulated in the *Pell* v. *Procunier* decision, attempts to weigh the rights of an individual against the authority of states to make laws or otherwise restrict a person's freedom.

Chapter 14 concludes with a discussion of three issues facing prisons today. First, it discusses AIDS in prisons, describing the number of inmates infected and some of the strategies in place to reduce the transmission of this disease. Second, it discusses the growing geriatric offender population. With longer sentences, and the "graying" of the population, administrators must implement policies to deal with the special needs of geriatric and long-term inmates. Third, the special needs of mentally ill inmates are discussed.

Teaching Outline

I. Introduction (p. 526)

   A. Research on Prison Life—Total Institutions (p. 526)

Total Institution An enclosed facility separated from society both socially and physically, where the inhabitants share all aspects of their lives daily. (p. 526)

II. The Male Inmate's World (p. 527)
  • The inmate world is controlled by the prison subculture.

Prison Subculture The values and behavioral patterns characteristic of prison inmates. Prison subculture has been found to be surprisingly consistent across the country. (p. 527)

  • The socialization into the prison subculture is called *prisonization*.

Prisonization The process whereby newly institutionalized offenders come to accept prison lifestyles and criminal values. Although many inmates begin their prison experience with only a few values that support criminal behavior, the socialization experience they undergo while incarcerated leads to a much greater acceptance of such values. (p. 527)

  • Describe and articulate the rules of the inmate code.
  • Define *prison argot*.

Prison Argot The slang characteristic of prison subcultures and prison life. (p. 528)

  A. The Evolution of Prison Subcultures
    • Stastny and Tyrnauer describe four subcultures: Official, Traditional, Reform, and Revolutionary.

INSTRUCTIONAL CUE

Discuss subcultures, including the fact that they can be found in many occupations and different human environments. For example, when discussing law enforcement, the text describes the police subculture. Similarly, many cultures and subcultures exist on college campuses, such as the fraternity and sorority subcultures. Have students try to identify different subcultures in a class discussion.

INSTRUCTIONAL CUE LINKED TO THE STUDENT STUDY GUIDE

Student Activity 1 will help students appreciate how subcultures develop and are molded by different environments.

  B. The Functions of Prison Subcultures (p. 529)
    • Introduce Sykes's "pains of imprisonment."
    • Contrast the deprivation model with the importation model of prison culture.
  C. Prison Lifestyles and Inmate Types (p. 529)
    • Highlight some of the inmate types.
  D. Homosexuality in Prison (p. 532)
    • Argot terms that explain homosexuality include *wolf* (a male inmate who assumes the masculine role in homosexual relations), *punk* (an inmate who is forced into submitting to the female role), and *fag* (an inmate who has a proclivity toward homosexual activity and effeminate mannerisms).
    • Wolves and punks are committed to heterosexuality but participate in homosexual activity due to their situation.

INSTRUCTIONAL CUE

The text describes nine inmate types. Ask students to develop a hierarchy based on the descriptions of these inmate types. What inmate types have the most power in prison society? Who would have the least amount of power? Through this exercise, students will develop an appreciation for the different types. It will also help them understand various aspects of inmate society.

Student Activity 2 will help students understand the realities of prison life for male and female inmates.

III. The Female Inmate's World (p. 533)
- Women account for 6.8% of prison inmates.
  - Drugs and drug-related offenses are major contributors to the growing female prison population.
  - Growth can also be linked to the demise of the "chivalry factor."
  - The average female inmate is 29 to 30 years old, is black or Hispanic (57%), comes from a single-parent or broken home, and has family members who are incarcerated (50%).
  - Eighty percent of women in prison are mothers.
  A. Gender Responsiveness (p. 536)
  - Prisons only recently have been designed with meaningful programs for women.
  B. Institutions for Women (p. 536)
  C. Social Structure in Women's Prisons (p. 537)
  - Discuss female involvement in prison "families."
  D. Types of Female Inmates (p. 538)
  - Describe the *square*, the *cool*, the *life*, and *crack kids*.
  E. Violence in Women's Prisons (p. 539)
  - Violence is less frequent than violence in male prisons.
IV. The Staff World (p. 539)
- Like inmates, correctional officers undergo a socialization process.
- The primary concern among officers is custody and control.

Student Activity 3 will assist students in understanding the important issues that face prisons today.

  A. The Professionalization of Correctional Officers (p. 542)
  - Highlight the increased use of psychological screening and training programs.
V. Prison Riots (p. 543)
- Describe the Attica and Santa Fe prison riots, as well as some of the more recent riots.
  A. Causes of Riots (p. 544)
  - An insensitive prison administration and neglected inmates' demands.
  - The lifestyles most inmates are familiar with on the streets.
  - Dehumanizing prison conditions.
  - Discuss how riots regulate inmate society and redistribute power. Various inmate groups struggle for power in the institution. Riots provide opportunities to rebalance this structure, and some groups will gain power while others lose power.

Security Threat Group (STG) An inmate group, gang, or organization whose members act together to pose a threat to the safety of correctional staff or the public, or who prey upon other inmates, or who threaten the secure and orderly operation of a correctional institution. (p. 544)

- Power vacuums are created by a variety of factors. For example, through much of the twentieth century, Texas prisons relied on "building tenders." Building tenders are inmates given special privileges by administrators in exchange for helping monitor and control the rest of the prison population. When this system was terminated, it created a power vacuum in the prison and the amount of violence against inmates and guards increased dramatically.

B. Stages in Riots and Riot Control (p. 544)

- Explosion
- Organization (into inmate-led groups)
- Confrontation (with authority)
- Termination (through negotiation or physical confrontation)
- Reaction and explanation (usually by investigative commissions)

VI. Prisoners' Rights (p. 545)

Hands-Off Doctrine A policy of nonintervention with regard to prison management that U.S. courts tended to follow until the late 1960s. For the past 30 years the doctrine has languished as judicial intervention in prison administration dramatically increased, although there is now some evidence that a new hands-off era is approaching. (p. 545)

Civil Death The legal status of prisoners in some jurisdictions who are denied the opportunity to vote, hold public office, marry, or enter into contracts by virtue of their status as incarcerated felons. While civil death is primarily of historical interest, some jurisdictions still limit the contractual opportunities available to inmates. (p. 545)

A. The Legal Basis of Prisoners' Rights (p. 546)

Balancing Test A principle developed by the courts and applied to the corrections arena by *Pell* v. *Procunier* (1974), that attempts to weigh the rights of an individual as guaranteed by the Constitution against the authority of states to make laws or to otherwise restrict a person's freedom in order to protect the state's interests and its citizens. (p. 546)

B. Precedents in Prisoners' Rights (p. 547)

1. Communications and Visitation

- *Procunier* v. *Martinez*: A prisoner's mail may be censored if it is necessary to do so for security purposes.
- *McNamara* v. *Moody*: Mere institutional convenience does not provide sufficient basis to censor mail.
- *Mallery* v. *Lewis*: Magazines depicting deviant sexual behavior can be banned.
- *Block* v. *Rutherford*: In the interests of security, jails can prohibit all visits from friends and relatives.
- *Pell* v. *Procunier*: The Supreme Court established a "balancing test" to guide prison authorities in determining what rights an inmate should have. Inmates should have the same rights as nonincarcerated citizens, provided that the legitimate needs of the prison for security, custody, and safety are not compromised.
- *Houchins* v. *KQED*: News personnel cannot be denied correspondence with inmates, but they have no constitutional right to interview inmates or inspect correctional facilities beyond what is available to the general public.

2. Religious Freedom

- *Cruz* v. *Beto*: Inmates must be given a "reasonable opportunity" to pursue their religious faith even if it differs from traditional forms of worship.

- *Hill* v. *Blackwell*: A prison regulation prohibiting the wearing of beards, even if grown for religious reasons, was held to be acceptable for security reasons.

3. Access to the Courts and Legal Assistance
   - *Bounds* v. *Smith*: Not only confirms the right of prisoners to have access to the courts and to legal assistance but also requires states to assist inmates in the preparation and filing of legal papers. This assistance can be given through trained personnel or through the creation and availability of a law library for inmates.
   - *Johnson* v. *Avery*: Inmates have a right to consult "jailhouse lawyers" for advice if assistance from trained legal professionals is not available.

4. Medical Care
   - *Estelle* v. *Gamble*: Requires prison officials to provide for inmates' medical care, and establishes the concept of "deliberate indifference" in determining whether prison administrators are meeting the medical needs of prisoners.

Deliberate Indifference   A wanton disregard by correctional personnel for the well-being of inmates. Deliberate indifference requires both actual knowledge that a harm is occurring and disregard of the risk of harm. A prison official may be held liable under the Eighth Amendment for acting with deliberate indifference to inmates' health or safety only if he or she knows that inmates face a substantial risk of serious harm and disregards that risk by failing to take reasonable measures to abate it. (p. 551)

- *Hudson* v. *McMillan*: The Supreme Court clarified the concept of "deliberate indifference" by holding that it requires both actual knowledge and disregard of risk of harm.
- *Newman* v. *Alabama*: Found Alabama's prison medical services to be so inadequate as to be "shocking to the conscience."
- *Ruiz* v. *Estelle*: Challenged the structure of the Texas prison system and specifically required major changes in the handling of inmates' medical care. The court ordered an improvement in record keeping, physical facilities, and general medical care while it continued to monitor the progress of the department.

5. Protection from Harm
   - *Holt* v. *Sarver*: This case examined conditions at two Arkansas state prison farms, concluding that the conditions were disproportionate to any offense.
   - *Farmer* v. *Brennan*: The U.S. Supreme Court provided substantial protections to prison administration by holding that they cannot be held liable for the harm if they took steps to mitigate the risk.

6. Privacy
   - Fourth Ammendment rights are not extended to prisoners.
   - No expectation of privacy while incarcerated.
   - *Hudson* v. *Palmer*: The need for prison officials to conduct thorough and unannounced searches precludes inmates' right to privacy in personal possessions.
   - *Block* v. *Rutherford*: In the interests of security, jails can prohibit all visits from friends and relatives.

7. Institutional Punishment and Discipline

Grievance Procedure   A formalized arrangement, usually involving a neutral hearing board, whereby institutionalized individuals have the opportunity to register complaints about the conditions of their confinement. (p. 556)

- *Jones* v. *North Carolina Prisoners' Labor Union*: Prisons must establish some formal opportunity for the airing of inmate grievances.
- *Wolff* v. *McDonnell*: Sanctions cannot be levied against inmates without appropriate due process. Beginning of the concept of "state-created liberty interests."

C. A Return to the Hands-Off Doctrine? (p. 557)

- Recent rulings by the Supreme Court signal what appears to be a return to the hands-off doctrine.
- *Wilson* v. *Seiter*: The Court will hear an inmate's complaint if he or she can show "deliberate indifference" by the officials responsible for the existence of those conditions.
- *Sandin* v. *Conner*: Case set aside substantial portions of the *Wolff* v. *McDonnell* and *Hewitt* v. *Helms* rulings.

1. The Prison Litigation Reform Act of 1996

- This act represents an effort to restrict inmate filings of civil suits.

VII. Issues Facing Prisons Today (p. 559)

A. AIDS (p. 559)

- About 140 cases per 100,000 inmates
- Strategies to reduce the transmission of AIDS include segregation, education, and prevention.

B. Geriatric Offenders (p. 561)

- Discuss the growth of an older inmate population and the special problems this growth poses for correctional administrators.

C. Mentally Ill and Mentally Deficient Inmates (p. 565)

- Some may be undiagnosed at the time of trial or become symptomatic after incarceration.
- Mentally deficient inmates may have special needs, but not all facilities are equipped to deal with these needs.

D. Terrorism (p. 566)

- America's efforts to fight terrorism are affecting prisons.
- Correctional personnel need to be vigilant in gathering critical intelligence.

Instructional Cue Linked to the Student Study Guide

Student Activity 4 will help students understand local corrections officials' attempts to deal with significant prison and jail issues.

Learner Activities

Activity 1

Your text outlines in great detail the adaptation process that inmates go through when entering a prison setting and describes the prisonization process. How are these adaptations similar to and different from the adaptations that students have to make at a college campus? What subcultures exist on your campus? Is there an argot unique to college campuses?

_____
_____
_____

Activity 2

Mike and his sister Michelle committed several bank robberies together. After they were caught, tried, and convicted, the judge sentenced them both to 25 to 50 years in a maximum-security prison. Their sentencing hearing occurred about two years ago. Recently, they exchanged their first letters describing their lives in prison. What did each of them say? Be sure to discuss the physical characteristics of the prison, what needs are fulfilled by the prison, and the different social realities of prison.

_____
_____
_____
_____
_____
_____

Activity 3

Visit the Prison Issues Desk at www.prisonactivist.org. Click on the Issues section. This section includes research information and data on issues such as the prison crisis, political prisoners, women and prison, medical neglect in prison, and children in prison. Choose one of these topics, and in the space below write a summary of the information provided.

_____
_____
_____
_____
_____

Activity 4

Contact a local correctional facility (either a prison or a jail). Interview an administrator of that facility about the issues discussed in Chapter 14. How is that facility responding to AIDS? How is it managing the aging inmate population? Mentally ill inmates? In the space below, discuss what you learn.

_____
_____
_____
_____
_____

Internet Activity

Read **Library Extras 14–8** and **14–9**. Describe the medical issues facing corrections officials in the space below. Your instructor may request that you submit this material.

_____

_____

_____

_____

_____

_____

Distance Learning Activity

Write a short essay about life in prison from the perspective of a correctional officer or from the perspective of an inmate. Search the World Wide Web for materials to be included in your essay. The following websites will be helpful: (1) New York State Correctional Officer Informational Page: http://www.geocities.com/MotorCity/Downs/3548, (2) 15 Years to Life: http://www.15yearstolife.com, (3) Prison Life Inside: http://www.inmate.com/inmates/davidcdc.htm. If your instructor asks you to do so, share your essay with other students in the class.

_____

_____

_____

_____

_____

_____

Learning Activities Utilizing the World Wide Web

There are student-based activities in the Student Study Guide (Internet Activity, Distance Learning Activity, CJ Today on the World Wide Web) that are similar in focus to those that follow. However, the following are presented as instructor-led activities, to be used in a classroom with online access.

Search the World Wide Web for stories about life in prison from the perspective of a correctional officer or from the perspective of an inmate. The following websites will be helpful: New York State Correctional Officer Informational Page at http://www.geocities.com/MotorCity/Downs/3548, or 15 Years to Life: http://www.15yearstolife.com or Prison Life Inside: http://www.inmate.com/inmates/davidcdc.htm. After displaying an overview of this information, lead a discussion on the different prison life perspectives.

Other websites for organizations and agencies related to the material in Chapter 14 include:

Prison Legal News	http://www.prisonlegalnews.org
Stop Prisoner Rape	http://www.spr.org/index.html
Attica Prison Riot	http://www.pbs.org/wgbh/amex/rockefellers/sfeature/sf_5.html

Weight Lifting and Recreation	http://www.strengthtech.com/ index.htm
15 Years to Life	http://www.15yearstolife.com
Prison Life Inside	http://www.inmate.com/inmates/ davidcdc.htm
Pennsylvania Department of Corrections	http://www.cor.state.pa.us

Suggested Answers to Chapter Discussion Questions

1. **What are prison subcultures, and how do they influence prison life? How do they develop, and what purpose do they serve?**

   Prison subcultures reflect the values and behavioral patterns characteristic of prison inmates. They are the mechanisms that inmates develop in the population to cope with the realities of prison life. Subcultures likely derive from a drive to have some control over one's environment, or at least some small segment of one's environment. Because prison authorities control all aspects of an inmate's life in the conventional world, the development of subcultures that cannot be controlled by those authorities gives inmates a means of exercising control in their "real" world.

2. **What does *prisonization* mean?**

   Prisonization is the adaptive process each inmate undergoes soon after arrival into a prison setting. During prisonization, inmates learn the prison lifestyle and criminal values.

   Describe the U-shaped curve developed by Stanton Wheeler to illustrate the concept of prisonization.

   Wheeler's U-shaped curve represents the process through which inmates abandon conventional values held at the beginning of their incarceration and increasingly adopt the criminal values they encounter in the prison setting. As offenders near release, however, commitment to prison values lessens. Since the curve reflects the degree of commitment to subcultural values characteristic of the prison, it is shaped like the letter *U*.

3. **How do women's prisons differ from men's? Why have women's prisons been studied less often than institutions for men?**

   Although there are far more males in prison than females, the number of women incarcerated continues to grow. The most significant difference between male and female prisons is in the social structure. Research has produced inconsistent results, but many scholars argue that women inmates construct pseudofamilies. The sexual relationships between inmates also differ, and staff and inmates are significantly more likely to have sexual relationships in women's prisons. Finally, violence in women's prison is less frequent.

   Reasons for not studying women's prisons as frequently include differences in the size of prison populations and differences in their involvement in criminal activities. In addition, the fact that the field of criminal justice was male dominated during the early days of the development of the discipline also had an impact.

4. **What are the primary concerns of prison staff? Do you agree that those concerns are important? What other goals might staff members focus on?**

   Custody and security remain the primary concerns of prison staff, and rightfully so. Other worthwhile goals might include the maintenance of fairness in prison operations and the creation of an environment that encourages rehabilitative efforts by the inmates.

5. **What causes prison riots? Through what stages do most riots progress? How might riots be prevented?**

Causes of prison riots include

- An insensitive prison administration and neglected inmates' demands.
- The lifestyles most inmates are familiar with on the streets.
- Dehumanizing prison conditions.
- To regulate inmate society and redistribute power balances among inmate groups.
- Power vacuums created by change in prison administration, the transfer of inmates, or court-order injunctions.

The stages in riots include

- Explosion.
- Organization (into inmate-led groups).
- Confrontation (with authority).
- Termination (through negotiation or physical confrontation).
- Reaction and explanation (usually by investigative commissions).

Prison administrators can attempt to prevent riots by having incident-management procedures in place when triggering events happen in order to quell disturbances.

6. What is the hands-off doctrine? What is the status of that doctrine today?

The hands-off doctrine is a policy of nonintervention with regard to prison management that U.S. courts tended to follow until the late 1960s. For the past 30 years the doctrine has languished as judicial intervention in prison administration dramatically increased, although there is now some evidence that a new hands-off era is approaching. It is important to note that most of the landmark cases discussed in this chapter were decided in the late 1960s and 1970s.

7. What are the commonly accepted rights of prisoners in the United States? Where do these rights come from?

Due process entitlements extend to all people within the jurisdiction of the United States or of the individual states. Those rights are constitutionally mandated and protected. Further, the U.S. Supreme Court enforces them in its interpretation of those constitutional mandates.

What U.S. Supreme Court cases are especially significant in this regard? Do inmates have too many rights? Explain.

Important Supreme Court cases include:

- *Block* v. *Rutherford*: In the interests of security, jails can prohibit all visits from friends and relatives.
- *Bounds* v. *Smith*: Not only confirmed the right of prisoners to have access to the courts and to legal assistance but also required states to assist inmates in the preparation and filing of legal papers. This assistance can be given through trained personnel or through the creation and availability of a law library for inmates.
- *Cruz* v. *Beto*: Inmates must be given a "reasonable opportunity" to pursue their religious faith even if it differs from traditional forms of worship.
- *Estelle* v. *Gamble*: Requires prison officials to provide for inmates' medical care, and established the concept of "deliberate indifference" in determining whether prison administrators are meeting the medical needs of prisoners.
- *Houchins* v. *KQED*: News personnel cannot be denied correspondence with inmates, but they have no constitutional right to interview inmates or inspect correctional facilities beyond what is available to the general public.
- *Hudson* v. *Palmer*: The need for prison officials to conduct thorough and unannounced searches precludes inmates' right to privacy in personal possessions.

- *Johnson* v. *Avery*: Inmates have a right to consult "jailhouse lawyers" for advice if assistance from trained legal professionals is not available.
- *Jones* v. *North Carolina Prisoners' Labor Union*: Prisons must establish some formal opportunity for the airing of inmates' grievances.
- *Pell* v. *Procunier*: Supreme Court established a "balancing test" to guide prison authorities in determining what rights an inmate should have. Inmates should have the same rights as nonincarcerated citizens, provided that the legitimate needs of the prison for security, custody, and safety are not compromised.
- *Ruiz* v. *Estelle*: Challenged the structure of the Texas prison system and specifically required major changes in the handling of inmates' medical care. The Court ordered an improvement in record keeping, physical facilities, and general medical care while it continued to monitor the progress of the department.
- *Wolff* v. *McDonnell*: Sanctions cannot be levied against inmates without appropriate due process. Beginning of concept of "state-created liberty interests."

Some argue that inmates should have no rights because they should forfeit them as a consequence of their criminal convictions. Courts in this country, however, have consistently opposed that notion.

The rights prisoners do have, however, are constitutionally provided. Since constitutional provisions are open to court interpretation, and since political considerations frequently play a role in court appointments, the extent to which inmates' rights are recognized tends to vary over time. Whereas federal courts followed a hands-off doctrine of nonintervention in the running of state prisons until 1969, federal court intervention in prison administration has greatly increased during the past three decades. Some people suggest that, as a consequence, prisoners now have too many court-created "rights" and that those rights are merely court-authored fictions with no bases in constitutional mandates.

8. **Explain the "balancing test" established by the Supreme Court in deciding issues of prisoners' rights.**

Applied to the corrections arena in the 1974 ruling in *Pell* v. *Procunier*, the "balancing test" is a principle developed by the courts that seeks to weigh a prisoner's constitutionally guaranteed rights against the state's authority to make laws or otherwise restrict a person's freedom in order to protect its interests and its citizens.

How might such a test apply to the emerging area of inmate privacy?

As a gauge for determining regulatory limits on inmates' privacy, the balancing test can be used to identify limitations that unduly restrict inmates' privacy rights without an articulable and significant adverse impact on the state's protective interests. In the absence of such a balance, the limitation can be seen as a violation of prisoners' protected liberties.

9. **What does the term *state-created rights* mean within the context of corrections? What do you predict for the future of state-created rights?**

The term *state-created rights* (also called *protected liberties*) evolved from court decisions recognizing prisoner entitlements based on provisions contained in prison regulations. If, for example, a regulation mandated a hearing before movement of a prisoner from the general population to solitary confinement, the courts found a violation of the prisoner's state-created liberty if solitary confinement was imposed without the hearing being held.

In response to extremely aggressive litigation by prisoners over everything from the color of the shoes they are issued to the flavor of the pie they are served at dinner, present-day prison administrators have become very cautious about the implementation of new regulations. Each is scrutinized so closely for legal compliance that it is unlikely a regulation will be enacted that inadvertently creates new prisoner entitlements.

10. **What are some of the major problems and issues that prisons face today? What new problems might the future bring?**

Three special problems facing corrections administrators today are health threats related to AIDS (acquired immunodeficiency syndrome), the aging of the prison population and the consequent health issues, and the unique problems of mentally ill prisoners. Each carries a spectacular price tag for health and treatment services that results in the consumption of disproportionate amounts of most prison budgets.

In the future, special problems may include the housing of foreign terrorists, the emergence of new diseases that further tax prison health systems, or changes in public policy or the law that lead to increases in inmate populations (a condition that might overwhelm already crowded prisons and jails).

Key—Student Study Guide Questions

True or False

_____ 14-1. Few states have substantial capacity for the psychiatric treatment of mentally disturbed inmates. **(True, p. 565)**

_____ 14-2. In 1935, an Indiana University sociology professor completed a groundbreaking study of prison life when he voluntarily served three months in prison as a participant-observer to discover what being an inmate was really like. **(True, p. 526)**

_____ 14-3. Prison argot is a secret language prisoners use to communicate that no one except the prisoners knows. **(False, p. 528)**

_____ 14-4. In all state and federal prison facilities combined, the number of incarcerated male prisoners is greater than the number of females incarcerated by a ratio of slightly more than two to one. **(False, p. 533)**

_____ 14-5. Most female prison inmates have been convicted of violent crime. **(False, p. 534)**

_____ 14-6. A prisoner's private mail from immediate family members may not be opened and censored by prison authorities. **(False, p. 549)**

_____ 14-7. Prison riots are generally unplanned and tend to occur spontaneously, the result of some relatively minor precipitating event. **(True, p. 544)**

_____ 14-8. Most male sexual aggressors in prisons do not consider themselves heterosexual. **(False, p. 532)**

_____ 14-9. Inmates have a right to consult "jailhouse lawyers" for advice if the prison does not provide assistance from trained legal professionals. **(True, p. 551)**

_____ 14-10. The U.S. Supreme Court case of *Hudson* v. *Palmer* asserts that the need for prison officials to conduct thorough and unannounced searches is greater than inmates' right to privacy in personal possessions. **(True, p. 555)**

Multiple Choice

14-11. _____ develop independently of the plans of prison administrators.
   a. Prison subcultures (p. 527)
   b. Total institutions
   c. Women's prisons
   d. Parole boards

14-12. The _____ established by the U.S. Supreme Court in *Pell* v. *Procunier* has served as a guideline generally applicable to all prison operations.
   a. either-or doctrine
   b. balancing test (p. 546)
   c. writ of *habeas corpus*
   d. prisonization process

14-13. Prison gangs who pose a threat to the safety of the correctional staff and the public are defined as:
   a. riot initiators
   b. wolves
   c. security threat groups (p. 544)
   d. terrorists

14-14. The policy followed by the courts until the 1960s in refusing to hear inmate complaints about the conditions of incarceration and the constitutional deprivations of inmate life was called the
   a. fingers-crossed model.
   b. bloody codes.
   c. hands-off doctrine. (p. 557)
   d. inmate code.

14-15. The hands-off doctrine ended when the federal court declared that the entire prison system in the state of _____ was in violation of the constitutional ban against cruel and unusual punishment.
   a. Arkansas (p. 557)
   b. New Mexico
   c. Indiana
   d. New York

14-16. An inmate who is quick to fight and fights like a wild man is referred to as the
   a. opportunist.
   b. mean dude. (p. 530)
   c. hedonist.
   d. retreatist.

14-17. In *The Society of Captives*, Gresham Sykes claims that prisoners are deprived of all of the following except
   a. liberty.
   b. goods and services.
   c. homosexual relationships. (p. 529)
   d. autonomy.

14-18. All of the following are listed as contributing to the "graying" of America's prison population except
   a. increasing crime among those over 50.
   b. the gradual aging of the society from which prisoners come.
   c. a trend toward longer sentences.
   d. the reduction in the number of older habitual offenders in prison. (p. 561)

14-19. Inmates adopt a series of lifestyles in an attempt to survive the prison experience. _____ build their lifestyle around the limited pleasures that can be had within the confines of prison.
   a. Mean dudes
   b. Hedonists (p. 530)
   c. Opportunists
   d. Retreatists

14-20. Correctional officers can be classified according to certain categories. If an officer tries to fraternize with inmates, attempting to be "one of the guys," he or she would be classified as a(n)
   a. dictator.
   b. friend. (p. 539)
   c. merchant.
   d. indifferent officer.

Fill-In

14-21. _____ is the slang characteristic of prison subcultures and prison life. **(Prison argot, p. 528)**

14-22. _____ are enclosed facilities where the inhabitants share all aspects of their lives. **(Total institutions, p. 526)**

14-23. _____ is the case that required that inmates be given a "reasonable opportunity" to pursue their religious faith even if it differs from traditional forms of worship. **(*Cruz* v. *Beto*, p. 550)**

14-24. _____ are formalized arrangements prisoners have to register complaints about the conditions of their confinement. **(Grievance procedures, p. 556)**

14-25. The _____ attempts to weigh the constitutional rights of an individual against the authority of the state to make laws to protect its interests and its citizens. **(balancing test, p. 546)**

14-26. The values and behavioral patterns characteristic of prison inmates comprise the _____. **(prison subculture, p. 527)**

14-27. The _____ was a policy of nonintervention with regard to prison management that American courts tended to follow until the late 1960s. **(hands-off doctrine, p. 577)**

14-28. _____ is the process whereby institutionalized individuals come to accept prison lifestyles and criminal values. **(Prisonization, p. 527)**

14-29. _____ is the legal status of prisoners in some jurisdictions who are denied the opportunity to vote, hold public office, marry, or enter into contracts by virtue of their status as incarcerated felons. **(Civil death, p. 545)**

14-30. The legislation that attempts to restrict the number of suits filed by inmates is the _____. **(Prison Litigation Reform Act of 1996, p. 558)**

Key—Crossword Puzzle

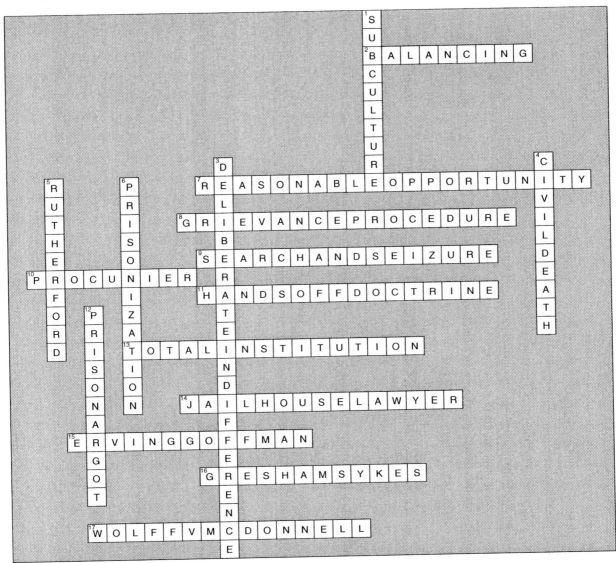

Across

2. Test established by *Pell* v. *Procunier*.
7. Standard set by *Cruz* v. *Beto*.
8. Official way prisoners can complain about the conditions of their confinement.
9. *Hudson* v. *Palmer* focuses on this issue.
10. *Pell* v. _____.
11. Policy of nonintervention of prison management.
13. Enclosed facility, separated from society both socially and physically, where the inhabitants share all aspects of their daily lives.
14. Inmate lawyer.
15. Scholar who coined the term *total institution*.
16. Author of *The Society of Captives*.
17. Case beginning the concept of state-created liberty interests.

Down

1. Values and behavioral patterns of prison inmates.
3. Standard set by *Estelle* v. *Gamble*.
4. State of prisoners denied the opportunity to vote and hold public office.
5. *Block* v. _____.
6. Process whereby newly institutionalized offenders come to accept prison lifestyles and criminal values.
12. Language of inmates.

Key—Word Search Puzzle

```
N J G P S C Z B A O I M A E B E A T R D Y T G F A C W G D D
M I G J K W E S E L Q F H I W V J S N S M Z G H H H Q M C A
P H V A Z C J J B S E H E Z C U A I A E R R I A Y E I T R T
I S S X Q X S D A L F F T F J M I F S E C U R I T Y R T E C
B E N P P G R C U A M T R D P M L I D N N U D B D I N A A I
J C G B R H D Z M E K C Y I C N H X H H E P X B P B T U S B
W U D R D I S F C O B M D K C L O Y E A L B H N C A V C O D
Z R W Q I B S C Z H X K O F F K U P Q N D B R S M Y E I N T
L I S A T E G O O W W T D K Y L S K T D Y Y I T E S A V A M
B T A S J M V T N W X O H J X O E M F S I L M T S M I I B Y
X Y A E U I D A O R F J S I P N L T J O E C U P T E K L P P
M T X O Q B M G N T I Y B M X Q A L H F E P X B E N Z E O L
I H V E J G C C D C A O A T Q D W U W F U O X A R T B E O W
Q R C V A V J U B E E L T T L X Y E C D R Z J L A L I P P O
C E Z P F I V R L P L P I B A J E I P O M A T A C L I T W O
N A T I R S X S C T Q A R N I F R W I C M U F N C U Y P R T
T T G R B I Q R L J U R B O S R H H O T F E N C U Y O W U N
I G P I C T S J B I K R G K C T Y O S R N O F I J I A E T I
V R H I G A L O E L K Z E K X E I D V I I R V N O L S G U T
G O V I S T Q N N P W I X Q O S D T X N Y G T G Z L Q T N U
Q U A W N I S J Y I K O M Q U O F U U E B Z M T X I P L I E
G P X A N O V I H N Z T I D O P N C R T M M X E U N J C T X
M S F N H N G O R O J A B V Z C X X Q E I V U S J M Q I Y X
L T R V F K Q R G W N I T I L Y Y O Q V H O L T E A X R H Z
D E L I B E R A T E I N D I F F E R E N C E N C T T M T U R
Z D L W K V O D W M N Q E X O N W A L I S B Z G X E Y T S V
B R L D M W S E D J F C R S K N S T U Q O O E J M S G T K N
P Z L I E D I O E B A T E R N K I S F E H E N W E W R E S P
Z C P C J L M D B A I E T N Z J Q W A A J H M K L N U W S B
E M O U W Y E P M C M D U K X E K J U A G F L K O C V V C O
```

Argot
Balancing Test
Civil Death
Deliberate Indifference
Grievance Procedure
Hands-Off Doctrine
Jailhouse Lawyer
Mentally Ill Inmates

Prisonization
Prison Riot
Reasonable Opportunity
Security
Security Threat Groups
Subculture
Total Institution
Visitation

Juvenile Justice

LEARNING OBJECTIVES

After reading this chapter, you should be able to:

- Describe the history and evolution of the juvenile justice system in the Western world
- List and define the categories of children in today's juvenile justice system
- Describe the nature of the problems that juveniles face in the United States today
- Name the important U.S. Supreme Court decisions of relevance to juvenile justice, and describe their impact on the handling of juveniles by the system
- Explain the similarities and differences between the juvenile and adult systems of justice

Chapter Summary

Juvenile crime is a perplexing problem for the criminal justice system. It is perplexing because research indicates that the amount of violent crime committed by juveniles is decreasing, but public demand for severe punishments for juveniles has increased. Moreover, the public's desire for a crackdown on juvenile crime, and the demand that juvenile punishments be equivalent to adult punishments, is inconsistent with the underlying philosophy of the juvenile court.

This chapter examines four areas of juvenile justice: First, it examines the historical development of the juvenile justice system; second, it compares the juvenile justice system to the adult system; third, it discusses the juvenile justice system process; and finally, it discusses several criticisms of the juvenile system.

The text discusses the historical beginnings of the juvenile justice system throughout the world and in America and traces this history through several important Supreme Court cases decided in the 1970s and 1980s. The text's examination of the historical evolution of the juvenile justice system begins with a discussion of treatment of juveniles in the earliest times, when they were treated differently from adults. For example, the laws of King Aethelbert made no special provisions for offenders because of age. The common law principle of **parens patriae** is important to an understanding of juvenile justice because it means that the state can assume the role of the parent and take custody of a child.

In America, the criminal justice response to juveniles began in the early nineteenth century with the development of houses of refuge. The child savers movement began in the mid-1800s, influencing the development of reform schools. The early model, embodied in the Chicago Reform School, focused on emulating family environments to provide security and build moral character, emphasizing traditional values such as hard work. Finally, the text discusses the beginnings of the juvenile court era from early legislation in Massachusetts and New York to the Illinois juvenile law that was modeled by most states and the federal government's Juvenile Court Act. Most legislation included six categories of children subject to the jurisdiction of the juvenile court: **delinquent children, undisciplined children, dependent children, neglected children, abused children**, and **status offenders**.

Chapter 15 also covers several theoretical explanations for juvenile delinquency. This discussion includes Shaw and McKay's **social ecology approach**, Cloward and Ohlin's **opportunity theory**, and Sykes and Matza's neutralization techniques. Moreover, the text discusses two significant research efforts to identify the determinants of delinquency. First, the text discusses research conducted by Marvin Wolfgang that traced the delinquent behavior of a birth **cohort** in Philadelphia. Second, it discusses the Program of Research on the Causes and Correlates of Juvenile Delinquency and its three coordinated projects.

Chapter 15 also provides an excellent overview of several important Court decisions affecting juveniles. The most significant is *In re Gault*. This decision guaranteed several procedural rights to juveniles including the right to have notice of the charges, the right to counsel, the right to confront and cross-examine witnesses, and the right to appeal. Other cases discussed include *In re Winship, McKeiver* v. *Pennsylvania, Breed* v. *Jones, Kent* v. *United States*, and *Schall* v. *Martin*. Juveniles, however, are not provided all the protections guaranteed to adult defendants. For example, juveniles do not have a constitutional right to a jury trial.

The juvenile justice system, as a process, involves four stages: intake, adjudication, **disposition**, and postadjudication review. **Intake** involves the filing of a juvenile petition by some party, such as the police, alleging illegal behavior by the juvenile. **Adjudication** is the trial process for juveniles. Adjudicatory hearings are similar to the adult trial, but with some exceptions. A **dispositionary hearing**, similar to an adult sentencing hearing, occurs to determine the action the court should take against a juvenile. Judges have several options at disposition, including outright release, probation, or confinement to a secure institution.

Chapter 15 concludes by considering the future of the juvenile justice system, acknowledging that it will increase penalties, reduce privacy, and eliminate diversionary opportunities for juveniles.

Teaching Outline

I. Introduction (p. 580)
  - Juveniles account for 15% of violent crimes and 30% of property crimes.
  - Discuss the decrease in juvenile violent crime, the increase in female delinquency, the increase in juvenile admissions to public facilities, and how minority juveniles are greatly overrepresented in the custody population.
  - Describe the juvenile justice system from its historical roots.

Juvenile Justice System Government agencies that function to investigate, supervise, adjudicate, care for, or confine youthful offenders and other children subject to the jurisdiction of the juvenile court. (p. 581)

  - Compare the juvenile and adult systems.
  - Describe in detail the agencies, the processes, and the problems of juvenile justice.
  - Raise several issues regarding the current juvenile system.

II. Juvenile Justice throughout History (p. 582)
  A. Earliest Times (p. 582)
    - No preferential treatment was given to juveniles.
    - Laws of King Aethelbert, the earliest legal document written in the English language, made no special allowances for age of the offender.
    - Little distinction was made between criminality and delinquency.

Delinquency In the broadest usage, juvenile actions or conduct in violation of criminal law, juvenile status offenses, and other juvenile misbehavior. (p. 582)

Parens Patriae A common law principle that allows the state to assume a parental role and to take custody of a child when he or she becomes delinquent, is abandoned, or is in need of care that the natural parents are unable or unwilling to provide. (p. 582)

    - Later social conceptions of children were influenced by Christian churches.
  B. Juveniles in Early America (p. 583)
    - Early juvenile legislation reflected the Ten Commandments.
    - Severe punishment was the norm.
    - Concern for children increased during the Enlightenment (eighteenth century).
  C. The Institutional Era (p. 584)
    1. The House of Refuge (p. 584)
      - First developed in New York City in 1824
      - In the case *Ex parte Crouse*, the appeals court clarified the power that states had in committing children to institutions. The decision in this case was built around the doctrine of *parens patriae*.
    2. The Chicago Reform School (p. 585)
      - Reform schools were a product of the child savers movement.
      - These schools emphasized traditional family values and hard work.
      - However, an Illinois appellate case, *People ex rel. O'Connell* v. *Turner*, put the reform movement out of business.
  D. The Juvenile Court Era (p. 585)
    - Although other laws existed prior to it, the codification of Illinois juvenile law in 1899 is the model most states relied on when enacting similar legislation.

- This legislation applied the term *delinquent* rather than *criminal*, specified the best interests of the child, and emphasized that concerns with guilt took second place to the betterment of the child.
- In 1938 the federal government passed the Juvenile Court Act, modeled after the Illinois legislation.
- Discuss the philosophical principles of the juvenile court movement:
  - The state is the "higher or ultimate parent."
  - Children are worth saving.
  - Children should be nurtured.
  - Justice needs to be individualized.
  - The needs of the child mandate use of noncriminal procedures.

INSTRUCTIONAL CUE LINKED TO THE STUDENT STUDY GUIDE

Student Activity 1 will help students think about problems associated with having a separate juvenile justice system.

---

1. Categories of Children in the Juvenile Justice System

Delinquent Child   A child who has engaged in activity that would be considered a crime if the child were an adult. The term *delinquent* is used to avoid the stigma associated with the term *criminal*. (p. 586)

Undisciplined Child   A child who is beyond parental control, as evidenced by his or her refusal to obey legitimate authorities, such as school officials and teachers. (p. 586)

Dependent Child   A child who has no parents or whose parents are unable to care for him or her. (p. 586)

Neglected Child   A child who is not receiving the proper level of physical or psychological care from his or her parents or guardians or who has been placed up for adoption in violation of the law. (p. 586)

Abused Child   A child who has been physically, sexually, or mentally abused. Most states also consider a child who is forced into delinquent activity by a parent or guardian to be abused. (p. 586)

Status Offender   A child who commits an act that is contrary to the law by virtue of the juvenile's status as a child. Purchasing cigarettes, buying alcohol, and being truant are examples of such behavior. (p. 586)

Status Offense   An act or conduct that is declared by statute to be an offense, but only when committed by or engaged in by a juvenile, and that can be adjudicated only by a juvenile court. (pp. 586–587)

INSTRUCTIONAL CUE

Use the following matching exercise during classtime to help students learn the six categories of children in the juvenile justice system.

  a. status offender   b. dependent child
  c. undisciplined child   d. neglected child
  e. abused child   f. delinquent child

- A child who has been physically, sexually, or mentally abused (e)
- A child who is beyond parental control, as evidenced by refusal to obey legitimate authorities such as school officials and teachers (c)
- A child who has no parents or whose parents are unable to care for him or her (b)

- A child who is not receiving the proper level of physical or psychological care from his or her parents (d)
- A child who has engaged in activity that would be a crime if the child were an adult (f)
- A child who commits an act that is contrary to the law by virtue of the juvenile's status as a child (a)

    2. Explanation of Delinquency

INSTRUCTIONAL CUE

It is important that you remind students about the various theoretical perspectives on the causes of crime discussed in Chapter 3. Provide a brief review of some of the important perspectives. This will help students develop an appreciation of the links among the theories discussed in Chapter 15 and Chapter 3.

- Shaw and McKay's Social Ecology Theory

Social Ecology A criminological approach that focuses on the misbehavior of lower-class youth and sees delinquency primarily as the result of social disorganization. (p. 587)

- Eventually replaced by Cloward and Ohlin's opportunity theory

Opportunity Theory A perspective that sees delinquency as the result of limited legitimate opportunities for success available to most lower-class youth. (p. 587)

- Sykes and Matza's neutralization of responsibility claims that delinquents drift between conformity and law and will choose the latter when social norms can be explained away.
- Describe cohort studies, and provide examples of this type of study.

Cohort A group of individuals sharing similarities of age, place of birth, and residence. Cohort analysis is a social science technique that tracks cohorts over time to identify the unique and observable behavioral traits that characterize them. (p. 587)

INSTRUCTIONAL CUE LINKED TO THE STUDENT STUDY GUIDE

Student Activity 2 will help students link the explanations of delinquency in Chapter 15 with other theoretical explanations.

  III. The Problems of Children Today (p. 588)
    A. Drug and Alcohol Abuse (p. 588)
- Drug use is widespread among young people. Over half have tried an illicit drug.
- Marijuana is the most widely used drug.
- Juvenile drug arrests are also on the rise. The number of drug arrests more than doubled from 1970 to 2000.

    B. Violence (p. 590)
- Childhood violence is growing. Nearly 800 homicides are committed by juveniles annually.
- The third leading cause of death for children ages one to four and five to 14.

    C. Gangs (p. 591)
- Close to 3,330 jurisdictions throughout the country have active youth gangs.

- Gangs are generally male-dominated; racial composition includes 47% Hispanic, 31% African-American, 13% white, and 7% Asian. Fifty percent were defined as underclass.
- According to Project Gangfact, gangs are heavily involved in crime.

D. Runaways (p. 595)

- According to the National Incidence Study of Missing, Abducted, Runaway, and Thrownaway Children report, the number of children missing each year is 800,000. The largest subgroup of this number is runaways.
- Runaways leave home for a variety of reasons, including sexual abuse, physical abuse, lack of love and affection, and disputes over activities within the home.
- Of the children who run away, 20% come into contact with the police or another social service agency.

E. Sexual Abuse (p. 596)

- Recently headline news

F. Other Forms of Abuse (p. 597)

- Neglect, physical abuse, emotional or psychological abuse, and abandonment are other forms of abuse.

IV. The Legal Environment (p. 599)

INSTRUCTIONAL CUE

Review the Fourth, Fifth, and Sixth Amendment cases discussed in the police and court section. Remind students of the protections provided to adults against unreasonable searches and seizures, protections against self-incrimination, and right to counsel. This review will set the stage for the discussion of juvenile case law.

A. *Kent* v. *U.S.* (1966) (p. 599)

- This case ended the hands-off era in juvenile justice and recognized that at least minimal due process must be provided in juvenile court hearings.

B. *In re Gault* (1967) (p. 599)

- The Court decided that juveniles have a right to notice of charges, a right to counsel, a right to confront and to cross-examine witnesses, and constitutional protections against self-incrimination.

C. *In re Winship* (1970) (p. 601)

- Allegations of delinquency must be established beyond a reasonable doubt. Status offenses, however, can be established with the preponderance of the evidence standard.

D. *McKeiver* v. *Pennsylvania* (1971) (p. 601)

- This case held that juveniles do not have the constitutional right to a jury trial.

E. *Breed* v. *Jones* (1975) (p. 602)

- This case severely restricted the conditions under which transfers from juvenile to adult court may occur. Such transfers must occur prior to an adjudicatory hearing in juvenile court.

F. *Schall* v. *Martin* (1984) (p. 602)

- This case upheld the practice of preventive detention but stated that it cannot be imposed without prior notice, an equitable detention hearing, and a statement by the judge setting the reasons for the detention.

G. *Illinois* v. *Montanez* (1996) (p. 602)

- In this case the Supreme Court let stand a state court ruling that threw out a voluntary confession made by a juvenile suspect who had been tried as an adult.

   H. Legislation Concerning Juvenile Justice (p. 603)
- The Omnibus Crime Control and Safe Streets Act of 1968
- The Juvenile Justice and Delinquency Prevention Act of 1974
- Also, discuss more recent changes to move away from the emphasis on treatment of juvenile offenders.

   I. The Legal Rights of Juveniles (p. 604)
- Most states have statutes extending *Miranda* provisions to juveniles.
- In *New Jersey* v. *T.L.O.*, the Supreme Court ruled that schoolchildren have a reasonable expectation of privacy in personal property.

V. The Juvenile Justice Process Today (p. 604)
- Describe the differences among exclusive, original, and concurrent jurisdiction.
    - *Exclusive jurisdiction* applies when the juvenile court is the only court with statutory authority to deal with children (e.g., status offenses).
    - *Original jurisdiction* means that a particular offense must originate with juvenile court authorities.
    - *Concurrent jurisdiction* exists where other courts have equal statutory authority to originate proceedings.

   A. Adult and Juvenile Justice Compared (p. 606)
- Although juveniles are provided several protections, they do not have the right to all the due process protections afforded adult defendants.
- Among the important differences are a reduced concern with guilt, an emphasis on treatment, privacy and protection from public scrutiny, use of techniques of social science, and no long-term confinement.

   B. How the System Works (p. 606)
      1. Intake and Detention Hearings

Juvenile Petition A document filed in juvenile court alleging that a juvenile is a delinquent, a status offender, or a dependent and asking that the court assume jurisdiction over the juvenile or that an alleged delinquent be transferred to a criminal court for prosecution as an adult. (p. 608)

- Detention hearing: Intake officers have substantial discretion, from full detention to dismissal.

Intake The first step in decision making regarding a juvenile whose behavior or alleged behavior is in violation of the law or could otherwise cause a juvenile court to assume jurisdiction. (p. 609)

- Preliminary hearing: The purpose is to determine if there is probable cause to believe the juvenile committed the alleged act.

      2. Adjudication

Adjudicatory Hearing The fact-finding process wherein the juvenile court determines whether there is sufficient evidence to sustain the allegations in a petition. (p. 609)

- Differences between the juvenile and adult systems include that the juvenile has no right to trial by jury, the emphasis on privacy, informality, speed, evidentiary standard, and the different philosophies of the courts.

Teen Court An alternative approach to juvenile justice in which alleged juvenile offenders are judged and sentenced by a jury of their peers. (p. 610)

INSTRUCTIONAL CUE LINKED TO THE STUDENT STUDY GUIDE

Student Activity 3 examines sentencing decisions for juvenile offenders. After students complete this exercise, have them revisit their sentencing decisions in Chapter 11. Ask them whether they treated juveniles and adults differently, and explore reasons for the differences.

---

3. Disposition

Dispositional Hearing   The final stage in the processing of adjudicated juveniles in which a decision is made on the form of treatment or penalty that should be imposed on the child. (p. 611)

Juvenile Disposition   The decision of a juvenile court, concluding a disposition hearing, that an adjudicated juvenile be committed to a juvenile correctional facility; be placed in a juvenile residence, shelter, or care or treatment program; be required to meet certain standards of conduct; or be released. (p. 611)

- Secure institutions for juveniles: Institutions for serious juvenile offenders.
- As of January 2002, approximately 104,400 juveniles were being held under custodial supervision.
- Characteristics of juveniles in confinement: Statistics from the Bureau of Justice on institutionalized youth indicate that 85.5% were male; 38.9% were black, 39.4% were white, and 17.3% were Hispanic; 42.4% were in residential facilities; and 1% were charged with murder.
- Overcrowding in juvenile facilities: Half of the juvenile facilities in the United States are overcrowded, and 22 states are operating at more than 50% over capacity.

4. Postadjudicatory Review

VI. The Post–Juvenile Court Era (p. 614)

- Juvenile courts are beginning to look very similar to adult courts.
- Common themes of new state juvenile justice laws include:
  - Targeting serious and violent juvenile offenders
  - Changes in jurisdictional authority (waiver to adult court)
  - Changes in sentencing authority
  - Development of programs to serve violent juveniles
  - Revision of traditional confidentiality provisions
  - Inclusion of victims as active participants in the justice process

---

INSTRUCTIONAL CUE LINKED TO THE STUDENT STUDY GUIDE

Student Activity 4 examines reforming the juvenile justice system.

Learner Activities

Activity 1

Youth violence has long been a concern for the criminal justice system. In the early 1900s, for example, legislators across the country decided that juvenile delinquents who commit a crime should be treated differently from adult criminals. Thus, the juvenile justice system was created with the important purpose of providing opportunities for juveniles to reform rather than strictly punishing them for their acts.

However, an increasing number of juveniles, some as young as 13, have been waived out of the juvenile justice system into adult court. Thirteen- and 14-year-old children are being sent to maximum-security prisons. Currently, it appears that the system is more concerned with punishing delinquents than reforming them. After reading about the juvenile justice system in Chapter 15, combined with what you learned about criminal justice in this class, do you think the juvenile justice system should be abolished? Why or why not?

_____

_____

_____

_____

_____

_____

Activity 2

Chapter 15 provides an excellent overview of several important theories designed to explain juvenile delinquency. Social disorganization, opportunity theory, and neutralization techniques are discussed. There are other theories that might be helpful in attempting to explain juvenile delinquency. For example, some critics argue that the reliance on various sources of media by children is a major contributing cause of delinquency. Video games, cartoons, music—especially rap and heavy metal—and violence on television have all been criticized for poisoning the minds of youth. Do you think media images of violence cause children to become delinquents? Why or why not? What types of media images do you think are most harmful to children? Explain your answer. (*Note:* There is a very large body of research examining the links between viewing violence and committing violence. It may be helpful to visit the World Wide Web or your library to do some background reading on this topic.)

_____

_____

_____

_____

_____

Activity 3

Judge Gayle Garner has the following three juvenile cases on her docket:

1. Jarred Owens is a 17-year-old high school dropout. He has recently been convicted of two burglaries. His criminal record includes three other crimes: two shoplifting incidents and a theft. His parents are frustrated with his behavior and admit to having trouble controlling him. Jarred's two brothers are well behaved and have no criminal records.

2. Anne Yeerns is 15 years old and was convicted of attempting to steal a car. This was her first offense. However, she is also a runaway. On two prior occasions, she has run away from her father. The first time she went back home after three days, the second time the police brought her back after one week, and this time she claims she was stealing the car to get as far away as possible. Anne's father did not attend the dispositional hearing.

3. Patrick Darvy is 12 years old and was recently initiated into a juvenile gang. He was caught selling drugs; it was his first offense. Patrick lives with his mother, who is divorced. Ms. Darvy is very concerned about recent changes in his behavior and would like the court's help in changing his behavior.

Make a recommendation to Judge Garner for the dispositions of these three cases. Discuss the sentences you would recommend, and provide the rationale for your recommendations.

_____

_____

_____

_____

_____

_____

Activity 4

Near the end of Chapter 15, the text discusses three ongoing efforts directed at reforming the juvenile justice system. These efforts include lessening the degree of privacy, increasing penalties for certain kinds of delinquent acts, and reducing diversionary opportunities for habitual, violent, and serious offenders. The President's Commission on Juvenile Justice would like you to recommend one of these reform efforts. In the space provided below, discuss which one of these reforms you think would have the most positive impact on the juvenile justice system, and provide your rationale for excluding the other two reforms.

_____

_____

_____

_____

_____

_____

Internet Activity

Visit the Cybrary at http://www.cybrary.info. Click on the topic "Juvenile Justice," and review the sites that appear. Which of those sites is identified as one of the "Top 100" sites? Are there other juvenile justice sites that you think should be among the "Top 100" identified by the Cybrary? If so, use the feedback link at the bottom of the Cybrary's home page to tell the Cybrary staff what you think. Submit your findings to your instructor if requested to do so.

_____

_____

_____

_____

_____

_____

Distance Learning Activity

Visit the American Bar Association's website on juvenile justice issues at http://www.abanet.org/crimjust/juvjus/jjnews.html. Read one of the essays posted, and provide a summary of its key ideas. If your instructor asks you to do so, participate in a class discussion that compares and contrasts the findings from the different essays.

_____
_____
_____
_____
_____

Learning Activities Utilizing the World Wide Web

There are student-based activities in the Student Study Guide (Internet Activity, Distance Learning Activity, CJ Today on the World Wide Web) that are similar in focus to those that follow. However, the following are presented as instructor-led activities, to be used in a classroom with online access.

Visit the Cybrary at http://www.cybrary.info. Click on the topic "Juvenile Justice," and review the sites that appear. Choose a few of the sites to display in class. Highlight some of the sites identified as the "Top 100" sites. Ask the students if there other juvenile justice sites that they think should be among the "Top 100" identified by the Cybrary. If so, use the feedback link at the bottom of the Cybrary's home page to tell the Cybrary staff what your students think.

Visit the American Bar Association's website on juvenile justice issues at http://www.abanet.org/crimjust/juvjus/jjnews.html. Read one of the essays posted, and provide a summary of its key ideas for display in class. Lead a class discussion that compares and contrasts the findings from the different essays.

Other websites for organizations and agencies related to the material in Chapter 15 include:

American Bar Association's Juvenile Justice Center	http://www.abanet.org/crimjust/juvjus/home.html
Center on Juvenile and Criminal Justice (CJCJ)	http://www.cjcj.org
Juvenile Court Section Juvenile Justice (NCJRS)	http://virlib.ncjrs.org/JuvenileJustice.asp
Juvenile Justice Magazine Online	http://www.juvenilejustice.com
National Council on Crime and Delinquency	http://www.nccd-crc.org
Office of Juvenile Justice and Delinquency Prevention (OJJDP)	http://ojjdp.ncjrs.org
Juvenile Justice Clearinghouse	http://www.fsu.edu/~crimdo/jjclearinghouse
Urban Ethnography of Latino Street Gangs	http://www.csun.edu/~hcchs006/gang.html
National Youth Gang Center (NYGC)	http://www.iir.com/nygc

Suggested Answers to Chapter Discussion Questions

1. **Describe the history and evolution of the juvenile justice system in the Western world.**

   In past centuries, children who committed crimes could expect no preferential treatment because of their youth. There was little distinction between delinquency and criminality. Early American solutions were strongly influenced by churches and the Ten Commandments. By the end of the eighteenth century, when the Enlightenment occurred, people started to revisit the role of children in society. America changed dramatically in the early nineteenth century, and many children were victimized and abandoned. These changes pressured government officials to consider how best to help children in society. Most of the pressure to change came from the child savers movement. This movement created the reform school for children. As the needs of children were more broadly recognized, states began to adopt legislation requiring separate hearings for juveniles. In 1899, the Illinois juvenile law was passed, creating a juvenile system separate from the adult system and serving as a model throughout the nation.

2. **Describe the six categories of children recognized by the laws of most states.**

   In most jurisdictions, children subject to juvenile court jurisdiction are categorized as follows:

   - Delinquent (those who violate the criminal law)
   - Undisciplined (those said to be beyond parental control)
   - Dependent (those without parents or a guardian to care for them)
   - Neglected (those not receiving proper care from their parents or guardian)
   - Abused (those who suffered physical abuse at the hands of their custodian)
   - Status offenders (those who violated laws written only for children)

3. **What problems do juveniles face in the United States today? Do these problems necessitate the development of new legal categories for some children handled by the courts? If so, what categories are needed? If not, how can existing categories adequately address illicit drug use by juveniles or the repeated and vicious delinquency of some inner-city gang members?**

   Problems include drug and alcohol abuse, violence, gangs, runaways, sexual abuse and other forms of abuse, and teen suicide.

   Most consider the existing list of categories to be sufficient and see no need to establish new categories. Behavior such as drug use and vicious delinquency fit into the delinquent child category as violations of criminal law. Rather than create new categories, it is probably best that habitual or especially vicious juvenile offenders be transferred to adult criminal court for processing—an alternative available in all states today.

4. **What was the impact of the *Gault* decision on juvenile justice in America? What adult rights were not accorded to juveniles by *Gault*? What other U.S. Supreme Court decisions have had a substantial impact on the handling of juvenile offenders by the justice system?**

   As a result of the Court's ruling in *Gault*, juveniles are now guaranteed many of the same procedural rights as adults. The only adult rights not included in the decision were the right of appeal and the right to a transcript of any legal proceedings. Other Supreme Court decisions include *In re Winship*, *McKeiver v. Pennsylvania*, *Breed v. Jones*, *Schall v. Martin*, and *Illinois v. Montanez*.

5. **What are the major similarities and differences between the juvenile and adult systems of justice? In your opinion, should children continue to receive what many regard as preferential treatment from the courts? Explain.**

The following table illustrates the main similarities and differences between the philosophies of the adult and juvenile justice systems:

Adult Justice System	**Juvenile Justice System**
Focuses on legal issues of guilt or innocence	Emphasizes the best interests of the child, with reduced concern for legal issues
Emphasizes punishment for offenses	Emphasizes treatment rather than punishment
Arrests, tries, and imprisons offenders in open procedures without concern for offenders' privacy	Emphasizes privacy of offenders and protection from public scrutiny
Uses sentences determined by a need to punish	Emphasizes the techniques of social science in dispositional decision making
Sentencing options may include life terms	No long-term confinement, with most released by their twenty-first birthday
Sentenced to the appropriate available facility	Institutionalized in facilities separate from adults
Limited discretion throughout the process	Broad discretionary alternatives at all points in the process

The problem with the juvenile justice system is that most of the public thinks it is flawed because the public focuses on the violent gang member who committed a murder at age 12. Most of the children in the juvenile justice system need the help of the courts and deserve the preferential treatment. Society should not punish juveniles because the system is flawed.

Key—Student Study Guide Questions

True or False

_____ 15-1. Juveniles have a constitutional right to a jury trial. **(False, p. 606)**

_____ 15-2. Most chronic juvenile offenders begin their offending career before the age of 12. **(True, p. 580)**

_____ 15-3. Gresham Sykes and David Matza developed opportunity theory in the 1960s, arguing that delinquency results from the lack of legitimate opportunities for success available to most lower-class youth. **(False, p. 587)**

_____ 15-4. Violence among teenagers and teenage suicide continue to decrease at a rapid rate. **(False, p. 596)**

_____ 15-5. Very few juvenile correctional institutions are overcrowded. **(False, p. 612)**

_____ 15-6. A delinquent child is one who has no parents or whose parents are unable to care for him or her. **(False, p. 586)**

_____ 15-7. Juveniles charged with a status offense have the same procedural rights afforded to adults charged with a criminal offense. **(False, p. 587)**

_____ 15-8. If a juvenile is charged as a status offender, his or her guilt must be proved using a preponderance of evidence standard. **(True, p. 587)**

_____ 15-9. Juvenile trials are open to the public and to the news media. **(False, p. 606)**

_____ 15-10. If a juvenile is charged with a criminal offense, his or her guilt must be proved beyond a reasonable doubt. **(True, p. 606)**

Multiple Choice

15-11. Which of the following was not emphasized by the reform school movement?
  a. worth of hard work
  b. wholesome family environments
  c. affection necessary to build moral character
  d. all of the above emphasized by the reform school movement (p. 585)

15-12. Which theory sees delinquency as the result of social disorganization?
  a. social ecology (p. 587)
  b. opportunity
  c. neutralization
  d. strain

15-13. Which of the following is not a status offense?
  a. truancy
  b. running away from home
  c. robbery (p. 586)
  d. incorrigibility

15-14. What is the evidentiary standard that must be met at a delinquency hearing?
  a. preponderance of the evidence
  b. beyond a reasonable doubt (p. 609)
  c. in most instances
  d. the "feel good" standard

15-15. Which of the following U.S. Supreme Court cases ruled that juveniles are entitled to representation by attorneys who must have access to their records when the juveniles are being transferred to adult court?
  a. _Breed_ v. _Jones_ (p. 602)
  b. _Schall_ v. _Martin_
  c. _Kent_ v. _U.S._
  d. _Ex parte Crouse_

15-16. _____ children are defined as those who do not receive proper care from their parents or guardians.
  a. Dependent
  b. Neglected (p. 586)
  c. Abused
  d. Undisciplined

15-17. Teen court is
  a. a place where status offenders are given due process.
  b. another name of the juvenile justice system.
  c. a place where children ages 13–17 are tried.
  d. a place where alleged offenders are judged and sentenced by a jury of their peers. (p. 610)

15-18. Which step of the juvenile court process is similar to an adult trial?
  a. intake
  b. adjudication (p. 606)
  c. disposition
  d. postadjudicatory review

15-19. A common law principle that allows the state to assume a parental role and to take custody of a child who becomes delinquent, is abandoned, or is in need of care that the natural parents are unable or unwilling to provide is
    a. arrest.
    b. community outreach.
    c. *parens patriae*. (p. 582)
    d. intake.

15-20. Most states' juvenile court systems were modeled after the court system in what state?
    a. Indiana
    b. Illinois (p. 586)
    c. New York
    d. Ohio

Fill-In

15-21. The term applied to a child in order to avoid the stigma that comes from application of the term *criminal* is _____. **(delinquent child, p. 586)**

15-22. A child who is beyond parental control, as evidenced by refusal to obey legitimate authorities such as school officials and teachers, is termed a(n) _____. **(undisciplined child, p. 586)**

15-23. _____ theory views delinquency as the result of limited legitimate avenues to be successful. **(Opportunity, p. 587)**

15-24. A child who has been forced into delinquent activity by a parent or guardian is termed a(n) _____. **(abused child, p. 586)**

15-25. _____ is the principle that allows the state to assume a parental role. **(*Parens patriae*, p. 582)**

15-26. _____ is the fact-finding process in which the court determines whether or not there is sufficient evidence to sustain the allegations in a petition. **(Adjudicatory hearing, p. 609)**

15-27. A document filed in juvenile court alleging that a juvenile is delinquent, a status offender, or a dependent and asking that the court assume jurisdiction over the child is a(n) _____. **(juvenile petition, p. 608)**

15-28. A child who commits an act that is contrary to the law by virtue of the juvenile's status as a child is a(n) _____. **(status offender, p. 586)**

15-29. A child not receiving the proper level of physical or psychological care from parents is a(n) _____. **(neglected child, p. 586)**

15-30. A child who has no parent(s) or whose parent(s) is (are) unable to care for him or her is a(n) _____. **(dependent child, p. 586)**

Key—Crossword Puzzle

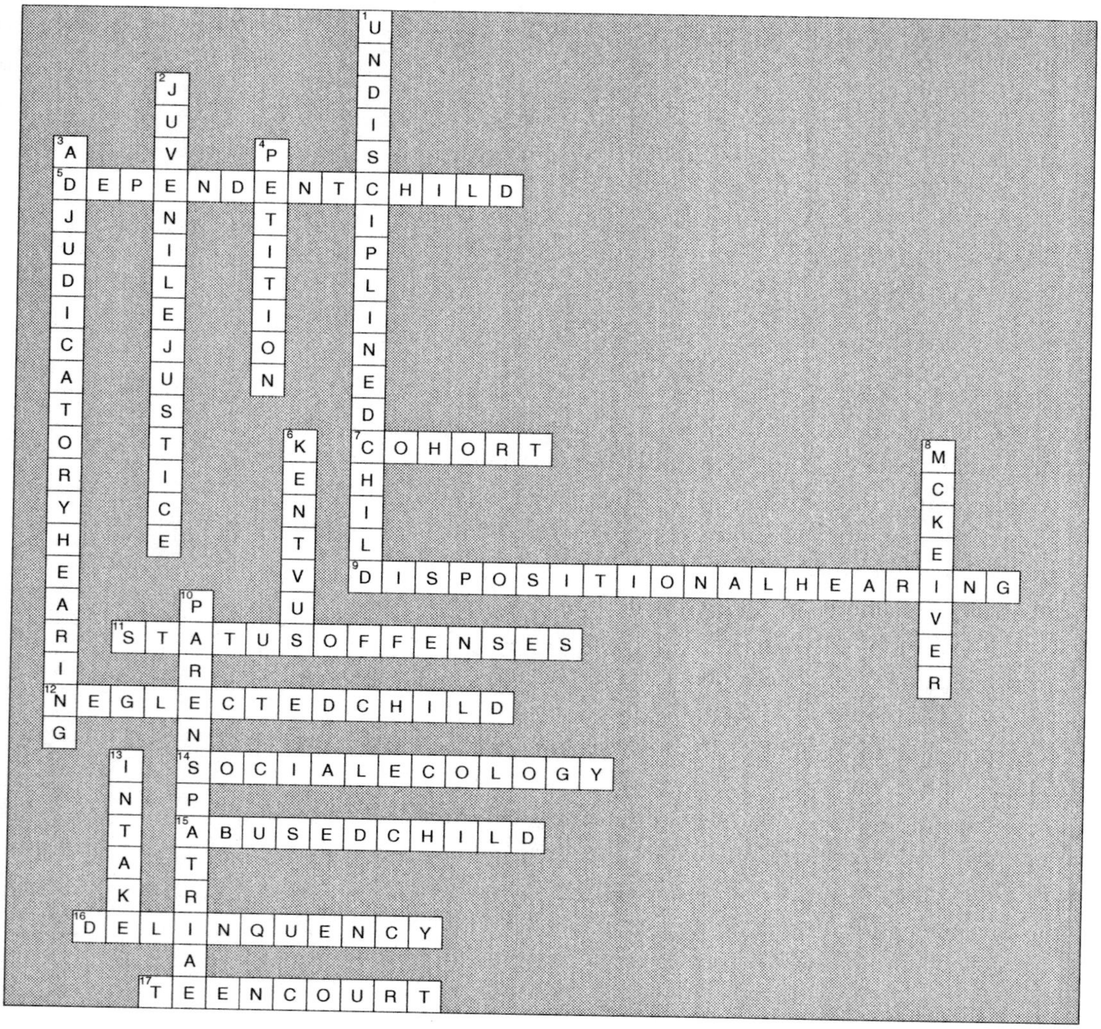

The crossword puzzle solution grid contains the following answers:

- 1 Down: UNDISPLINED (UNDISPLINED — reading: U-N-D-I-S-P-L-I-N-E-D)
- 2 Down: JUVENILEJUSTICE
- 3 Down: ADJUDICATORYHEARING
- 4 Down: PETITION
- 5 Across: DEPENDENTCHILD
- 6 Down: KENTVU
- 7 Across: COHORT
- 8 Down: MCKEIVER
- 9 Across: DISPOSITIONALHEARING
- 10 Down: PRAT (PART...)
- 11 Across: STATUSOFFENSES
- 12 Across: NEGLECTEDCHILD
- 13 Down: INTAKE
- 14 Across: SOCIALECOLOGY
- 15 Across: ABUSEDCHILD
- 16 Across: DELINQUENCY
- 17 Across: TEENCOURT

Across

5. Child who has no parents or whose parents are unable to care for him or her.
7. Group of individuals sharing similarities of age, place of birth, and residence.
9. Final stage of the juvenile justice process.
11. Purchasing cigarettes, buying alcohol, and being truant are examples.
12. Child who is not receiving the proper level of physical or psychological care from his or her parents.
14. Theory that explains delinquency primarily as the result of social disorganization.
15. Child who has been physically, sexually, or mentally abused.
16. When a juvenile breaks the law.
17. Alternative approach to juvenile justice in which juvenile offenders are judged and sentenced by a jury of their peers.

Down

1. Child who is beyond parental control.
2. System that responds to crimes committed by youthful offenders.
3. Juvenile justice hearing to determine whether there is sufficient evidence to sustain allegations.
4. Juvenile court document.
6. Case that ended the Supreme Court's hands-off era in juvenile justice.
8. _____ v. *Pennsylvania.*
10. Term for when the state assumes responsibility for the welfare of problem children.
13. First step of the juvenile justice process.

Key—Word Search Puzzle

```
I P G Y E Z S X O W I R F L T V D K D X G V H I U N Y X U Y
K O E U P T B X K Q V G E K I V J E V N T L A B J V K W V G
M P G A W T C B N R U Y R U X O C E I W J D R M D K O Y R X
Q P C Y L V J I N T A K E L Q A U R C N O U L E E M J X E X
S O I Y Y B V U R D E W Y Y F W A T O Z F H F O P A U J Y W
A R K T A H N P V O P Q B I I E U R H L W X F L E K V U G O
D T D J P J V E P E K C E V H B E J O K Y L Q T N B E N F Z
J U T R W W J C G T N I A L S D F Y R J R O O G D K N E V E
U I E E Y G X Q P H I A D N Q U H T M S U O M E Y I N O N
D T J T B R A X C L A N L E Y D K L Z U L F S Y N D L I U W
I Y C N H N P V Z A O B F E S P E L F V P U S H T E E L N
C T U N E H Z P C I F F K V D S L W H R E D G C E J E R R L
A H S M U B L I E S A M Z S R A S P O N M C F V I B S E S P
T E O S E T S E U J M G Q Y G G V P C Q Q A I S L K T T E I
O R X Z P O G T C S W A P C U K D T O A U U V P D A I I T J
R Y L M P R A X M T T E E N C O U R T S U Q E C E B C T D Z
H P Z S P T P R D K E H K Q E Q E S Y S I H O N U S E I V V
E I A S I B G V H Y D S B Y F I L S B M T J N C J S O G G
A D H A B Q E F N Z K L C Z A O S J O B V S I H M Y Y N E P
R K Z U E R Y L G A L G J H T J G G L O O A A O N Q S N V K
I T X L X T N D U H U Q V K I O N D N R I A C I N E T A E F
N Q L Q U C J I U F U P M U H L Z G J X D G Y B S A E G Q X
G X F A B U S E D C H I L D V M D U L W V X F F U T M U F C
S T N W V I N J K T O N F L M M S J R Y I K V Y D V P Z T P
V F G V P X D F U F H G K Y L L L P A R E N S P A T R I A E
K K N B U D H O S L U N D I S C I P L I N E D C H I L D H X
R K E O N L B C P R T L P G S O C I A L E C O L O G Y W F B
B G K E I K B R D E L I N Q U E N T C H I L D S L I M X P S
M J C G W U Y D E K U L E U R V X I A Z W Z F V Z Y C N P V
```

Abused Child
Adjudicatory Hearing
Cohort
Delinquency
Delinquent Child
Dependent Child
Dispositional Hearing
Intake
Juvenile Disposition

Juvenile Justice System
Juvenile Petition
Neglected Child
Opportunity Theory
Parens Patriae
Social Ecology
Status Offender
Teen Court
Undisciplined Child

Drugs and Crime

LEARNING OBJECTIVES

After reading this chapter, you should be able to:

- Discuss the history of drug abuse in America
- Discuss the history of antidrug legislation in America
- Identify the different types of drugs that are illegally used in this country, as well as the effects and legal classifications of each
- Explain the link between drugs and other social problems, including different forms of criminal activity
- Describe the various efforts to respond to the drug problem, and assess the effectiveness of each

Chapter Summary

The textbook examines the important issue of drugs and crime in Chapter 16. Drug use, drug-related crime, drug laws, and drug-enforcement efforts significantly affect processes of criminal justice. A large proportion of the financial and personnel resources of the criminal justice system is used to respond to the drug problem in the United States. For example, police departments utilize undercover operations to increase the number of arrests of drug offenders, prosecutions for drug offenses overwhelm court dockets, and the number of defendants incarcerated for drug offenses continues to grow.

Chapter 16 begins with an overview of the drug problem. First, it illustrates the importance of the topic by highlighting the specific impacts of drugs on the criminal justice system. The text also provides essential background information with a discussion of the question "What is a drug?" It also examines alcohol abuse and the criminal justice system's response to alcohol-related offenses.

The text then traces the history of drug abuse, covering the use of opium, morphine, and heroin in the 1800s and early 1900s, the response to marijuana in the 1900s, the use of LSD in the 1960s and 1970s, the use of crack cocaine in the 1980s, and the increased use of club drugs in the 1990s. The text further discusses the corresponding history of anti–drug abuse legislation in the United States. The first significant piece of federal antidrug legislation was the Harrison Act of 1914. The text describes the Marijuana Tax Act of 1937, the Narcotic Control Act of 1956, the Comprehensive Drug Abuse Prevention and Control Act of 1970, and the Anti-Drug Abuse Act of 1988. This latter piece of legislation created the position of drug czar within the Office of National Drug Control Policy.

A detailed explanation of four major drug types, marijuana, cocaine, heroin, and club drugs, follows the discussion of antidrug legislation. The text describes how these drugs are produced, consumed, and trafficked into the United States. Cocaine, for example, is extracted from the leaves of the coca plant, produces intense psychological effects, and typically enters the United States from Peru, Bolivia, Colombia, or Ecuador.

Chapter 16 then examines social problems related to drugs. The chapter discusses the link between drugs and crime and **money laundering**. For example, the link between drugs and crime has at least three dimensions: crimes specifically related to the use or sale of drugs; crimes committed by drug users, such as the addict who commits robberies to maintain his or her habit; and the organized criminal and gang activities that support the drug trade.

Chapter 16 concludes with a discussion of various criminal justice strategies used to respond to the drug problem. These strategies have very different philosophical orientations. On the one hand, several methods focus on the supply side of drug use. Strict enforcement, **forfeiture, interdiction**, and crop-control efforts concentrate on responding to the problem by attacking the selling and production of drugs through increased efforts by police, courts, and correctional institutions. Strict enforcement efforts include calls for imposing harsher punishments and increasing the number of police officers responding to the problem. Forfeiture involves seizing the assets of individuals involved in drug trafficking, and interdiction involves international efforts to prevent drugs from entering the United States and to destroy crops. On the other hand, education, treatment, and counseling efforts focus on prevention and the drug user. For example, project DARE attempts to educate school children, focusing on decision-making skills, peer pressure, and choices. The chapter concludes with a discussion of **legalization** and **decriminalization** efforts.

Teaching Outline

    I. Introduction (p. 622)

Drug Abuse   Illicit drug use that results in social, economic, psychological, or legal problems for the user. *Source*: Bureau of Justice Statistics, *Drugs, Crime, and the Justice System* (Washington, D.C.: Bureau of Justice Statistics, 1992), p. 20. (p. 622)

       • Explain the impact that drugs have had on the criminal justice system during the last 20 years.

- Emphasize clogged court dockets and huge increases in prison populations.
A. Drug Abuse: More Than an Individual Choice (p. 622)
    - Drug crimes may be the major challenge of criminal justice practitioners and of state and federal policymakers.
    - List the destructive consequences of drugs:
        - Lost productivity
        - Inequitable distribution of economic resources
        - Disease
        - Wasted human potential
        - Fragmented families
        - Violence
        - Other crimes

Controlled Substance A specifically defined bioactive or psychoactive chemical substance proscribed by law. (p. 623)

INSTRUCTIONAL CUE

Emphasize the "victimless" nature of drug crimes. Like other victimless crimes, such as prostitution and gambling, the consensual nature of these crimes poses a unique challenge to the criminal justice system. Law enforcement and other criminal justice practitioners have had to develop innovative approaches to respond to these types of crime.

II. What Is a Drug? (p. 623)

Drug Any chemical substance defined by social convention as bioactive or psychoactive. (p. 623)

Recreational Drug User A person who uses drugs relatively infrequently and whose use occurs primarily with friends and in social contexts that define drug use as pleasurable. Most addicts begin as recreational users. (p. 623)

- Highlight that the definition of drugs and the labeling of substances as drugs occur through a process of social construction.

Psychoactive Substance A chemical substance that affects cognition, feeling, or awareness. (p. 624)

A. Alcohol Abuse (p. 624)
    - Alcohol, in combination with other drugs, is often a factor in the commission of crimes.
    - Discuss the crackdown on drunk drivers.

INSTRUCTIONAL CUE

Discuss the impact that Mothers Against Drunk Driving (MADD) has had on policymakers and criminal justice practitioners.

III. A History of Drug Abuse in America (p. 626)
    A. Drug Use and Social Awareness (p. 627)
        - Elements that have cast drug use in a different light from that of the past include:
            - The conceptualization of addiction as a physical and/or medical condition
            - The understanding that drug use is associated with other kinds of activity

- Widespread social condemnation of drug use as a waste of economic resources
- Comprehensive and detailed federal and state laws
- A large involvement with drugs among the urban poor and socially disenfranchised
- A shift from the definition of drug abuse as a medical problem to the view that it is a law enforcement problem
- Describe the three schools of thought that form the basis for current drug policy.
  - "Public health generalism": This perspective holds that all controlled substances are harmful and that the disease victimizes drug abusers.
  - "Cost-benefit specifism": Drug policy should be built around a balancing of the social costs of drug abuse with the costs of enforcement.
  - "Legalist": Suggests that drug policies are necessary to prevent the collapse of social order.

INSTRUCTIONAL CUE LINKED TO THE STUDENT STUDY GUIDE

Use Student Activity 1 in the Student Study Guide to illustrate characteristics of current drug-control policy. After students complete this assignment, contrast current policy with drug policy when President Reagan and President George Bush were in office.

B. Antidrug Legislation (p. 628)
- Harrison Narcotics Act (1914)

Harrison Narcotics Act The first major piece of federal antidrug legislation, passed in 1914. (p. 628)

- Persons dealing in opium, morphine, heroin, and cocaine had to register with the federal government and pay a $1.00 tax every year.
- Marijuana Tax Act (1937)
  - This act placed a tax of $100 per ounce on cannabis.
- Boggs Act (1951)
  - This act made marijuana and several other drugs federally prohibited controlled substances.
- Narcotic Control Act (1956)
  - This act increased penalties for drug trafficking and possession and made the sale of heroin to anyone under age 18 a capital offense.
1. Comprehensive Drug Abuse Prevention and Control Act of 1970
  - This act still forms the basis of federal enforcement efforts today.

Controlled Substances Act (CSA) Title II of the Comprehensive Drug Abuse Prevention and Control Act of 1970, which established schedules classifying psychoactive drugs according to their degree of psychoactivity. (p. 629)

- Discuss the five schedules used to classify psychoactive drugs.

Psychological Dependence A craving for a specific drug that results from long-term substance abuse. Psychological dependence on drugs is marked by the belief that drugs are needed to achieve a feeling of well-being. *Source*: Bureau of Justice Statistics, *Drugs, Crime, and the Justice System* (Washington, D.C.: Bureau of Justice Statistics, 1992), p. 21. (p. 629)

Physical Dependence A biologically based craving for a specific drug that results from frequent use of the substance. Physical dependence on drugs is marked by a growing tolerance of a drug's effects, so that increased amounts of the drug are needed to obtain the desired effect, and by the onset of withdrawal symptoms over periods of prolonged abstinence. *Source*: Bureau of Justice Statistics, *Drugs, Crime, and the Justice System* (Washington, D.C.: Bureau of Justice Statistics, 1992), p. 21. (p. 629)

    2. Anti-Drug Abuse Act of 1988
- This act created a cabinet-level post, a drug czar to be in charge of federal initiatives.

Drug Czar The popular name for the head of the Office of National Drug Control Policy (ONDCP), a federal cabinet-level position that was created during the Reagan presidency to organize federal drug-fighting efforts. (p. 632)

- Penalties for recreational drug users increased substantially.
- The Anti-Drug Abuse Act denied federal benefits to convicted drug offenders.
- Civil penalties of up to $10,000 may be assessed against convicted recreational users.
- Legislation also included the possibility of capital punishment for drug-related murders.

    3. Other Federal Antidrug Legislation
- Crime Control Act of 1990
- Violent Crime Control and Law Enforcement Act of 1994
- Drug-Free Communities Act of 1997

INSTRUCTIONAL CUE LINKED TO THE STUDENT STUDY GUIDE

After you complete the discussion of the various types of drug-control legislation, assign Student Activity 2. Discuss the fact that most drug policy has focused on increased enforcement rather than on increased treatment opportunities.

    C. The Investigation of Drug Abuse and Manufacturing (p. 632)
- Abandonment
    - Property, once clearly thrown away, ceases to fall under Fourth Amendment protections.
    - *California* v. *Greenwood*: In this case the Court held that there is no reasonable expectation of privacy in trash left for collection. It is considered abandoned property.
    - *Abel* v. *U.S.*: The Supreme Court found that a warrantless search of a motel room immediately after it had been vacated was acceptable.

Curtilage In legal usage, the area surrounding a residence that can reasonably be said to be a part of the residence for Fourth Amendment purposes. (p. 633)

- *Oliver* v. *U.S.*: This case was the first to clearly recognize the term *curtilage*. Here, the Court ruled that territory within the curtilage of a residence is accorded the same Fourth Amendment protections as that within the walls of the house.

INSTRUCTIONAL CUE LINKED TO THE STUDENT STUDY GUIDE

Review some of the important Fourth and Fifth Amendment decisions from earlier in the semester, and then have students complete Student Activity 3.

- Open Fields Doctrine
  - *Hester* v. *U.S.*: The Supreme Court held that law enforcement officers could search an open field without a warrant.
  - *U.S.* v. *Dunn*: The Court held that even if an area is fenced, it is not within the curtilage if sufficiently distant from the household.

INSTRUCTIONAL CUE

Use the following situation to explore issues of abandonment and curtilage. Officer Shuren and Officer Neron went to 1165 State Road after receiving a complaint from a neighbor of a loud party. Shelly Thomas answered the door when they knocked, apologized for the noise, but explained that the party had broken up and she was going to bed. The officers were satisfied with her response but decided to look in a trash can before getting back in their police car. The trash can was leaning against the house. Officer Neron removed the lid of the trash can and saw what appeared to be a half-smoked joint on top of a garbage bag. Is the seizure of this joint an unreasonable search and seizure? It probably is, because the trash can was in the curtilage of the house and the officers had to remove the lid to see the contents of the can. If, however, there had not been a lid, it probably would have been a good seizure because of the plain-view doctrine. Furthermore, if she had put the trash can on the street corner, it would be considered abandoned property.

IV. The Most Common Drugs—And Who Is Using Them (p. 634)

    A. Drug Trafficking

Drug Trafficking   Trading or dealing in controlled substances, to include the transporting, storage, importing, or sale of controlled substance. (p. 636)

- Nearly $60 billion annual industry
- Nearly 20 million Americans are users.
- Fiscal year 2004 expenditures on drug-control activities were about $11.7 billion.

    B. Marijuana (p. 637)

- Marijuana is usually smoked, although it may be eaten or made into a tea.
- Most users are recreational.

    C. Cocaine (p. 639)

- Produces intense psychological effects
- Is the most dangerous common drug

    D. Heroin (p. 640)

- Produces euphoria
- Risks include overdose because of dosage uncertainties, AIDS, and hepatitis.

    E. Club Drugs (p. 641)

Club Drug   A synthetic psychoactive substance often found at nightclubs, bars, "raves," and dance parties. Club drugs include MDMA (ecstasy), ketamine, methamphetamine (meth), GBL, PCP, GHB, and Rohypnol. (p. 641)

Pharmaceutical Diversion   The transfer of prescription medicines controlled by the Controlled Substance Act by theft, deception, and/or fraudulent means for other than their intended purposes. (p. 643)

    V. Costs of Abuse (p. 644)

        A. Indirect Costs of Abuse (p. 644)

- Annual national cost of illicit drug use is estimated at $180.9 billion.

- Includes costs of lost productivity, health care and justice system and social welfare expenditures.

B. Drug-Related Crime (p. 644)

- Three dimensions of the links between drugs and crime:
  - Economic losses
  - Costs from transactions, actual crimes committed by drug users
  - Organized crime activities to support the drug trade

Money Laundering   The process by which criminals or criminal organizations seek to disguise the illicit nature of their proceeds by introducing them into the stream of legitimate commerce and finance. *Source*: U.S. Department of Treasury, *2000–2005 Strategic Plan* (Washington, D.C.: U.S. Government Printing Office, 2000), p. 1.

- Estimates of the amount of drug money laundered are as high as $300 billion.
- *Ratzlaf* v. *U.S.*: The Court ruled that no one can be convicted of trying to evade bank-reporting requirements unless authorities can prove that offenders knew they were violating the law.
- The International Money Laundering Abatement and Anti-Terrorist Financing Act of 2001 (Title III of the USA PATRIOT Act) requires banks to make considerable effort in determining the sources of monies in overseas accounts.

VI. Solving the Drug Problem (p. 647)

A. Strict Enforcement (p. 647)

- Antidrug law enforcement and long drug sentences
- Goal is to remove dealers from the streets, disrupt supply lines, and eliminate sources of supply.

B. Asset Forfeiture (p. 648)

Forfeiture   The authorized seizure of money, negotiable instruments, securities, or other things of value. In federal antidrug laws, judicial representatives are authorized to seize all cash, negotiable instruments, securities, or other things of value furnished or intended to be furnished by any person in exchange for a controlled substance, as well as all proceeds traceable to such an exchange. (p. 648)

Racketeer Influenced and Corrupt Organization (RICO)   A federal statute that allows for the federal seizure of assets derived from illegal enterprise. (p. 648)

- Discuss the important Supreme Court decisions on forfeiture.
  - *U.S.* v. *92 Buena Vista Ave.*: This case established the "innocent owner defense" in forfeiture cases.
  - *Austin* v. *U.S.*: This case put limits on the government's authority to seize property, stating that any seizure must not be excessive when compared to the seriousness of the charge.
  - *Alexander* v. *U.S.*: The Court found that forfeitures under the RICO statute must be limited according to the rules established in *Austin* v. *U.S.*
  - *U.S.* v. *Ursery*: The Court rejected claims that civil forfeiture laws constitute double jeopardy.

C. Interdiction (p. 649)

Interdiction   The interception of drug traffic at the nation's borders. Interdiction is one of the many strategies used to stem the flow of illegal drugs into the United States. (p. 650)

- Interdiction efforts have been attacked because of ineffectiveness and concern that using military personnel in these efforts is a violation of the law.

   D. Crop Control (p. 650)
       • The purpose of crop control is to limit availability by targeting foreign producers.
   E. Prevention and Treatment (p. 650)
       • Prevention primarily focuses on education programs aimed at preventing drug use and abuse.
       • Examples include the National Youth Anti-Drug Media Campaign and Project DARE.

INSTRUCTIONAL CUE

In January 2000, the White House drug-policy office came under attack because it used financial incentives to force television networks to include antidrug messages in their shows. On several occasions, it even asked to review television scripts before a program was aired. In response to the criticism, policy was implemented that prevented it from viewing episodes before airing.

       • Discuss the research evidence indicating that DARE is not effective.
       1. Drug Courts

Drug Court   A special state, county, or municipal court that offers first-time substance-abuse offenders judicially mandated and court-supervised treatment alternatives to prison. (p. 652)

   F. Legalization and Decriminalization (p. 652)
       • Explain the difference between legalization and decriminalization.

Legalization   Elimination of the laws and associated criminal penalties associated with certain behaviors—usually the production, sale, distribution, and possession of a controlled substance. (p. 653)

Decriminalization   The redefinition of certain previously criminal behaviors into regulated activities that become "ticketable" rather than "arrestable." (p. 653)

       • Explain the arguments for and against both legalization and decriminalization.
       • One compromise approach is the limitation model. This model would make drugs legally available, but with clearly defined limits.

INSTRUCTIONAL CUE LINKED TO THE STUDENT STUDY GUIDE

Assign Student Activity 4. After students complete the assignment, arrange a class debate on the legalization of marijuana.

Learner Activities

Activity 1

Read the National Drug Control Strategy posted as **Library Extra 16–9**. Describe the strategy in the space below. What aspects of drug enforcement does the strategy focus on? What are its key characteristics?

LIBRARY EXTRA

_____

_____

_____

_____

_____

_____

Activity 2

Historically, political policy on drug enforcement has approached the problem with two different responses. One response is to focus on cracking down on the sellers, increasing the number of arrests, and advocating stricter punishments. The second response focuses on rehabilitating the user with treatment and counseling. Which approach, or combination of approaches, would you recommend as the most effective response to drugs? Discuss how this approach would impact the criminal justice system.

_____

_____

_____

_____

_____

_____

Activity 3

The war on drugs, fought through the 1980s and early 1990s, focused primarily on a strict enforcement approach. The strict enforcement approach provides police with wide latitude in formulating how best to respond to the drug problem. The U.S. Supreme Court supported these efforts with several important decisions that limited the rights of individuals. For example, the Supreme Court used several drug cases to redefine Fourth Amendment protections against unreasonable searches and seizures and to redefine Fifth Amendment protections against self-incrimination. Review the legal cases presented in the text. Find three cases discussed earlier in the text that addressed a legal question in a drug case. Describe the facts of the cases, and the Court's rulings, in the space provided below.

_____

_____

_____

_____

_____

_____

Activity 4

A political consulting firm has requested your assistance in writing a memorandum on the legalization of marijuana. Write a memorandum that discusses the advantages and disadvantages of the legalization of marijuana.

_____

_____

_____

_____

_____

_____

Internet Activity

Research drug and alcohol information on the Web using the Cybrary at http://www. cybrary.info. Search the Cybrary listings to find sites that contain suggestions and ideas on how to solve the drug problems facing this country. Describe the various strategies that are proposed. Which do you think are the most useful? Why? Submit your findings to your instructor if requested to do so.

_____

_____

_____

_____

_____

_____

Distance Learning Activity

What is your opinion about the legalization of "soft" drugs such as marijuana? Visit three or four websites to search for evidentiary support for your position. The following websites should be helpful: (1) American Council for Drug Education: http://www.acde.org; (2) Drugs and Crime: http://www.virlib.ncjrs.org/DrugsAnd-Crime.asp; (3) Marijuana Policy Project: http://www.mpp.org; (4) National Drug Intelligence Center: http://www.usdoj.gov/ndic; and (5) National Institute on Drug Abuse: http://www.nida.nih.gov. If your instructor asks you to so do, participate in a class discussion about the legalization of drugs.

_____

_____

_____

_____

_____

Learning Activities Utilizing the World Wide Web

There are student-based activities in the Student Study Guide (Internet Activity, Distance Learning Activity, CJ Today on the World Wide Web) that are similar in focus to those that follow. However, the following are presented as instructor-led activities, to be used in a classroom with online access.

Research drug and alcohol information on the Web using the Cybrary at http://www.cybrary.info. Search the Cybrary listings to find sites that contain suggestions and ideas on how to solve the drug problems facing this country. Display the various strategies that are proposed. In class, ask students: Which do you think are the most useful? Why?

Prepare for a class discussion focused on various opinions about the legalization of "soft" drugs such as marijuana. Visit three or four websites to search for evidentiary support for the various positions. The following websites should be helpful: (1) American Council for Drug Education: http://www.acde.org; (2) Center for Education and Drug Abuse Research: http://www.cedar.pharmacy.pitt.edu/main.html; (3) Drugs and Crime: http://www.virlib.ncjrs.org/DrugsAndCrime.asp; (4) Marijuana Policy Project: http://www.mpp.org; (5) National Drug Intelligence Center: http://www.usdoj.gov/ndic; and (6) National Institute on Drug Abuse: http://www.nida.nih.gov.

Other websites for organizations and agencies related to the material in Chapter 16 include:

Addiction Resource Guide	http://www.addictionresource guide.com
Alcohol and Drug Information	http://www.health.org
American Council for Drug Education	http://www.acde.org
Center for Education and Drug Abuse Research	http://cedar.pharmacy.pitt.edu/ main.html
Drug Abuse Resistance Education (DARE)	http://www.dare.com
Drug Enforcement Administration (DEA)	http://www.usdoj.gov/dea
Drugs and Crime	http://www.virlib.ncjrs.org/Drugs AndCrime.asp
MADD (Mothers Against Drunk Driving)	http://www.madd.org
National Drug Intelligence Center	http://www.usdoj.gov/ndic
National Institute on Drug Abuse	http://www.nida.nih.gov
Executive Office for Weed and Seed	http://www.ojp.usdoj.gov/eows

Suggested Answers to Chapter Discussion Questions

1. How long have substances that today would be considered illicit been used in the United States? For what purposes?

An examination of the history of drug abuse in America reveals that many substances considered illegal today have been used for a variety of purposes. For example:

- Opium was widely available in medicines of the nineteenth and early twentieth centuries.
- Morphine was widely prescribed and used by physicians.
- Marijuana was imported by Mexican immigrants in this country but was quickly criminalized.
- LSD has been used for the treatment of psychiatric disorders.
- Cocaine was also used for the treatment of psychiatric disorders. Cocaine was also put in medicine and beverages.

2. List and describe some of the most important pieces of federal drug-control legislation.

Harrison Narcotics Act (1914). This was the first major piece of federal antidrug legislation, requiring that persons dealing in opium, morphine, heroin, and cocaine had to register with the federal government and pay a $1.00 tax every year.

Marijuana Tax Act (1937). This act placed a tax of $100 per ounce on cannabis.

Boggs Act (1951). This act made marijuana and several other drugs federally prohibited controlled substances.

Narcotic Control Act (1956). This act increased penalties for drug trafficking and possession and made the sale of heroin to anyone under age 18 a capital offense.

Comprehensive Drug Abuse Prevention and Control Act of 1970. Established schedules classifying psychoactive drugs according to their degree of psychoactivity.

Anti-Drug Abuse Act of 1988. This act created a cabinet-level post (a drug czar to be in charge of federal initiatives), increased penalties for recreational drug users, denied federal benefits to convicted drug offenders, and included the possibility of capital punishment for drug-related murders.

Crime Control Act of 1990. This act doubled the appropriations for drug-law enforcement grants, enhanced drug-control and drug-education programs, assisted rural states in drug-enforcement efforts, sanctioned steroids under the Controlled Substances Act, and created "drug-free school zones."

Violent Crime Control and Law Enforcement Act of 1994. This act accomplished many objectives, including providing funding to rural areas for anticrime and drug efforts, provided money for treatment and education programs, required postconviction drug testing of all federal prisoners, and tripled penalties for using children to deal drugs in drug-free zones.

Drug-Free Communities Act of 1997. This act provided support to local communities to reduce substance abuse among youth.

3. **What are the major types of drugs that are illegally used in this country? Describe the effects and legal classification of each.**

- Marijuana. Produces euphoria, relaxation, intoxication, time distortion, memory alteration, and focused awareness. It is a Schedule I controlled substance.

- Cocaine. Produces excitability and feelings of competence and power. It is a Schedule II controlled substance.

- Heroin. Produces pleasure, euphoria, lack of concern, and a general feeling of well-being. It is a Schedule I controlled substance.

- Club Drugs. Varies by type of drug, but generally includes mild intoxication, hallucinations, and amnesia. They are Schedule I controlled substances.

4. **What is the relationship between drug use and other social problems? What kinds of crimes might be linked to drug use?**

Money is the chief reason why drug users migrate to other types of criminal behavior. Addiction to most drugs is extraordinarily expensive, and most users do not earn enough legitimately to support their habit and meet their other living expenses, too. The pull of addiction is so strong that it often leads users into crimes such as shoplifting, robbery, burglary, auto theft, and prostitution.

5. **What strategies have been used or suggested as ways of responding to the drug problem? Which of these strategies seem to hold the most potential?**

The six identified types of strategies for attacking the drug problem include:

- Strict enforcement. A feel-good approach that has cost a fortune to sustain but that has done little to reduce the use and manufacture of controlled substances.

- Asset forfeiture. An aggressive approach that yields great monetary return but often ensnares truly innocent property owners.

- Interdiction. An almost futile effort to seal the borders of the United States to drug shipments.

- Crop control. Theoretically it is a good idea, but in practice it is more show than substance. Major obstacles include the inability to overcome the potentially huge profits for farmers of illegal plants and difficulties involved in getting foreign governments to cooperate in eradication efforts.

- Education and treatment. These are seen by some as the key to resolving the drug problem but are inherently long-term solutions that do little to reduce the problem now.

- Legalization or decriminalization. An approach that would likely reduce criminal justice expenditure, with commensurate expenditure increases for health care and attendant problems. Some say, however, that the additional costs to society resulting from erosion of the social and moral fabric would be immeasurable, making this the least attractive strategy.

Some say getting tougher is the only solution. Their rather idealistic stance, however, often fails to address the problems that getting tougher brings on, such as ever-growing prison systems (and the staggering cost of running them) and growing inmate populations comprised of a large segment of an entire generation.

Others favor the opposite approach: legalization or decriminalization of all illicit drugs. They cite the fact that drug use in America has become epidemic and believe it should be treated as a medical emergency, not a criminal emergency.

Key—Student Study Guide Questions

True or False

_____ 16-1. The limitation model pertains to law enforcement strategies to limit the amount of drugs brought into the United States. **(False, p. 650)**

_____ 16-2. The Marijuana Tax Act of 1937 created a special assistant to the president on drug issues known as a "drug czar." **(False, p. 629)**

_____ 16-3. Most federal prisoners are incarcerated for drug offenses. **(True, p. 622)**

_____ 16-4. In many victimless crimes, society is the ultimate victim. **(True, p. 623)**

_____ 16-5. Although use of drugs continues to increase, alcohol abuse is declining rapidly. **(False, p. 624)**

_____ 16-6. Abandoned property is protected under the Fourth Amendment provisions against search and seizure. **(False, p. 634)**

_____ 16-7. Cocaine is considered a Schedule I drug by the criminal justice system, and crack is considered a Schedule IV drug. **(False, p. 629)**

_____ 16-8. Because of the Anti-Drug Abuse Act of 1988, an offender who commits a drug-related murder can be sentenced to death. **(True, p. 632)**

_____ 16-9. Drug abuse has minimum social and personal costs beyond its impact on the criminal justice system. **(False, p. 623)**

_____ 16-10. Zimring and Hawkins' "legalist" category suggests that drug-control policies are necessary in order to prevent the collapse of social order and of society itself. **(True, p. 627)**

Multiple Choice

16-11. Which piece of antidrug legislation created the five schedules used to classify psychoactive drugs?
   a. The Anti-Drug Abuse Act of 1988
   b. The Comprehensive Drug Abuse Prevention and Control Act of 1970 (p. 629)
   c. The Boggs Act of 1951
   d. The Narcotic Control Act of 1956

16-12. The Anti-Drug Abuse Act of 1988 accomplished all of the following except
   a. it increased penalties for recreational drug use.
   b. it made it difficult for suspected drug dealers to purchase weapons.
   c. it denied federal benefits to convicted drug offenders.
   d. it eliminated the possibility of capital punishment for drug-related murders. (p. 632)

16-13. Which of the following is not a Schedule II drug?
   a. opium
   b. peyote (p. 629)
   c. morphine
   d. codeine
   e. cocaine

16-14. Which U.S. Supreme Court case established the open fields doctrine?
   a. *Hester* v. *United States* (p. 634)
   b. *United States* v. *Dunn*
   c. *California* v. *Greenwood*
   d. *Abel* v. *United States*

16-15. Under the Controlled Substances Act, cough medicine is considered a
   a. Schedule I drug.
   b. Schedule II drug.
   c. Schedule IV drug.
   d. Schedule V drug. (p. 630)

16-16. Zimring and Hawkins argue that current drug policy is based on three schools of thought. Which of these schools proposes that drug policy be built around a balancing of the social costs of drug abuse?
   a. public health generalist
   b. cost-benefit specifism (p. 627)
   c. legalist
   d. deterrence

16-17. Which of the following pieces of antidrug legislation required drug users to register with the federal government and to pay a tax of $1.00 per year?
   a. The Harrison Narcotics Act (p. 628)
   b. The Marijuana Tax Act
   c. The Narcotic Control Act
   d. The Comprehensive Drug Abuse Prevention and Control Act

16-18. _____ is a legal term that describes the area surrounding a residence that can reasonably be said to be a part of the residence for Fourth Amendment purposes.
   a. Innocent owner
   b. Open field
   c. Curtilage (p. 633)
   d. Abandoned property

16-19. Which of the following pieces of legislation made marijuana a federally prohibited controlled substance?
   a. The Boggs Act of 1951 (p. 628)
   b. The Comprehensive Drug Abuse Prevention and Control Act
   c. The Marijuana Tax Act of 1937
   d. The Narcotic Control Act of 1956

16-20. Which of the following strategies focuses on reducing penalties for drug offenses, treating a drug-related offense similarly to a traffic offense?
   a. legalization
   b. decriminalization (p. 653)
   c. crop control
   d. interdiction

Fill-In

16-21. Illicit drug use that results in social, economic, psychological, or legal problems for the user is called _____. **(drug abuse, p. 622)**

16-22. _____ is the interception of drug traffic at the nation's borders. **(Interdiction, p. 650)**

16-23. A federal cabinet-level position created during the Reagan presidency to organize federal drug-fighting efforts is called _____. **(drug czar, p. 632)**

16-24. _____ is the redefinition of certain criminal behaviors into regulated activities, which become "ticketable" rather than "arrestable." **(Decriminalization, p. 653)**

16-25. _____ is the authorized seizure of money, negotiable instruments, securities, or other things of value. **(Forfeiture, p. 648)**

16-26. Title II of the Comprehensive Drug Abuse Prevention and Control Act of 1970, which established schedules classifying psychotic drugs according to their degree of psychoactivity, is called the _____. **(Controlled Substances Act, p. 629)**

16-27. The _____, passed in 1914, was the first major piece of federal antidrug legislation. **(Harrison Narcotics Act, p. 628)**

16-28. _____ refers to legislation that allows the federal seizure of assets derived from illegal enterprise. **(RICO, p.648)**

16-29. A(n) _____ is a chemical substance defined by social convention as bioactive or psychoactive. **(drug, p. 623)**

16-30. _____ eliminates the laws and associated criminal penalties that prohibit the production, sale, distribution, and possession of a controlled substance. **(Legalization, p. 653)**

Key—Crossword Puzzle

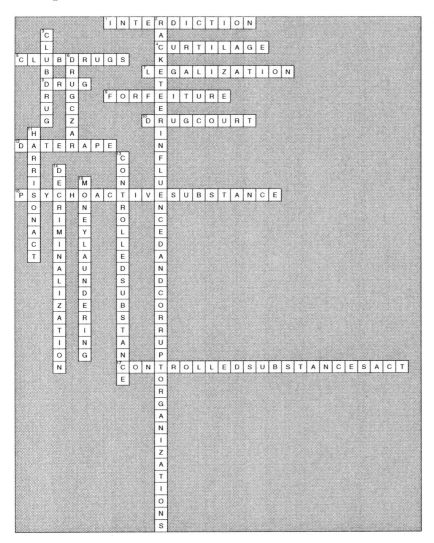

Across

1. Interception of drug traffic at the nation's borders.

4. Legal term for the area near a residence.

5. General term used for psychoactive substances found at nightclubs and raves,

7. Elimination of the laws and associated criminal penalties that prohibit the production, sale, distribution, and possession of a controlled substance.

8. Any chemical substance defined by social convention as bioactive or psychoactive.

9. Seizure of cash, instruments, and securities involved in a drug transaction.

10. Alternative to traditional court processes for first-time substance abuse offenders.

12. Rohypnol and GHB are considered this type of drug.

16. Chemical substance that affects cognition, feeling, and/or awareness.

17. Title II of the Comprehensive Drug Abuse Prevention and Control Act of 1970.

Down

2. Federal statute that allows the federal seizure of assets derived from an illegal enterprise.

3. Example includes ecstasy or GHB.

6. Popular name for the head of the Office of National Drug Control Policy.

11. First major piece of federal antidrug legislation.

13. Specifically defined bioactive or psychoactive chemical substance proscribed by law.

14. Redefinition of criminal behaviors into regulated activities.

15. Conversion of illegally earned assets to some other form.

Key—Word Search Puzzle

```
B E N Z Z F V W F L U N B A V S G S N Y W Y B D O J N Q I Q
Z O R J H F O O F Q Q S N Y Y O O D W Q U T D K M D F E W
H Q Z K P M H R U X O T D L R M I N L D R U G A B U S E K R
R B B J H D A D F X X S X D C T O W H M C I F D P L M B T D
E V C K Y C R V T E Q P H X C B B E E F O A A X M U M H P X
C X N O S G R W Q Q I O Z I D R U G T R A F F I C K I N G S
R R N K I D I P E D L T D P S M A P O R O F V O M U R P U U
E L R O C X S H J I E R U W J L H I F D B I K B A T Z D M F
A M Z H A L O B D B E C Y R I N J X E Q P P E U W A W J R L
T B K V L J N P N T X F R T E P L W N A V T I L K A X L V P
I W Y L D Y A W N U V Z R I G T E B E C Q K G M T J C Z M C
O V R T E N C I K W Z U Z G M G V G G Y F D R U G C Z A R O
N S Y B P U T D N B C I W W Z I S E O E Y V H Z V F T H A Y
A F K F E Q O Q N G M E O E A F N K Z X X Q S I Z J N O P J
L T W B N S C L Y V K Q U Q S H D A B O O S F R C E Q A S Z
D J D Q D J B J J T X A L X O S R H L O Z S B X G L P F T Q
R C M W E G R R F D C B T Z N S U G T I F J U A V X D F E H
U N I A N W H X O A K R T Y O L G M V Y Z J Z N N N K K T S
G Y E R C D F C H T U S W F J Y W U T A A A H Z R Z R I R S
U Q I I E S X A L O X K E P B E D R D P W Z T V B Q P G H X
S E D C B M S K C U L S B T V A E K V E X K Y I U R S Z U K
E V E O O T S G F J B N F D L T I Z R T P J Y M O R L H T F
R E C V A V U C A X Z D L E G A L I Z A T I O N X N H N E B
M U W U Z R A F X L I F R M O N E Y L A U N D E R I N G H I
P H L I D Z A X L W R T B U A N U O T N T O Q T J M D I D D
X V L F D W E O L Z N I L M G D Q D R B R G V F Q F Q J Y Y
X Z M X A U M P F C O N T R O L L E D S U B S T A N C E T I
F B C O N T R O L L E D S U B S T A N C E S A C T A Q L D H
E Z I X T O I N S P S Y C H O A C T I V E S U B S T A N C E
G R B X Q X I F T X P O Z J J W K C E D I K X U V S T R R H
```

Club Drug
Controlled Substance
Controlled Substances Act
Curtilage
Decriminalization
Drug
Drug Abuse
Drug Court
Drug Czar
Drug Trafficking

Forfeiture
Harrison Act
Interdiction
Legalization
Money Laundering
Physical Dependence
Psychoactive Substance
Recreational Drug User
RICO

Terrorism and Multinational Criminal Justice

LEARNING OBJECTIVES

After reading this chapter, you should be able to:

- Describe the nature of comparative criminal justice, and identify the potential benefits of, and problems inherent in, cross-cultural comparisons of crime
- Describe the principles that inform Islamic law
- Identify important international criminal justice organizations, and explain their role in fighting international crime
- Explain transnational crime, and explicate its possible relationship to terrorism
- Define terrorism, and identify two major types of terrorism
- Discuss the causes of terrorism and the U.S. government's attempts to prevent and control the spread of terrorism
- Explain why terrorism is a law enforcement concern and how it is a form of criminal activity

Chapter Summary

Thus far, the textbook has focused primarily on criminal justice in the United States. As you have discovered, the criminal justice process can be complex and confusing. However, the attention given to important criminal justice issues has provided the necessary foundation to cut through this complexity to develop a comprehensive understanding of the criminal justice system in the United States. Chapter 17 provides the opportunity to expand your understanding of these processes by first discussing the work of **comparative criminologists**. Comparative criminologists are interested in examining crime and criminal justice at a cross-national level. Chapter 17 provides considerable information on Islamic criminal justice system. Chapter 17 also discusses **terrorism** in the United States.

Although it is difficult to compare crime rates across countries because of the differences in the ways crimes are defined, diverse crime-reporting practices, and political influences, we can learn a great deal from investigating similarities and differences of criminal justice processing in different countries. Consider the Islamic criminal justice system. The four primary sources of Islamic law are the *Koran*, the teachings of the Prophet Muhammad, the consensus of the clergy, and reason or logic. A key distinction of Islamic law is the difference between *Hudud* and *Tazir* crimes. **Hudud crimes** are serious violations of Islamic law and regarded as offenses against God. These crimes are essentially violations of "natural law," and the punishment for committing one is severe. In contrast, **Tazir crimes** are minor violations of Islamic law. These offenses are regarded as offenses against society, not God. The three levels of the Islamic court system are also discussed.

The next section of Chapter 17 focuses on international criminal justice organizations and **transnational** crime. This section describes the International Society of Criminology (ISC) and the role of the United Nations in criminal justice. It also describes the activities of INTERPOL and Europol. **INTERPOL** is an acronym for International Criminal Police Organization, an international law enforcement organization that began operations in 1946. **Europol** is the integrated police intelligence-gathering and dissemination arm of the member nations of the European Union. Transnational crime has been influenced by the ongoing process of globalization. **Globalization** refers to the internationalization of trade, services, investment, information, and other forms of human social activity.

The final section of Chapter 17 discusses terrorism in the United States. Since the attacks on the World Trade Center and the Pentagon, terrorism has become a top-priority political and criminal justice issue. For example, significant legislation has been passed to improve the response to both domestic and international terrorism. **Domestic terrorism** refers to the unlawful use of force by an individual or group operating entirely in the United States. **International terrorism** refers to the unlawful use of force or violence by a group or individual with some connection to a foreign power. Other types of terrorism discussed in this section include **cyberterrorism** and **narcoterrorism**. When considering how best to combat terrorism, the chapter discusses the role of the Department of Homeland Security. The chapter concludes with a discussion of **foreign terrorist organizations** and the future of international terrorism.

Teaching Outline

I. Introduction (p. 662)

Comparative Criminologist One who studies crime and criminal justice on a cross-national level. (p. 662)

A. Ethnocentrism and the Study of Criminal Justice (p. 662)

Ethnocentric Holding a belief in the superiority of one's own social or ethnic group and culture. (p. 662)

- Recently, interest has grown in comparing the justice systems of the United States and those of other cultures.

    B. Problems with Data (p. 662)
- It is difficult to compare crime rates of different nations.
  - Crimes are defined differently.
  - There are diverse crime-reporting practices.
  - There are political and other social influences on the reporting to international agencies.

  II. Islamic Criminal Justice (p. 664)

    A. The *Hudud* Crimes (p. 665)
- Islamic law is based on the Koran, the teachings of the prophet Muhammad, the consensus of the clergy, and reason or logic.

Islamic Law A system of laws, operative in some Arab countries, based upon the Muslim religion and especially the holy book of Islam, the Koran. (p. 665)

- Islamic law recognizes seven *Hudud* crimes—crimes based on religious strictures.

Hudud Crime A serious violation of Islamic law regarded as an offense against God. *Hudud* crimes include such behavior as theft, adultery, sodomy, alcohol consumption, and robbery. (p. 665)

- These crimes are essentially violations of "natural law."
- Committing a *Hudud* offense results in severe punishment.
- All crimes other than *Hudud* are called *Tazir*.

    B. The *Tazir* Crimes (p. 666)

Tazir Crime A minor violation of Islamic law regarded as an offense against society, not God. (p. 666)

- *Tazir* crimes are regarded as any action not considered acceptable in a spiritual society.
- *Tazir* crimes may call for *Quesas* (retribution) or *Diyas* (compensation or fines).

    C. Islamic Courts (p. 667)
- Three Levels of Islamic Courts
  - The first level hears cases involving the potential for serious punishments.
  - The second level deals with relatively minor matters.
  - The third level consists of special courts.

INSTRUCTIONAL CUE

As you describe the various components of the Islamic justice system, contrast them with the U.S. criminal justice system.

  III. International Criminal Justice Organizations (p. 667)

    A. The Role of the United Nations in Criminal Justice (p. 668)
- The UN makes significant efforts in international crime prevention and bringing together world criminal justice systems.
- The UN also is responsible for the World Crime Survey, which reports official crime statistics from nearly 100 countries.
- A complementary source of data is the International Victim Survey.
- The UN is attempting to advance understanding of crime prevention through the dissemination of criminal justice information through its Crime Prevention and Criminal Justice Program.
- The UN also holds an international congress on crime every five years.

B. INTERPOL and Europol (p. 671)

International Criminal Police Organization (INTERPOL) An international law enforcement support organization that began operations in 1946 and today has 182 members. (p. 671)

European Police Office (Europol) The integrated police-intelligence gathering and dissemination arm of the member nations of the European Union. (p. 671)

C. The International Criminal Court (p. 672)
- Was created under the auspices of the United Nations on April 12, 2000
- Is intended to be a permanent court for trying individuals committing the most serious crimes of concern to the international community

IV. Transnational Crime (p. 673)

Transnational crime Unlawful activity undertaken and supported by organized criminal groups operating across national boundaries. (p. 673)

- Transnational crime is one of the most pressing problems of criminal justice today.
- The problems of transnational crime have revealed a need for coordination of law enforcement efforts throughout the world

A. Globalization and Crime (p. 673)

Globalization The internationalization of trade, services, investment, information, and other forms of human social activity. (p. 673)

V. Terrorism (p. 674)

Terrorism A violent act or an act dangerous to human life in violation of the criminal laws of the United States or of any state committed to intimidate or coerce a government, the civilian population, or any segment thereof, in furtherance of political or social objectives. *Source*: Federal Bureau of Investigation, Counterterrorism Section, *Terrorism in the United States, 1987* (Washington, D.C.: FBI, 1987). (p. 674)

- The "rules" of terrorism include:
  - No rules
  - No innocents
  - Economy
  - Publicity
  - Meaning
  - No clarity

A. Types of Terrorism (p. 675)

Domestic Terrorism The unlawful use of force or violence by a group or an individual who is based and operates entirely within the United States and its territories without foreign direction and whose acts are directed at elements of the U.S. government or population. *Source*: Adapted from Federal Bureau of Investigation, *FBI Policy and Guidelines: Counterterrorism*. Web posted at http://www.fbi.gov/contact/fo/jackson /cntrterr.htm. Accessed March 4, 2002. (p. 675)

International Terrorism The unlawful use of force or violence by a group or an individual who has some connection to a foreign power, or whose activities transcend national boundaries, against people or property in order to intimidate or coerce a government, the civilian population, or any segment thereof, in furtherance of political or social objectives. *Source*: Adapted from Federal Bureau of Investigation, *FBI Policy and Guidelines: Counterterrorism*. Web posted at http://www.fbi.gov/contact/fo/jackson/ cntrterr.htm. Accessed March 4, 2002. (p. 675)

1. Domestic Terrorism
2. International Terrorism
3. Cyberterrorism

Cyberterrorism   A form of terrorism that makes use of high technology, especially computers and the Internet, in the planning and carrying out of terrorist attacks. (p. 680)

Infrastructure   The basic facilities, services, and installations that a country needs to function. Transportation and communications systems, water and power lines, and institutions that serve the public, including banks, schools, post offices, and prisons, are all part of a country's infrastructure. *Source*: Adapted from Dictionary.com, Web posted at http://dictionary.reference.com/search?q=infrastructure. Accessed January 10, 2003. (p. 680)

4. Narcoterrorism

Narcoterrorism   A political alliance between terrorist organizations and drug-supplying cartels. The cartels provide financing for the terrorists, who in turn provide quasi-military protection to the drug dealers. (p. 683)

B. Causes of Terrorism (p. 683)
   - The underlying conditions that lead to terrorism include poverty, political corruption, religious and ideational conflict, and ethnic strife.
   - Other important elements of the process leading to international terrorism include the international environment, states, organization, and leadership.
C. Combating Terrorism (p. 684)
   - Describe the 1996 Antiterrorism and Effective Death Penalty Act.
   - Describe the 2001 USA PATRIOT Act.
D. Antiterrorism Committees and Reports (p. 785)
   1. The Department of Homeland Security
      - Introduce the five directorates and their responsibilities.
   2. The National Strategy for Combating Terrorism
      - Describe the multipronged initiative aimed at reducing terrorism.
E. Foreign Terrorist Organizations (p. 791)

Foreign Terrorist Organization (FTO)   A foreign organization that engages in terrorist activity that threatens the security of U.S. nationals or the national security of the United States and is so designated by the U.S. secretary of state. (p. 691)

F. The Future of International Terrorism (p. 693)

Learner Activities

Activity 1

Compare and contrast the United States and other countries that have attempted to respond to terrorism. What types of strategies are common? What about the response by the United States is unique?

_____

_____

_____

_____

_____

_____

_____

Activity 2

Should some attempt be made to create a worldwide code of criminal behavior? Why or why not? What types of criminal behavior can be globally forbidden?

_____

_____

_____

_____

_____

_____

Activity 3

LIBRARY EXTRA

Read the "National Strategy for Combating Terrorism," posted as **Library Extra 17–18**. What strategies directly involve the police, courts, and corrections components of the criminal justice system? What strategies do you think are the most promising?

_____

_____

_____

_____

_____

_____

Activity 4

LIBRARY EXTRA

Choose a country not discussed in Chapter 17, and then research how criminal justice operates in that country using the Web and library resources. **Library Extra 17–1** is a good place to start. Gather information about policing, courts, and corrections in that country. Describe that criminal justice system in the space provided below.

_____

_____

_____

_____

_____

_____

Internet Activity

Search the cybrary for information about internatioal criminal justice issues. What types of websites are listed? What types of issues are discussed on these websites?

_____

_____

_____

_____

_____

Distance Learning Activity

Visit the websites of criminal justice agencies located outside the United States. You can use any search engine to discover these agencies. In the space below, describe the major characteristics of the agencies from the country you selected. Assess the amount and type of criminal justice information posted on the World Wide Web for that country.

_____

_____

_____

_____

_____

Learning Activities Utilizing the World Wide Web

There are student-based activities in the Student Study Guide (Internet Activity, Distance Learning Activity, CJ Today on the World Wide Web) that are similar in focus to those that follow. However, the following are presented as instructor-led activities, to be used in a classroom with online access.

Visit the Talk Justice message boards at http://www.cybrary.info. Click on Begin and then log in to register as a new user (unless you have previously registered, in which case you can use your existing user name and password to enter the site). After creating a user name and a password, enter the message board area and look for the topic "International Criminal Justice." Display this message board in class, and have small groups of students write responses to prompts in which they are interested.

Visit the websites of criminal justice agencies located outside the United States. You can use any search engine to discover these agencies. Prepare a representative sample of these agencies for display in class.

Other websites for organizations and agencies related to the material in Chapter 17 include:

Central and East European Law Initiative	http://www.abanet.org/ceeli/home.html
Justice Resources for England	http://arapaho.nsuok.edu/~dreveskr/eng.html-ssi
Criminal Justice Resources for France	http://arapaho.nsuok.edu/~dreveskr/fra.html-ssi

International Association of Women Police	http://www.iawp.org
International Centre for Criminal Law Reform and Criminal Justice Policy	http://www.icclr.law.ubc.ca
International Centre for the Prevention of Crime	http://www.crime-prevention-intl.org
International Court of Justice	http://www.icj-cij.org
International Criminal Justice References	http://www.uncjin.org
Criminal Justice Resources for Japan	http://arapaho.nsuok.edu/ ~dreveskr/jap.html-ssi
Scotland Yard (United Kingdom)	http://www.met.police.uk
World Factbook of Criminal Justice	http://www.ojp.usdoj.gov/bjs/ abstract/wfcj.htm

Suggested Answers to Chapter Discussion Questions

1. **What are the potential benefits of studying criminal justice systems in other countries? What problems are inherent in such study?**

   Comparative criminal justice is becoming increasingly valued for the insights it provides. By contrasting native institutions of justice with similar institutions in other countries, procedures and problems that have been taken for granted under one system can be reevaluated in the light of world experience. Such reevaluation may yield information we can use to improve our own system. It is also possible, of course, that such study may lead to the discovery of domestic inequities that would place America in a difficult political position, as some say has happened in the area of the death penalty.

   Difficulties are often encountered in the comparison of crime rates from one country to another because of differences in the way a specific crime is defined, diversities in crime-reporting practices, and political and other influences on the reporting of statistics to international agencies.

   Definitional differences create what may be the biggest problem. For cross-national comparisons of crime data to be meaningful, reported data must share conceptual similarities. Unfortunately, that is rarely the case. Nations report offenses according to the legal criteria by which arrests are made and under which prosecution can occur. When legal criteria differ between nations, data are inherently inaccurate.

   Social, cultural, and economic differences among countries compound the difficulties. Auto theft statistics, for example, when compared between countries such as the United States and China, need to be placed in an economic as well as demographic context. While the United States has two automobiles for every three people, China has only one car per 100 citizens. For the Chinese auto theft rate to equal that of the United States, every automobile in the country would have to be stolen nearly twice each year!

   Reporting practices vary substantially between nations, and no mechanism exists for confirming the accuracy of reported data. Many countries simply do not disclose requested information, and those that do often make only partial reports. International reports of crime are also often delayed. Complete up-to-date data are rare, since the information made available to agencies such as the United Nations and INTERPOL is reported at different times and according to schedules that vary from nation to nation.

   Crime statistics also reflect political biases and national values. Some nations do not accurately admit to the frequency of certain kinds of culturally reprehensible crimes. Communist countries, for example, appear loath to report property crimes such as theft, burglary, and robbery because the very existence of such offenses demonstrates felt inequities within the Communist system.

2. **What are the principles that inform Islamic law? How do these principles contribute to the structure and activities of the criminal justice systems of Muslim nations that follow Islamic law?**

   Islamic law is a system of duties and rituals founded on legal and moral obligations that are sanctioned by the authority of a religious leader, who may issue commands that the faithful are bound to obey. Four aspects of justice include (1) a sacred trust, a duty imposed on humans to be discharged sincerely and honestly; (2) a mutual respect by one human being for another; (3) an aspect of the social bond that holds society together; and (4) a command from God. Items 3 and 4 are the ones most commonly invoked in Islamic jurisprudence and form the basis of criminal justice practice in many Middle Eastern countries.

3. **What important international criminal justice organizations does this chapter discuss? Describe the role of each in fighting international crime.**

   INTERPOL is an international law enforcement support organization that began operations in 1946 and today has 137 members. INTERPOL acts as a clearinghouse for information on offenses and suspects who operate across national boundaries. Europol is the integrated police-oriented intelligence-gathering and dissemination arm of the member nations of the European Union. Its mission is to improve the effectiveness and cooperation within the member states of the European Union.

4. **What is transnational crime? What possible relationships might exist between transnational crime and terrorism?**

   Transnational crime is the unlawful activity undertaken and supported by organized criminal groups operating across national boundaries. Transnational crime is similar to organized crime in many respects, and individuals participating are very opportunistic in deciding what types of crimes to commit. These organizations will certainly consider using terrorism or supporting terrorist organizations in order to accomplish their objectives.

5. **What is terrorism? What are the two major types of terrorism?**

   Terrorism is a violent act or an act dangerous to human life, in violation of the criminal laws of the United States or of any state, committed to intimidate or coerce a government, the civilian population, or any segment thereof, in furtherance of political or social objectives. *Domestic terrorism* is the unlawful use of force or violence by a group or an individual who is based and operates entirely within the United States and its territories without foreign direction and whose acts are directed at elements of the U.S. government or population. *International terrorism* is the unlawful use of force or violence by a group or an individual who has some connection to a foreign power, or whose activities transcend national boundaries, against people or property in order to intimidate or coerce a government, the civilian population, or any segment thereof, in furtherance of political or social objectives.

6. **What causes terrorism? What efforts is the U.S. government making to prevent and control the spread of terrorism?**

   Terrorism generally builds on a process that begins with considering underlying social conditions, such as poverty and political corruption. At the second level is the international environment relating to the differences between nations. Nations might provide the physical assets and bases for terrorist organizations to grow and function, and leadership provides direction to the organization. The efforts to prevent and combat terrorism include the passage of legislation providing resources and enhancing punishment of terrorists; creating government agencies, such as the Department of Homeland Security; and issuing reports suggesting strategies to respond to terrorism. The U.S. government is spending an incredible amount of money in an attempt to prevent and respond to terrorism.

7. **Why is terrorism a law enforcement concern?**

   American law enforcement agencies are responsible for combating threats to public safety. Since terrorist actions inherently jeopardize public safety, they clearly are a specific concern of law enforcement.

How is terrorism a violation of the criminal law?

Terrorism consists of acts perpetrated for the express purpose of inducing a degree of fear in a target population sufficient to cause that population to pressure its leaders to capitulate to the terrorists' demands. To achieve this goal, the typical terrorist act involves actions that expose members of the target population to violent death or physical injury. Such acts, therefore, violate the criminal codes of all American jurisdictions.

What can the American criminal justice system do to better prepare for future terrorist crimes?

The following table depicts concerns within each area of the American criminal justice system that must be addressed if the system is to adequately prepare for effective responses to future terrorist crimes. By no means is this a comprehensive list. It does, however, illustrate the scope and complexity of the task facing local, state, and national leaders.

The Area Of	Requires Action To
Law enforcement	Intensify training in riot, traffic, and panicked-population control; mass-casualty response; operations in chemically; biologically, or radiologically contaminated environments; and the handling and securing of massive amounts of evidentiary material.
	Prioritize and upgrade plans for the physical security of community leaders, hospitals, power-generation resources, computer networks, communications resources (e.g., radio and television stations, telephone systems, and linguists), water treatment and storage facilities, food sources (e.g., supermarkets, warehouse facilities), and transportation routes and mass transit assets.
	Prepare key personnel rosters with telephone contact data. These should include all command, reserve, or auxiliary officers, dispatchers and communications specialists, linguists, and personnel with American Sign Language abilities.
	Prepare alternate command-post sites equipped with redundant power, computing, and communications capabilities (including linguists and personnel with American Sign Language abilities).
	Coordinate operational protocols with other public-service and emergency-response agencies. This should include the exchange of key personnel rosters, telephone rosters, and radio frequencies and call-sign lists and advance resolution of any potential jurisdictional disputes via memoranda of agreement specifying who bears responsibility for what actions and the structure of an emergency chain of command.
Courts	Upgrade plans for the processing of potentially large numbers of defendants.
	Review and upgrade administrative resources to streamline the preparation of required documents.
	Prepare key personnel rosters with telephone contact data. These should include all judges and magistrates, bailiffs, essential court administrators, clerical support personnel, attorneys eligible for appointment as public defenders, linguists, and personnel with American Sign Language abilities.

The Area Of	**Requires Action To**
	Prepare alternate sites equipped with redundant power, computing, and communications capabilities.
Corrections	Upgrade plans for the incarceration of potentially large numbers of inmates.
	Prepare alternate sites to serve as temporary confinement facilities. These sites must be secure and should include adequate housing, hygiene, food-preparation facilities, medical-treatment resources, and redundant power and communications capabilities.
	Prepare key personnel rosters with telephone contact data. These should include all command, reserve, or auxiliary correctional officers, medical personnel, linguists, and personnel with American Sign Language abilities.

The expectation is that law enforcement will be primarily responsible for responding to terrorism. Federal agencies, especially the Federal Bureau of Investigation, have the resources and manpower to coordinate national and international intelligence and responses. Terrorist acts are often tied to other types of criminal activity, such as organized crime, computer crime, and drug trafficking, which makes them difficult to respond to as well as making it hard to decide which appropriate laws to enforce. Gathering information and intelligence, training, and conducting preparedness exercises are probably the best ways to prepare for future terrorist crimes.

Key—Student Study Guide Questions

True or False

_____ 17-1. Narcoterrorism is the act of "spiking" drugs to give them a more dangerous effect. **(False, p. 683)**.

_____ 17-2. All countries are willing to extradite suspects wanted in the United States. **(False, p. 674)**

_____ 17-3. Crimes committed by the Weathermen, the Symbionese Liberation Army, and the Black Panters are considered acts of domestic terrorism. **(True, p. 676)**

_____ 17-4. Cyberterrorism makes use of high technology such as the Internet. **(True, p. 680)**

_____ 17-5. The USA PATRIOT Act was Passed in response to the bombing in Oklahoma City in April 1995. **(False, p. 685)**

_____ 17-6. Only the president can designate any group outside the United States as a foreign terrorist organization. **(False, p. 691)**

_____ 17-7. Islamic courts typically exist on six levels. **(False, p. 667)**

_____ 17-8. Terrorism is one form of transnational crime. **(True, p. 674)**

_____ 17-9. International terrorism and foreign terrorism can be used interchangeably when describing international terrorist acts. **(False, p. 675)**

_____ 17-10. Comparative criminology is becoming increasing valued for the insights it provides about crime and criminal justice. **(True, p. 662)**

Multiple Choice

17-11. The recent globalization of crime and terrorism is sometimes called:
    a. hyperglobalization
    b. globalization of insecurity (p. 674)
    c. narcoglobalization
    d. terrorist networks

17-12. Insurgents involved in the trafficking of narcotics are
    a. money launderers.
    b. mules.
    c. narcoterrorists. (p. 682)
    d. pseudoterrorists.

17-13. Using one's own culture as a benchmark against which to judge all other behavior patterns is
    a. ethnocentrism. (p. 662)
    b. Eurocentrism.
    c. hypersensitivity.
    d. fatalism.

17-14. According to Gwynn Nettler, all forms of terrorism share how many characteristics?
    a. six (p. 675)
    b. five
    c. four
    d. three

17-15. All of the following are problems in the utilization of crime data from other countries except
    a. differences in the definition of crime.
    b. diverse crime-reporting practices.
    c. lack of crimes to report. (p. 663)
    d. political and other influences on the reporting of crime.

17-16. How many agencies are coordinated by the Department of Homeland Security?
    a. 12
    b. 18
    c. 22 (p. 688)
    d. 30

17-17. All of the following are considered *Hudud* crimes under Islamic law except
    a. adultery.
    b. drinking alcohol.
    c. theft.
    d. murder. (p. 666))

17-18. What term describes a new kind of terrorism emphasizing technological attacks?
    a. infoterrorism
    b. cyberterrorism (p. 680)
    c. technoterrorism
    d. infraterrorism

17-19. The police agency being created by members of the European Union to share crime information among European countries and INTERPOL is
    a. Europol. (p. 671)
    b. Outerpol.
    c. Francopol.
    d. Commonpol.

17-20. Compensation or fines in Islamic law are called:
   a. diya (p. 667)
   b. quesa
   c. tazir
   d. hudad

Fill-In

17-21. A(n) person who studies crime and criminal justice on a cross-national level is called a(n) _____. **(comparative criminologist, p. 662)**

17-22. _____ is the belief that one's culture is superior to any other culture. **(Ethnocentrism, p. 662)**

17-23. A political alliance between terrorist organizations and drug-supplying cartels is called _____. **(narcoterrorism, p. 682)**

17-24. _____ includes the unlawful use of force or violence by a group or an individual who is based and operates entirely with the United States and whose acts are directed at elements of the U.S. government or population. **(domestic terrorism, p. 675)**

17-25. Unlawful activity undertaken and supported by organized criminal groups operating across national boundaries is called _____. **(transnational crime, p. 673)**

17-26. _____ is a system of laws based on the Muslim religion and especially the holy book of Islam. **(Islamic law, p. 665)**

17-27. _____ is a process of social homogenization by which the experiences of everyday life, marked by the diffusion of commodities and ideas, can foster a standardization of cultural expressions around the world. **(Globalization, p. 673)**

17-28. _____ is a form of terrorism that makes use of high technology, especially computers and the Internet, in the planning and carrying out of terrorist attacks. **(Cyberterrorism, p. 680)**

17-29. The international law enforcement support organization that began operations in 1946 is called _____. **(INTERPOL, p. 671)**

17-30. Minor violations of Islamic law that are offenses against society and against individuals, but not against God, are called _____. **(*Tazir* crimes, p. 666)**

Key—Crossword Puzzle

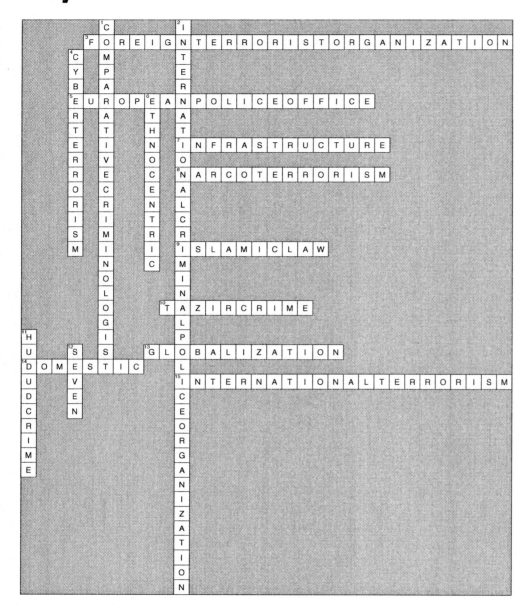

Across

3. Foreign organization that engages in terrorism.
5. Integrated police-oriented intelligence-gathering and -dissemination arm of the member nations of the European Union.
7. Basic facilities that a country needs to function.
8. When terrorists and drug cartels are linked.
9. System of laws based on the Muslim religion.
10. Minor violation of Islamic law.
13. Process of social homogenization.
14. Timothy McVeigh's type of terrorism.
15. September 11 attack is an example of this type of terrorism.

Down

1. One who studies crime and criminal justice on a cross-national level.
2. Organization with 182 members.
4. Terrorism plus high technology.
6. Type of belief that holds the superiority of one's own social or ethnic group and culture.
11. Serious violation of Islamic law.
12. Number of *Hudud* crimes recognized by Islamic law.

Key—Word Search Puzzle

```
I P N B M G E B B J W D B F I U E Q V N Z T H J Z J X U S D
U X F T A Z I R C R I M E L P R P Z P X I M G I H Z W C N V
T F Z Q X T L P C C Z J A V U W U U J K C L Y B U A V F A C
A O H X G X P D D E L P H T H F C S B Q G A J P E H Y X R O
Y R J X Z N L A U V C F C I U U H N B R G R N C U L V H C M
B E L W B F G A A V Q U M P G V D I A E K S Z M R P X L O P
K I D S G B K O J M R N C Y U E J H Q A O Z Z I O R Q A T A
O G X H T E Z X I T O L G C E T T R I O N A L T P K O F E R
N N D D N L C C S V T L Z W X Q G H N Y B B J H O Y X E R A
V T T C I K S A V B M A Q V G D X B N N B R N L L R L X R T
S E E I B T R D O M E S T I C T E R R O R I S M O J N T O I
L R I K C F H V U B K D G V T S D H C C O O O G M O R A R V
K R T N N C Y B E R T E R R O R I S M U W E K W W P N A D I E
N O R I T U B Z F H T W N D P V J X E N C U N I Z S R D I S C
X R A K M E T L S E O O A D U I N F G X C H Z T P T X I T M R
I I N M P E R B N S I T R O N I L C A I L E N Z R P B T T I
T S S O G T N P I G D E T C D E N G P L U H Z G M I A I D M
V T N G X E A Z O J O R M O O K Q G M A Y I F B R Y C O U I
A O A I H X H E X L C R I F Z B Q O L Q V L W U Y E C N D N
O R T R U X G D M H F O T Q A Y T Z S O Q J X B H Y N U D O
J G I P D D J F N F Y R N N I T B N V B B H N D O G K L D L
N A O N A O G J G P I L C S C I M W L Y A W G D V M R F O O
K N A T D C V C L T O S X H L E U D C H B O L P W N T L K G
O I L Q C U V O O N O M B X A V O C C H I U K I X K J T G I
W Z P R A A K F G S S C A M W H G A W D E V H Z W X Q Z S S
E A C Y N D U T T R W B M I E B E W W F K X N D A X Y S T T
F T I M J X C J I L D T W C H E W K C I Y W N J S T N B S H
S I V E U C P D X A H Q O L I Y K G J L F H L X K P I Y H
V O M I N T E R N A T I O N A L T E R R O R I S M O D Z O W
G N E A E K O O D C H K R K W J S D U R R K W Y Z R B M M N
```

Comparative Criminologist

Cyberterrorism

Domestic Terrorism

Ethnocentric

Europol

Extradition

Foreign Terrorist Organization

Globalization

Hudud Crime

Infrastructure

International Terrorism

INTERPOL

Islamic Law

Narcoterrorism

Tazir Crime

Terrorism

Transnational Crime

The Future of Criminal Justice

LEARNING OBJECTIVES

After reading this chapter, you should be able to:

- Describe the historical relationship between technological advances and social and cultural change
- Explain the nature of high-technology crime, and list some forms that such crimes have taken in the past and that they might take in the future
- Explain the important role that technology has played, and will continue to play, in the fight against crime and the quest for justice
- Explain why laws defining criminal activity must change to keep pace with advancing technologies
- Provide an overview of criminalistics, and explain how evolving technology contributes to advances in that field
- Identify the threats to individual rights inherent in the ever-increasing use of advanced technology

Chapter Summary

The final chapter of the textbook focuses on issues critical to the future of the criminal justice system as it adapts to social, political, and cultural changes in society. In addition, as the level of technological sophistication in society grows and expands, regulating and responding to crimes that result from these changes become the responsibility of the criminal justice system.

The chapter begins with a discussion of various types of **technocrimes**. For example, it discusses **biocrime** and cybercrime. Biocrimes are those perpetrated through the use of some biologically active substance. Changes in technology have also provided opportunities to commit new types of crime. Any crime perpetrated through the use of computer technology is referred to as cybercrime. Offenders who hack computers, pirate software, engage in information piracy, destroy or manipulate data, and use computer technology to carry out theft of services are all committing cybercrimes.

Technological innovation is an important tool the criminal justice system uses to respond to crime. For example, the field of **criminalistics** has a long and distinguished history. The text provides some early examples of the use of criminalistics with a discussion of the system of personal identification created by Alphonse Bertillon, the use of fingerprints to identify suspects, and the reliance on **ballistics, forensic anthropology, forensic entomology**, and voiceprint identification.

Chapter 18 also describes emerging technologies in criminalistics. Perhaps the most significant scientific advance in the last decade is the development of **DNA profiling**. DNA profiling is the use of biological residue found at the scene of a crime for genetic comparisons, aiding the identification of criminal suspects. DNA profiling has been used by law enforcement to identify suspects but also has assisted accused persons. For example, in a National Institute of Justice report titled *Convicted by Juries, Exonerated by Science*, researchers describe 28 cases of defendants who were released from prison after DNA tests established their innocence. Other emerging technologies discussed in Chapter 18 include online clearinghouses, computer-aided investigations, and computer-based training.

The last section of Chapter 18 focuses on technology and individual rights. It focuses on the clash between fighting crimes committed with new technology and protecting individual rights.

Teaching Outline

   I. Introduction (p. 704)

      A. Technology and Crime (p. 704)

Technocrime   A criminal offense that employs advanced or emerging technology in its commission. (p. 705)

      B. Biocrime (p. 705)

Biocrime   A criminal offense perpetrated through the use of biologically active substances, including chemicals and toxins, disease-causing organisms, altered genetic material, and organic tissues and organs. Biocrimes unlawfully affect the metabolic, biochemical, genetic, physiological, or anatomical status of living organisms. (p. 705)

      C. Cybercrime (p. 706)

Computer Crime   Any crime perpetrated through the use of computer technology. Also, any violation of a federal or state computer-crime statute. Also called *cybercrime*. (p. 706)

Hacker   A computer hobbyist or professional, generally with advanced programming skills. Today, the term *hacker* has taken on a sinister connotation, referring to hobbyists who are bent on illegally accessing the computers of others or who attempt to demonstrate their technological prowess through computerized acts of vandalism. (p. 706)

Social Engineering A nontechnical kind of cyberintrusion that relies heavily on human interaction and often involves tricking people into breaking normal security procedures. (p. 707)

      1. Transnational Crime

      2. Types of Cybercrime

          • Describe Grabosky's nine broad categories of cybercrime.

Computer Virus A computer program designed to secretly invade systems and either modify the way in which they operate or alter the information they store. Viruses are destructive software programs that may effectively vandalize computers of all types and sizes. (p. 708)

Malware Malicious computer programs like viruses, worms, and Trojan horses. (p. 708)

Software Piracy The unauthorized duplication of software or the illegal transfer of data from one storage medium to another. Software piracy is one of the most prevalent computer crimes in the world. (p. 709)

Spam Unsolicited commercial bulk e-mail (UCBE), whose primary purpose is the commercial advertisement or promotion of a commercial product or service. (p. 710)

      D. Terrorism and Technology (p. 712)

Weapon of Mass Destruction (WMD) A chemical, biological, or nuclear weapon that has the potential to cause mass casualties. (p. 712)

Bioterrorism The intentional or threatened use of viruses, bacteria, fungi, or toxins from living organisms to produce death or disease in humans, animals, or plants. *Source*: Centers for Disease Control and Prevention, *Bioterrorism: An Overview*. Web posted at http://www.bt.cdc.gov/documents/PPTResponse/laboverview.pdf. Accessed August 5, 2003. (p. 713)

  II. Technology and Crime Control (p. 713)

     A. Leading Technical Organizations in Criminal Justice

          • National Law Enforcement and Corrections Technology Center (NLECTC)

          • Society of Police Futurists International (PFI)

             • Future Working Group (FWG)

  III. Criminalistics: Past, Present, and Future (p. 715)

Criminalistics The use of technology in the service of criminal investigation; the application of scientific techniques to the detection and evaluation of criminal evidence. (p. 715)

Criminalist A police crime-scene analyst or laboratory worker versed in criminalistics. (p. 715)

      • The first "modern" system of personal identification was created by Alphonse Bertillon.

          • Bertillon combined physical measurements with photography, creating the anthropometric system.

      • Herschel and Faulds, in the 1880s, discovered that each person's fingerprints are unique and unchangeable.

      • The use of fingerprints to identify offenders was popularized by Sir Francis Galton in the early 1900s.

      • Computerization and digitization have improved accuracy and speed in matching an offender's fingerprints with databases.

Biometrics   The science of recognizing people by physical characteristics and personal traits. (p. 717)

Ballistics   The analysis of firearms, ammunition, projectiles, bombs, and explosives. (p. 717)

Forensic Anthropology   The use of anthropological principles and techniques in criminal investigation. (p. 717)

Forensic Entomology   The study of insects to determine such matters as a person's time of death. (p. 717)

> A. New Technologies in Criminalistics (p. 720)
>> 1. DNA Profiling.

DNA Profiling   The use of biological residue, found at the scene of a crime, for genetic comparisons in aiding the identification of criminal suspects. (p. 720)

INSTRUCTIONAL CUE

Discuss the evidentiary value of DNA evidence. Illustrate its value by describing cases in which DNA evidence was used to identify the suspect of a cold case or to exonerate an innocent person.

- Introduce the Court's finding in the civil case of *Daubert* v. *Merrell Dow Pharmaceuticals, Inc.* This case revised the criteria for the admissibility of scientific evidence by rejecting the "general acceptance" test set in *Frye* v. *United States*. This case determined that admissibility of scientific evidence would be based on Rule 402 of the Federal Rules of Evidence.

***Daubert* Standard**   A test of scientific acceptability applicable to the gathering of evidence in criminal cases. (p. 722)

- The DNA Identification Act of 1994 provided substantial funding to improve the quality and availability of DNA analyses.
- Discuss the findings of the National Institute of Justice report titled *Convicted by Juries, Exonerated by Science*.

> 2. Online Databases
>> - Examples include the National Crime Information Center (NCIC), the Violent Criminal Apprehension Program (VICAP), state-operated police identification networks, and METAPOL.
>> - Law enforcement is also making information available to the public via the Internet.
> 3. Computer-Aided Investigations
>> - Highlight the use of computer models known as expert systems in investigations.

Expert System   Computer hardware and software that attempt to duplicate the decision-making processes used by skilled investigators in the analysis of evidence and in the recognition of patterns that such evidence might represent. (p. 725)

- Examples include HITMAN, Big Floyd, and ImAger.

> 4. Computer-Based Training
> B. On the Horizon (p. 727)
>> - Discuss some of the devices used to help secure the nation's borders.

Augmented Reality (AR)   The real-time and accurate overlay of digital information on a user's real-world experience, through visual, aural, and/or tactile interfaces. The computer readouts superimposed on the visual fields of the fictional cyborgs in the various *Robocop* and *Terminator* movies provide an example. *Source*: Thomas J. Cowper and Michael E. Buerger, *Improving Our View of the World: Police and Augmented Reality Technology* (Washington, D.C.: Federal Bureau of Investigation, 2003). Web posted at http://www.fbi.gov/publications/realitytech/realitytech.pdf. Accessed October 7, 2003. (p. 728)

    C. Problems in Implementing New Technologies (p. 729)
- The ability of law enforcement to adapt to technological change is limited.
- Technological capabilities raise concerns about violations of individual rights.
  1. Prosecution of Computer and High-Technology Crime.

Protected Computer   Under federal law, (1) a computer used exclusively by a financial institution or the U.S. government, (2) a computer used by or for a financial institution or the U.S. government, or (3) a computer used in interstate or foreign commerce or communication. (p. 731)

    D. Secure Identity Management (p. 732)

Identity Management   The comprehensive management and administration of a user's individual profile information, permissions, and privileges across a variety of social settings. *Source*: Adapted from Entrust, Inc., "Secure Identity Management: Challenges, Needs, and Solutions." Web posted at http://www.entrust.com, p. 1. Accessed August 5, 2003. (p. 732)

Smart Card   A plastic card or similar device, containing a computer chip and other sources of nonalterable information (such as a hologram or a laser-encoded memory strip), that is used to provide highly secure personal identification. (p. 732)

INSTRUCTIONAL CUE

Ask students to describe the type of person they think is most likely to commit computer crimes, and also have them speculate as to the motivation to commit these types of crimes. Have them contrast the person they describe with individuals who commit violent crimes.

    IV. Technology and Individual Rights (p. 734)
- Discuss the relationship between technology and the various constitutional amendments mentioned.
- In *Reno* v. *ACLU*, the Supreme Court upheld a lower court's ruling invalidating enforcement provisions of the Communications Decency Act. This rule accorded Internet content the same level of constitutional protection afforded print media.

Learner Activities

Activity 1

How much privacy are you willing to give up in the fight against crime? Would you be willing to be under constant video surveillance if it meant a 40% or 50% reduction in violent crime? Where would you draw the line to protect individual rights?

_____

_____

_____

_____

_____

_____

Activity 2

Throughout history, police have claimed that if they were just given the proper tools, they could really do something about crime. For example, law enforcement officials at the turn of the century argued that as soon as the police force became "motorized," they would be able to apprehend offenders with ease. The same claim was made for mobile radios, machine guns, mobile data terminals, cellular phones, and so forth. In some cities, equipping a police car with all of the electronic equipment and special features police claim are essential to their effectiveness costs nearly as much as the car itself! Do you think technology will ever be able to give police departments the edge they have been looking for in the fight against crime? Will the reactive nature of policing mean that cops will always be at least one step behind the offenders, or will police eventually get ahead of the offenders in the fight against crime?

_____

_____

_____

_____

_____

_____

Activity 3

What role do juries play in the court system? Will advances in technology make it easier for juries to arrive at decisions that represent the "truth"? Should technology be used to eliminate juries from the criminal justice system? Why or why not?

_____

_____

_____

_____

_____

Activity 4

Visit **Web Extra 18–3** and **18–4**, and read **Library Extra 18–5**. These links provide an opportunity to learn more about biological and chemical terrorism. In the space below, summarize the materials posted at these links. In your analysis, be sure to describe efforts to respond to biological and chemical terrorism.

WEB EXTRA

LIBRARY EXTRA

_____

_____

_____

_____

_____

_____

Internet Activity

Search the WWW for information about identity theft. In the space provided below, discuss some of the information that you found. Is identity theft a serious crime? What steps can a person take to reduce the likelihood of being a victim of identity theft?

_____

_____

_____

_____

_____

Distance Learning Activity

Write a short essay in the space below addressing how the criminal justice system can respond more effectively to crime in the United States. The following websites should be helpful: (1) Criminal Justice Policy Foundation: http://www.cjpf.org; (2) National Center for Policy Analysis: http://www.ncpa.org; and (3) Center for Policy Alternatives: http://www.cfpa.org.

_____

_____

_____

_____

_____

Learning Activities Utilizing the World Wide Web

There are student-based activities in the Student Study Guide (Internet Activity, Distance Learning Activity, CJ Today on the World Wide Web) that are similar in focus to those that follow. However, the following are presented as instructor-led activities, to be used in a classroom with online access.

Initiate a discussion addressing how the criminal justice system can respond more effectively to crime in the United States. Display the following websites during class time to support the discussion: (1) Criminal Justice Policy Foundation: http://www.cjpf.org; (2) National Center for Policy Analysis: http://www.ncpa.org; and (3) Center for Policy Alternatives: http://www.cfpa.org.

Other websites for organizations and agencies related to the material in Chapter 18 include:

Criminal Justice Policy Foundation	http://www.cjpf.org
International Centre for the Prevention of Crime	http://www.crime-prevention-intl.org

Justice Fellowship	http://www.justicefellowship.org
National Center for Policy Analysis	http://www.ncpa.org
Center for Policy Alternatives	http://www.cfpa.org
Future of DNA Evidence	http://www.ojp.usdoj.gov/nij/ dna/welcome.html
Cybercrime Page	http://www.cybercrime.gov
Court Technology Laboratory	http://www.ncsc.dni.us/ncsc/ ctl/ctl_main.htm
International Association of Crime Analysts	http://www.iaca.net
Society of Police Futurists International	http://www.policefuturists.org
Futures Working Group	http://www.fbi.gov/hq/td/fwg/ workhome.htm

Suggested Answers to Chapter Discussion Questions

1. **Historically speaking, how have advances in technology affected society and culture? Is the same relationship between technology and society likely to persist into the future?**

   Advances in technology can ignite social changes. These advances affect how people interact, communicate, learn, and profit. Such advances are likely to continue, and society will continue to evolve because of the changes.

2. **What is high-technology crime? What new kinds of crimes have technological advances made possible? Distinguish between new types of crimes produced by advancing technology and new ways of committing "old crimes" that have been facilitated by emerging technologies.**

   High-technology crimes focus on offenses that use advanced and emerging technologies. Biocrime, cybercrime, and bioterrorism are just a few examples of the new kinds of crimes created because of technological advances. Many high-tech crimes are simply "old wine in new bottles." Historically, criminals of all types have shown remarkable resourcefulness in adapting technological advances to their criminal pursuits. The recent surge of high-quality counterfeiting wrought by the advent of the color laser printer is a typical example. Similarly, theft, fraud, intimidation, and vandalism are age-old crime problems. Advances in technology have just provided new opportunities to use computers and other types of technology to commit these crimes.

3. **How has technology affected the practice of criminal justice in America over the past century? How has it affected the criminal law?**

   One hundred years ago, American police officers walked beats or rode horses and communicated by whistles and shouts. Criminal investigation was less scientific than intuitive, court cases were often resolved more on the popularity of the defendant than on the weight of the evidence, and American prisons were bleak edifices immersed in the industrial prison era.

   Today, American police officers walk beats or ride horses—or use automobiles, motorcycles, bicycles, boats, or aircraft. They have instant communication with other patrol members, their leaders at the precinct or departmental headquarters, the mayor, the governor, the Pentagon, or the president, if necessary, via an incredible communications network using satellite and computer communications. All manner of forensic and scientific resources remove guesswork from criminal investigations. Court cases are far more informed by precedent and constitutional considerations than ever before, but they are also often strongly influenced by the economic status of the accused.

4. **Why do criminal laws have to change to keep up with the changes in technology? What modifications in current laws defining criminal activity might soon be necessary to meet the criminal possibilities inherent in new technologies?**

   Criminal behavior evolves as technology evolves. Many offenders use new technologies in order to commit crimes, and often such behaviors have not been previously defined as being criminal. Criminal laws must be changed or created to account for these changes.

   The Office for Technology Assessment of the U.S. Congress notes that "What is judicially permissible and socially acceptable at one time has often been challenged when technology changes." When agencies of the justice system use cutting-edge technology, it inevitably provokes fears of a future in which citizens' rights are abrogated by advancing science. Individual rights, equal treatment under the law, and due process issues all require constant reinterpretation as technology improves. However, because some of the technology available today is so new, few court cases have yet directly addressed the issues involved.

5. **What is criminalistics? Explain the interplay between advancing technology and methods used to gather evidence in the fight against crime.**

   Criminalistics is the use of technology in the service of criminal investigation, the application of scientific techniques to the detection and evaluation of criminal evidence. Law enforcement and other criminal organizations attempt to put new technologies to use in their fight against crime. Similarly, criminalists also use scientific and technological advances in any way they can to identify suspects.

6. **What threats to individual rights might advanced technology create?**

   In this information age, the obvious threat is to the privacy of the individual. Many believe it is already too late because somebody, somewhere, has likely already created a comprehensive database containing your entire life in a thousand or so bytes. Might this be paranoia, or simply an accurate assessment of reality?

   Will our standards as to what constitutes admissible evidence, what is reasonable privacy, and so on undergo a reevaluation as a result of emerging technology?

   Here is an interesting scenario: A business competitor obtains damaging information about you, including evidence of your participation in a criminal activity. Seeking to eliminate you as a threat to his business, he posts the information on the Internet. A police investigator, after seeing the information on the Net, arrests you for the crime you committed. Can the investigator argue the admissibility of the evidence she or he found on the Internet on grounds that it was in the public domain?

   This scenario illustrates what lies ahead for investigators, courts, and ordinary citizens who may be victimized by the posting of false and malicious information that leads to their arrest. Technological advances will continue to yield dramatic improvements in all aspects of American life, including the functioning of the criminal justice system. But they also have tremendous potential for spawning nightmarish confusion that is incapable of being unraveled, with devastating consequences for the innocent.

Key—Student Study Guide Questions

True or False

_____ 18-1. One of the most prevalent computer crimes is the unauthorized duplication of copyrighted software. **(True, p. 709)**

_____ 18-2. Fingerprinting, which became widespread as a crime-fighting technique in the late 1800s, was the first nearly foolproof method of identification available to investigators. **(True, p. 716)**

____ 18-3. Modern criminalistics depends heavily on ballistics, which involves the reconstruction of the likeness of a decomposed or dismembered body. **(False, p. 717)**

____ 18-4. The "Pakistani Brain" is the nickname of an international terrorist bombing attack. **(False, p. 708)**

____ 18-5. Malware refers to malicious computer programs, such as viruses and worms. **(True, p. 708)**

____ 18-6. Fingerprinting is an early example of biometric technology. **(True, p. 717)**

____ 18-7. Most countries have effective computer-crime legislation in effect. **(False, p. 707)**

____ 18-8. Bioterrorism includes the use of technology in carrying out an act of terrorism. **(False, p. 713)**

____ 18-9. Smart cards are tools used by criminalists to identify illegal credit-card users. **(False, p. 732)**

____ 18-10. In *Convicted by Juries, Exonerated by Science*, DNA testing was called the most important technological breakthrough of twentieth-century forensic science. **(True, p. 722)**

Multiple Choice

18-11. The _____ performs yearly assessments of key technological needs and opportunities facing the justice system.
  a. Law Enforcement Assistance Administration (LEAA)
  b. National Law Enforcement and Corrections Technology Center (NLECTC) (p. 714)
  c. Office of Law Enforcement Organization (OLEO)
  d. International Technology Protection Program (ITPP)

18-12. The case of *Daubert* v. *Merrell Dow Pharmaceuticals* proved to be important in the acceptance of _____ in criminal trials.
  a. DNA profiles (p. 721)
  b. computer-enhanced images
  c. fingerprints
  d. serial killer profiles

18-13. About what percentage of software in Vietnam is copied illegally?
  a. 1
  b. 24
  c. 50
  d. 97 (p. 709)

18-14. Who coined the term "DNA fingerprints"?
  a. Alphonse Bertillon
  b. Michael Bloomberg
  c. Alec J. Jeffreys (p. 720)
  d. Henry Faulds

18-15. Which of the following is an example of malware?
  a. viruses
  b. worms
  c. Trojan horses
  d. all of the above (p. 708)

18-16. The constitutional amendment most concerned with "secure paper and effects."
  a. Eighth
  b. Fourteenth
  c. Fourth (p. 734)
  d. Fifth

18-17. According to the Computer Crime and Security Survey, how many large businesses and government agencies detected security-related breaches in 2002?
   a. 20
   b. 50
   c. 75
   d. 90 (p. 708)

18-18. What constitutional amendment pertains most directly to the issue of gun control?
   a. First
   b. Second (p. 734)
   c. Fourth
   d. Fifth

18-19. Crime that employ advanced or emerging technology in its commission is called:
   a. technocrime (p. 705)
   b. cybercrime
   c. biocrime
   d. profiling

18-20. A computer that is the property of the federal government or a financial institution, or is located in a state other than the one in which the criminal perpetrator is operating, is classified as a(n) _____.
   a. federated computer
   b. institutionalized computer
   c. protected computer (p. 731)
   d. interstate compact computer

Fill-In

18-21. _____ is another name for computer crime, or crime involving the use of computers. **(Cybercrime, p. 706)**

18-22. _____ is the use of a blood sample or other residue found at the scene of a crime for genetic comparisons in aiding the identification of criminal suspects. **(DNA profiling, p. 720)**

18-23. _____ are computer software models that attempt to replicate the decision-making processes used by skilled investigators in the analysis of evidence. **(Expert systems, p. 725)**

18-24. A(n) _____ is a destructive computer code designed to vandalize computers. **(computer virus, p. 708)**

18-25. _____ is the application of anthropological principles and techniques to a criminal investigation. **(Forensic anthropology, p. 717)**

18-26. A(n) _____ is a computer hobbyist who illegally accesses the computers of others to demonstrate technological superiority. **(hacker, p. 706)**

18-27. _____ refers to the study of insects to determine such matters as the time of death. **(Forensic entomology, p. 717)**

18-28. The application of scientific techniques to the detection and evaluation of criminal evidence is called _____. **(criminalistics, p. 715)**

18-29. The science of recognizing people by physical characteristics and personal traits is called _____. **(biometrics, p. 717)**

18-30. _____ is the analysis of firearms, ammunition, bombs, and explosives. **(Ballistics, p. 717)**

Key—Crossword Puzzle

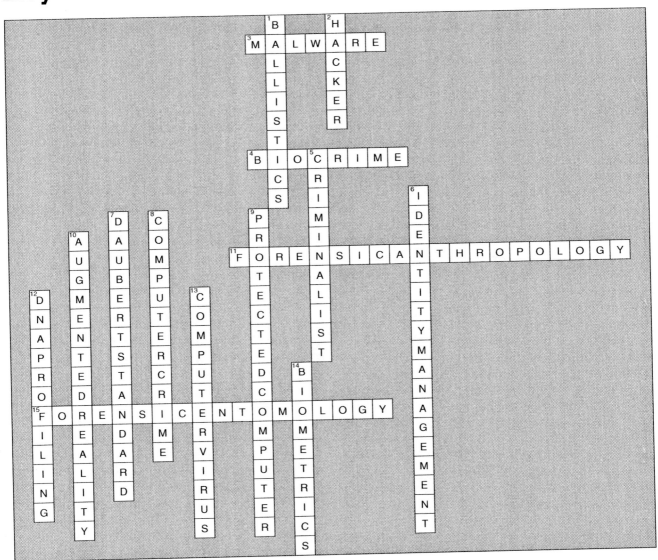

Across

3. Malicious computer programs.
4. Criminal offense using biologically active substances.
11. Use of anthropological principles and techniques in criminal investigation.
15. Study of insects to determine issues such as a person's time of death.

Down

1. Analysis of firearms, ammunition, projectiles, bombs, and explosives.
2. Computer hobbyist.
5. Police crime-scene analyst or laboratory worker versed in criminalistics.

6. Administration and control over a user's individual profile information.
7. Test of scientific acceptability applicable to the gathering of evidence in criminal cases.
8. Also called cybercrime.
9. Under federal law, a computer exclusively for the use of a financial institution or the U.S. government.
10. Examples include the movies *Robocop* and *Terminator*.
12. Scientific technique often used in rape cases.
13. Computer program that invades another system to destroy it.
14. Approach used to recognize people by physical characteristics and personal traits.

Key—Word Search Puzzle

```
G F Q Z F T A M X R M B I O M E T R I C S N R N S M Q I X Z
U A Q D N O E C R I M I N A L I S T I C S Q B V O D D V E A
X U A U G W R C A T P C Z N G X S L D H R Y Y W B N N G L F
X N T U C Z O E H D P S Y H U X M O H J H W K O R G A X K J
R C N F G R C B N N N M S I D M A P L G X T Z H J G P Q V J
J O K O Q I R H B S O E N P T F R V R K W Y K R B M R Y I T
E M S R E B M M I U I C H F B X T S G N D K O M O A O Z H Q
B P T E A A C D O P L C R A F V C N H D N C K O F L F E B T
S U H N P L M Q T R D A I C O A G F G V V Y Q R W I N Q A
O T L S L L I L E Y R O T N M U R I D G X Z T U C A L L V W
F E C I Y I I D R H G F T V T E D Q F F U B L M E R I M F U
T R F C Y S E W R L D D T E M H T I T O P B G C A E N J F D
W C A E D T D Z O W I M T E C I R Y K W E C X U P G G H I E
A R D N K I D U R Z U B T K B T C O M P U T E R V I R U S O
R I A T B C B A I Q I S N J I A E U P L L S W L Q K O P O H
E M U O J S V O S E Y R B V O R Y D W O R M P B H U N R U G
P E B M X F C G M S T N K M C I U T C I L G O A A N M H K T
I K E O X E M I T W K I C M R B J N D O Z O S R C J J N T N
R W R L A O J R Q C J V R X I A A C A B M X G M K Z O B D S
A U T O R C E X R S Z Z I I M X Q A I V F P E Y E Q O H W N
C I S G N P G I E W B G M L E T U I K H W L U Z R W B A L Q
Y G T Y X B X Z M P T H I P R O W F A Y W P R T Z B M Q K Q
L N A E V J H L F H M E N S O C I A L E N G I N E E R I N G
I U N I D E N T I T Y M A N A G E M E N T I Q V M R Y D V B
R N D Q Z F G X N S I Q L C N H F K P M Q C Q N G I U K N Q
R G A S E N T L X D N Y I R G U D S F R P S S J R E T P H I
Q M R X G W N X F N H R S Z M Z O I S L E K D A U G I D T X
Y L D J Y Q T Q B O S O T K B E R O Y A D Y T E Q R G J N W
D F I K V V J W E A P O N O F M A S S D E S T R U C T I O N
O R X M X Q Q W A U G M E N T E D R E A L I T Y S B U Z U Q
```

Augmented Reality

Ballistics

Biocrime

Biometrics

Bioterrorism

Computer Crime

Computer Virus

Criminalist

Criminalistics

Daubert Standard

DNA Profiling

Expert System

Forensic Anthropology

Forensic Entomology

Hacker

Identity Management

Malware

Protected Computer

Smart Card

Social Engineering

Software Piracy

Spam

Technocrime

Weapon of Mass Destruction

APPENDIX A

Popular Media in the Classroom

There are so many resources to choose from in current popular media. What follows are suggestions, grouped by chapter, for you to choose from as you prepare for your classroom teaching. The list of media can be endless, so I recommend you also check out two websites that provide current information and updated rankings by genre, in this case Crime Movies. The sites are:

Internet Movie Database (IMDb)   http://www.imdb.com/chart/crime
British Film Institute (BFI)   http://www.bfi.org.uk

The challenge remains only in choosing the best media, from those that are relevant to the topic, to support your teaching. *Note*: Some of the movies listed may contain graphic violence or explicit sexual activity. Also, make sure to respect copyright restrictions on any media you show in the classroom.

Chapter 1

What Is Criminal Justice?

In Student Activity 4, students list television programs that depict the various stages of the criminal justice process. The purpose of the assignment is to get students thinking about the various stages of the process and how the realities of processing criminal justice cases differ from media images.

A good activity that uses popular media is to assign students to view an episode of the popular show *Law & Order*, either assigning it as a homework or perhaps using some class time to show an episode or part of an episode. A typical episode spends about half of the time on the police stages of the process, following an incident from occurrence to investigation and arrest. The second part of the program usually shows the court stages, including a bail hearing, motion hearings, and the trial. You should be able to use characteristics of the episode to illustrate the stages of the criminal justice process. In addition, you will be able to discuss the relationship between the police and the prosecutor's office, illustrating the conflict between the two agencies. In addition, the cases presented on this show are typically interesting and thought-provoking and often present an ethical or moral dilemma. You will be able to generate discussion by asking students how they would have responded to the dilemma presented. Classic movies, such as *To Kill a Mockingbird*, illustrate various stages of the criminal justice process. Truman Capote's classic *In Cold Blood* can be linked to various aspects of Chapter 1, including the balance of individual rights and public order and of due process and crime control. A long list of television programs from the past and present illustrates the various stages of the process: *NYPD Blue, Homicide, The Practice, Ally McBeal, Pacific Blue, Perry Mason, Murder, She Wrote, COPS,* and *FirstWatch*. In addition, students could read *Death of a Little Princess: The Tragic Story of the Murder of JonBenet Ramsey* by Carlton Smith.

Chapter 2

The Crime Picture

Mostly due to news media and their portrayal of the criminal justice system, it is difficult to convey to students a picture of crime that is not sensationalized. Some of your students will have been touched by a crime as a victim, as a witness, or sometimes even as a suspect. If this has not been their personal experience, your students will know of someone who has had these experiences. To stress an accurate picture of crime in society, local and national news stories that focus on current crime problems and patterns can be viewed and then compared to expanded factual information from UCR, NCVS, and BJS.

Chapter 3

The Search for Causes

Two of the most popular and acclaimed modern-day films focused on criminal justice are *Silence of the Lambs* and *Hannibal*. In the first film, a psychotic serial murderer, Hannibal "The Cannibal" Lecter, agrees to help an FBI agent (Clarice Starling) track down another serial killer called Buffalo Bill. The second film focuses primarily on Hannibal. You can use these movies to highlight psychological theories of crime, or you can use the Hannibal character to illustrate any of the theories presented in Chapter 3. How would biological approaches explain Hannibal's cannibalism? Sociological approaches? The 2003 film *Monster* is the story of Aileen Wuornos, one of America's first female serial killers. Wuornos had a difficult and cruel childhood plagued by abuse and drug use in Michigan. The movie focuses on the nine-month period between 1989 and 1990 during which Wuornos maintained a lesbian relationship and also began murdering her clientele in order to get money without using sex. This turned the tables on a rather common phenomenon of female highway prostitutes being the victims of serial killers—instead Wuornos herself carried out the deeds of a cold-blooded killer.

An incredible number of books, movies, and other media resources are available that deal with serial murder and serial murderers. For example, other serial murder movies include *Natural Born Killers, Badlands, Wild at Heart*, and *Copy Cat*. There are also many novels that discuss serial murder, such as *Blood Lust: Portrait of a Serial Sex Killer* by Gary King. If your students are interested in the profiling of serial murderers, refer them to *The Anatomy of Motive: The FBI's Legendary Mindhunter Explores the Key to Understanding and Catching Violent Criminals* by John Douglas and Mark Olshaker. Other movies that might be helpful include *A Clockwork Orange* and *Do the Right Thing*. In addition, an excellent novel illustrating sociological theories of crime is *There Are No Children Here* by Alex Kotlowitz.

Violence is also a staple issue in heavy-metal and rap music. Some musicians whose music includes violent lyrics are Marilyn Manson, Korn, Black Sabbath, Ice-T, and 2 Live Crew. Finally, the song *Dirty Boulevard*, by Lou Reed, is a good example of sociological theories.

Chapter 4

Criminal Law

A Time to Kill by John Grisham is a good novel that can be used to illustrate several issues presented in Chapter 4. Have students read specific parts of the novel to illustrate these points, or assign students to view the movie based on the novel. The novel focuses on the trial of Carl Lee Hailey, who is charged with murdering two men. He committed these murders after the two men raped his ten-year-old daughter. The novel describes the tension that often accompanies an interracial incident. Carl Lee, an African-American, killed two white men. During the trial, the Ku Klux Klan, civil rights activists, and high-profile members of the faith-based community attempt to use the trial to further their respective causes. In addition, the novel would be very useful as a tool to explain the insanity defense. The trial testimony of the attorneys and the psychiatrists for the state and the defense is incredible. Two psychiatrists, after looking at the same set of facts, come to different conclusions: One argues that Carl Lee was insane at the time of the offense; the other argues that he was not.

There are many courtroom dramas that may be effective tools to illustrate criminal law processes. These dramas are discussed later, in the court chapters. Two movies, *A Civil Action* and *The Sweet Hereafter*, are good examples of civil law. Finally, if students believe that the insanity defense provides defendants with an easy way to escape justice, show the movie *One Flew over the Cuckoo's Nest*.

Chapter 5

Policing: History and Structure

One federal law enforcement agency of particular interest to students is the Federal Bureau of Investigation. Students are usually curious about the type of work that the FBI does, and many have an interest in pursuing a career in federal law enforcement. A television show students are probably familiar with is *X-Files*, which focuses on the investigations completed by fictional FBI agents. The agents work on "X Files"; these are usually odd cases that are difficult to explain. You can assign students to watch an episode of this program or rent and show the movie of the same title. You can then discuss the activities of these two special agents and contrast them with the types of activities that actually occur at the FBI as discussed in Chapter 5. Three new television series that focus on FBI operations are *Numbers*, *Criminal Minds*, and *Without a Trace*.

A good way to illustrate the problems with the early frontier and vigilantism is to rely on movies of the Western genre. For example, the movie *Unforgiven*, starring Clint Eastwood, would be an outstanding resource to demonstrate these issues. In this film, Eastwood plays a gunfighter who comes out of retirement to kill a couple of men who disfigured a prostitute. Other movies relevant to the issues discussed in Chapter 5 include *U.S. Marshals*, *Ransom*, *Mulholland Falls*, and *Fargo*.

An interesting book that describes the operations of the New York City Police Department is *Turnaround: How America's Top Cop Reversed the Crime Epidemic* by William Bratton and Peter Knobler. Law enforcement is a staple prime-time television subject. Other classic television shows relevant to the subject matter of Chapter 5 are *Mayberry R.F.D.*, *Charlie's Angels*, and the *Rockford Files*.

Chapter 6

Policing: Purpose and Organization

One of the most difficult aspects of teaching students about policing is combating the stereotypes they possess. Many of the students who walk into your classroom probably have not had much face-to-face contact with the police. Instead, their understanding of police work is based primarily on what they have seen on television or in popular movies. The use of force is standard police practice for the main character. The work of detectives and rogue cops is glamorized in movies, and the work of the line-level officer is typically excluded. In addition, very complex crimes are solved in the time frame of the program. An effective way to combat the myths that students have about police work is to show a movie or part of a movie that depicts Hollywood's portrayal of policing. An excellent example is *Dirty Harry*, starring Clint Eastwood. In the first 20 minutes of the movie, Harry Callahan (Eastwood) is insubordinate to his boss and the mayor, arrests several bank robbers, and uses deadly force quite effectively. After students have seen the movie, discuss how it misrepresents police work.

A good example of how law enforcement agencies continue to have challenges in sharing information is the movie *Catch Me If You Can* starring Leonardo DiCaprio. It is based on the real life story of Frank Abagnale, Jr., a successful con artist who managed to elude arrest as he assumed several different identities.

There is a large supply of movies, television shows, and novels depicting law enforcement issues. Both the *Lethal Weapon* and *Die Hard* series demonstrate the same themes as the Eastwood movies. *Beverly Hills Cop* can also be an effective teaching tool. Ask your students about the law enforcement programs on television. They will probably identify many programs, including *NYPD Blue, First Watch*, and *Law & Order*. In addition, probably the most popular current television crime dramas include the *CSI* series. The three television shows, which take place in Las Vegas, Miami, and New York City, focus on the work of crime-scene investigators.

Chapter 7
Policing: Legal Aspects

The television show *NYPD Blue* often provides interrogation footage. The characters often use either psychological or physical coercion to elicit a confession from a suspect. Ask students to view an episode, or show a brief clip of an interrogation in class, to illustrate the tactics used by police to get confessions from suspects.

One of the more popular "infotainment" programs dealing with criminal justice and police issues is *COPS*. Television crews ride with a group of officers, usually from the patrol unit, and record their interactions with citizens. There are typically four or five incidents in a half-hour show. Ask students to view two or three episodes of this program, and then have them write a short paper describing what aspects of policing are presented, whether they believe this is an accurate representation of policing, and whether the rights of suspects were violated during the show.

Entertainment media typically misrepresent the constitutional limitations of police evidence gathering and interrogation. One of the common misconceptions that students have is that *Miranda* is read on arrest. Reading *Miranda* at arrest provides good entertainment, but it is inaccurate. Most police shows emphasize the ways police officers and detectives get around the law rather than follow the law. Have students view any of the police shows on television (for example, *NYPD Blue* and *Law & Order*), and ask them to describe how arrests are presented and identify when *Miranda* is read. Cable TV stations may show reruns of shows such as *Hill Street Blues, Cagney and Lacey, Hawaii Five-O*, and *Homicide* that illustrate various legal aspects of policing.

Chapter 8
Policing: Issues and Challenges

Police corruption is frequently presented in film. Often, the plot revolves around a good cop working to overcome adversity and a "blue wall" of silence to expose corruption. *Serpico*, starring Al Pacino, focuses on the work of Frank Serpico, who exposed widespread corruption in the New York City Police Department in the early 1970s. Another film to watch is *Training Day*. Denzel Washington plays detective Alonzo Harris, a well-decorated veteran narcotics detective, who is asked to train Jake Hoyt (played by Ethan Hawke). The film is set in Los Angeles and focuses on the corrupt practices of Harris and the struggles of the rookie to solve several ethical dilemmas. It depicts an intense 24-hour period in which Harris ultimately attempts to murder Hoyt because he threatens to expose the corruption. Hoyt escapes, and Harris is later murdered. Ask students to watch the film and find examples of the different types of corruption depicted in Figure 8-1 in this chapter.

Joseph Wambaugh, a former Los Angeles police officer, is a very popular author who writes about law enforcement. One of his books, *The Choirboys*, effectively illustrates the police subculture and the working personality. Also, ask students to watch any television law enforcement program. Ask them to find incidents of police corruption and questionable police practices.

Chapter 9

The Courts: Structure and Participants

A good novel to link to several of the issues presented in Chapter 9 is *The Bonfire of the Vanities* by Tom Wolfe. Published in 1987, it provides an excellent portrayal of criminal justice processes in New York City. Moreover, large portions of this novel are devoted to court processes and decision making. The story focuses on the trials, tribulations, and triumphs of Sherman McCoy, a high-priced bond trader on Wall Street. McCoy's life takes a terrible turn when he and his mistress end up lost in the South Bronx. In an effort to escape from some "menacing" young males, McCoy hits one of them with his car. Most of the book focuses on the apprehension, pretrial processes, and trial processes in McCoy's case. The novel provides an outstanding look at the impact of a high-profile media case on criminal justice processes. It also follows the case from its earliest stages through the trial and appellate processes, providing an opportunity to discuss many of the important issues in Chapter 9. Furthermore, *The Bonfire of the Vanities* is available on film. You could assign students to view this film outside class or show a portion of the film during class and have students discuss the film in terms of the issues presented in Chapter 9.

Supreme Court decision making and many historic cases are presented in Bob Woodword's book *The Brethren*. Most movies and television shows focus on the trial stage of the court process. These media resources are discussed in the next chapter. However, a movie that illustrates some of the negative aspects of plea bargaining, as well as how the court process affects sexual assault victims, is *The Accused*. This movie depicts the impact of sexual assault on a victim and also shows the "second victimization" often experienced in the criminal justice system.

Chapter 10

Pretrial Activities and the Criminal Trial

The criminal trial is one of the most familiar public images of court processing. Films, television shows, and other entertainment sources glamorize the trial. Moreover, the role of the defense attorney is usually emphasized. Popular media's defense attorney is an incredibly skilled trial advocate. Indeed, it is only through the skill, determination, and investigative abilities of the defense attorney that justice is achieved. Probably the best example of this skilled attorney is Erle Stanley Gardner's Perry Mason character. Gardner published more than 150 novels using the Mason character as the ultimate defense attorney. Mason had incredible trial prowess and was usually able to use his cross-examination skills to force a witness to admit to the crime that his client was on trial for committing. Gardner's novels are typically short and easy to read. In addition, *Perry Mason* was a popular television show, and reruns are shown often. Encourage your students to read one of these novels or view an episode, and then discuss how Mason, although he may be representative of some of the highest-priced celebrity attorneys, is not the typical attorney one would find in many courtrooms today.

To Kill a Mockingbird, A Time to Kill, Ghosts of Mississippi, 12 Angry Men, The Caine Mutiny, The Practice, Law & Order, Murder One, L.A. Law, The Star Chamber, Judge Judy, Judge Brown, and *Matlock* can all be used in various ways to illustrate courtroom work group and trial practices.

Chapter 11

Sentencing

The Green Mile, the film adaptation of the serialized novel by Stephen King, is a good movie to illustrate death penalty issues. The film is set in Cold Mountain Penitentiary in the mid-1930s. Tom Hanks, who plays guard Paul Edgecomb, is responsible for seeing that "the Mile" (death row) runs smoothly. Three inmates are executed during the film.

The movie depicts the relationships that can emerge between guards and inmates on death row, difficulties in staffing death row, and the effects of death by electrocution. In addition, the movie concludes with the execution of John Coffey, sentenced to death for a crime he did not commit.

The death penalty is a popular entertainment topic. For example, *The Executioner's Song* by Norman Mailer discusses the life and execution of Gary Gilmore—the first prisoner executed after the moratorium on capital punishment was lifted after *Gregg* v. *Georgia*. Other novels on capital punishment include *Native Son* by Richard Wright, *Knock on Any Door* by William Motley, *Billy Budd* by Herman Melville, *Dead Man Walking* by Helen Prejean, and *The Chamber* by John Grisham. These novels are also available as movies.

Chapter 12

Probation, Parole, and Community Corrections

The popular media have not given much attention to community corrections. Instead, the media have focused on capital punishment, as discussed in the previous chapter, and life behind bars (discussed in the chapters that follow). The exclusion of community corrections as sanctions is an interesting point that you can discuss with your class. Why aren't community corrections presented in the news? The text stresses the large number of offenders sentenced to these types of programs and the continued growth of such programs. The exclusion of community corrections from popular entertainment is of course tied to the types of crime preferred by audiences. Murders and rapes are emphasized, and conviction usually ends in long prison terms. Because of this exclusion, however, the public is rarely exposed to community corrections.

The news media coverage of presidential campaigns provides a good illustration of public criticism of community-based corrections. Although the 1988 election occurred more than 15 years ago, the Bush-Dukakis run for the presidency provides one of the more unfortunate examples of media coverage of politics. Remember the Willie Horton advertisements that the Bush campaign used to show that Dukakis was "soft on crime"? Horton was a convicted murderer who, on a weekend furlough from prison, committed a rape. The use of the Horton advertisement helped George Bush win the presidency, but it was also an important factor in eliminating the use of furloughs in many states.

Chapter 13

Prisons and Jails

Prisons, especially maximum-security prisons, have been a staple topic in Hollywood for some time. Classics include *The Big House* (1930), *Cool Hand Luke* (1967), and *The Shawshank Redemption* (1994). Several movies illustrate the different types of prisons highlighted in Chapter 13. For example, a movie depicting life in a juvenile correctional facility is *Bad Boys*, starring Sean Penn. Penn plays juvenile delinquent Mick O'Brien, sentenced to a juvenile facility after killing a young boy in a hit-and-run incident. This movie focuses on how O'Brien survives in prison, giving special attention to the violence and brutality of the facility. The movie also demonstrates the inmate hierarchy. Another movie is *Slam*. This excellent film follows a young African-American male through the District of Columbia's jail system. *Cool Hand Luke* and *I Am a Fugitive from a Chain Gang* depict Southern prison farms. *A Clockwork Orange*, based on the novel by Anthony Burgess, provides a fascinating view of crime and aversion therapy. Finally, *Murder in the First*, starring Kevin Bacon, provides graphic imagery of America's most symbolic prison—Alcatraz. Be careful to respect copyright restrictions on any media you show in the classroom.

Other movies include *Life, Brubaker, White Heat, Jailhouse Rock, Escape from Alcatraz, American Me, Chained Heat, The Longest Yard, Birdman of Alcatraz, Caged, The Rock, The Green Mile*, and *Double Jeopardy*. In addition, the HBO television series *Oz* provides an excellent depiction of prisons and prison life. Popular music also covers many prison and prisoner themes. Some examples include "Folsom Prison Blues" (Johnny Cash), "Prison Song" (Crosby, Stills, and Nash), "Phone Call from Leavenworth" (Chris Whitley), "The Tower" (Ice-T), and "Letters from Earth" (Black Sabbath).

Chapter 14
Prison Life

One of the interesting aspects of the Attica prison riot was that inmates requested, and were granted permission, to have the news media present during negotiations with correctional administrators. A substantial amount of riot footage exists because television cameras were present. For example, some very powerful footage can be seen in the *Eyes on the Prize* video series.

Encourage your students to watch *The Shawshank Redemption*, based on Stephen King's novel *Rita Hayworth and the Shawshank Redemption*. It is an outstanding movie that can be linked to many issues described in Chapter 14. The movie stars Tim Robbins as Andy Dufresne, a prosperous banker sent to Shawshank Prison after being wrongfully convicted of a double homicide. The movie follows Dufresne from his entry into prison society to his eventual escape—20 years after arrival. It shows how new inmates are immediately deprived of all their worldly possessions and introduced to prison society first by corrections officials. It illustrates the powerful inmate subculture and the many social roles of inmates in prison. The movie shows the violence and rape that occur in prison. It also shows the development of an inmate economy, which is run by a few inmates (it focuses particularly on Red Redding [Morgan Freeman]).

The Hurricane, a recently released movie starring Denzel Washington, also illustrates aspects of life in prison. The movie tells the story of Rubin "Hurricane" Carter, a middleweight boxing contender who spent close to 20 years in prison for a crime he did not commit. The film shows the day-to-day monotony of prison life, solitary confinement, and the isolation experienced by inmates. It is an outstanding story and movie. Carter is an author himself and speaks frequently on criminal justice and prison issues. His book, *The 16th Round*, was written while he was incarcerated.

Chapter 15
Juvenile Justice

Scared Straight is a documentary available on videotape that illustrates different responses to juvenile delinquency. The documentary describes a program implemented in Rahway Prison in the 1970s to "scare juveniles straight" by giving them a taste of prison. In this program, juveniles spend a day in Rahway to listen to stories about life in prison from older adult inmates. Many policymakers claimed that the program offered a miraculous cure for delinquency, and many states adopted some version of this program because they believed it would reduce crime. Have your students view the documentary, and then ask them what they think: Are programs such as *Scared Straight* an effective way to deter juveniles from committing crime? Why or why not? Should the *Scared Straight* video be required viewing for all elementary school children? Be careful to respect copyright restrictions on any media you show in the classroom.

Other movies include *Bad Boys, The Newton Boys, Young Guns, The Outsiders, The Warriors, Suburbia, True Crime, American History X, South Central, Marked for Murder*, and *Drugstore Cowboy*.

Chapter 16
Drugs and Crime

Depictions of drug and alcohol abuse are presently in all types of popular media. Different drugs, the link between drugs and crime, and alcohol can be seen in television programs, movies, music videos, and music. Drugs are portrayed as either a primary criminal activity, such as in *Drugstore Cowboy* starring Matt Dillon, or a supplemental criminal activity. Drugs are often portrayed as part of the criminal lifestyle. For example, a movie such as *Casino* focuses on organized crime but still provides significant attention to drug use and abuse by one of the characters in the movie. *Traffic* provides an outstanding critique of the drug war. Other movies showing drug abuse include *Blow, Dead Presidents, Private Parts, 2 Days in the Valley, Gross Pointe Blank, Jade, Less Than Zero, High School High, People v. Larry Flynt, Donnie Brasco, Scarface, Rush, Carlito's Way, New Jack City, Studio 54, Leaving Las Vegas, Pulp Fiction,* and Cheech and Chong's *Up in Smoke.*

Drug and alcohol abuse are also frequent themes in popular music. For example, both Eric Clapton and Jackson Browne sing about "Cocaine," Lou Reed has a song about "Heroin," the band Urge Overkill sings about "Crackbabies," Robert Cray sings about alcohol abuse in the song titled "I Got Loaded," and John Lee Hooker sings "One Bourbon, One Scotch, and One Beer." Other songs include "Mr. Brownstone" by Guns n' Roses and "Rainy Day Women #12 & 35" whose lyrics include "everybody must get stoned" by Bob Dylan. "Lucy in the Sky with Diamonds" by the Beatles is popularly believed to be about drugs, specifically LSD.

Chapter 17
Terrorism and Multinational Criminal Justice

The movie *Red Corner*, starring Richard Gere, provides an excellent overview of the Chinese justice system. Gere plays Jack Moore, an American businessman visiting China to close a communications deal. However, he wakes up one morning, after meeting a beautiful woman at a bar, covered in blood. He is then arrested for murder and rape—crimes he did not commit. The movie focuses on Moore's attempts to prove his innocence in a system that is biased toward conviction. Moore is provided a court-appointed defense counsel, Shen Yuelin (Bai Ling), but she immediately files a guilty plea, stating that it is the only way to receive leniency. He eventually convinces her that he did not commit these crimes, and the movie focuses on how difficult it is to prove innocence in a system not concerned with individual rights. Recall that Chapter 17 describes the Chinese defense attorney's responsibility as first to the country and then to the accused. The conversations between Moore and Yuelin, and the pressure she exerts on him to accept responsibility for crimes he did not commit, illustrate the defense attorney's role in the system very well. This movie also illustrates the functions of the courts of the Chinese justice system, the links between the political and justice systems, and prison conditions.

There are many popular media sources depicting terrorism. A list of relevant films includes *Black Sunday* (1977), *Chain Reaction* (1996), *Delta Force III: The Killing Game* (1991), *Executive Decision* (1996), *Navy Seals* (1990), *The Siege* (1998), and *True Lies* (1994).

Chapter 18
The Future of Criminal Justice

In the mid-1990s, Sylvester Stallone was in two movies with futuristic criminal justice themes. First, Stallone and Wesley Snipes starred in *Demolition Man*. Both Stallone, who plays a Los Angeles police officer, and Snipes, who plays a sophisticated criminal, are cryogenically incarcerated in 1996. Snipes, however, escapes from his parole hearing in

2033. Since the futuristic police department is unable to capture the escaped Snipes, they must release Stallone for assistance. The movie then centers on Stallone's pursuit and capture of Snipes. His second movie was called *Judge Dredd*, based on the comic-book character of the same name. This movie is set in the year 2139, when technology and crime run rampant. "Justice" is the responsibility of armor-covered judges who respond to incidents and make quick punishment decisions. The populace is enamored with Dredd, but after being arrested and convicted for a murder he did not commit, he is banished to the "Cursed Earth." Dredd eventually returns to save the world from a psychopathic criminal named Rico (Armand Assante). More recently, *Minority Report* starred Tom Cruise and depicted a time in the future when crime was predicted and then suspects arrested prior to the crime being committed. All three of these movies provide opportunities to forecast and imagine the criminal justice system of the future and society's response to crime.

    The Terminator and *RoboCop* are good examples of augmented reality discussed in this chapter. Other futuristic crime and justice movies include *Blade Runner, Mad Max, The Matrix, Johnny Mnemonic, Waterworld, The Running Man, Hackers,* and *The Net.* There are also several very good authors who write crime novels and rely on forensic technology to solve crimes. Perhaps the most popular is Patricia Cornwell. Cornwell's main character is Dr. Kay Scarpetta, Chief Medical Examiner of Richmond, Virginia. Cornwell's books, including *The Body Farm, Cause of Death, Black Notice,* and *Southern Cross* (among many others), focus on Scarpetta's ability to solve complex crimes using advanced criminalistic techniques and her training as both a physician and an attorney.

Video Library

Teaching with the ABC News Video Library That Accompanies *Criminal Justice Today*

Criminal Justice Today is accompanied by a growing library of ABC News video segments individually selected by the textbook author, Frank Schmalleger. New videos have been added with each edition of *Criminal Justice Today* so that the entire video library now consists of more than 50 informative shows covering topics as diverse as police subculture, the death penalty, women in prison, racial profiling, three-strikes laws, private prisons, the changing juvenile justice system, computer crime, community policing, victims and victims' rights, and civil rights violations by law enforcement officers. Some shows focus on specific crimes such as rape.

Descriptions of each video segment, organized by edition, are provided in the following pages. Each description is followed by questions that can be used to stimulate discussion following the showing of that segment.

Ninth Edition

CRIME AND PUNISHMENT (*NIGHTLINE*)

Suggested Use

Chapter Four—Criminal Law
Chapter Seven—Policing: Legal Aspects
Chapter Nine—The Courts: Structure and Participants
Chapter Ten—Pretrial Activities and the Criminal Trial
Chapter Eleven—Sentencing
Chapter Thirteen—Prisons and Jails
Chapter Fourteen—Prison Life

Summary

Wilbert Rideau, who became famous as the editor of the prison magazine *The Angolite*. was incarcerated for 44 years in the Louisiana State Penitentiary in Angola, longer than any criminal offender in the history of Calcasieu Parish.

On December 22, 2000, the U.S. 5th Circuit Court of Appeals in New Orleans threw out the 1961 indictment and subsequent murder conviction of award-winning prison journalist Wilbert Rideau. The Appeals Court cited racial discrimination in the selection of the grand jury, noting that five white jury commissioners in Calcasieu Parish, Louisiana, used race-coded cards to handpick whomever they wanted in the jury pool.

The only African-American they put in the jury pool that indicted Rideau worked as a yardman for one of the jury commissioners. On June 18, 2001, the U.S. Supreme Court refused to review the 5th Circuit's decision. The state had to then decide whether to retry or settle the case. In his fourth trial, the defense sought a manslaughter verdict, which allowed him to be released for time already served. Rideau's attorney argued that racism played a role in Rideau's earlier convictions.

Wilbert Rideau was set free from Louisiana State Prison after 44 years. This interview takes place a few days after his release.

Discussion Prompts

1. Wilbert Rideau admitted to his crime, that of stabbing a woman after a botched bank robbery. Do you think he should have been released from prison?
2. Rideau was tried for the same crime four times. On what legalities were the appeals based? Why was the case allowed to come to trial four times?
3. What challenges do you think Rideau will face as a free man, after spending most of his life in prison?
4. Wilbert Rideau became known as "the Most Rehabilitated Prisoner in America." How did he earn this title?

For more information on this topic:

> http://www.wilbertrideau.com/
>
> http://crime.about.com/b/a/139611.htm?iam=metaresults&terms=wilbert
>
> http://crime.about.com/gi/dynamic/offsite.htm?site=http://www.thenation.com/doc.mhtml%253Fi=20020121%26s=bach

BOMB SQUAD 101 (*NIGHTLINE*)

Suggested Use

Chapter Five—Policing: History and Structure
Chapter Six—Policing: Purpose and Organization
Chapter Seven—Policing: Legal Aspects
Chapter Eight—Policing: Issues and Challenges
Chapter Sixteen—Drugs and Crime
Chapter Seventeen—Terrorism and Multinational Criminal Justice
Chapter Eighteen—The Future of Criminal Justice

Summary

Members of the nation's most elite bomb squads attend training in Huntsville, Alabama, the only bomb squad school in the country. The Hazardous Devices School is a joint project of the FBI and the U.S. Army, designed to train public-safety personnel in the art of bomb disposal. This interview takes place during a recent class.

Discussion Prompts

1. The term *bomb squad* no longer describes the many circumstances that might require these services. What are other calls for service that depend on the expertise of the bomb squad?
2. The officers interviewed in this segment mention the mental aspect of this specialty more than the physical. Do you agree that this is the case?
3. One of the officers talks about more calls and greater awareness by the public. What caused this?

For more information on this topic:

> www.pbs.org/nova/robots/
>
> www.defensetech.org/archives/001916.html

THE FINAL REPORT (*NIGHTLINE*)

Suggested Use

Chapter Six—Policing: Purpose and Organization
Chapter Seven—Policing: Legal Aspects
Chapter Eight—Policing: Issues and Challenges
Chapter Fourteen—Prison Life
Chapter Seventeen—Terrorism and Multinational Criminal Justice
Chapter Eighteen—The Future of Criminal Justice

Summary

The National Commission on Terrorist Attacks upon the United States, known as the 9-11 Commission, was an independent bipartisan commission created in late 2002. Its charter was to prepare a full and complete account of the circumstances surrounding the September 11, 2001, terrorist attacks, including preparedness for and the immediate response to the attacks. The commission was also mandated to provide recommendations designed to guard against future attacks. The 9/11 Commission issued its final report on July 22, 2004. Major themes of dysfunction were identified as poor communication and a lack of clear duties and responsibilities within and among federal agencies. Overall, the commission found that even almost three years after the attacks, the United States only earns C+ to B– grades for being prepared for another major attack. This interview took place within days of the report's release.

Discussion Prompts

1. As stressed by the 9/11 Commission, al-Qaeda represents an ideology, not a finite group of people, and as such will continue to grow and adapt in order to fulfill its mission. How can we protect ourselves from an opponent we cannot really describe?

2. Since the report was completed in 2004, other updates have been released. What is our state of preparedness now as compared to 9/11/2001 and 7/22/2004?

3. Many reforms have been suggested as a result of this report. List and describe some of them. Are there others that should be added?

For more information on this topic:

http://www.gpoaccess.gov/911/
http://www.9-11pdp.org/
http://www.9-11commission.gov/

THE PATRIOT ACT (*NIGHTLINE*)

Suggested Use

Chapter Six—Policing: Purpose and Organization
Chapter Seven—Policing: Legal Aspects
Chapter Eight—Policing: Issues and Challenges
Chapter Fourteen—Prison Life
Chapter Seventeen—Terrorism and Multinational Criminal Justice
Chapter Eighteen—The Future of Criminal Justice

Summary

The PATRIOT Act, an expansion of powers for law enforcement, was drafted and passed by Congress and then signed into law by President Bush within seven weeks of September 11, 2001. The law gives government the ability to conduct searches into library, business, and medical records and obtain wiretaps that pertain to persons instead of specific phones. It also makes it easier to obtain entry into private homes to conduct secret searches with delayed notification. At the time of this interview, two years had passed since the PATRIOT Act was made law.

Discussion Prompts

1. Opponents of the PATRIOT Act want the government to ensure the safety of its citizenry without taking away civil liberties. In a post 9/11 world, is it possible to protect the nation without disregarding the Constitution?

2. Why did Attorney General Ashcroft find it necessary to personally present further information, nationwide, two years after the passage of the PATRIOT Act? Was this a good decision, or was there a better way that the importance of this law could have been clarified?

3. What are ACLU's main points of contention with the PATRIOT Act?

4. How can a nation such as the United States continue to respect the rights provided to us by the Constitution yet ward off terrorist attacks?

For more information on this topic:

> http://www.epic.org/privacy/terrorism/hr3162.html
>
> http://www.lifeandliberty.gov

DIVINE LAW (*NIGHTLINE*)

Suggested Use

Chapter One—What Is Criminal Justice?
Chapter Seventeen—Terrorism and Multinational Criminal Justice
Chapter Eighteen—The Future of Criminal Justice

Summary

The majority of Muslim populations are very traditional, patriarchal, and tribal. Amina Lawal was a 32-year-old poor young woman who could not read or write. She lived in the remote village of Kurami in northern Nigeria. Amina and her infant daughter lived in a small hut with mud floors and walls and a thatched roof. In January 2002, she was taken from her village to court, where she was charged with adultery. If convicted of adultery and sentenced under *sharia* law (a strict interpretation of Islamic justice), she would be buried up to the waist and then stoned to death. This interview takes place while the conviction was going through the appeal process in late 2003.

Discussion Prompts

1. *Sharia* law was imposed in many parts of Nigeria in an attempt to quell high crime rates and general lawlessness. Discuss the impact of this strict Islamic law on the crime rate in Nigeria.

2. What rights for the arrested were lacking for Amina Lawal as compared to what exist under American criminal justice.

For more information on this topic:

> http://www.nigerdeltacongress.com/articles/amina_lawal.htm
> http://www.oprah.com/tows/pastshows/tows_2002/tows_past_20021004_
>   b.jhtml
> http://www.cnn.com/2003/WORLD/africa/09/25/nigeria.stoning/

Eighth Edition

DR. LEE

Summary

This video segment profiles Dr. Henry Lee, one of the world's premiere crime-scene investigators. Over the past 40 years, Dr. Lee has investigated more than 6,000 cases. He established his reputation by testifying as a key witness for the O.J. Simpson defense team but also played roles in the William Kennedy Smith trial and in the case of Jon-Benet Ramsey. In his latest book, *The Science of Solving Crimes*, Dr. Lee reveals clues that were missed in those cases.

Discussion Prompts

1. What rationale does Dr. Lee offer to support his belief that crime-scene investigation is very important work?
2. Would you consider working as a crime-scene investigator? What rewards might such a career offer? What difficulties might it present?

AN INNOCENT MAN

Summary

In recent years, there have been stories about people who were wrongly convicted of a crime they didn't commit. One of them is Joseph Salvati, a convicted murderer and the subject of this video segment. At the time of Salvati's trial, the FBI apparently knew that he was innocent. Nonetheless, the bureau allowed Salvati to go to prison for 30 years in an effort to protect the real murderers. Free today as a result of the efforts of defense attorney Victor Garo, Salvati is suing the government for $300 million.

Discussion Prompts

1. Did FBI agents know that Salvati was innocent at the time of his trial? If so, why didn't they prevent his conviction and imprisonment?
2. Could the kind of injustice described in this video segment happen today? How might the system be changed to prevent it from happening?

CRIME & PUNISHMENT: A MATTER OF LIFE AND DEATH, PART 1

Summary

Nightline looks at the case of Marcus Pressley, who sits on Alabama's death row. Pressley has been found guilty of several murders, and this episode (which is Part 1 of a four-part series) examines whether it was appropriate to sentence him to death. Ted Koppel speaks to the governor of Alabama and asks whether people there are seeing justice done.

Discussion Prompts

1. Do you believe that a sentence of death was appropriate in the case of Marcus Pressley? Why or why not?
2. Is the death penalty ever appropriate as a criminal sanction? Why or why not?

CRIME & PUNISHMENT: A MATTER OF LIFE AND DEATH, PART 2

Summary

What drives the decision to target a killer for the death penalty? In this episode (which is Part 2 of a four-part series), John Donvan reports on the prosecutors. The process can be very subjective, depending on the prosecutors' own values and life experiences. The video portrays two prosecutors in Maryland with very different views on the death penalty.

Discussion Prompts

1. What are the two different views on the death penalty that the Maryland prosecutors portrayed in this video represent?
2. Which of the two views do you find more appealing? Why?

CRIME & PUNISHMENT: A MATTER OF LIFE AND DEATH, PART 3

Summary

Ted Koppel talks with the governors of Illinois and Virginia, both Republicans, who favor capital punishment but have very different attitudes about the fairness of the death penalty. In Illinois, executions were suspended by action of the governor, while Virginia ranks second (Texas is first) in the nation in the total number of executions. This episode is Part 3 of a four-part series.

Discussion Prompts

1. Why did the governor of Illinois impose a moratorium on capital punishment? Why did he think that the system that was then in place in Illinois for the determination of guilt and the imposition of punishments was fundamentally unfair?

2. Virginia Governor James Gilmore tells interviewers, "The criminal justice system...is the best that we can humanly do...to bring justice and to separate us out from anarchy and lynch mobs and total injustice everywhere. We do the best we can. And we do exceedingly well." Should it be acceptable, then, for an innocent person to be occasionally convicted and sentenced to die? Why or why not?

CRIME & PUNISHMENT: A MATTER OF LIFE AND DEATH, PART 4

Summary

Texas has the lowest reversal rate of death sentences in the country. In this episode (which is Part 4 of a four-part series), *Nightline* looks at the role of the Texas Criminal Court of Appeals, the highest criminal court in the state, in an effort to examine whether the system has been fair. Mike McCormick, the court's judge, is interviewed along with several death-row inmates.

Discussion Prompts

1. The video points out that Texas seems to have a series of fail-safe devices in place "to insure that no innocent man or woman goes to the death chamber." What are these "devices"? How might they fail?

2. How can trial procedures in death penalty cases be changed to prevent conviction of the innocent? Can such procedures ever be made 100% effective? That is, can we ever be certain that innocent people will not be convicted and sentenced to die?

MIND OF A RAPIST

Summary

In 1989 the "Central Park jogger case" made headlines nationwide because of the brutality of the rapists who committed the crime. The young female victim was savagely beaten, raped, and left for dead. That same night, another 11 people were assaulted at random, apparently by the same perpetrators. Soon afterward, police investigators arrested a group of teenagers and charged them with the rape, saying that the young men involved had spent the evening "wilding." Five young black men faced prosecution, and all of them confessed to rape. Most of the confessions were made on camera. In 2002, however, Matias Reyes, an imprisoned convicted murderer and serial rapist, came forward to say that he committed the notorious Central Park rape and that he had acted alone. Reyes provided vivid details of the crime, and DNA evidence supported his story. He claimed that he is sorry for his crimes, but a psychologist who examined him says he doesn't buy Reyes' story.

Discussion Prompts

1. Who do you think committed the Central Park rape? Was it the five teenagers who were arrested or Matias Reyes, who later confessed to being the perpetrator? Why?

2. Why might the accused teenagers have made false confessions? How can investigators know when confessions are legitimate?

Seventh Edition

CIVIL RIGHTS

Summary

This segment focuses on the issue of ethnic profiling in the wake of the September 11, 2001, terrorist attacks. Of the three million Arabs and Muslims in the United States, many have been singled out for interrogation by federal investigators seeking information related to terrorism. More than 500 people, overwhelmingly Arab and Muslim, were detained as material witnesses or on various charges in the days following the terrorist attacks. Many of these people claim to have been harassed, intimidated, and threatened by investigators. Questions are raised relating to the constitutionality of ethnic profiling for purposes of law enforcement and terrorism investigations. The negative impact of profiling is explored, including the possibility of reduced cooperation with future investigations among Arabs and Muslims in the United States.

Discussion Prompts

1. What are some ways that federal investigators can retrieve information related to terrorism without the use of ethnic profiling? Would the use of profiling make those techniques more effective?

2. Do you believe that ethnic profiling can be a constitutional method for obtaining information in police investigations? Is there a workable alternative for obtaining such information?

LOS ANGELES POLICE DEPARTMENT

Summary

Public outrage following the LAPD's assault on Rodney King in 1992 led to a number of proposed reforms within American policing. Many of these reforms, however, were not fully implemented. The arrest in 2000 of LAPD Officer Rafael Perez, who was caught stealing cocaine from the LAPD's Rampart Division's evidence locker, again brought the attention of the American public to the dark underbelly of law enforcement. Perez plead guilty and admitted to planting evidence, abusing suspects, and lying in court. Perez's testimony led to the dismissal of 30 officers and the overturning of 73 criminal convictions—mostly for drug dealing. The LAPD's antigang task force, known as the "Crash Squad," became the center of a number of investigations into widespread corruption and abuse of police power. One estimate put the possible dollar loss at more than $200 million in lawsuits against the city of Los Angeles due to systemic police corruption in the city's Rampart Division.

Discussion Prompts

1. The LAPD has had long-standing problems in the area of police brutality and civil rights violations. What are some tactics federal investigators can use to put a stop to problems such as this?

2. In the video, peace officers express their fear of what might happen if they were to tell investigating officials of the ongoing criminal offenses within the LAPD. How might internal threats to cooperative officers be controlled?

50,000-VOLT STUN BELT TO CONTROL PRISONERS

Summary

Stun belts, already used in dozens of states across America, are now facing serious criticism. These 50,000-volt belts are activated by remote control and do not leave any marks on prisoners, making the belts more susceptible to abuse by enforcement agents. Amnesty International is pushing for a ban on stun belts, calling them "high-tech torture devices." The video shows two documented cases of abuse involving these devices. In one case, a judge in Los Angeles ordered a prisoner to be shocked for refusing to remain quiet. In New Orleans, a prisoner was shocked when a prison guard accidentally pushed the remote trigger. The video notes that stun belts have already been banned in three states but are still being used by police and corrections officials elsewhere.

Discussion Prompts

1. Does the ability to restrain a prisoner without causing lasting physical harm outweigh the possibility of abuse of stun belts by enforcement agents?
2. What kind of supervision can the federal court system provide, if any, to help prevent future stun-belt abuse?

PLEA BARGAINS

Summary

Court systems in many parts of the country are overworked, and backlogs are not unusual. The San Francisco District Attorney's office, which is the focus of this segment, files 20,000 misdemeanor cases each year. With only five courtrooms available for trying such cases, each available judge would have to try 11 cases a day, 365 days a year, if all went to trial. Plea bargains are used in San Francisco and across the country to speed up case processing. Using bargained pleas, prosecutors (with judicial approval) offer a lesser sentence in return for a certain conviction, thus avoiding trial. The practice, however, creates a problem for felony defendants who have prior convictions—especially in California and other three-strikes jurisdictions that impose mandatory minimum sentences on repeat offenders.

Discussion Prompts

1. Do you believe that plea bargains provide a useful justice system tool? Why or why not?
2. Might state court systems be able to change in order to quicken the pace of trials? If so, how?

KIDS IN COURT

Summary

Californians are voting on Proposition 21, which will take juveniles who commit serious crimes out of juvenile court and place them in criminal court. The video documents the case of Thomas, a 14-year-old Californian who is processed through the California juvenile justice system under pre-Proposition 21 standards. Thomas allegedly robbed, then stabbed to death, the owner of a convenience store and was arrested and questioned by officers without his mother or an attorney present—a legal practice under California statutes. A determination was made by the judge in a fitness hearing that Thomas should be tried as an adult. At fitness hearings the sophistication and gravity of the crime, prior offenses, and the likelihood of rehabilitation are weighed in an attempt to assess whether a juvenile offender should be tried as a juvenile or an adult. The burden in such hearings is on the defense to show that the juvenile is capable of being rehabilitated and effectively dealt with in the juvenile system.

Discussion Prompts

1. Should parents bear any criminal responsibility for the actions of children who become juvenile offenders?

2. Can a 14-year-old serious offender be rehabilitated within the juvenile justice system? Will imprisonment be more effective if the juvenile is tried as an adult and ordered to confinement?

3. The prior "criminal activity" the judge used in determining that Thomas exhibited a pattern of delinquency as "crimes" based on age: possession of a .22-caliber pistol and a history of drinking. If Thomas had been an adult, possession of a weapon and drinking would not necessarily have been considered criminal behavior. Should juveniles be held to the same standards as adults?

DRUG COURTS

Summary

There are approximately two million people in jails and prisons in the United States, at a cost ranging from $20,000 to $50,000 per year for each prisoner. Many of the nation's inmates are incarcerated for drug-related offenses, and recidivism rates are high. Moreover, drugs are readily available in many prisons, but drug-treatment programs are offered in only a few. Drug courts, which can be an alternative to imprisonment, are showing excellent results through the court-ordered treatment of drug offenders, resulting in low recidivism rates. This video highlights a drug court in Tucson, Arizona, showing a judge, prosecutor, defense attorney, therapist, and caseworker cooperating in the treatment of drug offenders. As the segment shows, two-thirds of Tucson drug-court participants succeed. Of those who have completed the program over the past two years, none have been rearrested.

Discussion Prompts

1. Some people say that drug court is an "easy way out" for drug offenders. Do you agree? Why or why not?

2. Drug courts have proven to be effective in selected locations. Do you feel that they would be as effective if instituted nationwide? Why or why not?

CYBERSTALKER

Summary

Internet stalking has become a fairly widespread problem. However, fewer than half of all states have laws making this form of stalking a crime. This segment follows three cases in which perpetrators used the Internet as a weapon but were either found not guilty due to the lack of laws necessary for effective prosecution or were found guilty only of a misdemeanor and punished with a small fine and no prison time.

Discussion Prompts

1. Should cyberstalking be a crime? Why or why not?

2. Should the federal government attempt to mandate that all states enact laws criminalizing cyberstalking (perhaps by reducing federal funding available to states that do not)? Can preexisting laws be used effectively to prosecute cyberstalkers?

Sixth Edition

CRIME AND PUNISHMENT, PART 1 (*NIGHTLINE*; AUGUST 6, 1998)
CRIME AND PUNISHMENT, PART 2 (*NIGHTLINE*; AUGUST 13, 1998)
CRIME AND PUNISHMENT, PART 3 (*NIGHTLINE*; AUGUST 20, 1998)
CRIME AND PUNISHMENT, PART 4 (*NIGHTLINE*; AUGUST 27, 1998)
CRIME AND PUNISHMENT, PART 5 (*NIGHTLINE*; SEPTEMBER 3, 1998)

Summary

A five-part *Nightline Special Edition* series about American attitudes toward crime and the increased use of imprisonment as a criminal sanction examines the consequences of "get tough on crime" policies recently enacted in many states across the country and takes viewers on a tour of maximum-security prisons. Using interviews with victims, inmates, policymakers, and correctional officers, the series asks just what "criminal punishment" means in today's world.

The series begins with a close examination of North Carolina's prison system, with special emphasis on Raleigh's Central Prison and the death-row inmates housed there. The Texas prison system becomes the focus of the last two segments, with the final segment detailing the course of an execution in Texas.

Discussion Prompts

1. What does society expect of prisons today? After watching this series, does it seem to you as though society is getting what it expects?

2. How do the inmates shown in this series adjust to prison life? Can you discern different modes of adjustment among different inmates? If so, what are they?

3. How did you feel after watching the final segment (on capital punishment)? Did the show influence your attitudes toward capital punishment? If so, how? Do you now feel that capital punishment is justified or not?

Fifth Edition

THE BLUE WALL, PART 1 (*NIGHTLINE*; AUGUST 21, 1997; 5:55)
THE BLUE WALL, PART 2 (*NIGHTLINE*; AUGUST 22, 1997; 9:13)

Summary

In the wake of the horrific attack on Haitian immigrant Abner Louima by two white New York City police officers, public reaction builds to outrage. This segment focuses on a disturbing element of this tragic affair: Despite the common knowledge of this attack among officers assigned to the 70th Precinct, more than two days passed before any police officer came forward with the story. Precinct members seemed to close ranks, first in an effort to prevent the story from getting out and then in an effort to protect the officers accused of committing the attack.

Discussion Prompts

1. What can be done to make police officers understand that it is okay to be intolerant of wrongful, unethical, or criminal behavior by fellow officers and that speaking out about it to one's superiors is the right—and preferred—response?

2. Is the fear of being labeled a tattletale an American cultural phenomenon so strongly embedded in our national psyche as children that it taints our judgment as adults?

3. Is the infamous "blue wall" the result of an "us against them" mentality among police officers?

WOMEN DOING TIME
(*PRIMETIME LIVE*; JANUARY 24, 1996; 12:59)

Summary

This segment examines the phenomenal growth of the female prison population in the United States. News correspondent Diane Sawyer spent two days as a prisoner in the Louisiana Correctional Institute for Women and, through interviews with individual prisoners, presents a compelling picture of anger and despair.

Discussion Prompts

1. What social factors are contributing to the growing population of female inmates?
2. Has the criminal justice system changed the way it views sentencing models for female offenders?

GIRLS IN THE HOOD
(*PRIMETIME LIVE*; JANUARY 24, 1997; 8:02)

Summary

A look at gangbangers, both male and female, is achieved through the use of candid home-movie footage recorded by gang members at the behest of the ABC News affiliate in Los Angeles. Interviews with gang members reveal a disturbing acceptance of violence and lawlessness as the preferred alternative to living the "boring" existence of conventional, socially acceptable behavior.

Discussion Prompts

1. What factors make gang membership attractive to American youth?
2. What can we do to counteract the attraction of gang membership?
3. Does the gravitation to gang membership represent failures of the American family, the educational system, or such institutions as churches and government? Or must these failures be shared by all?

CRIMINAL INJUSTICE (*20/20*; FEBRUARY 16, 1996; 13:38)

Summary

The ongoing conflict between the interests of society and constitutional protections of the individual are illustrated in a variety of cases wherein judges made seemingly senseless rulings regarding the admissibility of evidence. In each case, accused offenders were released because law enforcement officials failed to correctly interpret or apply very complex rules of search and seizure. One judge opposed to such releases points out that the rule book governing such searches is more than 4,000 pages thick. He asserts that even a chief judge accompanying police officers on patrol would be unable to guide them in the conduct of a legal search "with any degree of confidence."

Discussion Prompts

1. Should the rules of search and seizure be clarified and simplified?
2. Should the courts throw out cases because police officers cannot properly interpret rules of evidence that even law scholars are unable to interpret?
3. One judge in this segment calls for modifying the *Miranda* protections by changing the point at which counsel is required. Currently, if a suspect demands counsel, she or he cannot even be interrogated until counsel is present, and counsel, of course, simply advises the suspect to say nothing. This, says the judge, completely negates an investigator's ability to conduct an effec-

tive interrogation and, says the same judge, simply makes no sense. Instead, he suggests that justice would be better served by permitting the conduct of normal investigative interrogations whether or not counsel is present. What do you think?

THE COLOR OF JUSTICE (*20/20*; DECEMBER 12, 1997; 8:31)

Summary

A George Washington University law professor advocates race-based jury nullification (in nonviolent cases) as an appropriate African-American response to what he considers a criminal justice system hopelessly biased against black citizens. Even if they believe the defendant is guilty, he says, black jurors should vote for acquittal as a means of balancing past injustice.

Discussion Prompts

1. Do you agree or disagree with this professor's notion of contemporary justice?
2. How do you feel about the proponent of such radical views teaching law to generations of future lawyers?
3. Do you agree or disagree with the trial judge's effort to counter the jury nullification by dismissing the obstinate juror? Do you agree or disagree with the appellate judge's reversal of the trial judge's action?

Fourth Edition

THREE STRIKES: IS IT WORKING?
(*NIGHTLINE*; MARCH 7, 1995; 20:14)

Summary

Analysis of the effects of California's "three strikes and you're out" law in the first year of its existence shows it to be a somewhat mixed blessing. A committee charged with evaluating the effects of the legislation computed actual reduction of more than 70,000 crimes in one year. But the extraordinary costs associated with the law seem to support opponents' claims that it is simply too expensive. Critics point to the fact that defendants' demands for jury trials have increased more than 70 percent, hopelessly bogging down an overburdened court system and resulting in lengthy delays of prosecution. They also charge that the law reduces judicial discretion and is ensnaring too many nonviolent offenders rather than the violent repeat offenders it was meant to target.

Discussion Prompts

1. Arguments against three-strikes laws frequently focus on the financial costs of the law. Are the costs worth it?
2. On the surface, a reduction of more than 70,000 crimes in a single year in one state seems to be significant. But has that reduction translated to a greater feeling of security and improved quality of life for the citizenry?
3. Are criticisms of the three-strikes law based on flaws in the law itself, or are they based on perceived flaws in the practical application of the law by prosecutors?

THE ACCOMPLICE?
(*PRIMETIME LIVE*; AUGUST 2, 1995; 12:54)

Summary

A Tacoma, Washington, bar owner is shot and killed during a robbery. When the killer is arrested eight days later, police are not surprised to learn that he is on parole from a Massachusetts prison. They are disturbed, however, when they discover the extensive violent criminal record of the accused, and they question the wisdom of the Massachusetts parole board's release decision in this case. Their questions turn to outrage when they find that parole was granted at the behest of the Federal Bureau of Investigation, which sought the release of the man so that he could be used as an informant.

Discussion Prompts

1. Should violent felons be so aggressively recruited as informants that existing prison terms are shortened?
2. Do you think that either the Massachusetts parole board or the Federal Bureau of Investigation or both bear responsibility for the death resulting from their actions to obtain the release of this killer?

THE SHERIFF AND THE POSSE
(*20/20*; OCTOBER 7, 1994; 11:16)

Summary

Controversial hard-line Maricopa County, Arizona, Sheriff Joe Arpaio enlists volunteer support from county citizens as an armed posse to support his aggressive law enforcement tactics. Arpaio's innovative approach includes housing jailed offenders in a "tent city" annex to the overcrowded county jail. He firmly states his position and refuses to back down: "It is not a question of *if* I'll be sued," he says, "it's a question of *when* I'll be sued. My job is to protect the people of this county. I'll accept the risk of lawsuit to do that job."

Discussion Prompts

1. Hero—or wacko? Sheriff Arpaio's supporters laud his aggressive style and commitment to law enforcement. His detractors call him a loose cannon whose practices are unjust and predict inevitable tragedy. What do you think?
2. Arpaio's hard-line tactics strike an emotional chord in the "get tough" atmosphere of America in the mid-1990s. But are they safe? Are they sensible? Are they humane? Are they what Americans want from their law enforcement agencies?
3. Sheriff Arpaio says that law-abiding citizens are at war with the criminal elements of American society and that fact alone justifies the adoption of all-out measures to win that war. Do you agree?

WHO'S WATCHING THE GUARDS?
(*20/20*; MARCH 11, 1994; 11:03)

Summary

This segment exposes widespread deficiencies in the hiring practices of private security companies that enable clearly unqualified applicants to become armed security guards. Numerous examples of such laxity are presented, such as the case of a man with an extensive felony record, including prior convictions for rape and assault. After being hired to patrol an apartment complex, the man abducted, raped, and shot a 14-year-old girl. Industry-wide laxity in screening and hiring practices is shown to be placing the public at great risk.

Discussion Prompts

1. Should verification of criminal records through the National Crime Information Center (NCIC), with an appropriate waiting period to allow receipt of a response, be a mandatory component of private security hiring practices?

2. Should a felony conviction bar a candidate from employment in the private security industry?

3. Should standardization in hiring practices be imposed on the private security industry?

JUVENILE JUSTICE SYSTEM
(*WORLD NEWS TONIGHT*; FEBRUARY 21, 1995; 5:26)

Summary

This segment of *ABC News American Agenda* castigates the juvenile justice system. One prosecutor simply states: "It does not work, it does not work, it does not work!" The segment calls the juvenile justice system in New York "the finest crime school in the country," where relatively inexperienced youthful offenders learn techniques for committing more serious crimes. Styled after a juvenile justice concept originally put in place in 1899, contemporary programs are portrayed as grossly outmoded and unrealistic in the face of the sophistication and callous worldliness of today's youth.

Discussion Prompts

1. Is a major overhaul of the juvenile justice system due?

2. At the time of his arrest for murder, a 12-year-old boy in Florida had a record of 57 prior felony arrests. That's 57 times the boy was cycled through the juvenile justice system before—what a surprise!—he made the big time. But he made the big time at the expense of a man's life. Is it the government's role to protect citizens or merely to take appropriate action after the citizens are harmed?

LAW AND ORDER ON THE INFORMATION SUPERHIGHWAY
(*NIGHTLINE*; MAY 2, 1994; 19:13)

Summary

How to police cyberspace is the focus of this segment. Examples of problems include the pending case of a Massachusetts Institute of Technology (MIT) student who posted software to an electronic bulletin board for free downloading by anybody who chose to do so. Now facing charges of software piracy, the student's defenders claim he cannot be held responsible for what others do with the material he provided access to on his bulletin board. "That's like holding the telephone company responsible if someone uses the phone to commit a crime," says one law professor.

Discussion Prompts

1. All of the MIT students queried during the development of this report stated that their fellow student was wrong and deserved punishment. Do you agree?

2. Should theft of intellectual property be addressed in civil or criminal courts?

3. Do you agree with the professor quoted in the synopsis above?

Third Edition

OXNARD, CA, REDUCTIONS IN CRIME
(*PRIMETIME LIVE*; NOVEMBER 11, 1993; 6:27)

Summary

This segment shows how Oxnard, California, employed a program called SHO—Serious Habitual Offender—to significantly reduce crime citywide. SHO targets the 2% of the city's juvenile population that is known to be responsible for committing almost 50% of the felony offenses in the city.

Discussion Prompts

1. Methods employed in the SHO program appear to be an expansion of the much-reviled "profiling" process, considered by many to be the embodiment of systemic racism. Does the success realized by SHO validate profiling?

2. SHO is an example of proactive crime management by progressive community leaders. What other methods might there be for citywide intervention before crimes occur?

COMMUNITY POLICING
(*PRIMETIME LIVE*; NOVEMBER 11, 1993; 4:26)

Summary

Security measures being adopted by neighborhoods and communities across America are discussed. Physical protections ranging from the emplacement of fencing and gated entryways to the hiring of roving security guards are described. Proactive measures undertaken by members of the Riverside Park community in Fort Lauderdale, Florida, are reviewed, including efforts to close off roadway access to drug dealers and prostitutes.

Discussion Prompts

1. This segment highlights the fact that the desire for feeling secure in one's home is not unique to the wealthy and that cities can take measures to improve security for members of the lower economic class. Are such measures the responsibility of community leaders, or does the primary responsibility rest with the individual citizens? Could it be that the responsibility should be shared?

2. Regarding the portion of this segment that addressed safe rooms in homes: Are they a manifestation of growing paranoia or a practical response to a very real threat?

THE GREAT PRISON PASTIME
(*20/20*; SEPTEMBER 24, 1993; 16:13)

Summary

Civil courts throughout the country are experiencing massive increases in the number of lawsuits being brought against corrections officials by inmates. In some court systems, such as in Illinois, prisoners brought almost 50% of pending civil cases. The problem addressed in this segment is that most of these cases are so frivolous as to be ridiculous. Viewer response to this segment is invariably indignant outrage. (*Note:* Recent passage of the Prisoner Litigation Reform Act has significantly reduced inmates' abilities to clog the various court systems with frivolous lawsuits.)

Discussion Prompts

1. Should taxpayers bear the costs of lawsuits brought by prisoners?
2. Should prisoners' access to the courts be limited or constrained in some manner to prevent abuses such as those depicted in this segment?
3. Should the concept of civil death, wherein convicted felons lose entitlement to many civil legal procedures, be reinstated?

PUBLIC DEFENDERS
(*DAY ONE*; JUNE 14, 1993; 15:39)

Summary

An unending flow of new defendants into overwhelming caseloads and severely limited resources for conducting essential investigations are common constraints on the public-defense systems in most American cities. This segment shows the adverse effects those constraints have on defendants who are unable to afford a private defense attorney.

Discussion Prompts

1. Many members of the economic lower class perceive inequality in the criminal justice system. Does the kind of rubber-stamp, assembly-line processing of defendants by public defenders shown in this segment support that perception?
2. Is justice truly being served by this blatantly overloaded system?
3. Should state and local governments be required to allocate more funding to public-defender programs?

DEADLY DECISIONS
(*20/20*; AUGUST 21, 1992; 16:52)

Summary

The need for increased courthouse and courtroom security is discussed in this segment. Numerous cases of courtroom shootings are presented, most committed in response to adverse rulings in divorce or child-custody cases. Included is an interview with one convicted murderer who states that the shooting was simply the only response left to him after the court stripped him of his home and most of his income in a divorce ruling.

Discussion Prompts

1. Some judges have taken to carrying weapons for self-defense in their own courtrooms. Should they?
2. A common response to new incidents of courthouse/courtroom attacks is often a media call for stiffer penalties. Would they be an effective deterrent? Why or why not?

CUSTODY OF THE STATE
(*DAY ONE*; MARCH 14, 1993; 35:08)

Summary

This segment exposes long-term widespread sexual abuse of female inmates in the Georgia Women's Correctional Institution at Milledgeville. More than 160 inmates joined in a class-action suit against the state and individual correctional officers. Allegations included charges of consensual and forced sex, prostitution, drug trafficking to the inmates by correctional officers, and even murder. Ultimately, firing, reassignment, or criminal indictment removed more than 50 correctional administrators, guards, and staff members.

Discussion Prompts

1. The corruption and sexual abuse depicted in this segment are alleged to have gone on for more than 13 years. Do you believe that could happen without the knowledge and at least the tacit approval of senior administrators at the prison?

2. The former warden disavows any knowledge of prisoner sexual abuse during his tenure. Given the fact that almost the entire prisoner population and most of the guard force were aware of these activities, is his denial credible?

3. Does public apathy toward prison conditions create an environment in which corruption and abuse can flourish?

BLACKS AND THE CRIMINAL JUSTICE SYSTEM (*NIGHTLINE*; SEPTEMBER 2, 1992; 9:45)

Summary

Charges of institutional racism in the criminal justice system are supported by a dizzying, disturbing, and compelling array of statistics gleaned from reports on arrest rates in Washington, D.C., and Baltimore. The evident systemic bias is addressed in commentaries by civic leaders who label it "a national tragedy."

Discussion Prompts

1. The majority of drug abusers are white, but the majority of offenders arrested for drug violations are black. Why do you think that is the case?

2. Is the criminal justice system racially biased? Support your response.

Second Edition, Tape One

A LOOK AT AMERICA'S FASTEST GROWING CRIME: RAPE (*WORLD NEWS TONIGHT*; 3:50)
SEATTLE'S FIGHT TO PREVENT RAPE AND HELP VICTIMS (JANUARY 7, 8, and 10, 1991; 3:55)
SUCCESSFUL PROGRAM THAT REHABILITATES RAPISTS (4:00)

Summary

Three segments of *ABC News American Agenda* examine various aspects of the increasing incidence of rape in major cities across America. Influences such as the portrayal of women as sex objects in advertising and movies are discussed, as is the growth of self-defense class enrollments by women. Legal and educational measures adopted by the city of Seattle, Washington, to combat the growing rape problem are described. A sex offender treatment program in the Vermont prison system is described.

Discussion Prompts

1. Do you support or oppose the practice of public notification when a convicted sex offender is paroled into a community? Support your position.

2. Do you support or oppose such radical treatment methods as chemical castration? Why or why not?

NEW REPORT CRITICAL OF L.A. POLICE
(*NIGHTLINE*; JULY 9, 1991; 20:52)

Summary

An independent commission found evidence of the routine use of excessive force by and widespread racism among members of the Los Angeles Police Department and called for the immediate resignation of the department's chief. They also cited poor performance by supervisors at all levels as a major contributing factor to the erosion of professionalism within the department. Included are discussions of cultural conflicts between the predominantly white police ranks and the large inner-city minority population and such existent social ills as poor educational systems and limited employment opportunities. (*Note:* Shortly after this tape segment aired, Los Angeles Police Chief Darryl Gates resigned.)

Discussion Prompts

1. What can be done to reduce the use of excessive force by street cops?
2. Can contemporary community policing models be applied effectively in a large urban area such as Los Angeles? What obstacles would be encountered? How could those obstacles be overcome?
3. How can the Los Angeles Police Department overcome its image as a racially biased institution?

VICTIM IMPACT STATEMENTS
(*NIGHTLINE*; FEBRUARY 13, 1989; 21:57)

Summary

Defense attorneys almost universally oppose the introduction of victim impact testimony during sentencing hearings on grounds that it is unduly prejudicial and inflammatory toward the defendant. Advocates for victim impact testimony characterize it as an essential counterbalance to the defendant's ability to introduce mitigating evidence. This provocative segment presents persuasive arguments from both sides of this controversial issue.

Discussion Prompts

1. Is it fair to provide defendants the opportunity to present matters in mitigation without permitting victims the opportunity to present matters in extenuation?
2. Defense attorneys argue that victim impact statements are prejudicial to the defendant because they unjustly inflame jurors' emotions. Is not a defendant's presentation of issues clearly designed to evoke juror sympathy for the defendant equally prejudicial toward the state's pursuit of justice for the victim?
3. Since this segment aired, the U.S. Supreme Court reversed its previous ruling banning the use of victim impact statements in criminal trials. Such statements are now routinely considered in courts throughout America. Do you support or oppose the use of such statements. Why or why not?

Second Edition, Tape Two

THE SUPREME COURT: END OF THE LIBERAL HOUR? (*THIS WEEK WITH DAVID BRINKLEY*; JUNE 30, 1991; 41:21)

Summary

The retirement of liberal U.S. Supreme Court Justice Thurgood Marshall presented President George Bush the opportunity to seat a conservative on the Court, potentially causing a shift in the Court's ideological perspective. A distinguished panel discusses relevant issues, including the need to nominate a candidate who will signal an effort to balance the Court.

Discussion Prompts

1. Ideological leanings in either the conservative or liberal direction are to be expected. Would it not be detrimental to the nation's best interests, however, if an impaneled U.S. Supreme Court were firmly committed to one ideology or the other and consistently and rigidly voted its perspective?

2. Is a moderate or balanced U.S. Supreme Court more likely to make rulings that are fair to the greatest percentage of the population?

KILLING MACHINE (*PRIMETIME LIVE*; JUNE 13, 1991; 14:04)

Summary

The phenomenon of serial murder is examined, including discussions of common characteristics of serial murderers. The Federal Bureau of Investigation's Behavioral Sciences Unit, headquartered at Quantico, Virginia, is highlighted, and the unit's use of profiling techniques to focus an investigation is discussed. This segment offers a rare opportunity to observe an actual investigation of serial murder, as *Primetime Live* correspondents are permitted unusual access to observe FBI and Delaware law enforcement authorities as they analyze clues in what came to be known as the Corridor Killer serial murder case.

Discussion Prompts

1. Profiling as an investigative tool has come under much scrutiny in the decade since this segment aired and has been harshly criticized as a racially biased process. Do you agree or disagree? Support your response.

2. The Corridor Killer changed his *modus operandi* after learning through the media that investigators were focusing on blue fibers found on his first victims. Subsequently, he dumped his victims in the river so that trace evidence would be washed away. Should the media be denied access to such investigative details? Would such restrictions constitute a violation of the public's right to know?

PICKING THE WILLIAM KENNEDY SMITH RAPE TRIAL JURY (*NIGHTLINE*; NOVEMBER 1, 1991; 20:37)

Summary

This tape segment examines jury selection in the sensational rape trial of a Kennedy family member. The defense team strategy of quizzing potential jurors regarding their knowledge of the Kennedy family itself and of Senator Ted Kennedy, a bit player in this drama, is discussed. Additionally, the potential effects of the extraordinary publicity surrounding the case are examined, and the various strategies for developing a profile of the "ideal" juror are described.

Discussion Prompts

1. Smith was ultimately found innocent of this charge. Do you agree? Why or why not?

2. Should jury-selection processes be limited to facts bearing directly on the case and the potential juror's ability to render an unbiased opinion, or should attorneys be permitted to explore seemingly extraneous matters, such as a potential juror's reaction to the celebrity status of the family of the accused?

3. At one point in this segment, the commentator remarked that the guilt or innocence of the accused might well have been decided during the jury-selection process itself. Do you agree or disagree?

First Edition, Tape One

WILDING (*NIGHTLINE*; MAY 16, 1989; 16:54)

Summary

Eight black teenagers brutally beat and gang-raped a white woman in Central Park. A shocking crime, it is sensationalized when the youths claim they were just "wilding," which they define as "when you go beat up somebody . . . for fun, or for money." The disturbing phenomenon of urban teen pack violence is examined. Elements such as the lack of adult supervision or positive male role models are discussed as contributing factors.

Discussion Prompts

1. Have television and movie violence played a role in the development of a culture of violence among urban youth?
2. What social factors have contributed to the development of a culture of violence among urban youth?
3. What measures can community leaders take to make violence unacceptable behavior?

DO-IT-YOURSELF JUSTICE (*20/20*; MAY 26, 1990; 11:24)

Summary

After witnessing the brutal murder of a woman in a shopping mall parking lot, a Dallas man shoots and kills the fleeing murderer. Fearful of arrest, the man initially flees the scene. Accompanied by his attorney, he then turns himself in to the authorities two days later. Ultimately, he is freed without being charged. Vigilante or hero? This compelling segment presents thought-provoking issues about the availability of guns in American society.

Discussion Prompts

1. Is Todd Broom a vigilante or a hero?
2. How do you feel about the fact that Broom initially fled the scene following the shooting? How did that affect your perception of him as a vigilante or hero?
3. Should private citizens become *de facto* law enforcement officers in situations like the one shown in this tape segment simply because they happen to have possession of the requisite armament?

TAWANA BRAWLEY AFFAIR (*NIGHTLINE*; JUNE 18, 1988; 8:37)

Summary

A 15-year-old black girl claimed she was abducted and raped by six white men. The case quickly became a *cause celebre* for black activists seeking to highlight the unwillingness or inability of both the criminal justice system and the white power structure to obtain justice for black victims. (*Note:* Events in the decade following this taped segment resulted in the girl's claim being ruled a hoax by a grand jury and major defamation of character civil suits being brought against the girl and the black activists by those accused of having committed the crime.)

Discussion Prompts

1. What is your opinion—was this a hoax or a miscarriage of justice for a black victim?

2. Does Ms. Brawley's refusal to cooperate with investigators strengthen or weaken the credibility of her story?

3. Should activists such as the Reverend Sharpton be permitted to disrupt ongoing criminal investigations?

WHY NOT WILBERT RIDEAU? (*20/20*; APRIL 14, 1989; 22:28)

Summary

Convicted murderer Wilbert Rideau has served 30 plus years in Louisiana's maximum-security State Penitentiary at Angola. Rideau earned national prominence as editor of the prison's award-winning magazine, for his effectiveness as an inmate leader, and for his articulate arguments for prison reform. Fully qualified for parole, Rideau is consistently denied parole or clemency while the typical murderer achieves parole in about eight years. Controversy centers on the political maneuverings of the state's governors, each of whom has ignored repeated release recommendations by the state's parole board, pardon boards, each of the penitentiary's former wardens, and the state's largest newspaper.

Discussion Prompts

1. Do you believe Wilbert Rideau should be released from prison?

2. What is your reaction to the explanations offered by both governors in defense of their refusals to grant parole or clemency to Wilbert Rideau?

3. Should such release decisions rest in the hands of one individual, or to reduce or prevent bias or corruption, should all such cases be ruled on by an independent board or panel?

First Edition, Tape Two

THE SATANIC VERSES UPROAR (*NIGHTLINE*; FEBRUARY 13, 1989; 21:57)

Summary

Author Salman Rushdie incurred the wrath of Islam upon publication of his fictional novel. Considered pure blasphemy by Muslim believers, the novel sparked riots throughout the Muslim world and brought innumerable death threats against the author, bomb threats against American bookstores where it was sold, and threats of worldwide blacklisting of all books marketed by the novel's publisher.

Discussion Prompts

1. The U.S. Constitution's protection of freedom of expression directly conflicts with the rigid controls on citizens' rights common in Muslim theocracies. As members of the world community, should Americans respect the views of the Muslim world, or should we ignore their agitation and support Rushdie's right to free expression? (Keep in mind that Rushdie was not under the protective umbrella of the U.S. Constitution when he wrote and published his controversial novel.)

2. As the world shrinks through technological advances in communications, it is reasonable to assume that we can expect more such cultural clashes. What should be the U.S. national policy on issues such as this?

3. Rushdie is in violation of Muslim law. If he were in the United States, would we be bound to honor an extradition request?

DRUG LEGALIZATION
(*THIS WEEK WITH DAVID BRINKLEY*; FEBRUARY 13, 1989; 5:56)

Summary

Critics call America's "war on drugs" ineffective, futile, as well as a monumental waste of money. Citing the exponentially growing inflow of illicit drugs even as federal money allocated to fight it is doubled and redoubled, they call for immediate legalization and diversion of those funds to educational programs.

Discussion Prompts

1. What are the most effective arguments for legalization?
2. What are the most effective arguments against legalization?
3. Considering the arguments presented in questions 1 and 2, should drugs be legalized?

Instructor Resources

Teaching with the *Criminal Justice Today* PowerPoint Presentation

The PowerPoint presentation that accompanies the annotated instructor's edition of *Criminal Justice Today* provides a comprehensive overview of key terms and concepts presented in the textbook. It also contains a number of important figures, charts, and graphs taken from the text. Organized according to the flow of material in the textbook, this entertaining CD-ROM-based presentation makes an excellent in-class tool for reviewing important points.

An online version of the presentation is available through the Prentice Hall instructors resource Website, and as part of the exciting WebCT and Blackboard courses that Prentice Hall has created in support of *Criminal Justice Today*. To access online instructor resources, go to www.prehnall.com and click the Instructor Resource Center link. Then click "Register" for an instructor access code. The code will be sent to you via email within 48 hours after you register.

Once you have received the code, follow the instructions below to access the instructor's resource material for this text:

1. Go to the Prentice Hall website at http://www.prenhall.com.
2. Browse or search the catalog to locate the instructors' resource you wish to download. If you search by main edition, please be sure to select Instructor Resources from the left navigation bar while on the product page.
3. Click the file name link.
4. Enter your login name and password.
5. Click the Log In button.
6. A new page will appear requesting you to acknowledge our terms of acceptance to ensure all users understand the proprietary nature of our products and the importance of keeping our resources in the hands of educators. Click *I Accept* to begin the download process.

Teaching with the *Criminal Justice Today* World Wide Web Sites

Criminal Justice Today is supported by a widely acclaimed, award-winning website accessible at http://www.cjtoday.com. The feature-rich ninth-edition site builds upon a strong tradition of standard-setting excellence in Web-based media. The site offers the following special features:

Electronic Syllabus. With this feature, you can create an online syllabus that students can use as their personal Web guide to assignments, test dates, term paper assignments and due dates, and other coursework. A sample electronic syllabus is available online, which you can modify easily to fit the needs of your class. The sample syllabus already includes all of the Web Extras, Library Extras, and Audio Extras found in *Criminal Justice Today*. It's easy to add assignments, important dates, and links to Web-based media such as your own online lectures, as well as to sites you've personally selected for your students to view.

Audio Chapter Introductions. Hear the author introduce each chapter with AudioExtras. Audio chapter introductions require Real Player or Windows Media Player software. The author's audio introductions can be used as the basis for essay questions, homework assignments, and in-class pop quizzes.

Chapter Learning Objectives. Set study goals for each chapter with the online chapter-specific learning objectives. Use these objectives to maintain your students' focus on important materials as they read the text material.

Practice Review Questions. Help your students prepare for tests and have them assess their knowledge of critical content with online review questions. Use these true-or-false and multiple-choice questions as homework assignments by asking students to test themselves and to print out and submit the results.

Electronic Homework. Ask your students to respond to online essay questions, and have them e-mail their answers to you for grading. Electronic homework makes it possible to demonstrate students' knowledge of core concepts while it helps save trees!

Chapter Summaries. Review chapter materials with online summaries of key points. Bulleted summaries allow quick and easy access to critical content and can help your students remember important information.

Web Quests Ask students to work their way through comprehensive Web-based chapter projects. These projects will help them learn how to research criminal justice on the Internet. Web Quests make studying enjoyable and open the door to a wealth of electronic information.

Web Extras Web Extras are written into the text material throughout the book. They direct students to sites that are closely related to the materials they are reading about. Web Extras provide a virtual criminal justice tour of the Internet, with visits to police, courts, and corrections sites on the Web.

Library Extras Students can read carefully selected documents from the Bureau of Justice Statistics, the National Institute of Justice, the Bureau of Justice Assistance, the FBI, and other agencies at the *Criminal Justice Today* electronic library. Library Extras, which appear at the end of every chapter in the textbook, are constantly updated to bring your students the latest in criminal justice research and information.

Crime and Justice News. Keep your students abreast of late-breaking crime and justice news via the *Criminal Justice Today* Companion Website. Continuously updated news stories provide complete coverage of current events in the crime and justice fields.

Careers Center. Your students can use the careers feature on the *Criminal Justice Today* website to find the best-paying jobs in the justice profession. The careers center can also help students make informed career choices.

E-mail Discussion List. Encourage your students to join our e-mail discussion list so that they can stay abreast of what other students are talking about. E-mail discussions are a handy way to stay current on issues in the field and to share thoughts. Students can also begin their own e-mail study group to review text materials with students in their classes or in other colleges.

The Prentice Hall Cybrary. Help your students find what they're looking for on the Web with the Prentice Hall cyber-library of criminal justice links. Containing more than 12,000 crime and justice sites in its fully searchable database, the Cybrary is well known on the Internet as "the World's Criminal Justice Directory." You can visit the Cybrary directly at http://www.cybrary .info.

CJ Blogs. Read what others are saying about important events and contemporary issues in criminal justice by visiting the CJToday Blogspace—where you will find links to the most relevant of today's crime and justice-related blogs.

Electronic Glossary. Your students can use this Web-based glossary as a ready-made study aid to help them learn key terms and other text materials. The glossary includes standardized terminology used in the fields of criminal justice, criminology, law, and corrections.

U.S. Constitution. Use this feature to review the full text of the U.S. Constitution, including all amendments, and to research the constitutionally protected rights of those facing processing by the justice system.

***Miranda* Revisited Site**. Our special *Miranda* Revisited site (at cjcentral.com/miranda) will help your students keep pace with possible changes in court-imposed *Miranda* requirements. This site provides all the background your students need to know about *Miranda* v. *Arizona* (1966), *Dickerson* v. *U.S.* (2000), and the federal statute on which the *Dickerson* case turned.

Using the *Time* Magazine Special Supplement with *Criminal Justice Today*

Professors have often found that requiring students to review print media in search of criminal justice–related stories can serve as a useful tool for integrating real events into the classroom study of the justice system. The supplements package that supports *Criminal Justice Today* facilitates such an approach through a special arrangement with *Time* magazine. Instructors who use *Criminal Justice Today* can receive a free *Time* special criminal justice supplement for distribution to their students. This special edition of *Time* contains articles that have been personally selected by Frank Schmalleger from recent issues of *Time*.

To receive free copies of this special supplement, please contact your Prentice Hall representative.

APPENDIX D

The Constitution of the United States

WE THE PEOPLE of the United States, in Order to form a more perfect Union, establish Justice, insure domestic Tranquility, provide for the common defence, promote the general Welfare, and secure the Blessings of Liberty to ourselves and our Posterity, do ordain and establish this CONSTITUTION for the United States of America.

Article I.

SECTION 1. All legislative Powers herein granted shall be vested in a Congress of the United States, which shall consist of a Senate and House of Representatives.

SECTION 2. The House of Representatives shall be composed of Members chosen every second Year by the People of the several States, and the Electors in each State shall have the Qualifications requisite for Electors of the most numerous Branch of the State Legislature.

No Person shall be a Representative who shall not have attained to the Age of twenty-five Years, and been seven Years a Citizen of the United States, and who shall not, when elected, be an Inhabitant of that State in which he shall be chosen.

Representatives and direct Taxes shall be apportioned among the several States which may be included within this Union, according to their respective Numbers, which shall be determined by adding to the whole Number of free Persons, including those bound to Service for a Term of Years, and excluding Indians not taxed, three fifths of all other Persons. The actual Enumeration shall be made within three Years after the first Meeting of the Congress of the United States, and within every subsequent Term of ten Years, in such Manner as they shall by Law direct. The Number of Representatives shall not exceed one for every thirty Thousand, but each State shall have at Least one Representative; and until such enumeration shall be made, the State of New Hampshire shall be entitled to chuse three, Massachusetts eight, Rhode-Island and Providence Plantations one, Connecticut five, New York six, New Jersey four, Pennsylvania eight, Delaware one, Maryland six, Virginia ten, North Carolina five, South Carolina five, and Georgia three.

When vacancies happen in the representation from any State, the Executive Authority thereof shall issue Writs of Election to fill such Vacancies.

The House of Representatives shall chuse their Speaker and other Officers; and shall have the sole Power of Impeachment.

SECTION 3. The Senate of the United States shall be composed of two Senators from each State, chosen by the Legislature thereof for six Years; and each Senator shall have one Vote.

Immediately after they shall be assembled in Consequence of the first Election, they shall be divided as equally as may be into three Classes. The Seats of the Senators of the first Class shall be vacated at the Expiration of the second Year, of the second Class at the Expiration of the fourth Year, and of the third Class at the Expiration of the sixth Year, so that one third may be chosen every second Year; and if Vacancies happen by

Resignation, or otherwise, during the recess of the Legislature of any State, the Executive thereof may make temporary Appointments until the next Meeting of the Legislature, which shall then fill such Vacancies.

No Person shall be Senator who shall not have attained to the Age of thirty Years, and been nine Years a Citizen of the United States, and who shall not, when elected, be an Inhabitant of that State for which he shall be chosen.

The Vice President of the United States shall be President of the Senate, but shall have no Vote, unless they be equally divided.

The Senate shall chuse their other Officers, and also a President pro tempore, in the absence of the Vice President, or when he shall exercise the Office of President of the United States.

The Senate shall have the sole Power to try all Impeachments. When sitting for that Purpose, they shall be on Oath or Affirmation. When the President of the United States is tried, the Chief Justice shall preside: And no Person shall be convicted without the Concurrence of two thirds of the Members present.

Judgment in Cases of Impeachment shall not extend further than to removal from Office, and disqualification to hold and enjoy any Office of honor, Trust, or Profit under the United States: but the Party convicted shall nevertheless be liable and subject to Indictment, Trial, Judgment and Punishment, according to Law.

SECTION 4. The Times, Places and Manner of holding Elections for Senators and Representatives, shall be prescribed in each State by the Legislature thereof; but the Congress may at any time by Law make or alter such Regulations, except as to the Place of chusing Senators.

The Congress shall assemble at least once in every Year, and such Meeting shall be on the first Monday in December, unless they shall by law appoint a different Day.

SECTION 5. Each House shall be the Judge of the Elections, Returns and Qualifications of its own Members, and a Majority of each shall constitute a Quorum to do Business; but a smaller Number may adjourn from day to day, and may be authorized to compel the Attendance of absent Members, in such Manner, and under such Penalties as each House may provide.

Each House may determine the Rules of its Proceedings, punish its Members for disorderly Behaviour, and, with the Concurrence of two thirds, expel a Member.

Each House shall keep a Journal of its Proceedings, and from time to time publish the same, excepting such Parts as may in their Judgment require Secrecy; and the Yeas and Nays of the Members of either House on any question shall, at the Desire of one fifth of those Present, be entered on the journal.

Neither House, during the Session of Congress, shall, without the Consent of the other, adjourn for more than three days, nor to any other Place than that in which the two Houses shall be sitting.

SECTION 6. The Senators and Representatives shall receive a Compensation for their Services, to be ascertained by Law, and paid out of the Treasury of the United States. They shall in all Cases, except Treason, Felony and Breach of the Peace, be privileged from Arrest during their Attendance at the Session of their respective Houses, and in going to and returning from the same; and for any Speech or Debate in either House, they shall not be questioned in any other Place.

No Senator or Representative shall, during the Time for which he was elected, be appointed to any civil Office under the Authority of the United States, which shall have been created, or the Emoluments whereof shall have been encreased during such time; and no Person holding any Office under the United States, shall be a Member of either House during his Continuance in Office.

SECTION 7. All Bills for raising Revenue shall originate in the House of Representatives; but the Senate may propose or concur with Amendments as on other Bills.

Every Bill which shall have passed the House of Representatives and the Senate, shall, before it become a Law, be presented to the President of the United States; If he approve he shall sign it, but if not he shall return it, with his Objections to that House in which it shall have originated, who shall enter the Objections at large on their Journal, and proceed to reconsider it. If after such Reconsideration two thirds of that House shall agree to pass the Bill, it shall be sent, together with the Objections, to the other House, by which it shall likewise be reconsidered, and if approved by two thirds of that House, it shall become a Law. But in all such Cases the Votes of both Houses shall be determined by Yeas and Nays, and the Names of the Persons voting for and against the

Bill shall be entered on the Journal of each House respectively. If any Bill shall not be returned by the President within ten Days (Sundays excepted) after it shall have been presented to him, the Same shall be a Law, in like Manner as if he had signed it, unless the Congress by their Adjournment prevent its Return, in which Case it shall not be a Law.

Every Order, Resolution, or Vote to which the Concurrence of the Senate and House of Representatives may be necessary (except on a question of Adjournment) shall be presented to the President of the United States; and before the Same shall take Effect, shall be approved by him, or being disapproved by him, shall be repassed by two thirds of the Senate and House of Representatives, according to the Rules and Limitations prescribed in the Case of a Bill.

SECTION 8. The Congress shall have Power to lay and collect Taxes, Duties, Imposts and Excises, to pay the Debts and provide for the common Defence and general Welfare of the United States; but all Duties, Imposts and Excises shall be uniform throughout the United States;

To borrow Money on the credit of the United States;

To regulate Commerce with foreign Nations, and among the several States, and with the Indian Tribes;

To establish an uniform Rule of Naturalization, and uniform Laws on the subject of Bankruptcies throughout the United States;

To coin Money, regulate the Value thereof, and of foreign Coin, and fix the Standard of Weights and Measures;

To provide for the Punishment of counterfeiting the Securities and current Coin of the United States;

To establish Post Offices and post Roads;

To promote the Progress of Science and useful Arts, by securing for limited times to Authors and Inventors the exclusive Right to their respective Writings and Discoveries;

To constitute Tribunals inferior to the supreme Court;

To define and punish Piracies and Felonies committed on the high Seas, and Offences against the Law of Nations;

To declare War, grant Letters of Marque and Reprisal, and make Rules concerning Captures on Land and Water;

To raise and support Armies, but no Appropriation of Money to that Use shall be for a longer Term than two Years;

To provide and maintain a Navy;

To make Rules for the Government and Regulation of the land and naval Forces;

To provide for calling forth the Militia to execute the Laws of the Union, suppress Insurrections and repel Invasions;

To provide for organizing, arming, and disciplining the Militia, and for governing such Part of them as may be employed in the Service of the United States, reserving to the States respectively, the Appointment of the Officers, and the Authority of training the Militia according to the discipline prescribed by Congress;

To exercise exclusive Legislation in all Cases whatsoever, over such District (not exceeding ten Miles square) as may, by Cession of particular States, and the Acceptance of Congress, become the Seat of the Government of the United States, and to exercise like Authority over all Places purchased by the Consent of the Legislature of the State in which the Same shall be, for the Erection of Forts, Magazines, and Arsenals, dock-Yards, and other needful Buildings;—And

To make all Laws which shall be necessary and proper for carrying into Execution the foregoing Powers, and all other Powers vested by this Constitution in the Government of the United States, or in any Department or Officer thereof.

SECTION 9. The Migration or Importation of such Persons as any of the States now existing shall think proper to admit, shall not be prohibited by the Congress prior to the Year one thousand eight hundred and eight, but a Tax or duty may be imposed on such Importation, not exceeding ten dollars for each Person.

The privilege of the Writ of Habeas Corpus shall not be suspended, unless when in Cases of Rebellion or Invasion the public Safety may require it.

No Bill of Attainder or ex post facto Law shall be passed.

No Capitation, or other direct, Tax shall be laid, unless in Proportion to the Census or Enumeration herein before directed to be taken.

No Tax or Duty shall be laid on Articles exported from any State.

No Preference shall be given by any Regulation of Commerce or Revenue to the Ports of one State over those of another: nor shall Vessels bound to, or from, one State, be obliged to enter, clear, or pay Duties in another.

No Money shall be drawn from the Treasury, but in Consequence of Appropriations made by Law; and a regular Statement and Account of the Receipts and Expenditures of all public Money shall be published from time to time.

No Title of Nobility shall be granted by the United States: And no Person holding any Office of Profit or Trust under them, shall, without the Consent of the Congress, accept of any present, Emolument, Office, or Title, of any kind whatever, from any King, Prince, or foreign State.

SECTION 10. No State shall enter into any Treaty, Alliance, or Confederation; grant Letters of Marque and Reprisal; coin Money; emit Bills of Credit; make any Thing but gold and silver Coin a Tender in Payment of Debts; pass any Bill of Attainder, ex post facto Law, or Law impairing the Obligation of Contracts, or grant any Title of Nobility.

No State shall, without the consent of the Congress, lay any Imposts or Duties on Imports or Exports, except what may be absolutely necessary for executing it's inspection Laws: and the net Produce of all Duties and Imposts, laid by any State on Imports or Exports, shall be for the Use of the Treasury of the United States; and all such Laws shall be subject to the Revision and Control of the Congress.

No State shall, without the Consent of Congress, lay any Duty of Tonnage, keep Troops, or Ships of War in time of Peace, enter into any Agreement or Compact with another State, or with a foreign Power, or engage in War, unless actually invaded, or in such imminent Danger as will not admit of delay.

Article II.

SECTION 1. The executive Power shall be vested in a President of the United States of America. He shall hold his Office during the Term of four Years, and, together with the Vice President, chosen for the same Term, be elected, as follows:

Each State shall appoint, in such Manner as the Legislature thereof may direct, a Number of Electors, equal to the whole Number of Senators and Representatives to which the State may be entitled in the Congress: but no Senator or Representative, or Person holding an Office of Trust or Profit under the United States, shall be appointed an Elector.

The Electors shall meet in their respective States, and vote by Ballot for two persons, of whom one at least shall not be an Inhabitant of the same State with themselves. And they shall make a List of all the Persons voted for, and of the Number of Votes for each; which List they shall sign and certify, and transmit sealed to the Seat of the Government of the United States, directed to the President of the Senate. The President of the Senate shall, in the Presence of the Senate and House of Representatives, open all the Certificates, and the Votes shall then be counted. The Person having the greatest Number of Votes shall be the President, if such Number be a Majority of the whole Number of Electors appointed; and if there be more than one who have such Majority, and have an equal Number of Votes, then the House of Representatives shall immediately chuse by Ballot one of them for President; and if no Person have a Majority, then from the five highest on the List the said House shall in like Manner chuse the President. But in choosing the President, the Votes shall be taken by States, the Representation from each State having one Vote; A quorum for this Purpose shall consist of a Member or Members from two thirds of the States, and a Majority of all the States shall be necessary to a Choice. In every Case, after the Choice of the President, the Person having the greatest Number of Votes of the Electors shall be the Vice President. But if there should remain two or more who have equal Votes, the Senate shall chuse from them by Ballot the Vice President.

The Congress may determine the Time of chusing the Electors, and the Day on which they shall give their Votes; which Day shall be the same throughout the United States.

No person except a natural born Citizen, or a Citizen of the United States, at the time of Adoption of this Constitution, shall be eligible to the Office of President; neither shall any Person be eligible to that Office who shall not have attained to the Age of thirty five Years, and been fourteen Years a Resident within the United States.

In Case of the Removal of the President from Office, or of his Death, Resignation, or Inability to discharge the Powers and Duties of the said Office, the same shall devolve on the Vice President, and the Congress may by Law provide for the Case of Removal, Death, Resignation or Inability, both of the President and Vice President, declaring what Officer shall then act as President, and such Officer shall act accordingly, until the Disability be removed, or a President shall be elected.

The President shall, at stated Times, receive for his Services, a Compensation, which shall neither be encreased nor diminished during the Period for which he shall have been elected, and he shall not receive within that Period any other Emolument from the United States, or any of them.

Before he enter on the Execution of his Office, he shall take the following Oath or Affirmation:—"I do solemnly swear (or affirm) that I will faithfully execute the Office of President of the United States, and will to the best of my Ability, preserve, protect and defend the Constitution of the United States."

SECTION 2. The President shall be Commander in Chief of the Army and Navy of the United States, and of the Militia of the several States, when called into the actual Service of the United States; he may require the Opinion in writing, of the principal Officer in each of the executive Departments, upon any subject relating to the Duties of their respective Offices, and he shall have Power to grant Reprieves and Pardons for Offenses against the United States, except in Cases of Impeachment.

He shall have Power, by and with the Advice and Consent of the Senate, to make Treaties, provided two thirds of the Senators present concur; and he shall nominate, and by and with the Advice and Consent of the Senate, shall appoint Ambassadors, other public Ministers and Consuls, Judges of the supreme Court, and all other Officers of the United States, whose Appointments are not herein otherwise provided for, and which shall be established by Law: but the Congress may by Law vest the Appointment of such inferior Officers, as they think proper, in the President alone, in the courts of Law, and in the Heads of Departments.

The President shall have Power to fill up all Vacancies that may happen during the Recess of the Senate, by granting Commissions which shall expire at the End of their next Session.

SECTION 3. He shall from time to time give to the Congress Information of the State of the Union, and recommend to their Consideration such Measures as he shall judge necessary and expedient; he may, on extraordinary Occasions, convene both Houses, or either of them, and in Case of Disagreement between them, with Respect to the Time of Adjournment, he may adjourn them to such Time as he shall think proper; he shall receive Ambassadors and other public Ministers; he shall take Care that the Laws be faithfully executed, and Shall Commission all the Officers of the United States.

SECTION 4. The President, Vice President and all civil Officers of the United States, shall be removed from Office on Impeachment for, and Conviction of, Treason, Bribery, or other high Crimes and Misdemeanors.

Article III.

SECTION 1. The judicial Power of the United States, shall be vested in one supreme Court, and in such inferior Courts as the Congress may from time to time ordain and establish. The Judges, both of the supreme and inferior Courts, shall hold their Offices during good Behavior, and shall, at stated Times, receive for their Services, a Compensation, which shall not be diminished during their Continuance in Office.

SECTION 2. The judicial Power shall extend to all Cases, in Law and Equity, arising under this Constitution, the Laws of the United States, and Treaties made, or which shall be made, under their Authority;—to all Cases affecting Ambassadors, other public Ministers and Consuls;—to all Cases of admiralty and maritime Jurisdiction;—to Controversies to which the United States shall be a Party;—to controversies between two or more States;—between a State and Citizens of another State;—between citizens of different States;—between Citizens of the same State claiming Lands under Grants of different States, and between a State, or the Citizens thereof, and foreign States, Citizens or Subjects.

In all Cases affecting Ambassadors, other public Ministers and Consuls, and those in which a State shall be Party, the supreme Court shall have original Jurisdiction. In all the other Cases before mentioned, the supreme Court shall have appellate Jurisdiction, both as to Law and Fact, with such exceptions, and under such Regulations as the Congress shall make.

The Trial of all Crimes, except in Cases of Impeachment, shall be by Jury; and such Trial shall be held in the State where the said Crimes shall have been committed; but when not committed within any State, the Trial shall be at such Place or Places as the Congress may by Law have directed.

SECTION 3. Treason against the United States, shall consist only in levying War against them, or in adhering to their Enemies, giving them Aid and Comfort. No Person shall be convicted of Treason unless on the Testimony of two Witnesses to the same overt Act, or on Confession in open Court.

The Congress shall have Power to declare the Punishment of Treason, but no Attainder of Treason shall work Corruption of Blood, or Forfeiture except during the Life of the Person attainted.

Article IV.

SECTION 1. Full Faith and Credit shall be given in each State to the public Acts, Records, and judicial Proceedings of every other State. And the Congress may by general Laws prescribe the Manner in which such Acts, Records and Proceedings shall be proved, and the Effect thereof.

SECTION 2. The Citizens of each State shall be entitled to all Privileges and Immunities of Citizens in the several States.

A Person charged in any State with Treason, Felony, or other Crime, who shall flee from Justice, and be found in another State, shall on Demand of the executive Authority of the State from which he fled, be delivered up, to be removed to the State having Jurisdiction of the Crime.

No Person held to Service or Labour in one State, under the Laws thereof, escaping into another, shall, in Consequence of any Law or Regulation therein, be discharged from such Service or Labour, but shall be delivered up on Claim of the Party to whom such Service or Labour may be due.

SECTION 3. New States may be admitted by the Congress into this Union; but no new State shall be formed or erected within the Jurisdiction of any other State; nor any State be formed by the Junction of two or more States, or parts of States, without the Consent of the Legislatures of the States concerned as well as of the Congress.

The Congress shall have Power to dispose of and make all needful Rules and Regulations respecting the Territory or other Property belonging to the United States; and nothing in this Constitution shall be so construed as to Prejudice any Claims of the United States, or of any particular State.

SECTION 4. The United States shall guarantee to every State in this Union a Republican Form of Government, and shall protect each of them against Invasion; and on Application of the Legislature, or of the Executive (when the Legislature cannot be convened) against domestic Violence.

Article V.

The Congress, whenever two thirds of both Houses shall deem it necessary, shall propose Amendments to this Constitution, or, on the Application of the Legislatures of two thirds of the several States, shall call a Convention for proposing Amendments, which, in either Case, shall be valid to all Intents and Purposes, as Part of this Constitution, when ratified by the Legislatures of three fourths of the several States, or by Conventions in three fourths thereof, as the one or the other Mode of Ratification may be proposed by the Congress; Provided that no Amendment which may be made prior to the Year One thousand eight hundred and eight shall in any Manner affect the first and fourth Clauses in the Ninth Section of the first Article; and that no State, without its Consent, shall be deprived of its equal Suffrage in the Senate.

Article VI.

All Debts contracted and Engagements entered into, before the Adoption of this Constitution, shall be as valid against the United States under this Constitution, as under the Confederation.

This Constitution, and the Laws of the United States which shall be made in Pursuance thereof; and all Treaties made, or which shall be made, under the Authority of the United States, shall be the supreme Law of the Land; and the Judges in every State shall be bound thereby; any Thing in the Constitution or Laws of any State to the Contrary notwithstanding.

The Senators and Representatives before mentioned, and the Members of the several State Legislatures, and all executive and judicial Officers, both of the United States and of the several States, shall be bound by Oath or Affirmation, to support this Constitution; but no religious Test shall ever be required as a Qualification to any Office or public Trust under the United States.

Article VII.

The Ratification of the Conventions of nine States shall be sufficient for the Establishment of this Constitution between the States so ratifying the Same.

Articles in Addition to, and Amendment of, the Constitution of the United States of America, Proposed by Congress, and Ratified by the Legislatures of the Several States, Pursuant to the Fifth Article of the Original Constitution.

Amendment I. (1791)

Congress shall make no law respecting an establishment of religion, or prohibiting the free exercise thereof; or abridging the freedom of speech, or of the press; or the right of the people peaceably to assemble, and to petition the Government for a redress of grievances.

Amendment II. (1791)

A well regulated Militia, being necessary to the security of a free State, the right of the people to keep and bear Arms, shall not be infringed.

Amendment III. (1791)

No Soldier shall, in time of peace be quartered in any house, without the consent of the Owner, nor in time of war, but in a manner to be prescribed by law.

Amendment IV. (1791)

The right of the people to be secure in their persons, houses, papers, and effects, against unreasonable searches and seizures, shall not be violated, and no Warrants shall issue, but upon probable cause, supported by Oath or affirmation, and particularly describing the place to be searched, and the persons or things to be seized.

Amendment V. (1791)

No person shall be held to answer for a capital, or otherwise infamous crime, unless on a presentment or indictment of a Grand Jury, except in cases arising in the land or naval forces, or in the Militia, when in actual service in time of War or public danger; nor shall any person be subject for the same offence to be twice put in jeopardy of life or limb; nor shall be compelled in any criminal case to be a witness against himself, nor be deprived of life, liberty, or property, without due process of law; nor shall private property be taken for public use, without just compensation.

Amendment VI. (1791)

In all criminal prosecutions, the accused shall enjoy the right to a speedy and public trial, by an impartial jury of the State and district wherein the crime shall have been committed, which district shall have been previously ascertained by law, and to be informed of the nature and cause of the accusation; to be confronted with the witnesses against him; to have compulsory process for obtaining Witnesses in his favor, and to have the Assistance of Counsel for his defense.

Amendment VII. (1791)

In Suits at common law, where the value in controversy shall exceed twenty dollars, the right of trial by jury shall be preserved, and no fact tried by a jury, shall be otherwise reexamined in any Court of the United States, than according to the rules of the common law.

Amendment VIII. (1791)

Excessive bail shall not be required, nor excessive fines imposed, nor cruel and unusual punishments inflicted.

Amendment IX. (1791)

The enumeration of the Constitution, of certain rights, shall not be construed to deny or disparage others retained by the people.

Amendment X. (1791)

The powers not delegated to the United States by the Constitution, nor prohibited by it to the States, are reserved to the States respectively, or to the people.

Amendment XI. (1798)

The Judicial power of the United States shall not be construed to extend to any suit in law or equity, commenced or prosecuted against one of the United States by Citizens of another State, or by Citizens or Subjects of any Foreign State.

Amendment XII. (1804)

The Electors shall meet in their respective states and vote by ballot for President and Vice-President, one of whom, at least, shall not be an inhabitant of the same state with themselves; they shall name in their ballots the person voted for as President, and in distinct ballots the person voted for as Vice-President, and they shall make distinct lists of all persons voted for as President, and of all persons voted for as Vice-President, and of the number of votes for each, which lists they shall sign and certify, and transmit sealed to the seat of the government of the United States, directed to the President of the Senate;—The President of the Senate shall, in the presence of the Senate and House of Representatives, open all the certificates and the votes shall then be counted;—The person having the greatest number of votes for President, shall be the President, if such number be a majority of the whole number of Electors appointed; and if no person have such majority, then from the persons having the highest numbers not exceeding three on the list of those voted for as President, the House of Representatives shall choose immediately, by ballot, the President. But in choosing the President, the votes shall be taken by states, the representation from each state having one vote; a quorum for this purpose shall consist of a member or members from two-thirds of the states, and a majority of all the states shall be necessary to a choice. And if the House of Representatives shall not choose a President whenever the right of choice shall devolve upon them, before the fourth day of March next following, then the Vice-President shall act as President, as in the case of the death or other constitutional disability of the President. The person having the greatest number of votes as Vice President, shall be the Vice President, if such number be a majority of the whole number of Electors appointed, and if no person have a majority, then from the two highest numbers on the list, the Senate shall choose the Vice President; a quorum for the purpose shall consist of two-thirds of the whole number of Senators, and a majority of the whole number shall be necessary to a choice. But no person constitutionally ineligible to the office of President shall be eligible to that of Vice President of the United States.

Amendment XIII. (1865)

SECTION 1. Neither slavery nor involuntary servitude, except as a punishment for crime whereof the party shall have been duly convicted, shall exist within the United States, or any place subject to their jurisdiction.

SECTION 2. Congress shall have power to enforce this article by appropriate legislation.

Amendment XIV. (1868)

SECTION 1. All persons born or naturalized in the United States, and subject to the jurisdiction thereof, are citizens of the United States and of the State wherein they reside. No State shall make or enforce any law which shall abridge the privileges or immunities of citizens of the United States; nor shall any State deprive any person of life, liberty, or property, without due process of law; nor deny to any person within its jurisdiction the equal protection of the law.

SECTION 2. Representatives shall be apportioned among the several States according to their respective numbers, counting the whole number of persons in each State, excluding Indians not taxed. But when the right to vote at any election for the choice of electors for President and Vice President of the United States, Representatives in Congress, the Executive and Judicial officers of a State, or the members of the Legislature thereof, is denied to any of the male inhabitants of such State, being twenty-one years of age, and citizens of the United States, or in any way abridged, except for participation in rebellion, or other crime, the basis of representation therein shall be reduced in the proportion which the number of such male citizens shall bear to the whole number of male citizens twenty-one years of age in such State.

SECTION 3. No person shall be a Senator or Representative in Congress, or elector of President and Vice President, or hold any office, civil or military, under the United States, or under any State, who, having previously taken an oath, as a member of Congress, or as an officer of the United States, or as a member of any State legislature, or as an executive or judicial officer of any State, to support the Constitution of the United States, shall have engaged in insurrection or rebellion against the same, or given aid or comfort to the enemies thereof. But Congress may by a vote of two-thirds of each House, remove such disability.

SECTION 4. The validity of the public debt of the United States, authorized by law, including debts incurred for payment of pensions and bounties for services in suppressing insurrection or rebellion, shall not be questioned. But neither the United States nor any State shall assume or pay any debt or obligation incurred in aid of insurrection or rebellion against the United States, or any claim for the loss or emancipation of any slave; but all such debts, obligations and claims shall be held illegal and void.

SECTION 5. The Congress shall have power to enforce, by appropriate legislation, the provisions of this article.

Amendment XV. (1870)

SECTION 1. The right of citizens of the United States to vote shall not be denied or abridged by the United States or by any State on account of race, color, or previous condition of servitude.

SECTION 2. The Congress shall have power to enforce this article by appropriate legislation.

Amendment XVI. (1913)

The Congress shall have power to lay and collect taxes on incomes, from whatever source derived, without apportionment among the several States, and without regard to any census or enumeration.

Amendment XVII. (1913)

The Senate of the United States shall be composed of two Senators from each State, elected by the people thereof, for six years; and each Senator shall have one vote. The electors in each State shall have the qualifications requisite for electors of the most numerous branch of the State legislatures.

When vacancies happen in the representation of any State in the Senate, the executive authority of such State shall issue writs of election to fill such vacancies: *Provided*, That the legislature of any State may empower the executive thereof to make temporary appointments until the people fill the vacancies by election as the legislature may direct.

This amendment shall not be so construed as to affect the election or term of any Senator chosen before it becomes valid as part of the Constitution.

Amendment XVIII. (1919)

SECTION 1. After one year from the ratification of this article the manufacture, sale, or transportation of intoxicating liquors within, the importation thereof into, or the exportation thereof from the United States and all territory subject to the jurisdiction thereof for beverage purposes is hereby prohibited.

SECTION 2. The Congress and the several States shall have concurrent power to enforce this article by appropriate legislation.

SECTION 3. This article shall be inoperative unless it shall have been ratified as an amendment to the Constitution by the legislatures of the several States, as provided in the Constitution, within seven years from the date of the submission hereof to the States by the Congress.

Amendment XIX. (1920)

The right of citizens of the United States to vote shall not be denied or abridged by the United States or by any State on account of sex.

Congress shall have power to enforce this article by appropriate legislation.

Amendment XX. (1933)

SECTION 1. The terms of the President and Vice President shall end at noon on the 20th day of January, and the terms of Senators and representatives at noon on the 3d day of January, of the years in which such terms would have ended if this article had not been ratified; and the terms of their successors shall then begin.

SECTION 2. The Congress shall assemble at least once in every year, and such meeting shall begin at noon on the 3d day of January, unless they shall by law appoint a different day.

SECTION 3. If, at the time fixed for the beginning of the term of the President, the President elect shall have died, the Vice President elect shall become President. If a President shall not have been chosen before the time fixed for the beginning of his term, or if the President elect shall have failed to qualify, then the Vice President elect shall act as President until a President shall have qualified; and the Congress may by law provide for the case wherein neither a President elect nor a Vice President elect shall have qualified, declaring who shall then act as President, or the manner in which one who is to act shall be selected, and such person shall act accordingly until a President or Vice President shall have qualified.

SECTION 4. The Congress may by law provide for the case of the death of any of the persons from whom the House of Representatives may choose a President whenever the right of choice shall have devolved upon them, and for the case of the death of any of the persons from whom the Senate may choose a Vice President whenever the right of choice shall have devolved upon them.

SECTION 5. Sections 1 and 2 shall take effect on the 15th day of October following the ratification of this article.

SECTION 6. This article shall be inoperative unless it shall have been ratified as an amendment to the Constitution by the legislatures of three-fourths of the several States within seven years from the date of submission.

Amendment XXI. (1933)

SECTION 1. The eighteenth article of amendment to the Constitution of the United States is hereby repealed.

SECTION 2. The transportation or importation into any State, Territory, or possession of the United States for delivery or use therein of intoxicating liquors, in violation of the laws thereof, is hereby prohibited.

SECTION 3. This article shall be inoperative unless it shall have been ratified as an amendment to the Constitution by conventions in the several States, as provided in the Constitution, within seven years from the date of the submission hereof to the States by the Congress.

Amendment XXII. (1951)

SECTION 1. No person shall be elected to the office of the President more than twice, and no person who has held the office of President, or acted as President, for more than two years of a term to which some other person was elected president shall be elected to the office of the President more than once. But this Article shall not apply to any person holding office of President when this Article was proposed by the Congress, and shall not prevent any person who may be holding the office of President, or acting as President, during the term within which this Article becomes operative from holding the office of President or acting as President during the remainder of such term.

SECTION 2. The article shall be inoperative unless it shall have been ratified as an amendment to the Constitution by the legislatures of three-fourths of the several States within seven years from the date of its submission to the States by the Congress.

Amendment XXIII. (1961)

SECTION 1. The District constituting the seat of Government of the United States shall appoint in such manner as the Congress may direct:

A number of electors of President and Vice President equal to the whole number of Senators and Representatives in Congress to which the District would be entitled if it were a State, but in no event more than the least populous State; they shall be in addition to those appointed by the States, but they shall be considered, for the purposes of the election of President and Vice President, to be electors appointed by a State; and they shall meet in the District and perform such duties as provided by the twelfth article of amendment.

SECTION 2. The Congress shall have power to enforce this article by appropriate legislation.

Amendment XXIV. (1964)

SECTION 1. The right of citizens of the United States to vote in any primary or other election for President or Vice President, for electors for President or Vice President, or for Senator or Representative in Congress, shall not be denied or abridged by the United States or any State by reason of failing to pay any poll tax or other tax.

SECTION 2. The Congress shall have power to enforce this article by appropriate legislation.

Amendment XXV. (1967)

SECTION 1. In case of the removal of the President from office or of his death or resignation, the Vice President shall become President.

SECTION 2. Whenever there is a vacancy in the office of the Vice President, the President shall nominate a Vice President who shall take office upon confirmation by a majority vote of both Houses of Congress.

SECTION 3. Whenever the President transmits to the President pro tempore of the Senate and the Speaker of the House of Representatives his written declaration that he is unable to discharge the powers and duties of his office, and until he transmits to them a written declaration to the contrary, such powers and duties shall be discharged by the Vice President as Acting President.

SECTION 4. Whenever the Vice President and a majority of either the principal officers of the executive departments or of such other body as Congress may by law provide, transmit to the President pro tempore of the Senate and the Speaker of the House of Representatives their written declaration that the President is unable to discharge the powers and duties of his office, the Vice President shall immediately assume the powers and duties of the office as Acting President.

Thereafter, when the President transmits to the President pro tempore of the Senate and the Speaker of the House of Representatives his written declaration that no inability exists, he shall resume the powers and duties of his office unless the Vice President and a majority of either the principal officers of the executive department or of such other body as Congress may by law provide, transmit within four days to the President pro tempore of the Senate and the Speaker of the House of Representatives their written declaration that the President is unable to discharge the powers and duties of his office. Thereupon Congress shall decide the issue, assembling within forty-eight hours for that purpose if not in session. If the Congress, within twenty-one days after receipt of the latter written declaration, or, if Congress is not in session, within twenty-one days after Congress is required to assemble, determines by two-thirds vote of both Houses that the President is unable to discharge the powers and duties of his office, the Vice President shall continue to discharge the same as Acting President; otherwise, the President shall resume the powers and duties of his office.

Amendment XXVI. (1971)

SECTION 1. The right of citizens of the United States, who are eighteen years of age or older, to vote shall not be denied or abridged by the United States or by any State on account of age.

SECTION 2. The Congress shall have power to enforce this article by appropriate legislation.

Amendment XXVII. (1992)

No law, varying the compensation for the services of the Senators and Representatives, shall take effect, until an election of Representatives shall have intervened.